OUT OF ITALY

OUT OF ITALY

THE STORY OF ITALIANS
IN NORTH EAST ENGLAND

HUGH SHANKLAND

t

Troubador Italian Series
Series Editor
Professor George Ferzoco
University of Bristol

Troubador Publishing Ltd
9 Priory Business Park
Kibworth Beauchamp
Leics LE8 0RX, UK
Tel: (+44) 116 279 2299
Email: books@troubador.co.uk
Web: www.troubador.co.uk

t

ISBN 978-1783063-765

Cover photo: Nico Arpone at La Stalla, Newcastle 1979, courtesy The Sunday People.

A Cataloguing-in-Publication (CIP) catalogue record for this book
is available from the British Library.

Typeset in 10pt Bembo by Troubador Publishing Ltd, Leics, UK

For Lotte, the perfect companion in all our years together in the North East and Italy

Contents

'A Certaine Italian'

Register of baptisms, St Nicholas church, Durham, 1569:

Memorandum: that a certaine Italian brought into the Cittie of Durham the 11th day of June in the year abovesayd A very greate, strange & monstrous serpent in length sixxteene feete, in quantitie & dimentions greater than a great horse. Which was taken & killed by speciall pollicie in Æthiopia within the Turke's dominions. But before it was killed, it had devoured (as it is credibly thought) more than 1000 persons. And allso destroyed a whole Countrey.

That is the only news item to break the placid record of parish christenings between 1540, when the register was begun, and a second intrusion in 1574 ('The new bridge was built this year'), as though in all that time nothing else noteworthy happened in the city of Durham – never mind that the last months of 1569 also saw a local rising against Queen Elizabeth's repression of Catholicism, opening with the storming of the cathedral and concluding with the public hanging of 66 of the rebels on a single day. The carcass of that 'greate serpent' (stuffed python?) accompanied no doubt by an almost equally strange and monstrous-seeming foreign person vividly mimicking its insatiable hunger for humans must have been displayed in the market place, just outside the door of St Nicholas church itself. Judging by the churchwarden's breathless report – and *he* could read and write – no end of other credulous natives must have paid for a peep that summer's day. And for the rest of their lives what scarifying tales did they pass on?

And he'd greet big teeth, a greet big gob, an' greet big goggle eyes...

Who was this mysterious stranger? Some enterprising mariner who stepped off a boat in Newcastle or Hartlepool to make a quick lucrative tour of the neighbourhood before sailing away again? Or had he been tramping the rough roads of England for years, hauling his 'Ethiopian' worm on a handcart all about the country, even right across Europe? Had it proved such a good earner that by the time he reached the North East he toured in style in a horse-drawn wagon packed with other precious exhibits, even an English-born wife and kids? What life in Italy did he leave behind, what drove him to depart, did he ever return? And what did he make of us, the foreigners all round him?

These are the kinds of questions this book seeks to answer. For I take that nameless adventurer living on his wits among us four and a half centuries ago as a compelling emblem and forerunner of countless other Italians who have found their way to these northern parts, each bringing with them something 'strange' which in fascinating ways has coloured the life of our region.

An Italian with performing bears entertaining a crowd at North Shields about 1900. (Beamish Museum)

Although the first chapter covers contacts between Italy and the North East from Roman times up to the eighteenth century, and another considers the singular history of local support for Italian freedom in the nineteenth century, the main focus of the book is the story of Italian settlement in our region from its tentative beginnings in about 1800 right up to the present day. Systematic study of Italian immigration into Britain is relatively new, as though people only woke up to it after its main phases were over. *Immigrants Ignored* was the apt title of one of the earliest studies, a dissertation on Italians in London completed in 1973 by Robin Palmer, a former student of Italian at Durham University. Only in 1975, under the imprint of the Centre for Emigration Studies in Rome, appeared the first book-length work since the 1890s, Umberto Marin's *Italiani in Gran Bretagna*, a concise survey of the two-thousand-year history of Italians in Britain and a useful insider's view of the contemporary migrant situation. Over the next ten years the Centre also brought out three penetrating studies, again by Italians, concerning the experiences of postwar Italian workers and their families in Bedford, the Bristol area, and Scotland. Finally, in the early 1990s, two books of larger scope, both in English, gained the subject a much wider audience here, crowning the pioneering phase of Italian immigration studies: Lucio Sponza's *Italian Immigrants in Nineteenth Century Britain*, which covers the first period of extensive Italian immigration and British attitudes to that presence; and Terri Colpi's *The Italian Factor*, which along with a 'visual history' companion volume of photographs carries on the story by exploring the various strands of regional migration and occupation which produced the multifarious 'community' as it exists today. These few works in Italian and English have in turn inspired further books and pamphlets, some more or less strictly sociological, but most, like *Out of Italy*, contributions to the more homely category of local history. From all of them I have learned a lot.

But my deepest debt of understanding is to the Italians and Anglo-Italians of the North East. Their recollections and photographs make this book theirs as much as mine, and form its chief appeal. I only regret it has taken so long to appear – too long, alas, for Louis and John.

Durham Market Place before its revamping in 2011, with St Nicholas church in the background. The original Norman church was replaced by the present building in the mid-nineteenth century. The striking equestrian statue of the 3rd Marquess of Londonderry, pitiless exploiter of the Durham miners, unveiled by his widow in 1861, is by Raffaele Monti of Milan who worked for many years in Britain. Contrary to the local tale that the sculptor committed suicide in despair after a blind man discovered his perfect horse possessed no tongue Signor Monti died from other causes in 1881.

Among all the many people who have been prodigious with their friendship and hospitality over the years I must single out Gino and Pauline Rossi of Bishop Auckland who gave us the freedom of the house they built in Valvori next to the home of Gino's much-missed parents, Adelinda and Alfonso; Franca and Italo Rigali who have so often made us welcome in both Easington and Barga; Maureen and Paul Risi of Houghton-le-Spring, ever enthusiastic in their support; Betty and Joe Risi and all in the Anglo-Italian Association of Newcastle who work to keep alive the sense of a shared history, especially Anna and Carlo Rea with all their good food and memories and photographs; Michael Minchella and his family in South Shields who gave me so much encouragement (and grappa) in the days when Michael was president of the Ice Cream Alliance; Teresa Atkinson and her brother Louis Ciaraldi with his encyclopedic memory of the old Italian community; Dolores Maggiore; John and Elena Valente; Vincenzo Riggio and Angelo Rago of the Middlesbrough Anglo-Italian Association and their colleagues and families. They are just a very few of the many, many good people whose company and reminiscences we have enjoyed all over the North East, and during several visits to Italy. For further help I thank consular agent Armando Angelucci, Chiara Ghilardi of Lucca who wrote her graduate dissertation on the Italians of North East England, Barry Redfern who passed on everything of interest he came across in the course of his own research into nineteenth century Newcastle, David Burnett, Roger Norris, John Smith, all of Durham University, and Lucio Sponza whose singular commitment to the history and welfare of the immigrant community is an inspiration to all who seek to understand the experience of Britain from an Italian point of view.

A grant from the Nuffield Foundation paid for the cost of transcribing many of the earliest interviews conducted here and in Italy in 1991-2 with the help of a team of good friends in Italian studies in the North East: Phil Daniels, Chris Flynn, Simonetta Manfredi, Carla Singh, Carole Shepherd, Lucina Stuart, Maria Pia Fontana. In October 1992, Lotte and I mounted an exhibition called 'The Story of the Italians in North East England' at the Central Library, Newcastle, later seen at other venues in the region and beyond. Gathering material for that exhibition was the spur to begin to research this book.

All photographs unless otherwise attributed have been generously made available by the families concerned, or are my own. For all errors please blame the author, who will be glad to be put right by anyone who cares to write to him via the publisher.

The 'North East' of the title embraces all territory east of the Pennine Way between Tweed and Tees: ancient 'Bernicia', still a very distinct region of Britain united by a shared history, ancient rivalries, and its own variable but unmistakable twang.

Principal books on Italians in Britain

U. Marin, *Italiani in Gran Bretagna* (1975)

R. Cavallaro, *Storie senza storia: indagine sull'emigrazione calabrese in Gran Bretagna* (1981)

B. Bottignolo, *Without a Bell Tower: A Study of the Italian Immigrants in South-West England* (1985)

S. Chistolini, *Donne italoscozzesi* (1986)

L. Sponza, *Italian Immigrants in Nineteenth Century Britain: Realities and Images* (1988)

T. Colpi, *The Italian Factor: The Italian Community in Great Britain* (1991)

T. Colpi, *Italians Forward! A Visual History of the Italian Community in Great Britain* (1991)

C. Hughes, *Lime, Lemon and Sarsaparilla: The Italian Community in South Wales 1881-1945* (1991)

A-M. Fortier, *Migrant belongings: Memory, Space and Identity* (2000)

L. Sponza, *Divided Loyalties: Italians in Britain during the Second World War* (2000)

A. Medaglia, *Patriarchal Structures and Ethnicity in the Italian Community in Great Britain* (2001)

Memoirs by Italians and Anglo-Italians

'Cagliardo Coraggioso', *Wandering Minstrel* (1938)

Peppino Leoni, *I Shall Die on the Carpet* (1966)

Cabisto Cavalli, *Ricordi di un emigrato* (1973)

Charles Forte, *The Autobiography of Charles Forte* (1986)

Piero Tognini, *A Mind at War* (1990)

Elena Salvoni, *Elena; A Life in Soho* (1990)

Les Servini, *A Boy from Bardi: My Life and Times* (1992)

Joe Pieri, *Isle of the Displaced. An Italian Scot's Memoir of Internment in the Second World War* (1997)

Mary Contini, *Dear Olivia: An Italian Journey of Love and Loss* (2007)

Bernard Moscardini, *La vacanza* (2009)

The Anglo-Italian family history society: www.anglo-italianfhs.com

1

EARLY ITALIANS: ROMANS TO ROCOCO

When Hadrian built the Roman Wall
Two thousand years ago
He was troubled by the Picts and Scots,
A never-ending flow;
His legions were quite fagged out
But wasted not their nights,
They were scouring the countryside
For likely ice cream sites...

(From a poem by Tommy Gow, as remembered by Michael Minchella)

Romans in the North

All used Latin, many were Roman citizens, but very few were Italian. Some high-ranking officers and officials were born in Italy, but the many thousands of soldiers who for three centuries served in the northern frontier region were almost all recruited from among the fifty provinces of the empire near and far, from Gaul to the Levant. This multinational army of occupation soon became so settled that its manpower was predominantly British-born, of mingled native and foreign descent.

THE SIXTH COHORT, THE CENTURY OF LOUSIUS SUAVIS (built this)

Around AD 400, just before the empire lost all Britannia, the last Romano-British troops still garrisoning the north were reinforced with mercenaries from barbarian Germanic tribes, the same who would eventually overrun much of England as Angles and Saxons.

Even armed with this knowledge it is hard to resist the impression that the North East was once not only ruled from Rome but occupied by multitudes of Italians, since Roman customs and culture united these disparate peoples and all who served the empire assumed Roman names or Romanised their native names. Visiting the fort at Chesters to photograph one of the very few surviving inscriptions in our region which indisputably commemorates an Italian, I found the atmospheric little museum everywhere haunted with name traces of the men who built the Wall or who came from all over the known world to guard it: Quintus, Lucius, Florus, Aelius Aelianus, Flavius Civilis, Claudius Cleonicus, Verus, Pompeius, even Valerius Maximus... All fake Italians, I told myself to keep their ghosts locked in the stones, when a transcription placed beneath one more crudely incised block made the great stretch of time contract inside me like a concertina: 'The sixth cohort, the century of Lousius Suavis (built this)':

COH VI – 7 LOUSI SUAVIS

Louis Soave's eldest son was the first person I interviewed for this book (see page 154). Mario had told me how his father Luigi, whom the Geordies all called Louis, was born into a shepherding family near the small southern Italian village of Belmonte Castello. As a young conscript he was with Mussolini's legions in North Africa, and in the lean years following the war he left home again on a rigorous four-year Ministry of Labour contract to work on a farm near Stirling. Within two years he had married Lucia, a girl from his same village bound by similar contract to a long established family from Belmonte Castello running a very successful fish and chip shop in the neighbourhood, and now in addition to his long hours on the farm Luigi took to pedalling an ice cream trike round the streets of Stirling at weekends to help put by enough for the two of them to set up together over here when both finally gained their freedom. Forty years on, when I first met Mario and his wife Carol, a native Briton, at their home near ancient Concangium (Chester-le-Street), 'Louis' and 'Lucy' Soave were the hard-working proprietors of the very popular 'Belmonte' fish and chip shop in Coatsworth Road, Gateshead.

As for the centurion Lousius Suavis, five inscribed building-stones, a record for the Wall, mark the labours of his 'centuria' of eighty men along various sections of the 20-mile stretch between Chesters and Birdoswald.

As many as 12,000 Roman auxiliaries were regularly stationed on or near the Wall. Twenty-five years was the normal length of service, and inevitably – like British servicemen stationed in Italy in the far shorter period 1943-7 – many started liaisons, and eventually families, with local women. Their genes will be with us still, yet the most we know about any of them as individuals are the bare letters of their names carved on building stones, votive altars and gravestones, or hacked directly into the rock where the material for the wall and forts was quarried. Unless they served at Vindolanda.

The discovery in 1973 of the Vindolanda writing tablets, hundreds of ink-written slivers of birch and alder hidden ten feet beneath a field near Chesterholm, has yielded the most detailed record of everyday army life in Roman Europe, excelled only by similar finds on papyrus in North Africa. The hands of numerous correspondents and scribes have been identified in this still accumulating cache of official and personal letters, duty reports, leave applications, petitions, accounts, and quartermasters' inventories which give precise if tantalisingly patchy glimpses into daily life at this remote frontier station between AD 90 and 120. Along with garrison commander Flavius Cerialis and his wife Sulpicia Lepidina and their domestic staff of freedmen and slaves, the large cast of officers and some two hundred other-rankers includes Ascanius the hornblower, Marcus the medic, Lucius the shieldmaker, the vets Viralis and Alio, Aebutius the cobbler, Vitalis the bathman, Candidus the pig-keeper, Atectus the brewer, and Tullio the waggon-man.

The very first Vindolanda fragment to be deciphered is still the best known: 'I have sent you... pairs wollen socks from Sattua, two pairs sandals and two pairs underpants... Greetings to... Elpis, Rhenus, Tetricus... and all your messmates with whom I pray you live in the greatest good fortune'. Its sheer banality makes it extraordinary at this remove in time, as heart-warming as the arrival of that thoughtful parcel some chilly day no more than seventy years after Christ's crucifixion. 'I write this to you from Vindolanda, our winter quarters,' another fragment ends. *Haec tibi a Vindolanda scribo...* Another squeeze of the concertina, another breath of life, three hundred years before the Romans in Britain pulled on their pants and socks and sandals for the last time.

'EX ITALIA': third-century votive altar dedicated to Jupiter and the genius praetori (guardian spirit of the commander's household) set up by 'Quintus Petronius Urbicus son of Quintus of the Fabian tribe, from Italy, his home town Brixia, prefect of the fourth cohort of Gauls' (Chesters Museum, found at Vindolanda). The erasure probably removed the name of a disgraced emperor. Brixia is modern-day Brescia, near Milan. Two other inscriptions in our region record the presence of Italian-born prefects (commanding officers) in charge of non-Italian forces: Lucius Caesius Frontinus, from Parma, prefect of the first cohort of Thracians (Bowes museum), and Quintus Terentius Firmus, from Siena, prefect of the camp of the sixth legion (Hexham Abbey).]

The second Roman conquest

The second Roman conquest of Britain lasted three times as long, almost a full thousand years. In 597 a small expeditionary force of Italian missionaries landed in Kent armed only with the power of faith and Pope Gregory the Great's orders to convert the natives – a people who worshipped 'mere sticks and stones', according to the Venerable Bede, the Northumbrian chronicler of how his heathen countrymen came to adopt the creed of Rome. Bede's bias in favour of Rome is so strong that it is easy to lose sight of the fact that Christianity, which Constantine had imposed at the beginning of the last full century of Roman occupation, was far from extinct in the British Isles. That may have been the case in areas of England invaded and settled by Angles and Saxons, the pagan 'English', but it still flourished in distinctive variations among the unconquered Celtic-speaking tribes of Wales and South-West England, and in all Ireland with its expanding sister church in Scotland.

The Venerable Bede, wood carving by Fenwick Lawson of Durham, in the Pontifical Beda College, one of two English seminaries in Rome.

The first bishop of Northumbria was Italian. Paulinus had come as a young cleric in 601 to work with his fellow evangelists to complete the Christianising of the south from their base in Canterbury where they enjoyed the protection of the converted king of Kent. Many years later, when the king's sister was betrothed to king Edwin of Northumbria, Paulinus went north with her as part of the marriage deal, treating it as a God-sent opportunity to win the kingdom for Christ and Rome. The prize was substantial. Northumbria, a large realm 'north of the Humber', extended far beyond Hadrian's Wall to the Forth-Clyde line deep inside what is now Scotland. Bede says it took Paulinus two years to overcome king Edwin's suspicions, but once the king and his chief priest had agreed to receive baptism 'all the nobility of his kingdom and a vast number of the common people' followed their overlord's example. Bishop Paulinus founded his see at Erboracum, or York, the old Roman capital of the north, naming his church St Peter's after the martyred missionary-saint's great basilica in Rome. But the redoubtable Italian's efforts to convert the Northumbrians were curtailed within three years when he was forced to flee back to Kent after his royal protector died in battle and the whole kingdom was overrun by neighbouring rulers, Christians among them.

'A VENERABLE AND AWE-INSPIRING PRESENCE'

So great was the fervour of faith and desire for baptism among the Northumbrian people that Paulinus is said to have accompanied the king and queen to the royal residence at Ad-Gefrin [Yeavering, near Wooler], remaining there thirty-six days constantly occupied in instructing and baptising. During this period he did nothing from dawn to dusk but proclaim Christ's saving message to the people, who gathered from all the surrounding villages and countryside; and after he had instructed them he washed them in the cleansing waters of baptism in the nearby river Glen. These events took place in the province of Bernicia. In the province of Deira [Yorkshire], where Paulinus often stayed with the king, he baptised in the river Swale, which flows near the village of Catterick... Paulinus also preached the word of God to the province of Lindsey [Lincolnshire], which lies immediately south of the Humber and extends to the sea. The priest Deda, abbot of the monastery of Partney and a most reliable authority, when relating the story of the Faith in this province, told me that one of the oldest inhabitants had described to him how he and many others had been baptised by Paulinus in the presence of King Edwin, and how the ceremony took place at noon in the river Trent, close to the city which the English call Tiowulfingacaestir [Littleborough]. He used to paint a verbal portrait of Paulinus as a tall man having a slight stoop, with black hair, an ascetic face, a thin hooked nose, and a venerable and awe-inspiring presence. (Bede, *Ecclesiastical History of the English People*, II, 14 & 16)

The full Christianising of Northumbria was finally the achievement of Celtic monks from Scotland and Ireland following the kingdom's reconquest by king Edwin's brother Oswald who had been raised in a Christian community on the Scottish island of Iona. Even so, at the historic Synod of Whitby (664) the majority of the Northumbrian clergy opted to break with the Celtic church and accept the authority of Rome. Now once again, after a gap of two hundred and fifty years, the whole of England was in thrall to an international power based in Rome and unified by a common ideology codified in the Latin language and script. Masons from France and possibly Italy itself were brought over to help raise the north's first stone-built churches in the 'Roman' (Romanesque) style which English travellers encountered along the great pilgrimage routes that took them through France and northern Italy to the heart of Western Christendom.

Paulinus window, south nave, Durham cathedral, circa 1850

Kings and bishops, monks and laymen made the journey, often for political as much as devotional reasons due to the universal prestige of the pope's word in matters of litigation, even an individual's right to rule. Wilfred, the most forceful spokesman for the pro-Rome faction at Whitby and founder of important churches in the new monumental style at Hexham and Ripon, had studied in Rome, and during his long life returned there twice more to secure papal backing for his controversial claim to the bishopric of York.

Another energetic agent of Roman cultural colonialism was Benedict Biscop, the wealthy founder of Benedictine monastries at Wearmouth (673) and Jarrow (681). Five times he visited the Holy City, and his memories of Italy and the numerous manuscripts and sacred paintings he brought back profoundly affected native traditions of art and worship. The Lindisfarne Gospels, created at Wearmouth-Jarrow, were inspired by an Italian exemplar probably procured by Biscop. Ceolfrid, his friend and successor and another avid book collector, set out on his second pilgrimage to Rome at the age of seventy-four only to die in France. Some of his fellow monks journeyed onward to fulfil his vow to present to the pope their magnificent 2000-page transcription of the bible. Known as the Codex Amiatinus, it is one of the greatest treasures of the Laurentian Library in Florence where for long it was taken to be Italian, so closely does it adhere to Italian models.

Traffic between England and Italy went both ways of course. Theologians and scholars were sent out from Rome to instruct the Anglo-Saxon clergy in the rudiments of Latin and the faith. Along with all the holy relics and icons and books which Benedict Biscop brought back from his fourth Rome pilgrimage in 680 came a certain Johannes, a Roman abbot who was also chief cantor at St Peter's. Abbot John, whose brief included ensuring that the young church in Northumbria had rooted out all heretical Celtic tendencies, taught the monks the Roman mode of singing and reading the services in Benedict's own little St Peter's at Monkwearmouth. The following year he too died on the long journey home.

'A MAN CALLED JOHN'

Benedict went on a fourth visit to Rome, returning with a greater variety of spiritual treasures than ever before. In the first place he returned with a great mass of books of every sort. Secondly, he brought back an abundant supply of the relics of the blessed apostles and Christian martyrs which were to prove such a boon for many churches in the land. Thirdly, he introduced in his monastery the order of chanting and singing the psalms and conducting the liturgy according to the practice in force at Rome. To this end Pope Agatho, at Benedict's request, offered him the services of the chief cantor of St Peter's and abbot of the monastery of St Martin, a man called John. Benedict brought him back to Britain to be choirmaster of the monastery... where he was to teach his monks the chant for the liturgical year as it was sung at St Peter's. In accordance with the pope's instructions, Abbot John taught the cantors of the monastery the theory and practice of singing and reading aloud, and he put into writing all that was necessary for the proper observance of festivals throughout the year. The document is still preserved in the monastery, and many copies have been made for other places. John's instruction was not limited to the brethren of this monastery alone; for men who were proficient singers came from nearly all the monasteries of the province to hear him, and he received many invitations to teach elsewhere. (Bede, *Lives of the Abbots of Wearmouth and Jarrow*, chapter 6, and *Ecclesiastical History of the English People*, IV,18.)

The Middle Ages: clergy and merchants

With the decline of papal authority in all northern Europe, and the occupation of much of the British Isles by pagan Danes and Norwegians, the north of England only resumed regular links with Italy in the wake of the Norman Conquest, in an era of church reform inspired by Lanfranc and Anselm, two successive Italian archbishops of Canterbury.

The seal of Cardinal Ottobono Fieschi, papal legate in England 1265-67, appointed to arbitrate between Henry III and the rebel barons under Simon de Montfort, later elected pope Hadrian V. (Durham cathedral chapter library)

The rival claims of Scotland and England to the earldom of Northumbria raised a bloody dispute which raged for centuries. Many times Rome sought to mediate. In 1139, for instance, cardinal Alberico of Ostia, papal legate, was in Durham to negotiate a treaty between king Stephen of England and king David of Scotland. Fourteen years earlier it had been the turn of cardinal Giovanni of Crema to come north on a similar mission. The following colourful account of his reception by bishop Ranulf Flambard, a man notorious for his wit and worldliness, may more or less correspond to the truth but is more likely an inspired fabrication to get back at a powerful foreign prelate who had made himself deeply unpopular as a tough enforcer of Rome's latest decree against clerical marriage and concubinage.

HOW THE BISHOP OF DURHAM TRICKED THE PAPAL LEGATE

In the year 1125 John of Crema summoned a general council in London at which bishop Ranulf Flambard was accused of sexual incontinence and many other things inappropriate to holy office. He denied the charges, defending himself vigorously and refusing to appear for trial. Yet when the legate arrived in Durham he was received with great honour. At table he was plied with wine and became so merry that he fell for the charms of the bishop's niece, a maid of exceptional beauty. Reaching an understanding with the girl, he arranged for her to come to his chamber and to his bed to be initiated in the ways of the Romans, and this she did, all in accordance with the bishop's instructions. Once she was in the legate's bed, the bishop and a throng of clergy and boys burst into the room carrying drinking vessels and torches that made the black of night as bright as day. Surrounding the bed they shouted as one: "Blessings upon you! Blessings!" The legate was stupefied. "By St Peter," he cried, "what's the meaning of this?" "My lord,' retorted the bishop, "here in our country before a gentleman embarks on holy wedlock his friends must do him the honour of paying their respects. So out of bed and sup this goblet. And if you refuse I'll gladly make you down the drink that guarantees you'll never thirst again." Like it or not, he finally got out, and standing there stark naked drank the health of his young 'bride', draining half the goblet. At this the bishop withdrew, no longer fearing for his post. Before daybreak the legate stole off with his concubine whom he had meantime shamefully seduced, making for Rome as fast as he could. (Annals of Winchester Monastery)

The resumption of the conflict between England and Scotland under Edward I brought the boom of a war economy to Newcastle but left the rest of our region the most desolate in England for long after the disaster of Bannockburn (1314). In 1317 cardinals Joscelin D'Osset and Luca Fieschi, papal legates on their way to Scotland with a large retinue to negotiate peace between Edward II and Robert Bruce, were ambushed and robbed of all their valuables by Sir Gilbert Middleton and his band of merry men at Rushyford, only eight miles from the city of Durham where the Frenchman and the Italian were to be guests of honour at the new bishop's enthronement on St Cuthbert's day. They were the highest foreign dignitaries in the land, D'Osset was the reigning pope's nephew and chancellor, and Fieschi's uncle was the short-lived pope Hadrian V. Sir Gilbert, who had turned against the king in protest at his neglect of the north, released the cardinals unharmed but carried off the bishop-elect and his brother. News of the double kidnapping must have been met with mixed feelings in Durham, since the monks had bitterly opposed the nomination of the illiterate Lewis de Beaumont whose only qualification for the lucrative post was that he chanced to be the queen's cousin. Heaping lavish gifts on the outraged cardinals failed to smooth the waters, for when taken to view the saint's shrine in the cathedral they burst out, 'Cuthbert, you shall answer for all we have lost!' vowing that otherwise they would see the mighty building reduced to rubble. Cathedral treasures were hurriedly sold off to raise the ransom fee, and following the release of the De Beaumont brothers and most of the cardinals' valuables Saint Cuthbert further obliged by seeing that Sir Gilbert and his outlaw brothers were duly betrayed and handed over for trial. They all finished hanged, drawn and quartered down in London before the eyes of the placated cardinals. Fieschi left for Italy further consoled by the bishop's written promise of an annual compensation of 'one hundred genuine florins of purest gold', which never materialised.

Bishop De Beaumont did attempt to honour a colossal papal fine imposed for the scandalous methods he had used to secure the bishopric, though it was still not fully paid off when he died fourteen years later. The first massive instalment of two thousand pounds was raised through Amerigo de True and Gerardo Lombardo, two Italian merchants in England who agreed to use their connections in the business community in Rome to advance the sum and deposit it in the papal treasury. In 1322 the bishop again borrowed heavily from Italians, probably to defray the costs of mobilising his Durham tenantry when Edward II finally did come north to muster an army against the Scots. As security he agreed to cede to his creditors, five associates of the Peruzzi merchant company of Florence, all revenues from his diocesan estates in Yorkshire for the next five years.

There was nothing unusual about turning to resident Italians for financial favours. By this time most international banking in Europe was in the hands of family-run merchant companies based in Lombardy and Venetia and in the prosperous city-states of Tuscany (Florence, Lucca, Siena). Known universally as 'Lombards' no matter where they originated, they or their agents were present in every major trading post from Greenland to Cairo. London possessed one of the largest colonies, where it lent its name to Lombard Street in the City (and by emulation centuries later to Lombard Street in the old business quarters of Newcastle and Middlesbrough). Several of these Italian 'societies' owed their prominence to the collection and transmission to Rome of papal exactions from every state in Christendom, an immensely prosperous business which found them perfectly positioned to cultivate influential international connections and penetrate local money markets.

For seventy years, under Edward I and Edward II and Edward III, successive Italian companies were chief bankers and financial agents to the sovereign, their individual fortunes rising and falling according to royal favour. Huge advances, particularly in times of war, were extracted from them in return for assorted concessions and privileges, the most coveted being the right to collect and retain all royal customs dues on wool exports out of English and Irish ports, including Newcastle. Wool was the kingdom's most valued commodity, with most production in the hands of the great monasteries and large estates. The Italians toured the country buying up best quality wool for export to the specialised textile industries of Flanders and Italy.

London, and Boston in Lincolnshire, were the chief ports for the wool export, followed by Southampton, Hull and Yarmouth, with Newcastle only in sixth place. Even so, during Edward I's reign all the major Tuscan companies – the Riccardi of Lucca, and six Florentine societies: the Cerchi Bianchi, the Cerchi Neri, the Pulci, Rimbertini, Frescobaldi, and Mozzi – were leading operators in Newcastle, handling raw wool from all over the north for shipment overseas. One Riccardi agent, Ugolino Gerarducci, traded long enough in Newcastle to be elected a burgess and marry a local widow, Isolda of Pampeden (Pandon). The union promised rich commercial rewards, for Isolda had built up her own thriving export business together with her late husband, one of the wealthiest commoners in Northumbria.

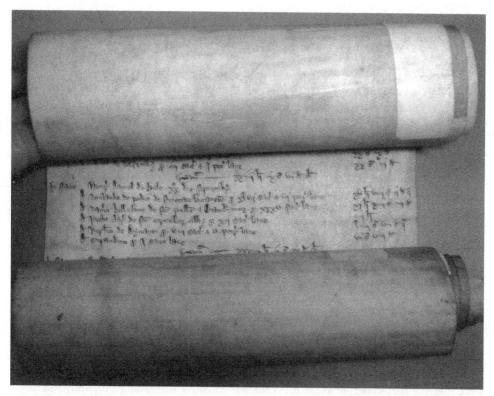

This Newcastle customs account roll for 1293 shows that on 20 September Orlando di Podio (Riccardi society), Ranier Bellinzoni (Pulci society) and Giacomo Chiari (Cerchi Bianchi) exported sixty-three sacks of wool (about four tons). The Italians probably combined to hire the same ship and split the costs. (National Archives).

Financial considerations also regularly brought Italian clerics to the north, in their case for the collection of papal taxes for remission to Rome or occasional levies to support a crusade. Barring a long French interlude in the fourteenth century when the papal court transferred to Avignon, the papal collector was almost always a high-ranking Italian prelate. Comfortably installed in London, he employed a team of sub-collectors, both English and Italian, to tour all the dioceses for him. As well as paying himself a percentage of the takings, the collector could expect to accumulate substantial 'provisions' in England, ecclesiastical offices and benefices which generally required no more commitment than checking that revenues kept rolling in. The wealthy fief of Bishopwearmouth was awarded to cardinal Orsini in 1325, and in the 1370s cardinal Flandrini was garnering the benefice of Houghton-le-Spring. In the wake of the Norman Conquest numerous Italian clerics had picked up English bishoprics and canonries.

Native resentment of these alien tax farmers and merchants and moneylenders sometimes boiled over into active blood-letting. Riccardi agents suffered kidnap and murder in Ireland. In Southampton a street battle between locals and the crew of a Venetian galley, with dead on both sides, persuaded Italian ships to avoid the port for years. As soon as news broke of Edward II's deposition mobs sacked the London headquarters of the Bardi and Peruzzi societies, chief underwriters of his unpopular regime. 'Dress plainly, act humble, dumb in appearance, subtle in deed,' counselled an experienced Tuscan traveller in a wry sonnet cautioning 'anyone going to England'.

Excluding the treatment of Jews and gypsies, and of course age-old antagonism toward our neighbours over the border, there is no record of similar xenophobic outbursts in the north, where in any case Italians and other foreign merchants (German, Flemish, French, Scandinavian) were fewer in number. Nonetheless, as elsewhere in the realm, local entrepreneurs banded together to lobby for financial penalties against all the foreigners on their patch and abolition of the hated royal privileges. The first national success came with the king's 'new custom' in 1303, a supplementary tax on wool exported by all alien dealers in England. Within twenty years all trade out of Newcastle was entirely in the hands of a consortium of home-grown merchants.

A century later, a remarkable Italian journeying through the north spent a memorable night among local 'barbarians' somewhere on the south bank of the Tweed in the winter of 1435-6. Years later, as Pope Pius II, he wrote it all up in his wonderfully candid memoirs, devoting more space to that one episode than to any other event in his adventurous early career. Aeneas Sylvius Piccolomini, as he then was, had just completed a brief visit to Scotland on behalf of his master, cardinal Albergati, the pope's leading representative at the Council of Basle and chief negotiator in a stalled peace settlement to end the Hundred Years War between England and France. Terrible gales during the crossing from Flanders to Scotland had persuaded Aeneas to make the return journey overland as far as possible. He took care to travel incognito since south of the border he knew Albergati was hated for persuading Burgundy to change sides in the English alliance against France, and furthermore it would be presumed his own mysterious mission to James I of Scotland was to incite the king to fresh hostilities on the Borders in order to force the English back to the negotiating table. 'Nothing delights the Scots more than to hear the English abused,' Aeneas noted, recalling how he found the king 'smallish, hot-tempered and craving revenge.'

'GRUESOME, SAVAGE PARTS, IN WINTER NEVER WARMED BY THE SUN'

Disguising himself as a merchant, Aeneas made his way from Scotland to England. A river running down from a high mountain marks the border between the two countries. After crossing it in a small boat he came to a large village around sunset and put up at a farmhouse where he dined with his host and the parish priest. Many dishes were served, including chicken and goose, but neither bread nor wine. The village men and women gathered round as if at some prodigy, and as our people marvel at Ethiopians or Indians these folk gaped spellbound at Aeneas, asking the priest where he came from, what was his business, and if he was a Christian.

Now it so happened that having heard what necessities would be lacking on his journey Aeneas had taken the precaution of procuring several loaves of bread and forty litres of red wine at a certain monastery, and when he had these brought to the table imagine the astonishment of these barbarians who had never before laid eyes on wine or white bread! Pregnant women and their husbands kept coming up to the table, fingering the bread and sniffing the wine and pleading for a taste, so that his entire stock of provisions was soon disposed of with their help. The meal lasted until the second hour of night, then the priest and his host together with all the men and children took their leave of Aeneas very evidently in a hurry to be gone, explaining that they intended taking refuge in a tower a long way off for fear of the Scots, who when the river was at low tide often crossed under cover of darkness to raid them. Aeneas begged to be taken with them but they would not relent, indeed they also left all their womenfolk behind although there were many good-looking maidens and wives among them. Seeing nothing wrong with rape, they believe they face no danger from the enemy.

So Aeneas was left alone with his two servants and his guide among a hundred women who formed a circle round the fire and settled down to sit out the night cleaning hemp and chatting on all subjects through the interpreter. But when a good part of the night had passed, Aeneas, who was by now dropping with sleep, was led to a straw-strewn chamber by two girls willing to sleep with him, as was the custom of the country, if asked. But Aeneas, with less thought for the women than the brigands whom he was terrified might appear at any moment, sent the girls away grumbling. In fact he feared that were he to commit a sin he would be punished for his guilt by the prompt arrival of the brigands. So he remained alone among the heifers and goats which prevented him from sleeping a wink

Aeneas Sylvius Piccolomini sets off for the Council of Basle: detail from a fresco series by Pinturicchio in the Piccolomini chapel, Siena cathedral, celebrating the life of Pope Pius II.

by stealthily plucking the straw from his pallet. *Some time after midnight there was a great din of dogs barking and geese hissing, at which the women scampered off in all directions to hide, and the guide similarly took to his heels, in short it was general pandemonium as if the enemy were at hand. Aeneas instead thought it best to await events in his chamber, or rather stable, so as not to fall victim to the first man he stumbled across if he were to rush outside not knowing the way. However it was not long before the women returned with the interpreter to report there was nothing the matter, the new arrivals were friends not enemies.* Aeneas thought this was nothing less than a reward for his continence.

At daybreak he continued on his way and came to Newcastle, which they say was founded by Julius Caesar. Here for the first time he seemed to see once more the semblance of a civilised world and a land inhabited by humans, for Scotland and the part of England nearest Scotland are utterly unlike the sort of country we live in: gruesome, savage parts, in winter never warmed by the sun.

Next he came to Durham where today men go to see the tomb of the venerable and saintly bishop Bede, deeply revered by the people of the region. He also visited York, a large and populous city where there is a church famous in all the world for its size and architecture, and for a brilliantly lit chapel whose glass walls are held together by astonishingly slender columns.

(The Commentaries of Pope Pius II, book I, 6. Aeneas, who always refers to himself in the third person, evidently muddled the Venerable Bede and the bishop Saint Cuthbert. The passages in Roman type were suppressed in the first edition since thought inappropriate in the memoirs of a Pope.)

Aeneas's choice of disguise suggests that Italian merchants were still occasionally met with in these parts even in the mid-fifteenth century, although the North East's economy had declined drastically ever since fine quality Cotswold wool had eclipsed demand for the north English product. Cloth was now the major export and its manufacture was southern-based, centred in East Anglia and the South West. Again Italian trading houses were heavily involved, and again their commercial acumen roused animosity. An eagerly read doggerel romance of the time celebrated the exploits of the doughty knight Sir Bevis of Hampton (Southampton) who after exterminating innumerable infidels comes to London to face the toughest challenge of his whole bloodthirsty career – the crafty Lombards – and butchers the lot. The reality was not a great deal better. In 1456, and again in 1457, ugly anti-Italian riots erupted in the City, so fearful that the Italian merchant colony considered decamping en masse to Winchester.

Yet within no more than fifty years Italy's domination of international trade was in terminal decline. One after another the rich Italian states fell prey to the colonising ambitions of neighbouring France and Spain, each now consolidated as large nation states. In the fragmented peninsula no unity met the aggressors and war was almost continuous for forty years. Lombardy and the entire south of the peninsula fell to Spain. Piedmont and Genoa, Venice and Florence somehow survived, though all impoverished. In 1527 Rome itself was sacked by Lutheran mercenaries. Italy's chief client states to the north, first France and then England and Holland, developed powerful commercial fleets of their own which out-competed Italian merchant shipping in the Atlantic, and finally even in the Mediterranean itself.

Italy's long commercial supremacy was over, but her unparalleled achievements in all the arts, both past and present, more than ever fired the imagination of her competitors and conquerors.

The Renaissance: mercenaries and military engineers

By the summer of 1569, when townsfolk flocked to gape at the 'strange and monstrous serpent' which a certain Italian displayed in Durham market place (see Preface), the English were relatively used to similar exotic figures, few in number yet conspicuous enough as roving showmen and fairground entertainers. In more exalted circles, at court and in the great houses and universities, the glamour associated with the revival of classical culture and style which we now call the Renaissance might accompany a Venetian ambassador or a Bolognese professor who had fled the ruthless stifling of dissent which was the papacy's response to the protestant revolution in northern Europe. Noble households competed to employ Italian lutanists and fencing-masters, one even boasted an Italian astrologer. Anything with an Italian label was fashionable, much as in our own day, though then it was exclusively a matter for the elite. Henry VIII engaged Italian artists to design his parents' tombs in Westminster Abbey and his own never-finished mausoleum, while others worked alongside craftsmen from France

Arquebusier with 'hackbutt' and gun rest. Italian and Spanish mercenaries based in the North East specialised in firing this cumbersome handgun even on horseback.

and Holland to embellish showpiece buildings like Nonsuch Palace and Hampton Court in a bid to outshine Francis I's extravagantly Italianate palace of Fontainebleau.

Despite reviving her father's anti-Rome policy, the vogue for things Italian continued under Elizabeth who had been brought up to speak and write Italian. Many of her courtiers knew Italy at first hand, and some could flatter her with sonnets and even epics in the Italian mode. Aspiring clerics and lawyers had for centuries gone to Padua or Bologna for university training, now civil servants and even humble artists found familiarity with Italy could do wonders for a career. The Duke of Northumberland helped to set a trend when in 1550 he paid a young protégé of his, John Shute, to go to Italy 'to view the ancient monumentes and to confer with the doings of ye skilful maisters in architecture.'

But the fascination with Italy also had a darker side. The very real threat of invasion from Catholic Europe bred general suspicion of compatriots sympathetic to new-fangled foreign ways, and age-old xenophobia and new Protestant paranoia combined to give true-blue Englishmen a fine nose for the faintest whiff of 'popery'. 'From the deceit and tyranny of the bishop of Rome, Lord deliver us!' was a routine chant in English church litanies, reported home Daniele Barbaro, the Venetian envoy. Popular playwrights such as Shakespeare and Webster plundered Italian chronicles and story-books for sensational plots to feed the public's hunger for tales of passion and treachery in an Italian setting.

Meanwhile, up here in the unsophisticated north, the land of moss troopers and freebooters and a near-feudal peasantry, four or five days hard ride from London, most of the population and its masters held true to the Old Religion. Henry VIII's suppression of the minor monasteries was taken as an attack on the people's faith, almost instantly triggering the 1536 northern rising known as the Pilgrimage of Grace, the most threatening of all the provincial rebellions against the Tudors. It took a massive army to break it. Within just a few years of the inevitable repression another formidable force gathered in the north, this time against Scotland. It was the start of Henry VIII's 'rough wooing' of Mary Queen of Scots, his brutal policy of laying waste to the Borders to force the infant queen's Scottish minders to betroth her to his own young son and heir, the short-lived future Edward VI, so binding the two countries together. Starting off from bases in the North East, the port of Leith was sacked and burned, and in 1544 Edinburgh too, though the great castle held out.

Next spring, after a humiliating English defeat at Ancrum Moor and reports of a large force assembling in France to aid the Scots, hundreds of Italian and other continental mercenaries were hastily recruited to reinforce the regular garrisons at the North East's main strategic points: Norham, Wark, Berwick, Newcastle, Durham. The 'Spanish Battery' at Tynemouth owes its name to Spanish mercenaries who were the largest component of this international force of military adventurers deployed in the region over the next five years. In that era before the introduction of costly national standing armies, professional soldiers like today's international footballers would join any team that paid good money. Scottish mercenaries fought on both the English and French sides in Henry VIII's concurrent struggle to conquer and hold Bologne.

From all over Europe soldiers of fortune flocked to join the English forces mired in France. Many were diverted across the Channel to strengthen south coast garrisons or to muster in London before proceeding northwards. Others were shipped straight to Newcastle. When all the 'strangers', as foreigners were termed, had gathered in the north they numbered over two thousand between cavalry and infantry, predominantly Spanish (under captain Pedro de Gamba) and Italian (captains Morgante and Muscovit), with a sprinkling of other nationalities. In early August, the earl of Hertford, field commander in the north, reported to the king from his Newcastle headquarters that he had deployed 'all the Spaniards, both horse and foot, at Morpeth and Alnwick, and Muscovit with his 150 Italian footmen within four miles of Berwick, and the rest of the strangers, horsemen, as the Italians, Albanians and Clevois, here at Newcastle and Durham, ready to set forward as needful'. The order to cross the Tweed was delayed until the corn was drying in the fields and easily fired. In the ensuing two-week campaign an army of some 15,000 English and foreigners torched numerous towns and hamlets as well as the great abbeys of Kelso, Melrose, Dryburgh and Jedburgh, all wrecks to this day. It is not hard to imagine the feelings of the people of Kelso who lynched three Italian stragglers. After this spree, which did nothing to advance the king's political cause, the campaigning season was over for another year, winter was coming and all 'strangers' but for the Spaniards were redeployed to Boulogne.

They were back in force in 1547, by which time Henry was dead and on the continent peace had broken out between England and France, leaving both countries free to focus on their rival ambitions in Scotland. The earl of Hertford, now duke of Somerset and protector of England during Edward VI's minority, was the first to move. His large force with its main body of mercenaries under count Piero Malatesta Baglione, an Italian condottiere, advanced in time to rout the Scots at the battle of Pinkie before the arrival of a French fleet packed with fresh troops and artillery under another notable Italian captain, Leo Strozzi. Next year, France committed a larger force of 10,000 men to the cause, which in turn drew yet more Italians and others across the Channel in pursuit of English contracts. By 1550 the massive French presence had tipped the scales in Scotland's favour and England sued for peace.

Over 7000 'strangers' served in the north during the Scottish wars, perhaps a third of them Italian. State papers preserve the names of many involved at various levels in the successive campaigns. In 1549, for example, the treasury noted payments to Gaspare Como 'and nine other Italians sent into the north,' Carlo Dado 'sent into the North,' Vincenzo Bellacci 'and others in his company, for service in the North,' Captain Battista Spinola 'serving in the North,' Cesare Dattilo 'and four servants, sent to the North'.

Italian expertise in the art of war, honed during the decades of international conflict in the peninsula, was universally deemed supreme in the field of military engineering. Specialists in fortifications, like the mercenaries, easily found patrons wherever their skills were needed. A new approach to fortification, technically known as *trace italienne*, had been pioneered during the Italian wars in response to the havoc wreaked on conventional high-built fortresses by more effective modern cannon. Features of the concept first appear in England from 1543 in connection with Henry VIII's overhaul of the system of coastal defences in expectation of a French invasion, an immensely costly project largely financed out of church revenues amassed after the break with Rome.

Though Henry did not employ Italian military engineers on the same scale as his continental rivals, a number were drafted into our region during the years of the 'rough wooing'. Three Italians surveyed Tynemouth in 1545 with a brief to improve its defences: Arcangelo Arcano, a gunnery expert who had already worked on the south coast, then Antonio da Bergamo and Gian Tommaso Scala of Venice, both described as 'Italians expert in fortifying'. These two went on to draw up plans for strengthening Wark castle and Lindisfarne harbour, and in 1547 were joined by Giovanni Rossetti, the earl of Hertford's chief military engineer during his last three years of Scottish campaigning. All the Italians worked in close consultation with Sir Richard Lee, the foremost English military architect who had studied Italianate fortifications in France.

Plan for the defences of Tynemouth by Gian Tommaso Scala, 1545, with notes in Italian. 'A revolutionary design for an English fortification and probably the earliest surviving drawing in the new Italianate idiom'
(H.M. Colvin). (British Library, Cotton Augustus I,ii,7.)

15

No fortification project in all England was more ambitious than the *trace italienne* modernising of the defences of Berwick in the early years of Elizabeth's reign, after the loss of Calais in 1558 again revived fears of a Franco-Scottish invasion. The first Italian to be summoned when work had already begun under Lee's supervision was Giovanni Portinari, a Florentine engineer and explosives expert who had made a long and varied career in England, blowing up church property for Henry VIII, overseeing work on the king's colossal Italian-designed mausoleum, and directing the English sappers in the siege of Boulogne. More recently he had been at work on French fortifications in Piedmont. He was in Berwick in 1560, and again in 1564 in the company of another Italian military engineer, Jacopo Aconcio, a protestant convert and important early theorist of religious tolerance who had fled Italy to escape persecution. On both occasions the Italians finished up locked in bitter dispute with Lee and his English associates over crucial features of the project. Some of their recommendations were carried out, but government alarm at spiralling costs put paid to their repeated advice to extend the system right round the south and west sides of the town where it was poorly protected by much older walls. Even so, the completed Elizabethan ramparts of Berwick are among the very finest examples outside Italy of the new methods of fortification, of stunning power even today.

In later centuries, when security finally came to the Borders with the union of the two crowns and soon the two countries of England and Scotland, the North East was to develop more peaceable connections with Italians.

The Italianate ramparts of Berwick: Cumberland bastion looking toward Brass bastion and the sea. The most evident trace italienne *features of the fortification system are these prominent but relatively low-lying triangular bastions at each corner projecting far beyond the curtain wall to give the fullest scope for both offensive fire and protective flanking fire. Windmill bastion was still in good enough condition to support a gun battery in World War II.*

The eighteenth century: Italian–Swiss stuccoists

The eighteenth century was the great era of the English country house, handsomely proportioned mansions set in orderly parkland and more or less directly inspired by the classic architecture of Andrea Palladio, the creator of luxurious country retreats for Venetian patricians two hundred years earlier. Veneration for Italy's artistic heritage, often stimulated by direct experience on the Grand Tour, flourished among the well-to-do who admired and collected originals or copies of Italian art and statuary and flocked to the Italian opera houses in London to applaud the celebrity castratos and prima donnas. In the decorative arts, generally more attentive to fashions in neighbouring France, a short vogue for monumental Baroque was soon superseded by a craze for French Rococo, a style as elegant and frivolous as a minuet, perfectly attuned to the tastes of the leisured classes of pre-revolutionary Europe. Among its most gifted practitioners were roaming Italian and Swiss-Italian master plasterers who handled stucco with a verve and

Great Hall, Seaton Delaval. Damage in the great fire of 1822 reveals the stuccadores' method of modelling on a base of 'rubble and tile cores, thin metal armatures, and hessian soaked in gypsum, folded and nailed to the figures to simulate, when set, classical drapery' (Geoffrey Beard).

freedom that reflected a long grounding in the eccentricities of their native baroque. In Britain they were called 'stuccadores', from the Italian *stuccatore*. Punctuated by rare visits home, some spent years in our region decorating the interiors of the stately homes and castles which fashionable architects like James Paine and Daniel Garrett created or restyled for the old landed gentry and the new men grown rich on coal and commerce.

Itinerant artisans with a particular specialist skill invariably come from areas with a long tradition in that craft. The masters and their young apprentices who took the secrets of stucco to northern Europe were almost all born in small towns and villages near Lugano and Como, a region of great lakes and precipitous mountains divided by the Swiss-Italian frontier but sharing the same language and a common history of deprivation and migration. For centuries the perpetual struggle against nature and poverty had compelled great numbers of males to leave home for a season or longer, hiring out their labour in the farms and cities of the plains, or developing a skill which might bring in some income from the wider world.

One common means of escape and advancement lay in the region's high reputation in every aspect of the building trade from stone-hewer to master builder. Ever since medieval times men from the lakes region had built and decorated palaces and churches and monasteries all over Italy and even as far north as the Rhineland, and in later centuries their experience and ingenuity helped to shape the townscapes of great cities like Rome, Vienna, Prague and St Petersburg. From around 1660 began an extraordinary exodus of home-grown talent from the Lake Lugano basin in Switzerland and the Intelvi valley (Val d'Intelvi) on the Italian side of the border: adventurous individuals, even entire families of architects, masons, sculptors, carvers, stuccoists and painters, carried the grand style of High Baroque and its playful off-shoot Rococo deep into central Europe and beyond. Glorious cream-and-gold churches and palaces in Austria, Germany, Bohemia, Poland, even Scandinavia, owe their inspiration to the men from the high valleys.

Baroque, the sumptuous style of papal Rome and Louis XIV's France, stood for everything England's Puritan revolution abhorred, so was only belatedly adopted after the restoration of the Stuart monarchy in 1660. Its foremost architects were Wren, Hawksmoor, and Vanbrugh. In the north of England, remote from the royal court, outstanding examples are few and more or less begin and end with Sir John Vanbrugh's solitary extravagant creations, Castle Howard in Yorkshire (1699-1726), and Seaton Delaval Hall, Northumbria (1718-28).

The central block at Seaton was gutted by fire in 1822 but the surviving shell still contains ravaged remnants of what looks like exceptionally fine work by Vanbrugh's stuccadores, Giovanni Bagutti and his assistant Giuseppe Plura, who had earlier worked at Castle Howard. Bagutti, from the small town of Rovio near lake Lugano, appears to have been the very first stuccadore to reach Britain, probably through Vanbrugh's friend Charles Montagu, Britain's ambassador in Venice, who recruited several artists for prestigious projects in England. The chance fact of Bagutti's Swiss origins explains why all who regularly worked stucco in Britain over the next sixty years were also from the canton of Ticino, despite the great reputation of their rivals over the border. Not that such fine distinctions troubled their lordly patrons over here for whom their Swiss workers were all 'Italians' because of their Italian names and speech. Word spread rapidly round Lugano that there were rich pickings in England, making the Swiss revival of British stucco in the eighteenth century a classic instance of so-called 'chain migration' (see map 1 on page 110).

In this Alpine heartland of the art of stucco (a durable modelling medium from classical times whose lost formula was rediscovered by Raphael's circle in Rome: powdered marble is added to the usual mix of gypsum, lime and sand) the craft was handed down through the family or by enrolling boys with relatives or friends in the trade for a rigorous five-year apprenticeship. With scant local employment opportunities they became used to working elsewhere in Italy or abroad from a very early age. Master and apprentices travelled with standard moulds and pattern books which could be freely adapted for all manner of ornamental schemes of their own devising or worked up from designs prepared by the architect. The most accomplished became superb sculptors in plaster, speedily executing anything from a low-relief garland of fruit and flowers to life-size portrait busts and figures. In Britain, though, where sober 'Palladianism' ruled the day, their creative flair had to be accommodated to the genteel code of restraint in art as well as manners that typified early Georgian England's reaction to 'affected and licentious' Baroque, as one of its leading exponents revealingly expressed it. As a consequence, apart from superb artists more in the baroque tradition such as Bagutti and Giuseppe Artari, another Swiss master who may have worked at Seaton, and indeed the North East's own favourite, Lafranchini, Britain proved most congenial to stuccoists with less flamboyant powers, inspired providers of the decorous and charming rather than anything too daringly individual. Another constraint was that their opulent style was considered inappropriate for church interiors (Catholic churches were of course still outlawed), yet this was a field in which they excelled in continental Europe.

After Seaton Delaval, the next master stuccoist to work in the North East was Francesco Vassalli, who came from Riva San Vitale at the south-eastern tip of Lake Lugano. Having also worked in Germany, Vassalli is thought to have been the first to bring the Italianate rococo style of stucco to Scotland. In 1734-6 he decorated the main rooms in a palatial bath house at Gibside near Gateshead for its new owner, the coal magnate George Bowes. Nothing of this work survives, nor of the reputedly magnificent rooms which Vasssalli created at Aske Hall near Richmond.

But the peak of the fashion for Italian stucco in our region came just a little later, in the two decades 1740-60 when two masters of the craft working quite independently picked up most of the many commissions. Giuseppe Cortese found his patrons in County Durham, while the prolific Pietro-Natale Lafranchini, who was the earlier arrival, worked all over the region. Born in 1705 at Bironico, some ten miles north of Lugano, he was the youngest of three brothers, all *stuccatori*, who found their way to Britain in the 1730s. After all three had worked in the south for the leading Palladian architect James Gibbs, the older brothers Paolo and Filippo became the first 'Italians' to secure commissions in Ireland where their example inspired the 'Dublin school' of stucco which famously distinguishes many Georgian houses in the capital.

In 1740, Sir Walter Calverley Blackett, MP for Newcastle and many times mayor of the city, initiated a Palladian-style modernisation of his country seat of Wallington in Northumbria. His architect, Daniel Garrett, who had no doubt appreciated the Lafranchini brothers' work when he too was employed in London, settled Pietro-Natale and his assistants on the Blackett estate at nearby Cambo village. Over the next eighteen months the little team completed all the exquisite plasterwork in the major rooms of the great house. Now owned by the National Trust, Wallington Hall has become a great favourite with the public, but not so well known is that equally fine examples of stucco décor by Swiss-Italian master-plasterers can be found all over the North East, though being mostly in domestic settings very few are so easily accessible. In London Daniel Garrett had been employed as clerk of works for Lord Burlington, the founding patron of British Palladianism, and this fortunate combination of useful professional connections and the Wallington showcase brought Pietro-Natale a string of commissions both in and beyond our region. One magnificent example open to the public is the sumptuous almost baroque decor of the Garrett-designed Garter Room at Lumley Castle, near Chester-le-Street. Fine rooms at privately owned Biddick Hall nearby are almost certainly also his work, presumably executed around the time he and his team decorated all the state rooms at Hylton Castle, just a few miles away, though every trace of that work disappeared long ago. Other Lafranchini losses are his original stuccowork inside Fenham Hall, Newcastle, and in Gosforth House (now Brandling House). Gone too are the most prestigious of all his commissions for great northern landowners, at the Duke of Cleveland's London residence, and in the Duke of Northumberland's huge mansion in the Strand, demolished to create Northumberland Avenue.

The full extent of Pietro-Natale Lafranchini's work in the North East can only be guessed at. Nikolaus Pevsner, the great connoisseur of English provincial architecture, was convinced he detected his trademark 'exuberant rococo' inside several more great houses in Northumbria – Callaly Castle, Bywell Hall, Nunwick House, Little Harle, Blagdon and Capheaton. The striking stuccowork at 55-57 Westgate Road, Newcastle, now under restoration, may also be Lafranchini's. On the other hand, an obscure contender for at least some of this plethora of expert work has now come to light. He is Filippo Danieli, whom records show worked stucco at Nunwick House around 1760. As 'Philip Daniel' he is also recorded on the workforce at Gibside, where a sample of his artistry can be viewed inside the restored Rococo-Gothick banqueting house.

Giuseppe Cortese, the other major Italian-Swiss master who became a favourite choice for many of the region's stately homes, was a native of Mendrisio, situated midway between Como and Lugano. As 'Joseph' Cortese he worked for over forty years in England, most often in Yorkshire for the architect John Carr. His County Durham commissions were executed over various visits between 1745 and 1766. His earliest work, at Hardwick Hall near Sedgefield, has all perished, but fine examples survive in Auckland Castle (notably the King Charles room), and at Elemore Hall and Croxdale Hall, both within a few miles of Durham City. On stylistic grounds several glorious stuccoed rooms in the city itself, at Aykley Heads House and at Castle Chare (now St Godric's Court), have also been confidently attributed to Cortese. An attested commission was the plasterwork at Coxhoe Hall, demolished in 1956 after serving as a camp for Italian prisoners-of-war (see chapter 7). A photograph of the drawing room survives. The bizarre heads in the whimsical chimneypiece and the placid goddess floating on clouds inside the ceiling arabesques must have been among the earliest delights of the poet Elizabeth Barrett Browning whose infancy was spent here (see illustration).

Other than the élan so evident in the work they left, nothing is known about the personalities of these foreign craftsmen who created such beguiling settings for the lives of the good, the bad and the ugly in so many of the North East's grandest homes. No memoirist of the time thought to record what it was like to see their 'exuberant' creations emerge under their expert touch. The value of their artistry was estimated by the yard, with standard higher fees for busts and figures. Account books show the sums they earned were not excessive. If recorded at all, their names were prefaced by 'Mr' to distinguish them from common labourers. One thing is certain though: these Italian Swiss were of the hardiest mountain stock. Vassalli worked far from home for half a century. Lafranchini died in Lugano aged 83. Cortese, who made York his permanent home, was touching seventy when he embarked on his last recorded commission. For anyone who has seen their best creations it is hard not to conclude that the secret of such longevity so unusual for their time was the delight they took in their joyous work and the delight they gave.

Delicate plasterwork by Pietro-Natale Lafranchini and his team of stuccadores in the drawing room, Wallington, Northumberland, 1741. (Photo courtesy the National Trust).

Detail of Lafranchini's more baroque decor in an upper corner of the vast Garter Room, Lumley Castle, 1745. Richard Lumley, having just been awarded the Order of the Garter, made sure the star of the order formed the centrepiece of this stupendous ceiling.

(Right) Stucco decor by Giuseppe Cortese in the drawing room at Coxhoe Hall (1749), demolished in 1956. (Photo preserved in Durham University library).

Cortese's bill for stuccowork executed for George Baker at Elemore Hall, 1752. The artist, who always signed 'Joseph Cortese', clearly worked hard at his English. The 'marble columns and pilasters' will have been made in scagliola, plaster pigmented and polished to imitate marble, another speciality of the stuccadores. (Baker Baker papers, Durham University library).

Detail of Cortese's 'ceiling of ye dining room', Elemore Hall. Much of the ceiling work and all 'ornaments of ye walls' are now lost.

BOOKS AND SOURCES

Romans in the North. The Vindolanda writing tablets can be consulted online at http://vindolanda.csad.ox.ac.uk. For 'Lousius Suavis' see R.G.Collingwood and R.P.Wright, *Roman Inscriptions of Britain* vol 1 (1995), RIB numbers 1499, 1506, 1681, 1859, 1861. We have been unable to trace the text of Tommy Gow's poem which goes on to tour the region's many Italian 'ice cream sites' still flourishing in the 1960s.

The second Roman conquest. Bede, *Ecclesiastical History of the English People* (Penguin Books, 1990). Peter Hunter Blair, *Northumbria in the Days of Bede* (1976). Nicholas Higham, *The Northern Counties to AD 1000* (1986).

The Middle Ages: clergy and merchants. W. Hutchinson, *The History and Antiquities of the County Palatine of Durham,* vol 1, (1825). A.D.M.Barrell, *The Papacy, Scotland and Northern England 1342-1378* (1993). R.A.Lomas, *North East England in the Middle Ages* (1992). M. Harvey, *England, Rome and the Papacy 1417-1464* (1993). Cardinal da Crema and Bishop Flambard: *Annales monasteri de Wintonia* in *Annales monastici* ii, 47-8 (ed. H.R.Luard, 1864-9). Documents relating to Bishop de Beaumont, the despoiled cardinals, and Italian money-lenders: *Historiae Dunelmensis scriptores tres,* ed. J. Raine, (Surtees Society n.9, 1839). The merchant-bankers: R.W.Kaeuper, *Bankers to the Crown: the Riccardi of Lucca and Edward I* (1973). T.H.Lloyd, *Alien Merchants in England in the High Middle Ages* (1982). J. Conway Davies, 'The Wool Customs Accounts for Newcastle-upon-Tyne for the Reign of Edward I' in *Archaeologia Aeliana,* 1954. Several English translations exist of Aeneas Sylvius Piccolomini's *Commentarii,* the Latin memoirs of Pope Pius II.

The Renaissance: mercenaries and military engineers. *Letters and Papers Foreign and Domestic: Henry VIII,* vols. 20 and 21. *Calendar of State Papers Domestic: Edward VI. Calendar of State Papers Scotland,* vol 1. M.L.Bush 'The Problem of the Far North' in *Northern History,* 6 (1971). G.J.Millar, *Tudor Mercenaries and Auxiliaries 1485-1547* (1980). G. Phillips, *The Anglo-Scots Wars 1513-1550* (1999). H.M. Colvin, *The History of the King's Works,* vol IV, pt 3 (1982), with much on the contribution of the Italians. I.MacIvor, 'The Elizabethan Fortification at Berwick-upon-Tweed', *Antiquaries Journal,* XLV (1965), and his many times reprinted illustrated pamphlet for the Department of the Environment, *The Fortifications of Berwick-upon-Tweed.* L. White, 'Jacopo Aconcio as an Engineer' in *The American Historical Review,* vol 72 (1967). 'Tudor Fortifications, 1495-1558' in J.R.Hale, *Renaissance War Studies* (1983).

Italian-Swiss stuccoists. For their provenance, working methods and achievements see *Decorative Plasterwork in Great Britain* (1975), *Stucco and Decorative Plasterwork in Europe* (1983), and the pamphlet *Italian Stuccoists in Yorkshire* (1986), all by Geoffrey Beard, the latter very useful on Cortese. On Vassalli and Daniel: Margaret Wills, *Gibside and the Bowes Family* (1995). On Lafranchini: Carlo Palumbo-Fossati, *Gli stuccatori ticinesi Lafranchini in Inghilterra e in Irlanda nel secolo XVIII* (1982). On the Wallington team: John Cornforth in *Country Life* vol 147 (March 12, and 16, 23 & 30 April 1970), and Peter Leach, 'The Architecture of Daniel Garrett', in *Country Life* vol 156 (September 12, 19 and 26). More on Cortese in John Gosden, 'Elemore

Hall Transformed' (*Transactions of the Architectural and Archaeological Society of Durham and Northumberland*, new series 6, 1982), and *Lost Houses of County Durham* (1993) by P. Meadows and E. Waterson.

Contacts with Italy and with Italian artists and architects made by local gentry in the era of the Grand Tour are expertly traced in Anne French's *Art Treasures in the North: Northern Families on the Grand Tour* (2009). Concert visits by Italian musicians figure in Roz Southey, *The Ingenious Mr Avison: Making Music and Money in Eighteenth Century Newcastle* (2009). As well as reviewing the season and the stars at the Italian opera houses in London and Paris, the *Newcastle Courant* habitually gave extensive coverage to local performances by visiting Italian artistes.

Stuccowork detail by Pietro-Natale Lafranchini,
Lumley Castle.

2

ARCHITECTS AND ARTISANS

I received your two letters. It is a relief to know you are both well, as I am too, and I can say I am glad to be in this country. Please do not be sad because dwelling on things too much could hurt your health and that is my greatest concern. For now I send greetings to all from the bottom of my heart, my dear father and mother and sisters and brother, and all my family and friends and all who ask after me.

Addio, addio

Your son

Matteo Tarelli

Newcastle, 20 May 1850.

The barometer makers of Newcastle

In the very last years of the eighteenth century a small community of skilled craftsmen from northern Italy began to put down roots in Newcastle. Metalwork, cabinet-making, and glass-blowing were the essentials of their craft. Best known for the production of barometers, they also made other precision instruments and optical devices such as thermometers, compasses, telescopes, microscopes, opera glasses, and simple eye glasses. Picture frames, ornamental mirrors, and clock-making were other staples. They came from the same mountainous region as the Swiss stuccadores, but on the Italian side of the border, from the many hill and lakeside communities dotted around Lake Como. As with their Swiss neighbours, a high proportion of Comasques left home for shorter or longer periods in pursuit of a living, since their patches of land in inhospitable terrain seldom produced enough to support an entire family

Barometer inscribed 'C. Tarelli, Newcastle'.[1]

for more than a few months of the year. Setting out for the first time, often as young as twelve, they left behind one of the most beautiful and dramatic landscapes in Europe but also a once stable peasant economy now acutely disrupted by overpopulation, loss of communal grazing rights, shrinking demand for raw silk (the main produce of many households), a high incidence of pellagra and lung disease, and punitive taxation. In general only the males left home, those of military age with the extra incentive of escaping conscription into the Austrian army (until 1860 Lombardy was part of the Austro-Hungarian empire). Their wives and sisters stayed behind to care for the very young and the very elderly, work the land and tend the animals.

Migration was mostly seasonal, spent peddling cheap merchandise or working on farms and building sites, anything to scrape together enough to fill bellies through the winter. The most adventurous struck out for unknown lands in the footsteps of near-legendary pioneers reportedly living like lords in Moscow or Madrid, or with visions of emulating some fabulous figure who after long years away had suddenly reappeared with a strange woman on his arm and money enough to buy half the village.

'I DISCOVERED HE HAD TRAVELLED ALL OVER'

There are people among us who wander to all nations selling barometers, thermometers, optical instruments and similar articles which they carry with them. There is not one district round the lake and in Valassina without them. Men back from abroad can always be seen about Como in large numbers, and by their appearance, demeanour, and the cut of their clothes, it is easy to tell which country they were in. Once, during a tour of inspection in the mountains of Pieve del Dongo, I had to spend part of the night in a shepherd's hovel, and falling into conversation with the peasant who accompanied me because he owned the mule I was riding I discovered he had travelled all over Germany, Denmark, Norway, Sweden and Russia, and had many apt things to say about these countries and knew the languages. They begin by selling barometers and then go on to specialise in some other form of portable merchandise. The man I mention sold maps. The custom is to set out at a tender age in the company of relatives or friends who are already experienced travellers. Some return for a year or two then depart again, others remain far from the homeland until of an age to marry. In this case they spend a few years at home, then set out once more. Generally all come back with money. Some have made considerable fortunes.

(Giuseppe Pecis, superintendant of roads and waterways for the government of Milan, 1774.)

Long before the first barometer maker (*barometaio*) settled in Newcastle around 1795, fellow Comasques had been tramping the roads of northern Europe, hawking their wares from door to door or bidding for custom at markets and fairs. No one knows when the first came to Britain. A glass-blower from Como called Molinari set up in Edinburgh as early as 1752, and by 1785 a weather-glass maker called Ronchetti was installed in Manchester. There were four barometer and thermometer businesses in London by 1810, and twenty-one by the mid-century. 'These poor Comasques issue forth to every country in Europe to carry on a petty commerce in which ingenuity is combined with great industry and frugality: these are they who everywhere are seen with barometers, looking-glasses, coloured prints, gilt frames, and other works which smack of the arts and ingenuity of their native country.' So wrote Lady Morgan in her 1821 bestseller *Italy*, knowing how they were a common sight for her readers at home. While holidaying on Lake Como in 1819 she had been struck by 'the singular fact that a vast number of the villages which rise above the lake are only inhabited by females.' Specific villages, she discovered, were designated 'Spanish, English, American &c, according to the favourite place of immigration of the inhabitants.'

Among these many wandering 'poor Comasques' were Giovanni Pochini, and Lorenzo and Giovanni Berti, the latter presumably brothers. All three lived long enough in Newcastle in the mid-1790s to start families with English partners. The Bertis, turning for home or moving on to some other centre with their young families, vanish from the record, but Pochini was still manufacturing and selling barometers at his premises in Dean Street in 1811. By then he was 'John Pochaine' in his adoptive city, and had started a sideline as a toy dealer.

During the last years of the Napoleonic wars – tough times for north Italians whose 'liberation' by French troops brought oppressive taxation and mass conscription into Bonaparte's armies – arrived young Francesco ('Francis') Bernasconi. Born in 1786, he and his Tyneside wife Isabella Murray and their many children resided in a home-cum-workshop near the quayside for over thirty years. Finally, in the 1840s, at the head of a small team consisting of one of his sons, his Comasque son-in-law, and a Comasque assistant, he moved to premises in the High Bridge, grandly advertising his skills as 'barometer, thermometer, glass hydrometer, and saccharimeter manufacturer'.

Soon after the peace of 1815 three more young Comasques opted for Newcastle. First came Giuseppe Falla ('Joseph Fallow'), a specialist in clocks as well as barometers, and Bernardo Paulucci ('Bernard Poulutchey'), jeweller, both with premises in crowded Pilgrim Street. The third arrival was Antonio Tarelli, born in 1795, presumably summoned by 'John Pochaine', since he is soon recorded installed at the old man's Dean Street address where customers found him combining the roles of barometer maker, optician, and toy dealer. Paulucci and Tarelli both married locally. Tarelli, who meantime had been joined by his younger brother Carlo, did so well that eventually he dwelled among the cream of society in Eldon Square. When in 1863 the British Association for the Advancement of Science decided to honour Newcastle's leading role in the industrial revolution by holding its annual conference in the city 'Tarelli and Son' in handsome Grey Street was the place to go for 'mathematical, nautical and philosophical instruments.'[2]

By the 1840s the small colony of *barometai* had expanded to some seven or eight core families who as their businesses prospered drew on a fund of new blood among their kith and kin in the homeland. Their own technical ingenuity, combined with the newcomers' fresh areas of expertise and everyone's general business flair, saw these small family enterprises branching out variously into the production of clocks and watches, jewellery, looking glasses, picture frames, and the retail of furniture and fancy goods. All operated from well-placed addresses in the city centre. Giambattista ('John Baptist') Bergna arrived in the early 1830s, setting up next to the Tarelli family in St Nicholas Churchyard, a few doors along from Thomas Bewick and Sons, printers and engravers. He found an outlet for his production in a 'jewellery and toy warehouse' at Giovanni Origoni's place in Dean Street, in a partnership which included his own brother Giuseppe Bergna and members of the Grassi family. Bergna descendants were to carry on in jewellery well into the next century, in both Newcastle and Sunderland.

Around 1838, four other newcomers pooled skills and resources to set up as 'barometer, thermometer and looking glass manufacturers' in fashionable Grainger Street soon after its completion. The partners were Angelo Molteni and his brother Natale (aka 'Christmas'!) from the village of Albese, near Como, a certain Fornelli, and Vittorio ('Victory') Mastaglio from Dosso del Liro, a hamlet perched high above the northern arm of the lake (see map on page 110). Manufacturing soon took second place as the business blossomed in the hands of Christmas and Victory into a 'London, Birmingham and Sheffield Warehouse' specialising in the retail of fancy goods, a success which inspired other *barometai* to move in the same direction. The Molteni-Mastaglio business links with the capital and two other major industrial cities imply that personal connections within the nationwide Comasque community were put to good use. In 1853, Victory, who maintained another shop and workshop in Carliol Square, went into partnership with 'John' Tacchi to open 'Noah's Ark Bazaar' in Sunderland High Street (see the advertisement of a later date when Tacchi was sole owner, still showing the Noah's Ark emblem above the entrance). The Carliol Square premises were later expanded into a large furniture business by Victory's sons John and Joseph, who in 1881 were employing a workforce of 24 men and boys, still including at least three specialists from Italy.

Anglicised names inevitably indicate some degree of assimilation within the host community, and indeed all these Italian-born men who settled here and married chose English wives, and most became British subjects. All the same, for as long as they thrived business remained as far as possible 'in the family'. Specialist craftsmen, journeymen assistants and shopmen continued to be recruited from the same small area of Italy, or found their way to Newcastle through the substantial Comasque network in Britain. It was with the second generation that links with the homeland became more tenuous. The ageing immigrants' children were English in all but name, and in any case in the land that pioneered mass production there were diminishing opportunities for independent artisans. Well before the end of the century the last families of Comasque descent still in business had all moved into the retail trade, and most of their staff was English.

Four or five of the original families cornered the lion's share of the city's toy trade, as importers and retailers rather than manufacturers, with extra outlets in Sunderland, Durham, and Darlington, run by other members of the circle. The pioneers had been Pochini and Tarelli, but the strongest business grew to be the partnership of Grassi and Rampoldi, 'general factors and importers of French and German toys', located in fashionable Grey Street in the 1840s. The Grassi and Rampoldi families were associates by sentiment and probably also kinship, for both hailed from the same hamlet of San Giorgio, near Bregnano, a dozen miles south of Como.

The Comasque colony – in the North East mostly confined to Newcastle – was never large. At the time of the 1851 census, the moment of its maximum expansion, no more than twenty-three Comasques were present in the city. They were without exception male, ten of them married, and all to English women. Even counting the wives and English-born children, the whole community amounted to hardly fifty souls yet they were disproportionately visible to the population at large, with some half-dozen flourishing businesses in the city centre.

One of the few surviving headstones in what little remains of St. Nicholas churchyard commemorates Luigi Grassi, 'Native of St. Giorgio near Como, Italy.' Aside from some unusual surnames still encountered around Tyne and Wear – Bernasconi, Bergna, Bianchi, Bregazzi, Inganni, Mastaglio, Molteni, Tacchi, Tarelli, Taroni – this nostalgic and surely also proud statement of provenance is today the last tangible public reminder of the city's venerable connection with Como.

John Tacchi's in High Street West, Sunderland, about 1870, gives some idea of the prosperity and prominence of these Italian-owned shops in the townscape. Along with a variety of desirable fancy goods Tacchi's elegant and capacious premises still offer typical Comasque products: barometers, thermometers, looking glasses, picture frames.

(Left) Barometer by 'A. Bernasconi, Newcastle', owned by John Bernasconi Jr, whose father discovered it in a Newcastle junkshop. Antonio Bernasconi, born 1836, received his training in the 34, Dean Street business run by his uncle 'John' Origoni.

(Right) 'Luigi Grassi' headstone outside the south wall of St Nicholas cathedral, Newcastle. The full inscription, now largely submerged, commemorates two family members interred in the same plot: Luigi Grassi, 'Native of St. Giorgio near Como, Italy', died April 16th 1835, aged 32, and Clement Grassi, 'Native of Como Italy,' died July 31st 1848, aged 38.

Tuscan plaster statuette makers

About the same time as the barometer men of Como, and from a similar tough mountain background, emerged another group of itinerants who were to become a familiar sight in the streets of nineteenth century England. Called *figurinai* or *stucchinai* in Italian, and known to the British census enumerators as 'figure-makers' or 'image-makers', they were makers and hawkers of painted plaster statuettes. Their homes lay in the northern Tuscan Apennines, high in the Serchio river valley in and around the ancient walled town of Barga, territory which was then part of the Duchy of Lucca (now province of Lucca: see map on page 110). Their trade and modes of operation were so modest that the impact on local business life of even those who settled here was nothing like that of the *barometai*. Even so, due to their greater number, their adaptability, and most of all the exceptional tenacity of their attachment to northern Britain, considerable colonies of 'Barghigiani' grew up during the last years of the nineteenth century in Glasgow and Edinburgh, and to a lesser extent in our own region. Former *figurinai* were prominent among the founders of the ice

Young Italian hawker of plaster statuettes, from Thomas Smith, Etchings of Remarkable Beggars, London 1815. Note the busts of Wellington and Napoleon. Smith writes of 'Lucchesi' (natives of the Duchy of Lucca) 'with fifty kilos of celebrities on their heads'.

cream trade in Scotland, and even more in the emerging fish and chip trade in which Italians north of the border were to develop a near monopoly. I have not come across a long-established family of Tuscan origin in the North East which does not claim some connection with Barga or its environs.

In bands of six or seven men and boys on 'campaigns' (*campagne*) lasting two or three years the statuette vendors wandered the length and breadth of Europe. The most adventurous had crossed the Atlantic before 1800, leading eventually to permanent settlements of Barghigiani in North America, Brazil and Argentina. Some might argue the *figurinai* were scarcely even artisans since their humble craft required only rudimentary skills, yet the master (the *capo*, or in later times *padrone*) was a man with formidable experience of the road and a good business head, and not without creativity in devising and adapting the wood and terracotta moulds required for the serial production of gilded or coloured plaster of Paris figurines turned out by himself and his workers: holy images, Christmas crib figures and animals, reproductions and miniatures of celebrated sculptures, classical gods, busts of heads of state and national heroes – the latter freely adapted or relabelled to suit whichever country they were in. The *capo*'s small team of *garzoni* or apprentice lads, some of them not yet teenagers, doubled as producers and street pedlars of the 'images'. Sometimes they were his own sons or nephews, more often men and youths from the same locality bound to him by written or verbal contract for the length of the tour. The 1841 census for Newcastle unearthed one of these teams lodging with a local glass-cutter's family in a crowded tenement in Silver Street near the Quayside. *Capo* of the six-man band was 56-year-old Giuseppe Laino, and since his *garzoni* ranged in age from twenty to thirty-two they were probably all veterans of many a foreign 'campaign'.

Because of their transient lifestyle it is impossible to pin down when the first statuette vendors found their way to our region. As with the *barometai*, all we have to go on before the first comprehensive census of 1841, besides one or two individuals sufficiently well-established to figure in the first trade directories, are the fleeting appearances of people with indicative surnames in the early Roman Catholic church records. On this evidence, the first *figurinaio* actually to settle in the North East was Jacopo Badini, born about 1790. The registers of St Andrew's RC church in Newcastle show he was living in the city with his English wife Margaret by at least 1815, and they were still resident in 1841. Jacopo was almost certainly never more than a street pedlar of his homemade wares, since he does not turn up in the trade directories, unlike later arrivals Giuseppe Brucciani, 'composition figure maker' in Bell's Court in 1833, and Federico Lundi, 'figure maker' in New Bridge Street in 1847, whose local descendants predictably anglicised to Lundy.

The English with their love of mantelshelves and dressers full of knick-knacks must have made good customers for these early settlers. Like the first resident barometer makers, they were single men far from home who in their twenties found English life partners and chose to chance it in the only trade they knew. Judging from the experience of Italians from similar backgrounds who struggled to establish themselves here in the early twentieth century, they would not have been in a position to return home for many a year. No doubt there was some business rivalry, but being used to operating collectively most teamed up in small working partnerships, such as fifty-year-old 'Guy' Pellegrini and the younger Michele Cardelli who shared an address in Picton Terrace in 1861, and the brothers (cousins?) Pancrazio and Daniele Stacchini who settled with their English wives and families next to each other in Pandon Dean. The names might change but numbers remained very steady. Seven 'figure and mould makers' were in Newcastle at the time of the 1861 census, ten in 1871, ten in 1881, nine in 1891, ten again in 1901.

Occasional bands of dark-haired Tuscans certainly trudged the roads and lanes of the North East well before even young 'Jacob' Badini with his tray of fragile 'figures' balanced on his head became a familiar sight to Geordie housewives. In 1851, Antonio Perotti, a 69-year-old bachelor and figure maker, was lodging with his colleague Federico Lundi and family in Newcastle. Lundi, scarcely half his guest's age but already a flourishing small businessman, was the doyen of all the Tuscans on Tyneside. Old Antonio, with a lifetime in the figurine trade behind him, must have tramped tens of thousands of miles and could have first crossed the Channel as a very young *garzone* well before anyone in England would have dreamed of asking for a bust of someone called Horatio Nelson.

Small firms in the upper Serchio valley still manufacture plaster (and plastic) statuettes for an international market in predominantly Catholic countries. These raw plaster products outside a workshop in the small town of Coreglia, near Barga, are stored in racks awaiting painting. Examining them is Italo Rigali, born in Barga, a retired fish fryer from Easington Colliery who first emigrated to Scotland and has an old family connection with the trade: 'My grandfather used to go from place to place making up these plaster figurines and selling them. The caricature of Italians when I came to this country was a man with a big black moustache and a barrel-organ with a monkey on his shoulder, and we resented that because people from our area didn't do that. Our people worked with their hands and sold an article. It was street trading, but it wasn't begging, and it needed a certain amount of art to make these figurines'. Coreglia has honoured its people's long history of emigration (largely to America) with a monument depicting an itinerant statuette maker and a fascinating museum dedicated entirely to the working lives and products of the figurinai.

Bonomi of Durham

Ever since the example set by Inigo Jones in the early seventeenth century no aspiring British architect was deemed fully trained without first-hand experience of Italy's formidable architectural heritage. In the mid-1750s, during their Italian years, the Scottish brothers Robert and James Adam struck up a friendship in Rome with Giuseppe Bonomi, a talented trainee architect like themselves. Ten years later Bonomi joined the Adam brothers' by then hugely successful London practice which also employed other Italian assistants and skilled draughtsmen. After fifteen years he quit the firm to start up his own practice, specialising in buildings in the neoclassical mode.

Ignatius Bonomi, architect, 1787-1870. Two outstanding architects of the Gothic revival, J.L.Pearson and J.A. Cory, worked for many years in the practice of Bonomi of Durham.

Historians of architecture single out as his finest works the spectacularly tall-steepled church at Packington, Warwickshire, and the nearby mansion for Lord Aylesbury.

In his mid-forties Giuseppe, by now Joseph, married the much younger Rosa Florini, a cousin and close friend of the renowned Swiss painter Angelica Kauffmann. They named the firstborn of their ten children Ignatius, and according to custom he trained for the profession in his father's practice. Joseph's death when his talented son was barely twenty put paid to Ignatius's hopes of studying in Italy, and although he did manage to see out some of his father's unfinished projects, in particular Skelton castle in Yorkshire, he was unable to sustain the firm. But then in 1813 he secured the post of Durham County bridge surveyor. No doubt this was on a nod from the influential Lambtons who had been on good terms with the family ever since Bonomi Sr had been engaged to convert relatively modest Harraton Hall on the banks of the Wear near Chester-le-Street into a suitably grand stately home for these fabulously rich coal owners. Years later, when John Lambton was well on his way to becoming the first Earl of Durham, Ignatius was commissioned to undo most of his own father's work and transform the building into a still grander sham medieval castle.

Ignatius Bonomi worked for nearly forty years in Durham, in independent practice as well as his salaried post. The chief Bonomi landmarks still to be seen in the city are Durham prison itself, his first major undertaking (central block and wings), St Cuthbert's RC church in Old Elvet, the first of that denomination in the city, and the Mechanics' Institute on Claypath (now an Indian restaurant). Elvet Hill House was the office and residence he built for himself, now neighbour to the Gulbenkian Museum of Oriental Art which contains items collected by his Egyptologist brother Joseph. Bonomi was also a dedicated philanthropist. Though he designed a treadmill for it, his early connection with the prison turned him into an advocate of penal reform and more humane policies toward young offenders. Always proud of his roots, he promoted Italian language classes at the Mechanics' Institute in 1848, the great year of revolution when reformers briefly wrested power from the autocratic regimes ruling the states of Italy.

Over one hundred works are attributed to Bonomi, some far beyond the borders of County Durham. Though not as adventurous an architect as his father, and the creator of nothing as stirring as his good friend John Dobson's central railway station in Newcastle, Bonomi's sturdy stone-built buildings and bridges in a variety of popular early Victorian styles are fine testimony to the versatile and hard-working professional he was. Burn Hall near Durham, Windlestone Hall near Darlington, and Eggleston Hall near Barnard Castle, are very handsome neo-classical mansions recalling his father's work in the same idiom. Though in poor shape now, his bridge over the river Skerne at Darlington, formed like a Roman triumphal arch and completed in 1825, was the world's first steam railway bridge and figured prominently on the old £5 note. Bonomi also carried out sensitive restoration work on Durham cathedral and rescued many a ruinous church in the parishes of County Durham. Others he designed afresh, generally in a plain Gothic style, all over the North East, most notably some half-dozen Roman Catholic churches during the building fever which followed the Catholic Emancipation Act of 1829. These commissions failed however to curb his loathing of papal autocracy, and in 1837 he finally renounced Catholicism. Fired by the outspoken views of his Anglican wife Charlotte Fielding, who once penned a long-forgotten anti-papist novel, and the campaigning zeal of their friend W.S. Gilly, vicar of Norham and canon of Durham, he went on to design three churches for the persecuted Waldensian (Italian Protestant) community in Italy. The most handsome of these is at Torre Pellice at the foot of the Italian Alps, in the historic heartland of the Waldensians.

FOUR NORTH-EAST LANDMARKS BY IGNATIUS BONOMI

Durham prison, 1810-11.

Lambton Castle, near Chester-le-Street: preparatory sketch by Bonomi, whose various commissions at the castle between 1815 and 1828 included landscaping the park and designing the bridge over the Wear.

The world's first steam railway bridge: Skerne Bridge, Darlington, built for the Stockton & Darlington Railway Company, 1824-25.

St Mary's RC church, Sunderland, 1835.

Alnwick Castle

Antonio Canaletto, the renowned painter of his native city of Venice, grew to be so popular with the English that a visit to his studio was one of the highlights of the Grand Tour. In his late forties, when the War of the Austrian Succession interrupted the tourist trade, the artist resolved to take his brushes to the land of his best customers. He stayed nine years. One of his keenest patrons was Sir Hugh Smithson, earl of Northumberland, who commissioned him to paint views of all the Percy family seats. In 1751 he came north to immortalise Alnwick Castle. As the delightful painting shows, it was then

Antonio Canaletto: Alnwick Castle, 1751. (The collection of the Duke of Northumberland)

little more than a picturesque ruin, however within months Sir Hugh set about transforming it into a luxurious country residence in the latest 'Gothick', or pseudo-medieval, style. Robert Adam's designs for the vast interior were among the most controversial and celebrated he ever produced. The 'profuse ornamentation in plasterwork' was executed by a roving team of stuccadores whose identity is now unknown, though the timing coincides with the presence of at least three of the Italian-Swiss masters discussed at the end of chapter 1.

Almost every trace of Adam's conception vanished in the castle's second total makeover in Victorian times. Algernon Percy, the fourth duke, spared no expense, finally outdoing the cost of Robert Stephenson's High Level Bridge over the Tyne. In 1854, with the more historically accurate Gothic Revival now in full swing, he set the Durham architect Anthony Salvin to give the rambling building a more convincing medieval look both inside and out, with all due allowance for 'the various luxuries and contrivances demanded by the nineteenth century cultivation'. Salvin was well into the work when the duke, a devout Catholic, wintering in Italy and enthused by all he saw, ordered drastic modifications – a change of mind which was to result in the most thoroughgoing tribute to the Italian artistic tradition in our region. As with ancient buildings in Italy refashioned according to the taste of later centuries, the exterior should remain medieval but the interior must now be turned into a perfect replica of a Roman palazzo of the High Renaissance. 'His Grace has made one of the most lamentable mistakes in the present day,' was the sour verdict of Gilbert Scott, the Gothic Revival's most influential exponent, after hearing Salvin outline the duke's intentions at the Institute of Architects. Some of today's visitors might not demur, but none can fail to appreciate the superb quality of workmanship in every detail they see.

Since designing an authentic Italianate interior was beyond Salvin's competence he had to accept an invasion of Italian expertise.[3] While still in Rome the duke recruited and despatched to Alnwick two leading connoisseurs of the grand tradition of Italian art, Luigi Canina, director of the Capitoline Museum, and Giovanni Montiroli, his talented young architect-assistant. In Alnwick the pair prepared detailed designs for the duke's approval, but when Canina suddenly died soon after their return to Italy all responsibility passed to Montiroli. The duke, a passionate antiquarian with the wealth to make his every aesthetic dream come true, stipulated in the final contract with Montiroli 'none but the best artists in Italy and the finest quality Italian materials'.

Over the next eight years, from his base in Rome and during long stays in Alnwick, Montiroli personally conceived, designed, and commissioned every feature and fitting, from the great gilded coffered ceiling and huge chandelier and the red and gold damask wallpaper in the Red Drawing Room (see illustration) right down to the intricate ornamentation of the boxwood frame for Raphael's 'Madonna of the Pinks'. True to the agreement, he engaged only top Italian or Rome-based internationally renowned sculptors and painters and carvers to work from his scores of meticulous preparatory drawings, many still preserved in the castle.

This Italian near-monopoly of talent and his Grace's extravagance produced an interesting local spin-off. Antonio Leone Bulletti, a Florentine woodcarver recruited on the recommendation of cardinal Antonelli, the formidably reactionary personal secretary of Pius IX, arrived in Alnwick to prepare models of Montiroli's designs for the ornate coffered ceilings. His presence struck Salvin as 'a most favourable opportunity for creating a school of carving in the Italian style' and he managed to convince Bulletti to stay. A consummate craftsman, the Florentine was given good studio space in the castle and over the next seven years supervised the execution of all the intricate wood carving *in situ*, passing on his skills to a team of initially twenty-six carvers and six talented boys recruited from Glasgow, Shields and Sunderland, under an Alnwick cabinet maker named John Brown. The duke, who fondly hoped the Italian example of Alnwick would inspire a national renewal of British craftsmanship, even arranged evening drawing classes for his workforce's education. When all their work was finished the entire 'Alnwick School' decamped to Cumberland to continue for several years under Bulletti on the decoration of the drawing-room and library at Muncaster Castle, this time to Salvin's designs.

The fame of Alnwick established Montiroli and Bulletti's reputations here. Montiroli secured several more commissions from aristocratic patrons, while Bulletti took up residence in Newcastle for many years, opening a much-visited studio in the High Bridge. His gratitude to his first patrons was expressed in the names he and his wife Thecla chose for their English-born children: Algernon after the Duke, Eleonora after the Duchess .

The Red Drawing Room, Alnwick Castle, designed by Giovanni Montiroli, with coffered ceiling made by Antonio Leone Bulletti and the 'Alnwick School'. (The collection of the Duke of Northumberland).

Letter from Montiroli in Rome to Fred Wilson, clerk of works, Alnwick Castle, stipulating a revision to the ceiling consoles in the library. (The collection of the Duke of Northumberland).

Eagle lectern at Holy Trinity church, Matfen, carved by Antonio Leone Bulletti in 1881.

Other early arrivals on Tyneside

The Musso family of artists are the only Italian residents in the North East before 1800 about whom anything much is known. Bonifacio Musso, a Piedmontese painter who had spent most of his twenties in London, moved to Newcastle with his English wife Mary in 1790 to make a living as a painter and drawing master, first in Newgate Street and later in Gateshead. He trained his son Charles and daughter Aurelia in the profession, and counted among his other pupils such future major figures as the painters William Nicholson and John Martin, and the architect John Dobson. Curiously, apart from traces of his helping hand in a moderately competent album of fifteen

Charles Muss, 'A View of Newcastle-upon-Tyne', aquatint, 1801, Laing Art Gallery (Tyne and Wear Archives and Museums).

engraved views of Newcastle by young Aurelia, no known works by Bonifacio survive. One reason might be Eneas Mackenzie's recollection of him as a very skilful artist 'though extremely indolent'. His industrious son Charles soon moved on to London where he gained a high reputation as a miniaturist and enameller, initially sharing digs with John Martin who was very deeply attached to the family and later generously recalled his far less talented old drawing master as 'an universal genius as well as the noblest of men, the most perfect of gentlemen, and the most disinterested of friends.'

That the Musso family were not lone Italians on Tyneside we know from the early record of the Comasque barometer makers, and also from three marriages of Italians to local women recorded at the cathedral church of St. Nicholas before the end of the eighteenth century: Domenico Minchi (1782), Antonio Perugia (1798), and Giuseppe Giobi (1799), whose Tyneside career is discussed at the end of this section. The early history of Italian settlement is however best traced through the records of the Catholic church of St. Andrew on Worswick Street, which runs from Pilgrim Street to Carliol Square in the heart of the district formerly most favoured by the city's Italians. The present church dates from only 1875 but stands near the site of an earlier St Andrew's, a chapel founded in 1798 by Fr. James Worswick whose congregation until then had made do with a room in Bell's Court off Newgate Street. (The earlier Catholic chapel in Nimm's Lane and a Jesuit chapel in Gateshead had been wrecked by anti-Catholic mobs at the time of the 1745 Jacobite Rising). The little chapel was to remain the only place of worship for the city's rapidly growing Catholic population until the consecration of St Mary's cathedral in 1844, Father Worswick's crowning achievement.

The earliest of the St. Andrew's records is the register of baptisms, dating from 1765 when services were still held in Bell's Court. Italian names however only first appear in December 1795 in connection with the christening of a son born to Lorenzo Berti and Mary Jones, when the godparents were Giovanni Pochini and Mary Banks. 1798 saw two further Italian christenings: a daughter of Giovanni Berti and a certain Charlotte, with English sponsors, and a daughter born to Giovanni Pochini and Joan Denton, whose godparents were Mary Burrell and Bartolommeo Lipe. Giovanni Pochini, as we saw, flourished for years in Newcastle as 'John Pochaine', its oldest resident barometer maker. Given the absence of a solid Italian community until well into the 1820s, and the special personal and social significance of godparenthood in Italy, it is a fair guess that the other three Italians were all fellow Comasques, trusted colleagues in the burgeoning barometer trade.

Newcastle's new centre for Catholic worship: St Andrew's chapel, off Carliol Square, 1798, by William Mettick.

Between them these few pre-nineteenth century marriages and christenings establish a pattern that remains more or less unbroken for the next seventy years: almost all Italian names in the St Andrew's registers are male and if married they have English (or Irish) partners. During the entire period 1795-1869 only thirteen out of the 110 Italian adults in the register are women, and of the 62 married men only five have Italian spouses. Migration was evidently almost exclusively male, a situation which hardly altered until the mass arrival of southern Italian migrants in the last decades of the nineteenth century (see chapter 4). As time went by, men who had left Italy as young bachelors felt remote enough to choose life partners from outside the clan, a step which risked disapproval back home where marriages were normally between close neighbours and sanctioned by elders. Still, their sense of isolation will have been mitigated by the presence of others living the same cross-cultural situation.

By noting the names of godparents at baptisms and witnesses at marriages in St Andrew's it is possible to map some of the main family and friendship networks which sustained this very small foreign Catholic colony in the first half of the nineteenth century. It was not one single homogeneous community. All attended the same place of worship but the record shows there were two distinct social groups, the Comasques and the Tuscans, each keeping to its own. Until 1860 Lombardy and Tuscany were separate countries, and like all Italians in the still disunited peninsula even these few emigrants far from home will have felt divided by strongly perceived differences of speech, cultural background, occupation, and economic status.

A family of some standing among the earliest settlers was Lazzari, still a familiar surname on Tyneside, though from early on some anglicised to Ladzrie. Angelo and Paolo Lazzari, presumably brothers, and both with English wives, were resident in Newcastle from the early 1800s. Paolo, who was born in Italy in 1776, must have been quite a fluent English speaker by 1810 when (according to a note in the registry of baptisms) he was appointed headmaster of St Andrew's School. This, the city's first Catholic school with already 250 pupils by 1827, was another of Worswick's admirable initiatives on behalf of his flock. The church registers show that the Lazzari family, presumably due to its leading role in the early Italian colony, formed close ties on both sides of the Comasque/Tuscan divide. In trade directories for the 1820s and 30s 'Paul Ladzrie' figures as a manufacturer of plaster of Paris and plaster ornaments, which would imply his background was Tuscan. On the other hand, Lazzari is a common surname around Lecco on Lake Como, and the registers suggest the family's earliest affiliations were indeed with the Comasque community.

The surname Bianchi is almost as common in Italy as White in England, yet all the Bianchis round Tyneside[4] seem to owe their existence to the fertilty of Carlo Bianchi and his two successive wives, Margaret Calvert and Isabelle Callender, who between them produced at least fifteen children. Carlo was born in Italy in 1791, probably in or around Como, and after meeting and marrying Margaret Calvert in York he appears in Newcastle around 1815 trading as an artificial flower maker under the patronage of Giuseppe Giobi, a flower maker and silk dyer who as we saw earlier was already settled and married in the city before the turn of the century. Their trade was not uncommon among street-vending Italians in Britain. In time both men graduated to the pages of the trade directories. By then Giobi had neatly anglicised to Jobey, but Bianchi retained the name, advertising his services as umbrella maker as well as artificial flower maker, and finally in the 1840s as 'ostrich feather dresser', exploiting a famous ladies' fashion of the time.

Some of today's Jobeys might be surprised to learn they may descend from founder members of Newcastle's oldest Italian colony. In September 1796 a certain 'Suanay Jobb' whose age is not recorded was interred in Ballast Hills cemetery. Zuani (or Zani) is the standard north Italian dialect form of Giovanni, so the puzzling name almost certainly conceals the identity of a certain Giovanni Giobi. Was he the brother or son or even the father of Giuseppe Giobi?

Joseph Bianchi's bootmaker's shop at 8, the Side, circa 1910. Joseph's grandfather Carlo came to Newcastle a century before this picture was taken. (Newcastle upon Tyne City Libraries and Arts)].

Glassworkers

In the 1870s, specialist craftsmen from the famous glass-making island of Murano in the Venetian lagoon were settled in Gateshead to work for Sowerby & Co, one of the country's foremost glassworks. The Italians had been recruited to help the firm to develop an exclusive line in 'art glass' to rival the novelty hand-blown products recently launched with great success by Salviati's Venice and Murano Glass Company in London. Exquisitely wrought examples of the kind of work these forgotten migrants produced in the styles of ancient Egyptian, Roman, and traditional Venetian glass are in the Shipley Art Gallery, Gateshead, and the Laing Art Gallery in Newcastle.

Sowerby 'Venetian' glass, Shipley Art Gallery, Gateshead (Tyne and Wear Archives and Museums)

A much earlier Italian connection with glass on Tyneside was the great Dagnia glass company. Edoardo Dagnia, almost certainly from Altare, a prominent glass-making centre near Savona, seems to have been one of several continental masters invited to England when the royal monopoly on glass was held by Robert Mansell, Admiral of the Fleet. In 1651 Dagnia was recorded as 'an ingenious Italian' running a glasshouse in Bristol. He had brought his four sons with him, all apprenticed to the trade, and over the next twenty years the family expanded its interests to include Stourbridge, the main glassmaking centre in the Midlands. In 1684 three Dagnia sons, Edward, John, and the leading partner Onesiphorus, set up a glassworks in the Closegate, Newcastle, with Benezar Durant, presumably a descendant of one of the original Huguenot families that had been manufacturing glass at Shields from around 1600. Among their distinctive output, Dagnia's flint glass works in Newcastle and South Shields developed the slender-stemmed clear wine glasses and goblets which became the trademark product of 'Newcastle glass'.

Mosaic and terrazzo workers

Some sixty miles north of Venice, in the Friuli countryside, is the small town of Sequals. Three hundred years ago it was the birthplace of a novel flooring technique. Crushed coloured pebbles from local streams were impacted with lime and polished flat to make a hard-wearing surface that was a cheap yet attractive alternative to marble paving in churches and great houses. In Venice, the ancient home of mosaic, the new method acquired the name of *terrazzo*. In time crushed marble in different hues came to replace crushed stone, and new techniques were explored for paving in coloured patterns and designs. In the

A team of local terrazzieri employed by Jaconello's for interior work at the Regal cinema, Sunderland, in the 1930s. (Photo: John Valente).

hands of specialised craftsmen from Sequals, and nearby hamlets like Fanna and Solimbergo, its usage spread to all Italy. As in the other Italian itinerant trades, apprentice boys travelled everywhere with them, one of their duties being to cut the mosaic pieces for their masters. By the mid-nineteenth century the Friulans had taken the art of terrazzo as far as Russia and across the Atlantic.

In Britain, from around 1875 and for the best part of the twentieth century, teams of Italian labourers under Friulan masters and foremen were commissioned to pave and mosaic innumerable churches, town halls, museums, theatres, cinema foyers, arcades, stations, banks, department stores and swimming pools. Hygienic and easy to clean, since its surface is smooth and continuous even in corners, it was also habitually laid in hospitals and operating theatres. Large companies with a nationwide clientele, notably Diespeker's in London and Toffolo-Jackson in Glasgow, employed workforces of several hundred Italians, invariably with Friulans in the leading roles. Another well-known Friulan firm, the Art Pavement Company of London, developed a specialist interest in the restoration of Roman mosaics.

In the North East these and other companies often worked in tandem with local teams of Italian skilled and unskilled labour. They laid terrazzo and tiled and mosaiced halls, walls, corridors and staircases all over the region in landmark buildings such as the Sunderland Empire Theatre, Ushaw College chapel, Newcastle General Hospital and the RVI, Sunderland Royal Infirmary, Monkwearmouth hospital, the Blyth and Stella power stations, ICI and Dorman Long, in addition to a host of smaller jobs in banks and libraries, cinemas and department stores, churches and schools. And yes, ice cream parlours too.

Cellini, Buzzeo, and Capocci were the leading names in terrazzo on Tyneside in the twentieth century, all families from southern Italy that had started out in ice cream and then presumably picked up the craft while employed by Friulans. The earliest arrival was Cesidio Cellini, who left Picinisco in 1889 at the age of fifteen to work in ice cream and went on to found the Terrazzo Tile Company. The brothers Angelo and Cesidio ('Joe') Buzzeo were born in Settefrati but grew up as boys in Newcastle working in their father Angelo's ice cream business, founded in 1899. Giovanni Capocci, also from Picinisco, creator of the Commercial and Marble Tile Company, arrived in 1904 when he was in his early twenties. A well-known genuine Friulan terrazzo family on Tyneside was that of Antonio Bertoia, whose eldest son Luigi was lost with the *Arandora Star* (see chapter 7). Two closely related Friulan families, Mion and Zanetti, dominated the trade on Wearside.

After World War II so much large-scale work was required on public buildings here that Toffolo-Jackson set up a Newcastle branch of the firm. As well as shipping the essential raw material, marble chippings, direct from their Italian quarries, the company also imported most of its essential manpower from Italy. When required, extra labour was recruited from among local Italian families already established here, young men who worked terrazzo in the winter months and went back to the family ice cream business during the hectic summer season.

Among the many local individuals and families involved in one way or another in this essentially Italian craft I have also noted: Androtti, Andrucci, Beltrami, Caligaro, Crolla, Fantozzi, Gabel, Ghiloni, Giordano, Grandini, Iannarelli, Mangulti, Manzuotto, Pacitti, Panzieri, Petrucco, Puttiglio, Riccardo, Risi, Tassi, Valente, Zari.

LOCAL EXAMPLES OF ITALIAN TERRAZZO AND MOSAIC

Sunderland Empire Theatre: foyer flooring.

Sunderland Royal Infirmary: entrance emblem.

Staircase, Sunderland Royal Infirmary.

Mosaic flooring by Antonio Iannarelli at his father Giuseppe's ice cream parlour, Skinnergate, Darlington.

'NO ENGLISH IN IT'

It was an Italian trade. The Italians brought it here and there were no English in it, not until about 1965 when they started to introduce young English lads into apprenticeships. The northern Italians, the Friulans, were always in charge. They were mainly the ones who set the jobs out and did the delicate work. The southern Italians did the fetching and carrying and the polishing. All us southern Italians used to have our bait to one side and the Friulans over the other side. My father, my elder brother, they accepted that, but we couldn't. The younger generation we said, No, you can't have that. Whether you have to mix or lay or polish doesn't matter, at the end of the day we're all equal. We're still one family, we're all Italian.

The 'Genoa' marble was the best and the hardest, a dark green. 'Verona' was the red. The basic was the white 'Carrara' because it was cheap and softer to polish. 'Dove' was a blue, actually a beautiful marble. 'Botticelli', a cream, was a hard marble too, always asleep, very difficult to polish.

You took your area of the floor, divided up and decided your levels and put down your guides, then screeded. On the old Roman floors, if you've noticed, you get a small inch of mosaic going right round the outside. That's your guide and you work your terrazzo up to it: two pails of marble chippings to one of white cement, so it's not fatty, laying it flat between the guides. Then you'll beat it and roll it with a steel roller to bring the cement up, sealing it with the cement that comes to the top. Then trowel it off. Next day you could walk on it, but it's better to leave it two or three days to set and dry, depending on the weather.

Paul Risi (centre) at work on in situ terrazzo at a Redcar showroom in the 1960s. His father Giuseppe, from Sant'Elia Fiumerapido near Cassino, worked for forty-two years in terrazzo in the North East, and at sixteen Paul started with him.

There were no machines then, the polishing was all done by hand. First you'd go over it with a raspin, a scraper with a broad sharpened blade, to take off the loose cement. To polish you'd have a galera, a great big long pole about four inches in diameter – the weight of it! – and you'd put your shoulder to it and push it up and down, up and down, with your big block of carborundum stone sitting inside. Galera means prison in Italian, and it was hard labour alright. For corners and coving you'd use a smaller one, a cagneta, meaning bitch – and it was a bitch! It was Stone Age, very hard on the hands, it made your fingers bleed, but that was it and you just got on with it.

The polish had to be right. You'd start off with a very rough carborundum, say a 16 grit, then come off that and use a 24 to smooth it, and then a 30 or a 40. Then grout, rubbing on cement in the same colour to seal up all the little holes. Leave it two or three days and finally put a very fine carborundum over, a 60 grade, even 80, depending on the quality they wanted. 'È lucido lucido!' they'd say, meaning it's shining, it's good. But if it wasn't polished right, the likes of my dad would come along and say, 'The marble's asleep, you can only see a little bit of its eyes!'

Like the ice cream men and their recipes, they could be secretive. They'd not let the English plasterers know the mix, how you can bind marble and cement without sand. Or how you polish a coving.

The skill is gone now. What killed terrazzo was the tiles, people wanted things quicker. Yes, it was hard work, sand and cement and marble chippings aren't butter. But the point is it wasn't just work, it was enjoyment, every day was exciting. I think the beauty of it was that your father and brothers were all in it, like you were one huge family.

(Paul Risi, Newbottle)

BOOKS AND SOURCES.

The barometer makers of Newcastle. Sources for this first account of the Comasque colony in the North East were trade directories, census records and, as explained, the registers of St Andrew's RC church, Newcastle, now held in Tyne and Wear Archives. In addition to the Grassi gravestone there is a large Mastaglio family crypt in Jesmond cemetery. The extensive correspondence between Giovanni Tarelli in Cardano and his son Matteo in Newcastle, which gave me many insights, was kindly loaned by Matteo's great-grandson Peter Tarelli. V. Lucati, 'I barometà del lago di Como' in *Periodico della società storica comense* 38 (1954) sketches the Italian background. For the Comasque immigrants elsewhere in Britain see Lucio Sponza, *Italian Immigrants in Nineteenth-Century Britain: Realities and Images* (1988), and Terri Colpi, *The Italian Factor* (1991).

Tuscan plaster statuette makers. North-East details from the same archival sources as the barometer men. More information on the spread of the *figurinai* in Bruno Sereni, *They Took the Low Road* (Barga 1974), and in Sponza and Colpi (above).

Bonomi of Durham. June Crosby, *Ignatius Bonomi of Durham, Architect* (Durham City Trust, 1987). P. Meadows, *Joseph Bonomi, Architect* 1739-1808 (exhibition catalogue, 1988). H.M.Colvin, *Biographical Dictionary of British Architects* (1978) for both Ignatius and Giuseppe, and T. Faulkner and A.Greg, *John Dobson, Architect of the North East* (Newcastle 2001) for Ignatius.

Alnwick Castle. Drawings and correspondence by Montiroli in the manuscript collection of the Duke of Northumberland, Alnwick Castle. *Papers of the Royal Institute of British Architects*, 1857, for Salvin's account. Jill Allibone, *Anthony Salvin, Pioneer of the Gothic Revival* (1988). Ettore Ferrari, *Giovanni Montiroli, architetto* (Spoleto 1892) includes a biographical memoir and Montiroli's engravings of his own designs for Alnwick. Frederick Wilson, clerk of works for Salvin, contributed personal recollections of the Italian transformation of the castle in George Tate, *The History of the Borough, Castle and Barony of Alnwick*, vol 1 (1866).

Mosaic and terrazzo workers. *Guida generale degli italiani in Gran Bretagna* (London 1939) has a short piece on the history of terrazzo and its application in major buildings in Britain up to that date. Almost all local information in this section is derived from oral sources.

Mosaic table by Paul Risi.

3

THE NORTH EAST AND ITALIAN UNIFICATION

Some North-East descendants of nineteenth-century settlers from northern Italy report that according to family tradition their forebears came to Britain to escape political persecution. This is said of Giovanni Calasca who settled in Newcastle in the 1830s and made a living in the city as a language teacher[1] and equally of some members of the Comasque network. The barometer maker Tommaso Angelo Ronchetti, for instance, is thought to have fled Austrian-held Como together with Enrico Negretti in the tumultuous year 1848, when Lombardy and almost every other Italian state and statelet was convulsed by revolution followed by harsh reprisal. Negretti joined Giorgio Zambra in a London partnership which was to become the celebrated Negretti and Zambra firm of precision instrument makers (a branch in Grey Street, Newcastle,

Giuseppe Mazzini, 1805-1872.
'When I think what I did for that man
my hair stands on end' – Joseph Cowen.

survived into the 1970s). Ronchetti made for Manchester where relatives were already engaged in barometer production, and there he acquired the business flair which took him to Teesside to cash in on Middlesbrough's extraordinary industrial expansion in the 1860s.

The vigilance of the Austrian police in pre-independence Italy and their notorious methods of intimidation may well have made emigration a prudent option for a few such men – and Britain was then the most secure haven in Europe for political exiles of all persuasions – nonetheless most who made their way here were, to use today's distinctions, economic migrants not asylum seekers. Lombardy was then the richest and best educated state in Italy but had scarcely begun to industrialise, so the number of comfortably-off customers for the kind of inessential items produced by the skilled artisans of Como was nothing next to the potential in cities like Vienna or Paris or far-off London and Manchester, then the world's two mightiest industrial cities.

Following the fall of Napoleon and the dismemberment of French-controlled Italy, Austria was once again the presiding superpower in the peninsula, directly or indirectly governing all the restored states and duchies in the north and centre saving Piedmont, and crucial ally and protector of the Papal States and the southern kingdom of Naples and Sicily. Jacobin and Carbonari secret brotherhoods stirred things up against the foreign occupier or the local absolutist ruler, but if ever the succession of fruitless risings which were a regular feature of post-1815 Italy received support from the mass of the population, the urban poor and the numberless peasants in the countryside, it sprang from age-old social grievances, not some fantasy of Italian nationhood. In fact these most deprived sections of society could more often be relied on by the forces of reaction to slaughter the 'patriots'. Even educated southerners had too little in common with what they perceived as the alien north to dream of a united peninsula. Northern views of the deep south were just as isolationist.

If one man can be said to have opened at least well-informed liberal minds to a more stirring vision it was Giuseppe Mazzini from Genoa, one of many leading European revolutionaries to find sanctuary in Britain. He was the founder and untiring propagandist of a new movement for national unity, *La Giovine Italia* ('Young Italy', 1831), almost a new religion for its prophet and his disciples, vaguely broad in its appeal to 'the people' but essentially driven by a few dedicated conspirators prepared to risk their lives to spread the Mazzinian gospel wherever it was proscribed and to foment or exploit unrest all over unfree Italy. A very early follower was Giuseppe Garibaldi, a young sailor from Nice (then Nizza, within the Italian kingdom of Piedmont and Sardinia), who vanished abroad under sentence of death for subversive activity in the fleet only to resurface in South America at the head of his famous red-shirted 'Italian Legion', a fearsome guerrilla band of Italian exile revolutionaries and local adventurers prepared to fight for any breakaway republic against its tyrannous neighbours.

Seeing the ancient institutions of monarchy and church and nobility everywhere collaborated to maintain rule by the privileged few, Mazzini's ultimate goal was a free democratic republic of Italy within a peaceful confederation of democratic European nations – hardly a threatening vision today because it has largely come about, if only after unparalleled suffering. In his other role as arch-conspirator the thinking behind his strategy of plotting constant unrest is also familiar enough today, though not yet debased to require the slaughter of innocents: a handful of zealots dedicated to armed struggle against overwhelming forces of oppression will produce more martyrs, more repression, more converts, more international sympathy.

Expelled for subversion from France, then Switzerland, Mazzini took refuge in England in 1837 and in his 'second country' as he called it promoted his cause well beyond the confines of the one-thousand strong Italian colony in London. His dream of national independence for all the 'enslaved peoples of Europe', whether languishing under theocratic rule in central Italy or under the heavy hand of the Austrian and Russian empires (no parallel was drawn with non-European peoples under British rule) struck a special chord of sympathy among radical and even moderate liberal elements in the fast-growing British middle class, and even some younger members of the aristocracy. These favoured people, like their counterparts in Italy, were progressive-minded and fiercely anti-papal.

In 1848, the great year of European revolution, when autocratic regimes were overthrown or shaken to the core in Palermo, Milan, Parma, Modena, Naples, Florence, Venice, Rome, before succumbing again to absolutism and military rule, the surge of solidarity in Britain and then appalled sympathy for the victims affected substantial sections of the working class as well. 'It was very natural that we should begin to pride ourselves on the unique position occupied by Britain as the only free country among the great powers of Europe,' wrote the liberal historian G.M. Trevelyan, looking back on those years in his *Garibaldi and the Thousand* (1909). 'Because we harboured the exiles, and held up in that night of time the beacon light of an ordered freedom... our national pride took fire for freedom, and under Palmerston's spirited lead those forces and passions which in a later generation were termed "Jingo" were enlisted on behalf of continental liberalism.'

Britain was of course no Mazzinian republic but a very 'ordered' constitutional monarchy, so open support for the cause of Italian emancipation only became acceptable for establishment politicians like Palmerston and Gladstone after the failure of revolutionary Chartism in Britain and the rout of the 1848 republican revolutionaries everywhere in Europe. Now even Garibaldi, the inspirational defender of Mazzini's doomed 'Roman Republic' which in 1848-9 had briefly dislodged the pope from Rome, seemed prepared to listen to the more moderate nationalists who shared the view of count Camillo Cavour, Piedmont's leading statesman, that the only realistic solution to independence from Austria lay with the one Italian ruler who still kept the throne of his ancestors, dreamed of aggrandizement, and possessed a well-trained army for the job: Victor Emmanuel II, the young king of Piedmont and Sardinia.

Joseph Cowen, patron of Italian revolutionaries

At the foot of Westgate Road, opposite the Assembly Rooms where until recently[2] the Anglo-Italian Association of Newcastle held its annual dinner dance get-togethers, stands a statue of Joseph Cowen, Liberal MP for Newcastle 1874-86: a nice coincidence, for Joe Cowen was the North East's most fervent agitator for Italian freedom. His unswerving Mazzinian republicanism and fiery denunciations of the iniquities of continental monarchs are said to have caused Queen Victoria to order the blinds of the royal train to be drawn whenever she passed through Newcastle en route for Balmoral. 'He was well known by repute to every despotic government, and viewed a danger by every tyrant of Europe,' enthused his friend and biographer E.R. Jones, reporting how police

Memorial statue to Joseph Cowen (1829-1900) in Westgate Road, Newcastle, unveiled in 1906. The Pinocchio restaurant across the street was originally Mario's, one of very few Italian restaurants in 1970s Newcastle. Mario Neri also later opened the Dolce Vita pizzeria next door, now Roberto's.

spies kept a close eye on him. A less well-disposed critic, the journalist F.W. Hirst, might have been invoking the bogeyman version of Mazzini himself when he wrote of Cowen: 'There was in his character something theatrical and mysterious. He loved secrecy and advertisement. Dark design and conspiracies appealed to him. His operations were mostly under the surface. His appearances above ground were carefully planned and premeditated in order to attract the maximum of attention'.

A plainer assessment would be that Joe Cowen was a wealthy businessman and newspaper owner with a rare humanitarian conscience, and even rarer commitment, who spent a great deal of his energy and cash on almost every radical cause of his time, from the education and emancipation of the North-East working class to the freedom struggles of the Poles, the Hungarians, the Italians, the Irish, and slaves in the United States. His attachment to his own region of England went deep, at times he was its most representative voice, and not even in parliament would he modify his Geordie speech of which Disraeli claimed not to understand a word. Like his heroes Mazzini and Garibaldi he was a radical democrat not a socialist, though this did not deter Frederick Engels, another wealthy factory owner dedicated to the emancipation of the proletariat, from calling him 'an old Chartist, half, if not a whole Communist, and a very fine fellow.'

Cowen's father – also Joseph – was one of the great self-made men of the era, a firebrick and gas pipe manufacturer from Blaydon Burn who began his working life as a blacksmith and rose to become chairman of the River Tyne Commissioners and Liberal MP for Newcastle, a position which after his death would pass to his son. In 1845, when just sixteen, Joseph junior penned his first letter to Mazzini, echoing public outrage at the revelation that in the land of free speech the contents of the Italian conspirator's mail were being secretly monitored and passed to 'a foreign government', i.e. Austria. (The post office, it turned out, had been routinely riffling people's mail for forty years). The gesture initiated a lifelong working friendship in which Cowen was one of the Italian's most trusted supporters and dependable fund-raisers. Soon he was smuggling abroad revolutionary propaganda (later pistols) for Mazzini, concealing them in shipments of Cowen bricks and other fireclay exports to the continent. Some of the inflammatory pamphlets were printed by hand press at Stella House, the family home at Blaydon Burn.

In 1854, just in time to cover a surprise visit by Garibaldi to Tyneside, Cowen made his first venture into publishing by launching a radical weekly called *Northern Tribune* with W J Linton, another prominent member of the Republican Brotherhood. When it folded he contrived to reach a far wider audience by underwriting the ailing *Newcastle Chronicle,* soon winning full personal control. By 1859, the year of northern Italy's decisive war of independence from Austria, his gifted editorial team had made it the most popular newspaper in the north. With its forthright support for workers' rights and education, trade unions and co-operatives, mechanics' institutes and the temperance movement, and not least its extensive racing coverage, the *Chronicle* secured the mass base on which also to build a genuine passion among working people for the cause of Italian freedom, as well as Hungarian and Polish independence. At Cowen's expense exiled revolutionary nationalists like Lajos Kossuth of Hungary and dedicated Mazzinian agitators for Italian independence such as Jessie White Mario, Aurelio Saffi, and the crowd-pulling pope-baiter Father Gavazzi, were brought to Tyneside to address packed fund-raising meetings which earned enthusiastic write-ups in the *Chronicle.*

Garibaldi on Tyneside

The most famous Italian ever to visit the North East was Giuseppe Garibaldi. A commemorative plaque on the Tynemouth house where he stayed (now King's School), and another in Nelson Street, central Newcastle, perpetuate the memory of the fortnight he spent on Tyneside during March–April 1854 while on his way home after five years in exile. His bold leadership of the Italian republicans' desperate last stand at Rome in 1849 against French and Neapolitan professional armies bent on reclaiming the city for the pope had made him a wanted man throughout the peninsula. On the run from the Austrians, expelled from his home town of Nice, he found refuge first in Gibraltar, then Tangier, and eventually among fellow émigrés in the Italian quarter of New York. Seeing no realistic prospects of another fight ('the Italians of today think of the belly not the soul') he resumed his old profession of merchant captain and sailed a trader round the world for a couple of years. Finally, at the news he would no longer be arrested on landing, he resolved to return to Nice and his family. Offered command of the brig *Commonwealth* by its Italian-American owners he sailed from Baltimore in February 1854 under an

Autographed photograph of Garibaldi formerly in South Shields Public Library.

American flag but with a crew of exile comrades of the Italian Legion. In London, where the ship discharged a cargo of flour and grain, her world-famous captain determinedly kept out of the public eye, though not without generating some speculation about the table talk when he attended a dinner at the home of the United States consul-general along with the cream of Europe's professional revolutionaries then resident in London: Mazzini and Orsini for Italy, Kossuth for Hungary, Alexander Herzen for Russia, and Stanislaw Worcell for Poland.

When Joe Cowen (still only twenty-four) learned presumably through Mazzini that the *Commonwealth* was next headed for the Tyne, he and his Committee of Friends of European Freedom prepared to mobilise a massive demonstration of pro-Italian sympathies with a view to using it also to protest against the government's grand alliance with 'the reactionary and absolutist potentates of Europe' in the run-up to the predicted war with Russia in the Crimea. When Garibaldi telegraphed back that he wanted no such fuss the committee quickly dreamed up an effective alternative stunt: a public appeal to Tynesiders for penny-a-head subscriptions towards a sword and a telescope and an illuminated address to be presented to 'the glorious defender of the Roman Republic'. The money was raised in just a few days by staging well-publicised meetings which attracted hundreds of subscribers.

The many hours which Cowen spent in the company of the great man cemented his commitment to the Italian cause and his abiding loyalty to the two very different individuals who – beyond the politicians who had little time for either of them – did most to achieve the unification of their country: Mazzini the intellectual visionary, and Garibaldi the soldier hero. When ashore Garibaldi lodged in Tynemouth or with the Cowens at Stella House, always

GENERAL GARIBALDI.

GOD AND THE PEOPLE.

At a Meeting of some FRIENDS OF EUROPEAN FREEDOM held in the Exhibition Room, Nelson Street, on Tuesday Night, the 28th inst., it was resolved to

PRESENT

THE

GLORIOUS DEFENDER OF THE ROMAN REPUBLIC

WITH A

SWORD!

Accompanied with an address of Welcome and Sympathy, on his visit to the Tyneside. The General (whose bravery in battle is only equalled by his modesty) having declined any public demonstration, the above was deemed the most appropriate mode of marking our regard for him as a Man, and our sympathy for the great cause which he loves so devoutly and serves so well.

It was further resolved to purchase the Sword by Subscriptions of one Penny.

Subscriptions will be received by J. Barlow, at the Northern Tribune Office; where collecting Lists can be had on application.

March 29th, 1854.

Printed by J. Barlow, at the Northern Tribune Office, 28, Grainger Street, Newcastle.

adamant that he wanted 'no public demonstration of any nature on my account'. He did however agree to informal meetings at the Nelson Street lecture room and at the Blaydon Mechanics' Institute, and besides posing for an oil portrait on board the *Commonwealth* also formally received a small farewell deputation of radical worthies, Polish exiles, and workers' representatives the day before sailing, 11th April. Each penny subscribed for the gold-hilted sword, Cowen assured him at the little ceremony, 'represents a heart which beats true to European freedom.' He then read out the presentation address which he himself had penned, concluding with a splendidly characteristic Cowen flourish: 'When they who drive out the Austrians build up again a Republican capital upon the Seven Hills, the heirs of Milton and Cromwell will not be the last to say, even from their deepest heart – God speed your work!' Garibaldi's reply, in the halting English he had picked up in America, was printed in full in the *Northern Tribune:*

> '*Gentlemen, I am very weak in the English language, and can but imperfectly express my acknowledgements for your over great kindness. You honour me beyond my deserts. My services are not worthy of all the favour you have shown me. You more than reward me for any sacrifices I may have made in the cause of freedom.*
>
> *One of the people – a workman like yourselves – I value very highly the expressions of your esteem, the more so because you testify thereby your sympathy for my poor, oppressed and downtrodden country. Speaking in a strange tongue, I feel most painfully my inability to thank you in terms sufficiently warm.*
>
> *The future will alone show how soon it will be before I am called on to unsheathe the noble gift I have just received, and again battle in behalf of that which lies nearest my heart – the freedom of my native land. But be sure of this: Italy will one day be a nation, and its free citizens will know how to acknowledge all the kindness shown her exiled sons in the days of their darkest troubles.*
>
> *Gentlemen, I would say more, but my bad English prevents me. You can appreciate my feelings and understand my hesitation. Again I thank you from my heart of hearts, and be confident of this – that whatever vicissitudes of fortune I may hereafter pass through, this handsome sword shall never be drawn by me except in the cause of liberty.'*

'The magical leader of men', as the star-struck Trevelyan called Garibaldi in his own magical biography of the man, sailed away to an adventurous future. Years later, writing in answer to one of those Geordie penny-subscribers, he confirmed that the chance to unsheathe his Tyneside sword in anger had come in 1859 when wielding it 'against the troops of the Austrian despot'. This was the ultimately successful if very bloody campaign fought in alliance with the French to wrest Lombardy from Austrian control during which Garibaldi, now a major-general in the royal army of Piedmont, conducted himself with his customary fearless flair at the head of his usual devoted band of irregulars. Today the sword and telescope and the oil portrait are all displayed in the Garibaldi house and museum on the little Sardinian island of Caprera, the general's modest home for the last twenty-five years of his life.[3]

Giuseppe Garibaldi: oil portrait by James Shotton inscribed "Painted on board of the ship Commonwealth A.D. 1854". Formerly in the North Shields Free Library, the painting now hangs in the Garibaldi museum on the island of Caprera. Shotton was the North Shields School of Art's first drawing master and a close friend of Holman Hunt, as is apparent from the rather dreamy rendition of the 47-year-old freedom fighter. (Photo: Museo Garibaldi, Caprera).

THE
EMANCIPATION OF ITALY!
A PUBLIC MEETING
will be held in the
LECTURE ROOM, NELSON STREET,
on **Monday night next, 29th Inst.,**
TO RECEIVE AN ADDRESS FROM THE ITALIAN WORKING-
MEN TO THE WORKING-MEN OF ENGLAND.
Communications will be read from

MAZZINI and GARIBALDI,
A REPLY TO THE ITALIAN ADDRESS

will be submitted for the adoption
of the Meeting,
AND A

SUBSCRIPTION
FOR THE EMANCIPATION OF ITALY
will be started.

DOORS OPEN AT 7. 30.—CHAIR TAKEN AT 8 O'CLOCK.

SEPTEMBER, 1856.

Flyer for a fund-raising meeting in Newcastle, 29 September 1856, chaired by Joseph Cowen. 'The Address from the Italian working men', an appeal by Mazzini's revolutionary followers in Genoa, was used to further his funding campaign in Britain. Cowen kicked off the Tyneside campaign with a massive donation of £100. (Cowen Collection, Tyne and Wear Archives).

'Evviva l'Italia! Evviva la libertà!' At the conclusion of the meeting Joseph Cowen, its main author, signs the Reply to the Italian Address 'on behalf of the working men of Tyneside'. 'The wrongs and the sufferings of Italy we deplore, the cruelties of her tyrants we execrate, the heroism of her sons we admire, and we recognise the duty, so far as in our power lies, of aiding in the holy work of effecting her Emancipation' (page one). (Cowen Collection)

Last page of a letter of 17 February 1859 to Cowen in which Mazzini appeals to his dependable friend for help in urgently raising 'some £2000' to fund a desperate last-ditch dream of uniting all Italians under one flag and the slogan 'Out with the Foreigner' to thwart the French and Piedmontese monarchies' combined designs on the peninsula: 'Englishmen ought to understand that to keep out Louis Napoleon, they have only two ways: killing him, or calling into action our own popular element.' (Cowen Collection).

Felice Orsini

The *Newcastle Courant* report (see next pages) of the rapturous response to an address by Felice Orsini in Newcastle is a vivid record of how successful were Cowen and his friends in fostering pro-Italian sentiment on Tyneside. Orsini, a fearless Mazzinian revolutionary, was touring the country with two lectures in English he had carefully committed to memory. A trial run in Brighton had gone down well, particularly with the ladies, so on Mazzini's recommendation he decided to open his national tour in the receptive North East, staying ten days with the Cowens at Stella House while starring in further appearances in South Shields and Sunderland. It is instructive to see how carefully his performance was crafted to flatter as well as rouse a patriotic Protestant audience with its fulsome tributes to British liberalism and imperialism and savage condemnation of popery and priestcraft.

Felice Orsini.

The dashing Orsini was already a celebrity in Britain for his thrilling prison escape described at length in his London-published bestseller *The Austrian Dungeons in Italy*. In its equally punchy sequel, *The Memoirs and Aventures of Felice Orsini,* he wrote amusingly of the agony of public speaking in a language he scarcely knew, quipping that it was worse than anything he had had to face from the Austrians. Of his North-East reception he wrote with special affection. 'It was a good school for me. I found a free and most intelligent population. When I finished the lecture the workmen took my hand in their horny palms and said, "We hope you will succeed in your good cause." I found in Mr. Cowen an excellent friend, a good father to his family, and a true lover of liberty, devoted to the Italian cause." He didn't mention that Cowen's wife Jane had spent hours helping him polish his speeches.

Little more than a year later, in January 1858, the good cause took Orsini to Paris where with two other Italian nationalists he carried out a horrendously blood-strewn bomb attempt on the life of emperor Louis Napoleon, a key hate figure for Europe's radicals owing to his dictatorial rule in France, his crushing of the Roman Republic of 1848, and his continuing military protection of the Papal States. By his desperate deed it seems Orsini hoped to ignite an 1848-style revolution in Paris to trigger similar uprisings in Italy and a war of liberation. Bumping off Napoleon had once been one of Mazzini's most cherished dreams and it is likely that by seizing the initiative in this way Orsini hoped to usurp his master as leader of the Italian cause, for he had come to deride the older man as outmoded and out of touch, shielded from reality by a cosy coterie of besotted English ladies. During the long weeks of Orsini's trial in Paris and his subsequent execution, both borne with a dignity that paradoxically won even the emperor to the cause of Italian liberty, the *Chronicle* preached that Orsini was a martyr for freedom while its Tory-owned rival, *The Northern Daily Express,* demanded the owner's prosecution for conspiracy to murder.

During the police hunt for the assassin's English backers suspicion did indeed fall on Cowen's circle of radical friends. Tyrannicide was not merely theorised among them. Only two years earlier Sydney Milne Hawkes, who later contributed a regular "Local Gossip" column for the *Chronicle*, had smuggled over to Paris the pistol used by Giovanni Pianori in a similar attempt to eliminate the emperor. Another close Cowen associate, George Jacob Holyoake, years later wrote a book confessing in vivid detail how he helped Orsini to test his bombs.

Joe Cowen saw a lot of Holyoake at this time since both men were regular speakers at public protests against the government's prosecution of Simon Bernard, a French communist exile in London accused of aiding Orsini. When the case collapsed, Cowen put up Bernard at Stella House to recuperate from his ordeal. According to Wemyss Reid, another journalist friend, Cowen once admitted to him he was indeed the mystery man who had funded the Orsini plot, though quite unwittingly, for he had acted 'in absolute ignorance of the fact that this was the purpose to which the money was to be appropriated.' He insisted he had understood it was merely 'for the equipment of another insurrectionary expedition against the Austrians in Italy.'

FELICE ORSINI IN NEWCASTLE

This celebrated Italian, whose extraordinary escape from the Austrian dungeon of St. Giorgio, Mantua, has rendered his name so familiar to the people of this country, delivered an address on Monday evening last, in the Lecture-room, Nelson Street, on "Italy". There was a numerous and respectable attendance, and Sir John Fife was called to the chair.

Plaque in Nelson Street, Newcastle. These premises, which hosted Felice Orsini in 1856, were a regular venue for talks and meetings for a whole variety of radical causes. The American publicist William Lloyd Garrison was a prominent anti-slavery campaigner and advocate of women's suffrage.

Signor Orsini stood forward amidst loud cheering. Glory (he said) to England, who was moved at the misfortune of Italy. Honour to the people of Newcastle, who first and always made demonstration of brotherhood towards the Italian exiles. Escaped from the tyranny of Austrian despotism, he came to this country – the only safe spot in Europe for the refugees – to relate the infamies employed by the despotic governments in Italy against the patriots.

Signor Orsini proceeded to speak of the wanton cruelty and heartless tyranny practised under the Austrian rule, of the universality of the spy system – spies being found in every grade of society. The office of these spies was to worm themselves into the homes and the secrets of the people, and report their every word and act to the police and government authorities. The power of the priesthood, the police, and the spies, was so uncontrollable that brothers and fathers were denounced and consigned to the dungeons and the galleys, because their daughters or sisters would not submit to the wishes of miscreant priests and police spies. Signor Orsini adverted to the cruelty and wantonness of the arrests of suspected persons; to the frequency with which persons were shot without trial; and to the fact of the prisons, large and numerous as they are, being too small to hold the accumulation of political prisoners. It was not seven months since he lay in the castle of St. Giorgio, infested by insects and scorpions, poisoned from the horrible exhalations of the water surrounding the castle, prostrated by fever, and so persecuted by frequent interrogatories that he really thought he must go mad. Several of his companions in that castle were taken from the next dungeon to his and led to the scaffold. Hundreds of thousands of noble-minded Italians were suffering in this way throughout Italy; and when they were released, if they were fortunate enough to be released, their health was broken, and they were never again the men they had been. Much as he had himself suffered, he was ready to endure everything, to pass through any trials and sufferings, if he could by so doing injure the oppressors of his country. (Loud applause.) *Although but a simple individual, yet while God granted him intellect and physical power he would always work in the firm hope of seeing at last every bloody foottrack of Austria cancelled from the soil of Italy.* (Vehement cheering.) *And if, with his latest breath, he could reflect that he had, with deeds, and not words only, done something to aid in the liberation of the land that gave him birth, he should die contented and happy.* (Applause.) *And what (asked Signor Orsini) is the cause of these our evils? It is the Pope, the centre of slavery in Italy! But (said Signor Orsini, in conclusion) the times are approaching in which we shall see the fall of priestly tyranny; in which the free nations by a sacred instinct, will aid us that we may live. The attitude of the free and liberal English people gives us hope that the wished-for time is near. I hear the name of Italy mentioned with sympathy from one end of your land to the other. It is a new and cheering fact to Italians. Seas separate us; our customs and our languages are different, and our governments have always tried to make the English name hateful to the land of DANTE. But the peoples understand each other; and the proud British islander, who fearlessly rules the waves wherever his ship can float, begins to reflect on our country's misery, and his generous heart is moved towards the classic land which gave Columbus to the world. The children of that soil whose heroes in ancient times were "Masters of the world, the lords of earth and sea", shall be allowed to work out their great destinies, and shall not for ever be bound by the keys of the Vatican and by all the despotic powers of Europe.* (Great and prolonged applause.)

Mr Wm. Cook, in a few remarks, proposed the following resolution:

"That the thanks of the meeting be rendered to Signor Felice Orsini for his able lecture this evening; and that it deplores the wrongs which his country suffers from the outrageous tyranny to which it is subjected. Further, that this meeting recognises the right of the Italian people to a natural existence, and believes it to be the duty of all free nations to aid them in their struggle to obtain it."

The Rev. James Pringle seconded the resolution. It was sad (he said) to think, – and he did not regard it as unfitting in a Christian minister to say so, – that the worst of evils was the evil which was embodied in a clerical form, and perpetrated in the name of what was wise, and just, and good. (Applause.)

The resolution was adopted unanimously.

Mr. Joseph Cowen moved a vote of thanks to the chairman.

(abridged from *The Newcastle Courant*, Friday October 24, 1856. Sir John Fife, a leading liberal and former mayor of Newcastle, espoused many of the radical causes dear to Cowen.)

'Who will fight for Garibaldi?'

Whatever the whole truth of Cowen's involvement in the Orsini affair, it is certain that he helped to fund another abortive Mazzini-planned rebellion in Genoa, and during the 1859 war of independence in which France and Piedmont teamed up against Austria to liberate Lombardy he procured both money and arms in aid of Garibaldi's appeal for 'a million rifles'. During the even more tumultuous events of 1860 he threw himself heart and soul and purse behind Garibaldi's almost miraculously successful campaigns in Sicily and southern Italy at the head of his 1,000 red-shirted volunteers.[4] The momentous story dominated the pages of the *Chronicle* with daily newsflashes, frequent editorials, calls for further funds, and lengthy well-informed reports from 'special correspondents' like Holyoake and Jessie White Mario, Garibaldi's spirited English friend who was organising the care of the wounded and had married an Italian patriot she met while imprisoned in Genoa.

On August 13th, when the self-styled Dictator of Sicily was poised to cross the Straits of Messina to invade mainland Italy, the paper opened a recruitment drive for local volunteers: 'Who Will Fight for Garibaldi?' The government had already declared the enlistment of Irish Catholics in the papal army a

THE GREATEST EVENT OF THE YEAR
IN DARLINGTON.
———
THE GARABALDI FUND SOIREE.
———
THE admirers of GARABALDI in Darlington and Neighbourhood are informed that a Committee has been formed for the purpose of raising funds, by means of

A SOIREE,

which will be held

EARLY IN SEPTEMBER,

IN THE

CENTRAL HALL, DARLINGTON,

the profits arising therefrom to be devoted to the

GARABALDI FUND,

which is being raised in England for the purpose of assisting him in his heroic endeavours to

LIBERATE ITALY

FROM THE

YOKE OF TYRANNY;

and it is to be hoped that

ALL LOVERS OF FREEDOM

will zealously respond to the appeal, and assist either by purchasing tickets for the Soiree or giving their mite towards the object.

TICKETS (now ready), 1s : sold by all Printers, Booksellers, the Committee, and by

W. J. OLIVER, Hon. Secretary,

who will give any information on the subject necessary.

Handbill, Darlington 1860. The spelling may be shaky, but there is no questioning the excitement generated by "Garibaldi"'s exploits. (Cowen Collection)

breach of the Foreign Enlistment Act, and now Cowen's flagrant contravention prompted the mayor of Gateshead, George Crawshay – instantly dubbed 'Don Quixote' by the *Chronicle* – to bring a summons against the paper's owner. The mayor, who was convinced the liberation of Italy was all a Tsarist plot and also happened to be Gateshead's chief magistrate, had already accused Cowen of 'corrupting the minds and hearts of the people of Blaydon with the ideas of Mazzini.' But the mood of the public was entirely behind Cowen, and Crawshay's case was quite literally laughed out of court. New elections had by now returned Lord Palmerston to power, well-known for his Italian sympathies not least because he calculated a strong Italy would impede French and Austrian ambitions in the Mediterranean which the British fleet both patrolled and policed. Despite his government's advocacy of non-intervention by any foreign power in Italy's affairs Palmerston had freely joked before parliament that he could hardly 'prevent excursionists from taking a peep at Mount Etna'. By then hundreds from all over the country were converging on London to sign up for the cause. Some thirty Britons had served in Garibaldi's famous Thousand right from the beginning, and some of their exploits had been made much of in all the press. 'To have fought with Garibaldi,' noted the London *Daily News* enticingly, 'will one day be thought one of the proudest memories a man can boast of.'

During the rest of August the *Chronicle* reported the departure of small parties of North-Easterners to join the 'excursionists' for whom, readers were informed, the London Garibaldi Committee (organised by Holyoake) 'have arranged for a free passage, costume, and means of self-defence together with all necessary provisions during the voyage.' By the time their ship reached Naples on 15th October Garibaldi was already master of the liberated city. A similar spirit of solidarity with people overseas fighting for their freedom was shown when more than 100 men from Northumberland and Durham volunteered for the International Brigade at the time of the Spanish Civil War after 1936. Even so, for all its idealism some first impressions of the English Legion in Italy were more like that of our soccer fans. 'They immediately distinguished themselves in a truly national manner by getting drunk and disorderly, and in sleeping on and under the tables in the principal cafes which have today been closed in consequence,' reported the British Minister in Naples. Their Catholic rivals, the Irish Papal Brigade, had similarly distinguished themselves after disembarking at Ancona in July, though there their drunken revels had been brutally curtailed by their supposed comrades-in-arms, the papal guard. One Geordie 'excursionist', J.E. Macklin, who readily admitted they were a 'mixed lot' with little or no military experience, left a less jaundiced account of their first day and night on Italian soil, before the contingent of 610 men made its way to the frontline near Caserta, just 20 miles north of Naples.

VIVA INGHILTERRA!

After many years, I can still remember every detail of our landing, and the enthusiastic reception given to the English Legion. The morning of October 15th, 1860, looked "drizzly" and threatened rain, but the glorious Italian sun came to the rescue, scattered the clouds, and beamed a kindly welcome. We were received by guards of honour composed of National Guards, with their bands playing and flags flying, as we paraded in front of the palace. An immense number of people crammed the spacious piazza. "Viva Inghilterra! Viva Inglesi!" saluted us on every side, while handsome young ladies, heading a procession of citizens, stuck flowers in our rifles. Some had flowers fixed in their caps, and a few favoured ones had garlands placed by fair hands round their necks. Nearly all of us were in the prime of life, "In youth's morning march when the bosom is young". Therefore the welcome from the ladies was not the least pleasant episode of our reception.

As we marched up the Toledo, one of the finest streets in Europe, every window was adorned with flags, tapestry, and all the adjuncts of a great fete. From many a balcony floated our national emblem, the Union Jack, which was also carried at the head of the National Guards. Escorted by our enthusiastic friends, we arrived at our temporary barracks, and, after receiving orders to hold ourselves in readiness for Caserta, were allowed to enjoy ourselves in the city. Having been so long cramped up on board ship, we felt like so many boys let loose from school. The theatres and all places of amusement were open to us free, and it was our own fault if the night was not passed pleasantly. "With youth at the prow and pleasure at the helm", we contrived to make our first visit to Naples something to remember. If in the early morning some of our men made "zigzaggy" strides when returning to barracks, and if others had hazy recollections as to how they reached their quarters, what matter, for were we not in a few hours to enter upon the stern realities of the campaign? Before the dawn the regiment was under arms, tramping along the dark streets en route to Caserta...

(John Eyre Macklin, from a series of articles about his experiences with the English Legion, in the *Weekly Chronicle*, Newcastle, 27 April-22 June 1889. Recruiting the legion was Garibaldi's idea, formulated in Milazzo in July 1860.)

On the battlefield the Legion acquitted itself well at a skirmish near Capua, and Garibaldi himself praised 'the brilliant courage they displayed in the slight engagement they shared with us on the Volturno.' This was not the great battle of the Volturno fought a fortnight earlier, the crowning victory of Garibaldi's campaign in the southern kingdom, but a later clash with Bourbon loyalist forces as he crossed the river to surrender all his territorial conquests to King Victor Emmanuel. The king was waiting to meet him on the other bank at the head of a Piedmontese army which had hastily invaded the Papal States to stop Garibaldi from seizing Rome and spreading more revolution.

(Advertisement from the Newcastle Chronicle, 1860)

Garibaldi mania, 1864

In April 1864, precisely ten years after his unobtrusive visit as skipper of the *Commonwealth*, Garibaldi made a spectacular return to Britain. Now almost all of Italy was finally one nation, a constitutional monarchy united – politically, but far from socially – under the royal house of Savoy. Only Venetia and a fraction of the old Papal State centred on Rome remained in other hands, the former still embedded in the Austrian empire, the latter in the care of a desperately beleaguered pope.

Never has a foreign visitor experienced anything like the spontaneous public welcome which greeted Garibaldi. 'The Hero of Two Worlds', 'the New Washington', had not even received an official invitation – he claimed he was only here to consult an eminent surgeon about an old wound to his foot (see next section) – though his many public appearances left no doubt that he meant to use his extraordinary

Head of Garibaldi, Blaydon public library.

popularity to pressure the government into favouring Italy's ongoing claims to Venice and Rome. Always for the underdog, he also repeatedly called for British aid in 'poor little' Denmark's war with Prussia over Schleswig-Holstein, and in Poland's equally doomed freedom struggle against mighty Russia. The ambassadors of every country except Turkey and the United States boycotted the big reception in his honour, the Queen ticked off the Prince of Wales for wanting to meet the 'revolutionist leader', and yet the six-hour progress of 'the Saviour of Italy' through the streets of London ushered by working men's committees and friendly societies and trade unions was watched by crowds of over half a million with the sort of rapturous scenes the British normally only reserve for royalty or one of their own conquering heroes. But he was their hero, for once a working class hero.

As soon as it was learned the great man next intended to tour the provinces, civic receptions were feverishly prepared up and down the country. The *Chronicle* proposed a general holiday and predicted huge turnouts on Tyneside. First to clap eyes on the 'Apostle of Liberty' in his famous red shirt and poncho would be the fortunate citizens of West Hartlepool when he stepped off a train from York for 'a hearty welcome of one of the noblest men the world ever knew.' The steamship *Garibaldi*[5] would then convey him to Sunderland for more mass adulation and lofty speeches. And next on by train to Newcastle to embrace his old friend Joe Cowen along with other dignitaries before concluding the memorable day with 'a great demonstration of the trades, a progress down the river, and an illumination.' South Shields and Blyth also laid plans to be in on the act. The notable exception was once again 'Don Quixote' George Crawshay of Gateshead. His mayoral veto on a civic reception, protested the *Gateshead Observer*, only gave more ammunition to those who already considered Gateshead inferior to other towns, for now it would be able to boast it truly was unique, being 'the only town to refuse to acknowledge Garibaldi's visit'.

But Giuseppe Garibaldi never returned to the North East, never even embarked on the triumphal tour of Britain which was scheduled to finish in Glasgow. Pleading deteriorating health, he suddenly issued apologies all round and quit the country, probably genuinely exhausted, and almost certainly bowing to government pressure, though this was strongly denied by Palmerston. The potentates of several 'friendly' powers had expressed alarm at his ecstatic popular reception and undiplomatic calls to overthrow them, and Queen Victoria, who had beaten a tactical retreat to Balmoral, let it be known she was appalled by the heady atmosphere of lower class jubilation. Joe Cowen, who had been one of the very first to welcome Garibaldi at Southampton docks, rushed south again to try to talk him into staying and then returned home to announce, 'the great guest of the nation, the liberator of Italy, the noblest soldier of our time, is to be thrust from our soil because our people love him.' Nowt to do with foreign interference, retorted the Tory *Newcastle Journal*, 'Garibaldi is being hurried off in order to get him out of the hands of the Red Republicans who at present have complete possession of him.'

In the afterglow of the 1864 visit Cowen strove to keep the special relationship alive on Tyneside by getting a terrace in Blaydon named after Garibaldi and by levying more pennies from his workers to pay for the raising of an 8-foot-high stone effigy of the Italian hero pointedly sporting his 1854 sword and telescope, his noble head gazing in the direction of his oppressed native land. Carved by George Burn of Newcastle, it was set up on Summerhouse Hill overlooking the site of Blaydon races. In the early years of the twentieth century persons unknown toppled the statue from its plinth and eventually even its whereabouts became a mystery. In 1941 the battered great head and lower limbs were unearthed by a local builder, Jack Thomas, at the site of an old refuse tip while excavating the foundations for army billets. For years they ornamented his garden. In 1977 he donated the head to Blaydon Public Library where it still enjoys a special place of honour. The legs are preserved in the grounds of St Joseph's primary school.

Up the Pope!

Depending on one's viewpoint, the ageing but resilient pope Pius IX, who after Italy's unification still ruled Rome from within a fragment of the old Papal State resolutely refusing to recognise the new nation, was either a tyrannical reactionary opposed to the unstoppable historic forces of liberalism and nationalism or else the inviolable Holy Father, Christ's vicar on earth menaced by rapacious heathens, the ruler of a patrimony held in trust for St Peter and assigned to him by Providence. Italy's new rulers made no secret of wanting Rome for capital but were wary of annexing the Holy City by force for fear of

Canon Thomas Wilkinson, Catholic priest of Crook and Wolsingham, and later Bishop of Hexham, flanked by the Weardale men he recruited for the pontifical army in 1867. The men are kitted out as papal Zouaves, the international brigade of 'crusaders' formed in 1860 by French and Belgian Catholics for the defence of the Papal State.

outraging world Catholic opinion and more dangerously France and Austria, the two Catholic great powers which had vetoed further expansion. The government had nonetheless seized nearly all territory outside Rome subject to the pope's temporal power, dissolved monasteries and sold off ecclesiastical estates all over Italy, and introduced secular education and civil marriage. Pius retaliated by excommunicating the king and all his ministers and forbidding Catholics to have any truck with Italian national politics. Liberalism and Catholicism were incompatible, he decreed, no one could 'embrace simultaneously God and the devil.'

In 1862 Napoleon III stepped up France's military presence in Rome after Garibaldi had been foiled in yet another unsanctioned attempt to take the Eternal City. Anti-French protests were orchestrated all over Britain. Cowen chaired angry meetings in Newcastle, Gateshead and Sunderland, and personally conveyed the resulting financial contributions to the organisers of the 'Garibaldi Surgical Aid Fund' in London which had appealed for £1,000 for specialist treatment to the general's right foot. In August, at Aspromonte in the Calabrian mountains, it had stopped a bullet fired by Italian royalist troops under orders to halt his progress at the head of a private army intent on storming Rome. He had used his legendary status in Sicily to raise a peasant army and lead it north, terrifying the king into supposing he meant to exploit southern resentment of the new northern rulers to start another revolution, seize Rome, and topple the monarchy.

The Aspromonte incident reignited enthusiasm for Garibaldi across the world, which in turn only aggravated Catholic indignation. The Italian nationalist cause always risked becoming a pretext for stoking the age-old quarrel between Papists and anti-Papists. Garibaldi's anti-clericalism was notorious: the papacy was 'the negation of God,' priests were 'black beetles, the scourge of Italy'. For many Protestants a large part of the appeal of the campaign for Italian freedom was that it had no support from Catholics. Each side routinely disrupted the other's meetings. At the time of the Aspromonte rumpus heavy heckling from Irish Catholics ('No Garibaldi! The Pope for ever!') at a huge pro-Garibaldi rally in Hyde Park ended in widespread rioting and the terrorising of London's Irish colonies. Cardinal Manning, head of the Catholic church in England, had vehemently protested against Garibaldi's planned visit in 1864 claiming it could stimulate 'the seditious and socialist revolution which at the present moment threatens every government, absolute or constitutional, throughout Europe.' During the Newcastle Race Week of 1866, a 300-strong group of Tyneside Irish paraded round the Town Moor threatening to beat in the brains of anyone who failed to give the appropriate retort to the challenge: "Garibaldi or the Pope?"

So by no means all North-Easterners shared Joe Cowen's outrage at the humbling of the 'hero of Aspromonte' by those who had benefitted so much from his victories, or would have joined him in echoing Garibaldi's war cry *Roma o morte!* (Rome or Die!). The opposition organised too. Ever since the crisis of 1860, in response to the papacy's call for 'an army of crusaders' from all over Europe leading British Catholics had been raising funds to send weapons and men to defend the pope against the menace of the godless new nation state. The immediate result, the 500-strong Irish Papal Brigade or 'Pope's Irish', had arrived in July 1860 in time to perform well in September against the invading Piedmontese forces, notably in the defence of Spoleto under major Myles O'Reilly, a graduate of Ushaw College, the celebrated Catholic seminary in County Durham. On a pilgrimage to Rome in 1867, canon Thomas Wilkinson, another product of Ushaw and later its president, was appalled to see four-fifths of the former papal lands under the dominion of 'the robber' (Italian troops). He returned home to recruit and personally sponsor a half-dozen young parishioners to 'defend the cause of God and to fight against the cause of Satan', as the chaplain of the English-speaking Zouaves in Rome portrayed the contest to him.

By this time, with Catholic Austria defeated in war by an Italo-Prussian alliance and finally forced to cede all Venetia to Italy, Pius IX looked still more desperately isolated. Garibaldi had another unlicensed go at Rome the year after Wilkinson's visit, but again Satan's irregulars were repelled by the pontifical army and the French garrison. Finally, in September 1870, following the hurried withdrawal of all French troops from the city during the crisis of the Franco-Prussian War, Rome was annexed almost without bloodshed and papal territory suddenly shrank to a 109-acre enclave inside the high walls of the Vatican. Garibaldi, incidentally, missed out on the final capture of Rome. He chanced to have business in France

Interior of 'Garibaldi' pink lustreware bowl, one of many similar items mass-produced by the Garrison Pottery, Sunderland, in response to the extraordinary popularity of the 'liberator of Italy.'
(Tyne and Wear Archives and Museums)

fighting for the new French Republic against the invading Prussians, too lame to walk by now but still gallantly heading a contingent of international volunteers. Victor Hugo claimed he was the only general on the French side to be undefeated in the entire war.

United Italy's first consul in Newcastle

An indication of the new Kingdom of Italy's arrival on the international scene was the appointment of a career diplomat as its consul in Newcastle in late 1862. Count Filippo De Mancini was the first person of Italian origin to hold the post. Overall it was not a happy experience. His chief grievances were the climate, his pay,

and his compatriots. Though prepared to concede his salary and expense allowance could only be a fraction of those of the consuls of wealthier countries like France and North America ('who nonetheless still complain of inadequate remuneration in view of the high cost of living and the execrable climate'), he still demanded to know how his masters could presume that the nation's honour and the dignity of his office were upheld by only permitting him to trim his uniform with silver and not 'first rank' gold. His straitened circumstances forced him to stoop to giving French and Italian lessons. Even so, at his own 'considerable' expense he rented chambers in the Quayside area and furnished a special room where Italian skippers could 'write and discuss business.'

Until his arrival the affairs of the principal states of Italy had been handled by Edward Bilton, a Newcastle insurance broker and coal exporter who also acted as consular agent for Spain, Portugal and Brazil. The count found him reluctant to step down and only prepared to part with his Italian records at a price. But that battle was nothing next to his efforts to regularise maritime procedure (i.e. levy unpopular new Italian state dues) which at once brought him into open conflict with a group of 'ignorant and coarse' Italian shipping brokers and interpreters downstream in North Shields, a base from which they could be first aboard Italian and other foreign vessels as they entered the Tyne. To judge by his sketch of one individual who gave him particular trouble they were indeed a pretty lawless bunch: 'Vincenzo Calì... in January this year [1863] was in the pay of a certain Bonaccini, shipping agent, who has since absconded abroad in a state of fraudulent bankruptcy. Not without suspicion of abetting the getaway, Calì then entered the service of a Mr Davison, an Englishman, who dismissed him reportedly for breach of trust. He was next employed by Messrs. Bruat & Co, French shipping brokers, who sacked him for dishonest dealings, and now he works for a certain Zaccheria, an Austrian subject, and both are accused of I know not what fraud and will be standing trial.' Zaccheria was also Italian, but from Venetia which was then still under Austrian rule. Apart from offering to pilot Italian skippers through the shoals of tiresome legal restrictions, the services of Calì and his associates, alleged the consul, included guided tours to the seamier side of Tyneside nightlife.

De Mancini's co-nationals in North Shields, who had never before had to deal with a meddling Italian bureaucrat in England, quickly came up with a ruse for keeping his nose out of their affairs once and for all. Compliant Italian merchant captains were persuaded to add their signatures to a collective appeal directed over his head straight to his boss, the Foreign Minister, petitioning for a special consular agent in North Shields, naturally chosen from among their ranks. To accede, raged the exasperated consul, would be tantamount to declaring him redundant. After perusing his six-page protestation Rome rejected the North Shields petition.

Next year, the count came to suspect the same North Shields gang was involved in a ring which specialised in inducing Italian seamen to jump ship 'with vain promises of better pay.' After helping the fugitives to lie low they would be passed on to safe houses in nearby ports like Sunderland or Hartlepool, even as far afield as London, before being 'as good as sold off' to foreign captains whose crews had been depleted by similar methods. Desertion was attaining alarming proportions, he reported, often after a long voyage almost the entire ship's complement might abscond. Poor pay and brutal treatment 'fortunately by few captains' were the chief causes, though many younger crewmen were also deserting to avoid conscription (generally three years in the new Italy). His efforts were not improved by the conduct of the local harbour police who all too often seemed ready to turn a blind eye when foreign seamen with bulky bundles were observed heading out of the dock area, 'perhaps in expectation of the money that will come their way if requested to go after them.' The consul cited the cases of Luigi Durazzano and Paolo Scotto, both from the island of Procida in the Bay of Naples, who deserted one night from the brig L'Indifferente with all their belongings. Notified early next morning, he alerted North Shields police who 'as usual' responded slowly, allowing the two men to be spirited to Sunderland. Even after picking up the scent 'they wasted precious time by calling on the captain to discuss the cost of the recovery expedition rather than instructing Sunderland police to make the arrest, thereby giving both men time to embark and depart.'

'The inclemency of the season, the humidity of the climate, the insalubrious nature' of his quayside quarters caused the count a long and painful illness during his first winter in Newcastle. The following spring he informed his masters that on doctor's orders he was forsaking 'the miasmas of the port, amidst the fogs of the river' and transferring office and residence to fashionable Eldon Square, next to the French consul and close to 'the other consuls who are not merchants'. After just over three years in his post count De Mancini managed to secure a position in sunnier Cadiz, and Italian consular affairs in Newcastle reverted to the care of Mr Edward Bilton, merchant.[6]

ROBBERY OF £9 10s FROM A NEAPOLITAN CAPTAIN

At the Hartlepool police court yesterday Catherine McDonald, Mary Ann Forster, and Elizabeth Winter, were charged with stealing £9 10s from the person of Michele Jannarino, captain of a Neapolitan brig at present lying in the Hartlepool dock. It appears from the evidence adduced that the prosecutor met McDonald in the street on the evening of the 4th inst., and she conducted him to the house of Winter. After going up stairs, Winter brought up the prisoner Forster, and after some drink had been obtained he had connections with her. During that time the other two prisoners retired; they presently returned; and while he was sitting on the bed with McDonald the other two closed round him, and entreated him to drink some brandy. He then suspected that he was in bad company; and his watch being in his waistcoat pocket, his attention was drawn to it, and whilst in the act of reaching over to get it, Forster and Winter held him down on the bed, and McDonald took his purse out of his pocket, emptied the gold into her hand, threw the empty purse into the bed, and made off. For some time the prosecutor could not obtain a release owing to Forster holding him down, but after so doing he went down stairs, but McDonald was not to be found. He gave information to the police, and the prisoners were apprehended, and severally sentenced to three months' imprisonment.

Daily Chronicle, 8 August 1860

The shipping connection

The bulk of foreign trade in the North East has always been with North Sea and Baltic ports. All the same, in consul De Mancini's time when with Liverpool the port of Newcastle was second only to London in volume of business, all the major Italian ports[7] were handling large shipments of coal and coke from the region, as well as lesser exports such as pig-iron, grindstones, firebricks, glass, chemicals, and machinery. De Mancini judged the potential for vastly increasing steel and

The Italian transport steamer Europa, the first vessel to pass through the Swing Bridge when it opened in 1876. Originally built by Palmer's of Jarrow, the Europa was bound for the Armstrong works at Elswick to load a huge 100-ton cannon for the Italian naval arsenal at La Spezia.

textile exports to Italy sufficient to recommend the appointment of consular agents in Sheffield and Leeds, despite the very small number of Italian settlers in these towns. Italy had one of the largest merchant fleets at this time, based mainly out of Naples and Genoa, and many Italian seamen served on British ships, some even being captained by Italians.

In the warmer months Italian-registered vessels were putting into the Tyne at the rate of almost one a day. In 1860, for instance, the North and South Shields Trinity House record of pilotage shows that 84 Italian-owned vessels, almost all registered in Naples, passed through their hands in the period July to September. This dropped to only 14 between October and November, after which there were virtually no sailings to or from Italian ports until the following spring. Before the advent of steamships Mediterranean traders were justifiably wary of winter gales in northern waters. The chief cargo of course was coal, as it had been for skipper Garibaldi of the *Commonwealth* in 1854, though competition was becoming intense from the great seams of 'smokeless' coal in South Wales which was so much better placed for Mediterranean trade.

In his first long commercial report extolling the industrial might of Tyneside and the opportunities for Italian business De Mancini claimed that Italian merchantmen were more favoured than any other foreign cargo vessels putting into the Tyne. But the looked-for busy commerce in Italian imports never materialised. Most Italian boats traded with other ports and nations before filling their holds with the North East's 'black diamonds' and turning for home. Italy's own still modest exports to Britain such as oil and wine and marble mostly continued to reach our region by train from the ports of Liverpool or Hull.

The vital coal connection with Italy, a country with almost no fossil fuels of its own, expanded enormously after unification, and the consequent increasing traffic of Italian colliers caused a small but colourful colony of Italians to grow up along the Tyne, particularly at the mouth of the river, as explained in the previous section. Italian and Dalmatian Italian-speaking ship brokers and chandlers and interpreters provided for the professional needs of the skippers, while Italian-owned eating houses and lodging houses particularly beside the quays along Clive Street in North Shields, most often run by old sea dogs who had married locally, catered for the flow of Italian crewmen ashore. Not infrequently the latter would sign off or simply desert to secure work with British vessels where the pay was significantly higher. They were not unwelcome, for due to a persisting shortfall in native manpower the National Sailors' Union was the one British union not wholly hostile to foreign labour.

A few well-educated young men from Italian port cities also found their way to the North East to work as commercial clerks for English ship owners and brokers. Three who prospered in this way were Francesco Marino who ran an import business in Tynemouth and a restaurant in Newcastle, the Neapolitan Tommaso Astarita who enjoyed a very long career as a ship owner and broker in North Shields, and Vittorio Amedeo Montaldi who made a fortune as a coal exporter and built himself and his family a fine villa in Forest Hall (see next chapter). Another long-term settler was Luigi De Scalzo, a commission agent from Chiavari, near Genoa, who also kept a general store for a while. He had been fully thirty years on Tyneside when consul De Mancini appointed him his official interpreter, and he went on to thrive another thirty working in a ship broker and insurance partnership with Vittorio Brosinovic on Tyne Street, North Shields.

By 1900 the score or so of Italian small maritime concerns along the Tyne and the colourful personalities that went with them were mostly no more. 'Some have vanished along with the sailing ships', reported Montaldi in 1902 in his new capacity as Italy's consular representative – 'the others took English wives and in abandoning their offspring to the mother's influence have themselves suffered the same consequence, and now all they possess of Italian is their name, having forgotten even the language!' The general fall in commerce persuaded him to shut down the Italian consular agents' offices in the ports of Sunderland, Hartlepool and Middlesbrough.

But Italian vessels – steamships mostly now – kept on calling at all the region's ports for coal. In 1901, for instance, well over a million tons of coal and coke from the North East entered Italy to fire the young nation's factories, locomotives and ships in its bid to catch up with northern European industrialisation. In addition, all the major yards on Tyne and Wear had long been engaged in building ships for the Italian merchant fleet and navy. Mitchell's and Whigham-Richardson on the Tyne, and Doxford and Laing on Wearside were the leading suppliers of transport and passenger steamers for Italian purchasers. As early as 1853, when no Italian yard was yet building iron ships, T & W Smith's, the Tyne's oldest shipyard, produced the great battleship *Carlo Alberto* for the Piedmontese navy. The launch, watched by 40,000, marked the start of what was destined to become an intense North-East involvement in the military requirements of the new Italian state.

Many vessels which were the pride of Italy's navy actually originated on Tyneside, such as the innovative light cruiser *Giovanni Bausan* engineered by Hawthorn and designed, built and armed by Armstrong Mitchell in 1885, or the same team's *Dogali* and *Piemonte* which for a while were the fastest steel-clad cruisers in the world. By this time, however, the Italians had vastly improved their own steel production and shipbuilding capacity, and not least for nationalistic reasons were looking less and less abroad for custom. To keep securing business both Armstrong and Hawthorn set up Italian-staffed subsidiaries in the Bay of Naples. Armstrong had for long been the leading foreign supplier of ordnance for the Italian naval arsenal, and Hawthorn for machinery. Armstrong Pozzuoli Ltd opened in 1885 for the production of guns and armour plates, and the following year Hawthorn-Leslie established a naval engineering works in partnership with Guppy & Co Napoli. However, once the boom years of the Great War were over, both foreign-owned firms found it hard to procure adequate Italian government patronage, and in the 1920s, in the face of the world economic recession and Mussolini's policy of Italian self-reliance they allowed themselves to be bought out by all-Italian concerns.

BOOKS AND SOURCES

Joseph Cowen and the Italian revolutionaries. Beside Cowen's own *Northern Tribune* and *Newcastle Daily Chronicle*, there is the very extensive Cowen Collection in the Tyne and Wear Archives which also contains Jane Cowen's notes for a memoir of her father. Disappointingly the vast archive possesses no originals of Cowen's letters from Orsini, and none from Mazzini or Garibaldi dating before 1859. His daughter provides the explanation: 'My father left a note which we found after his death saying that he had destroyed all the letters that he had received from the European revolutionaries prior to the execution of Felice Orsini – for fear of implicating anyone. All his correspondence bearing on Italian questions is dated years after the melancholy event.' Nigel Todd's *The Militant Democracy: Joseph Cowen and Victorian Radicalism* (1991) is an important re-evaluation of Cowen's remarkable career as a political campaigner and publicist, further expanded on in Joan Allen's *Joseph Cowen and Popular Radicalism on Tyneside 1829-1900* (2007). The best of several not very illuminating early biographies is E.R.Jones, *The Life and Speeches of Joseph Cowen, M.P.* (1886). Many thanks to Christopher Brunton for permission to use insights from his unpublished MA thesis (Newcastle University, 1991), *British Involvement in the Italian Risorgimento, with special reference to the contribution made by the North East of England*. Of further relevance: G.M.Trevelyan, *Garibaldi and the Making of Italy* (1911); D.F.Mackay, *The Influence of the Italian Risorgimento on British Public Opinion* (1958) and his 'Joseph Cowen e il Risorgimento' in *Rassegna storica del Risorgimento* (1964, vol. 51); Derek Beales, *England and Italy 1859-60* (1961); D. Mack Smith, *Mazzini* (1993); R. Sarti, *Mazzini, A Life for the Religion of Politics* (1997).

Garibaldi on Tyneside. *Northern Tribune,* vol. 1, 1854. G.M. Trevelyan, *Garibaldi and the Thousand* (1909). Christopher Hibbert, *Garibaldi and his Enemies* (1987). L. Riall, *Garibaldi, Invention of a Hero* (2007). Simonetta Manfredi, 'To General Garibaldi, from the Friends of Italian Freedom on Tyneside', *Journal of the Association of Teachers of Italian,* n.5, 1992. D. Beales, 'Garibaldi in England; The Politics of Italian Enthusiasm' in J.A. Davies and P. Ginsborg, *Society and Politics in the Age of the Risorgimento* (1991).

Felice Orsini. Felice Orsini, *The Austrian Dungeons of Italy* (1856); *Memorie politiche* (Turin 1858) issued in English as *The Memoirs and Adventures of Felice Orsini*. M. St John Packe, *The Bombs of Orsini*, (1957). G.J. Holyoake, *Sixty Years of an Agitator's Life* (1892).

Up the Pope! E.R.Norman, *Anti-Catholicism and Victorian England* (1968). C.T. McIntire, *England against the Papacy 1858-61* (1983). For Canon Wilkinson: *Ushaw Magazine*, 19 (1909).

United Italy's first consul. The Newcastle correspondence of consul De Mancini is held in the archives of the Ministry of Foreign Affairs in Rome: *Le scritture del ministero degli affari esteri del Regno d'Italia dal 1861 al 1887,* vol. VI, busta 892: 'Rapporto del consolato di Newcastle'.

The shipping connection. R.W. Johnson, *The making of the Tyne* (1895). D. Duggan, *The History of North East Shipbuilding* (1960). J.F. Clarke, *Building Ships on the North-East Coast (1997)*. K. Warren, *Armstrongs of Elswick* (1989) for the history of the Stabilimento Armstrong at Pozzuoli.

1873 opposition election cartoon depicting Joseph Cowen in the guise of an Italian barrel-organist, a wry allusion to the Liberal candidate's notorious Italian sympathies, no doubt also implying he was forever noisily grinding out the same old tunes. In fact Cowen is not known to have taken any interest in the many Italian street musicians in the North East, who of course played no part in the nationalist heroics. The artist evidently took as his model a well-known local Italian organ-grinder nicknamed Old Man Friday (compare the studio photo on page 85).

4

'THE HUMBLEST CLASS OF ITALIANS': THE NORTH EAST IN THE ERA OF ITALIAN MASS MIGRATION

The Italians of some social standing can be numbered almost on the fingers of one hand: in Newcastle two run coal companies, two have restaurants, three have a fancy goods shop, one a food and wine store; in North Shields there are two ship brokers; in Sunderland three Italians own a jewellery and fancy goods shop. From these, the colony's aristocracy, we descend straight to the humblest class of Italians, the street musicians who in certain seasons of the year switch to peddling ice cream. There are between 30 and 40 street musicians in Newcastle; perhaps 10 between North and South Shields, 5 in Sunderland. However piteous the reasons which compel these street musicians to come to England it must be said they do no honour to our nation; it is clear in what consideration such a class of people must be held in a country where there is a strong work ethic; they wander the streets with their barrel organs, sometimes they have monkeys with them, they live on whatever coins are tossed their way; some remain in one city or locality, others band together in groups to tour the whole United Kingdom; even when long resident in England they do not mix with the English; they keep their national dress and customs, they live together and all are known to each other; not always, in these circles, is the level of morality high; here in Newcastle the majority are from the south of Italy.

R.Rizzetto, Italian vice-consul, Newcastle, March 1892

Piteous indeed were the reasons which compelled 'the humblest class of Italians' in their millions to flee their own country, so soon after the achievement of national unification. For the governing class of the newly created kingdom of Italy, a fractious alliance of northern middle-class professionals and southern landlords with a near-feudal mentality, social reform was not a priority. They represented the interests of 'men of property', the less than two per cent of the population with a vote, and if they can be said to have had any common purpose it was to build a strong capitalist nation-state while upsetting the existing social order as little as possible. The disenfranchised poorest millions, foremost the 60 per cent who worked the land, were more and more heavily taxed to pay for the warships and railways and bureaucracy of a state whose official language most could neither speak nor read.

By every measure of well-being Italy in 1870 was one of the most backward and impoverished regions of Europe: high infant mortality (one in two children died before their fifth birthday), average adult life expectancy of little more than thirty years, widespread malnutrition and disease (malaria, pellagra, typhoid, cholera), and almost universal illiteracy outside the towns. The only early government initiatives which might have brought about real change – a fairer distribution of land, primary schooling for all – had little impact on the truly needy: the best lands ended up in the hands of the men with money and influence, and poor municipalities received no resources to invest in adequate schools. Even when the suffrage was widened in 1882 a literacy requirement purposely excluded two-thirds of the population. Where rural discontent was organised in effective collective action for reform, notably in the Po valley in the 1880s and Sicily in the 1890s, it was treated as insurrection and mercilessly crushed by the national army. Defeat drove thousands to emigrate as the last hope of bettering their lives.

From the 1880s the situation of the peasantry was aggravated by a succession of poor harvests and a long and damaging tariff war with France, Italy's chief trading partner, conducted for nationalistic reasons right in the midst of a European-wide agricultural depression. The falling value of staple produce like grain, wine, oil and livestock drove small peasant farmers to the wall and put out of work multitudes of rural labourers, precipitating a flight from hunger almost all over Italy. Now, for the first time, the majority headed overseas rather than to traditional destinations beyond the Alps, drawn like millions of other more or less pauperised Europeans by the magnet of the Americas.

Between 1851 and 1880 over five million people migrated from the British Isles, by no means only Irish, yet even measured against that sombre figure the statistics for the slightly later Italian diaspora are staggering. Between 1876 and 1915 fourteen million people left Italy, half of them never to return. At its peak, in the decade before the First World War, as many as 800,000 a year were leaving, or one in forty of the entire population. And still, for all the magnitude of the exodus the population grew faster, generating a labour surplus which the slowly improving economy could not absorb. Politicians spoke openly of emigration as an indispensable 'safety-valve', conveniently ridding the state of innumerable potential beggars, bandits and political subversives.

Mass emigration at first affected only northern regions, where mobility of labour had long been a way of life. For generations subsistence-farming upland communities in Piedmont and Lombardy and the Veneto had out of necessity practised seasonal or temporary migration to destinations elsewhere in northern Italy or to neighbouring European countries, but now hundreds of thousands from the plains too were departing for South America as more or less penniless proletarian colonists enticed by prospects of guaranteed work or cheap land. Brazil and Argentina each had over a million Italian settlers by 1900.

In Italy's central regions where the interdependence of landlord and tenant in the characteristic sharecropping farming system mitigated the effects of the recession the general exodus abroad was less intense, also because surplus labour was to some extent absorbed by the steady growth of cities like Florence and Bologna and the rapid expansion of Rome after it became the capital of the nation. However, in the southern third of the country, the territory of the former autonomous kingdom of Naples and Sicily, national unification proved calamitous for all classes. Under the old Bourbon monarchy protectionist trade policies had sustained industry and agriculture but when the tariff barriers came down with the amalgamation of all the old independent states of Italy the new northern rulers' liberal faith in free trade and market forces collapsed the south's fragile economy. Naples, then by far the largest city in Italy, lost its expanding textile and engineering concerns to northern competition. In the depths of the countryside, where so recently Garibaldi's vain promises of land reform had roused the peasantry to overthrow the Bourbons, the imposition of high taxation and mass conscription by the new Italian state which treated them as callously as colonial subjects led thousands to resort to armed resistance and brigandage. The 'pacification' of the southern interior by the national army was conducted with extreme brutality and resulted in more deaths than all the wars fought to achieve national unification.

Southern inland areas typically consisted of overpopulated remote hill towns where hard-working peasant families farmed a proliferation of meagre scattered plots, or immense private estates on malarial plains worked by day labourers for starvation wages. Due to their extreme isolation very few centres in these vast forgotten zones had any history of emigration, but when the great agrarian crisis of the 1880s hit the south even harder than the rest of Italy the resultant unemployment and rising food prices finally drove entire families to abandon the soil in favour of North America where well-paid jobs for the unskilled were reputed to be legion. The change from sail to steam had reduced transatlantic crossings from weeks to days, and competition between national and international shipping lines touting for the huge demand could make a passage in steerage from Naples to New York cheaper than boat and train to Paris.

At the same time, in the northern regions of the peninsula ever growing numbers were resorting to the traditional expedient of temporary migration to better-off neighbouring countries. France, Switzerland, Austria-Hungary and newly united Germany were each receiving well over 50,000 Italians a year by 1900. Most were seasonal workers who found employment in construction and in factories and mines, or on big public works projects such as roads and railways. France had a regular presence of 400,000 Italians, resented by the native workforce but appreciated by employers for their readiness to toil hard for low wages.

Given England's industrial might, the Italians' hunger for work, and the total absence of entry restrictions, it seems at first inexplicable that only a few hundred entered the country each year and of these only a minuscule proportion worked in industry and none in agriculture. But with ample surplus labour to draw on within the British Isles, particularly from Ireland and Scotland, there was no tradition of demand for workers from across the Channel and in any case the hostility of organised labour to foreign workers was implacable. Up to the First

A familiar figure in nineteenth century Europe: the Italian organ-grinder or 'hurdy-gurdy man'. Here barefoot bairns gather round a piano organ in Sandgate, Newcastle, about 1890. The organist's female companion, also Italian, has her back to camera. The piano organ, costlier but louder than the common hand organ, was a prized possession whether owned outright or hired from a padrone. (Photo: Newcastle Central Library).

'Those who walked it': members of the Scappaticci family of Santopadre and Middlesbrough back home in Italy, possibly photographed before setting out for England.

Francesca and Domenico Di Luoffo with their Newcastle-born adopted grandson Ernesto. According to the family, the couple worked 20 years in street music and ice cream in Middlesbrough before returning to Arpino in 1912 for fear 'someone would get killed' in the escalating territorial clashes between rival ice-creamers. Their savings amounted to 42,000 lira (£1,700), a considerable capital for that time, which like most return migrants they invested in land. Their daughter Rosalinda remained behind, having married Vincenzo Reale, a Newcastle ice cream worker (see start of next chapter).

Domenico Pacitti, from Picinisco, with his widowed mother Maddalena, his wife Rosa, and the first three of their eight children, all British born (Gateshead, about 1910). Domenico, who first accompanied his father to Britain in the 1880s, settled in Trafalgar Street, Newcastle, in 1897, working as an ice cream vendor and shipyard labourer. By the time of this studio portrait the couple had opened an ice cream business in Askew Road, Gateshead.

World War the total population of Italians in Britain reached little more than 24,000, or about ten per cent of all foreigners, and though they could be stigmatised as undesirable aliens their typical occupations were never much of a threat to the native labour market. Those from northern Italy and Italian Switzerland, about a quarter of the total, tended to fill low-paid jobs in the non-unionised service sector as waiters, cooks and domestic servants, the most ambitious hoping to make it to restaurant owners and hotel-keepers; while the majority from the central and southern Italian 'sending communities' (described in the next section) remained stubbornly self-reliant by earning a living on the streets as musicians, animal exhibitors, organ-grinders, plaster statuette sellers, and from around 1880 also as pedlars of home-made ice cream. Very few hotel and restaurant workers sought jobs beyond the great metropolis. It was therefore those in the wandering trades who first established small colonies in all the major provincial towns of the British Isles, reaching their greatest density in the great industrial cities of Manchester and Glasgow, and to a lesser extent in Edinburgh and Newcastle. All categories arrived via well-trodden routes through France, not infrequently with thoughts of a low-cost transatlantic passage out of Southampton or Liverpool if all else failed.

Although their government pressed for emigration to ameliorate Italy's economic and social woes, successive Italian consuls with responsibility for the north of England were invariably discouraging, negative about employment prospects in general, and consistently scathing about the calibre of most of their compatriots already here:

There is no strong history of Italian immigration in these parts. Italians only amount to a minute fraction mixed in with the great mass of the native population, and for the most part have come here only a few at a time or in small family groups, summoned by friends or drawn by the prospect of considerable financial rewards.

Our emigration here is permanent, or semi-permanent, in the sense that most do not plan to return home within a year or two. It stems mainly from our southern provinces, although there are also significant contingents from the provinces of Genoa, Lucca, Piacenza, and Parma.

Earnings are in general twice or even three times greater than for the equivalent work in Italy. Even the lowliest occupations, such as street musician or ice cream hawker – which unfortunately discredit our entire emigration – produce a considerable financial return for our co-nationals in these cities and smaller towns.

Even so, there is no notable exodus of Italian emigrants to the United Kingdom at present, nor is there ever likely to be; the national character is too reserved and impenetrable for our emigration; the sky less refulgent; workmates too dour and unforthcoming; the language is hard to learn, and it is not easy to adapt to the way of life, the food and drink; and, crucially, work is not easy to come by and is not as remunerative as in other lands much farther away but temperamentally far better suited to our people's character. (P. Bajnotti, Italian consul-general in Liverpool, 1901).

In the face of such attitudes a lowly emigrant electing to try his luck in Britain could expect little interest from those on high. He would need to rely on his own resources, and hopefully some support from fellow emigrants already established here. Still, one indubitably positive message was buried in there: even the most discredited occupations 'produce a considerable financial return'.

It is 1876 and mass emigration is well under way: this shipping agent's poster in the small town of Barga in the Tuscan Apennines advertises cut-price steamer passages to four continents. Substantial communities of 'Barghigiani' settled in Brazil and Argentina. Hundreds, following a longer established migration route, came to Britain.

'IN THE LAND OF THE FREE'

London, 20 April 1854.

Dear Marcello, on the 7th of this month after much walking we reached Paris, and on the 8th left for London first by train then by ship from Don Chierchi [Dunkirk], arriving in London at noon on the 9th. The journey went well, and on the road to Paris we made about thirty napoleons with the music. So here we are and here will stay a while until the chests with our things arrive from Livorno. For now we are working at the music which brings in enough for expenses and a little more, and an Italian who is very good on the bass tuba has joined our group for as long as we are here. We're not sure how the flowers will go but we mean to try, and have begun working with them. So now here we are, Marcello, in the land of the free. The city is huge, the language is a hindrance but hopefully with time we'll understand something. There is so much more I could tell you, if I had paper enough. I beg you, pray to God for our health and good fortune, and remain a good friend to us. Write with your news and what else is happening at home. Your faithful friend, Pausanio Corazzi.

Pausanio was the padrone of a seven-man 'campaign' of plaster statuette makers and vendors (figurinai) from Barga. The group had saved on travel expenses by sending their gear by sea from the Tuscan port of Livorno then tramping the whole way to Paris, busking as they moved along. The talented tuba-player was probably from one of the hill towns in the Val Taro or Val Ceno (see next section), some sixty miles north of Barga. Making and selling artificial flowers was a common sideline for the figurinai. Pausanio's later correspondence reveals the flowers did badly, the music-making fared scarcely better in the face of stiff competition from German bands, and even when the precious work chests finally arrived five weeks late the party found little demand for their plaster wares amid the rising cost of living brought on by the Crimean War. After enduring 'two months of constant rain' in the capital and with reserves dwindling to the point of having to beg Marcello to arrange a loan for them, the band sent their chests ahead by train and once more playing for survival set off to walk the 250 miles from London to Liverpool docks and take ship for hopefully better pastures in North America: 'And, Marcello, we'll write to you the day we embark, which will be a momentous day, when you think what a long and dangerous voyage.'

Early street entertainers

Chapter 2 described the peregrinations of the Tuscan figurine makers and the skilled artisans and tradesmen from the northern Lakes region. Other Italian itinerants had been wandering northern Europe for generations and reached Britain in more conspicuous numbers immediately after the Napoleonic wars, a time of severe economic depression throughout Europe. Like the *figurinai* and the barometer makers from around Como, they too came mostly from poor upland communities in northern and central Italy. There were knife-grinders from the Val Rendena near Trento, waiters from Lake Orta, confectioners from the Italian-Swiss Alps, and back again came the child chimney sweeps and their minders from the mountains of Savoy (then part of the Italian kingdom of Piedmont) who had

'Bear-Dancing at Rome' (from Charles Macfarlane, Popular Customs, Sports and Recollections of the South of Italy, 1846), featuring also a monkey and performing dogs, with music from a zampognaro (bagpiper). Bread and work were scarce in remote Apennine communities and one common way out was to entertain city folk with music and performing animals. The adventurous mentality fostered by the itinerant life led some to seek fresh markets all over Europe, and finally even the Americas. These were the pioneers of the mass migration to come.

first appeared in smoky London as long ago as the sixteenth century. Savoyards had also taken to making a living on the streets as musicians, their favoured instrument being the hurdy-gurdy, a small barrelled stringed instrument of ancient origin plucked by playing a keyboard with the left hand while the right turns a handle to vibrate the accompanying drone strings.

The Savoyards lent their name to other Italian street musicians who supplanted them in the course of the nineteenth century, and similarly 'hurdy-gurdy' became a common term for the purely mechanical street organ which came to dominate the field. The craze among street musicians for this portable hand-organ, or *organetto*, originally an Italian invention but very soon produced all over Europe, kept several small specialised Italian factories and workshops busy in London and Manchester and Leeds, building and maintaining the instruments and fitting new tunes.

About one in four Italians in Britain by the mid-nineteenth century was making a living by offering some form of street entertainment for a small reward or charitable donation. There were puppeteers and tumblers and numerous animal exhibitors, but most played a musical instrument or ground out Italian opera and English popular songs on a hand-organ. Many were just children, boys and girls who sang and danced with a tambourine, played the fiddle for farthings on street corners, or amused spectators with the antics of their pet white mice or performing dogs. Until numbers grew, these foreign 'wandering minstrels' in quaint costumes were well received or at least tolerated as colourful curiosities, even suitably sentimental inspiration for poets and artists who depicted them as picturesque primitives or heartbreakingly beautiful waifs sick for their sunny homeland.[1] To the English they were all either Savoyards or Neapolitans.

Aside from the fast dwindling numbers of true Savoyards, most of these early street performers hailed in fact from three very distinct areas of Italy. The animal exhibitors were subjects of the Duchy of Parma and Piacenza in central Italy, although they actually lived far from the relatively prosperous little cities of Parma and Piacenza high up in the neighbouring Taro and Ceno river valleys (Val Taro and Val Ceno) on the eastern slopes of the Apennines where the largest settlements are Borgo Val di Taro (present-day province of Parma) and Bardi (present-day province of Piacenza: see map on page 110). Necessity had long taught these mountain people roving ways of survival such as carting, peddling, seasonal work on lowland farms, charcoal burning and woodcutting on the island of Corsica, or smuggling goods across the high frontiers between the neighbouring duchies of Genoa, Modena and Lucca. The most derelict simply went begging. A few entrepreneurs, chiefly from Bedonia near Borgo Val di Taro, specialised in procuring and training wild animals for travelling circuses or as extra attractions to accompany small groups of local showmen and musicians on tours of Italian cities, and eventually as far as St Petersburg and New York. Most frequent were the bear trainers (*orsanti*) and monkey exhibitors (*scimmiari*). Some of these adventurous folk trekked the whole way to Britain, so opening up a special connection which over the course of time attracted many hundreds more from Val Ceno and Val Taro and nearby Apennine valleys inside Tuscany and Liguria (present-day provinces of Massa-Carrara, La Spezia, and Genoa), thus accounting for the third major historic strand in the regional composition of Italian immigration to Britain, with particularly strong representation in London and Wales. A number of families of Italian descent in our region, mainly in Northumbria, trace their origins to forebears from the Tuscan-Emilian uplands. (The two regional strands of slightly earlier date were examined in chapter 2: the *barometai* from Lombardy, and the *figurinai* from Tuscany)

Italian with dancing bear in Bondgate, Darlington, about 1900. (Centre for Local Studies, Darlington Library).

Performing bear with Italian keeper, St John's Chapel, Weardale, 1914 (Beamish Museum).

A zampognaro *and boy* pifferaro *perform outside Dinsdale rectory, County Durham, 1892.*
(Beamish Museum).

The southern Apennine area of Ciociaria, source of the majority of the North East's 'original Italians', owes its name to le cioce, the long-thonged sandals worn by the inhabitants. The sitter is Giacomo Forte of Casalattico who wandered through northern Europe with his family in the 1880s and 90s. His son Giovanni, born in London in 1883, later returned to work in the North East where he married within the immigrant community and was joined by his father and sister. The family founded Forte's café and billiard saloon in Washington, County Durham, which closed only very recently. (See illustration on page 117).

(Below) Italian couple with piano organ and songbird at Seaton Carew, about 1890.
(Beamish Museum)

From much further south, just inside the kingdom of Naples, came other bands of street musicians whose home villages lay near Montecassino in an Apennine zone known as Ciociaria, some one hundred miles south of Rome (present-day province of Frosinone, but formerly Caserta). For centuries, *zampognari* (bagpipers) and *pifferari* (fife and oboe players) from Picinisco and Sora and neighbouring villages had descended from the hills to busk in the streets of Rome and Naples, as is occasionally seen even today around Christmas time. Though the dialect is far closer to the speech of Naples than Rome, these people were country folk with a way of life remote from that of urban Neapolitans. As farmhands, herdsmen and foresters they were used to covering large distances on foot and spending long periods away from home. Some busked their way to Britain in the first decades of the nineteenth century, and these few pioneers with tales of fabulous winnings in the numberless streets of London finally prompted a large influx of fellow villagers (*paesani*) when mass migration from southern Italy took off in the 1880s. Their usual route to Britain, when not overland the whole way, was by ship from Naples to Marseilles, then on by foot or train via Paris. This later 'chain migration' of mostly street organists from Ciociaria rapidly led to the creation of the last major regional strand of early Italian immigration to this country, and it is to Ciociaria that the majority of the oldest Italian-name families in the North East trace their roots.

Another category of southern wandering minstrel to test the market in northern Europe came from well south of Naples in yet another relatively circumscribed area of the Apennines, this time in the inland region of Basilicata. Their homes lay in and around the mountain town of Viggiano (province of Potenza) and they were typically either violinists or harpists. Though never plentiful in Britain, the 'Viggianesi' were a significant component of the Italian population in Paris, and when harassed by clampdowns on vagrant activities or in the turmoil of the Franco-Prussian War of 1870 many crossed the Channel to continue their trade. I have not traced any who settled in the North East, but the two Italian boys discussed in the next section, a harpist and a violinist picked up by the Middlesbrough police for vagrancy in 1877, must have been from Viggiano or some neighbouring town since by then this fairly lucrative profession (for the childrens' minders, that is) had drawn in the entire area. In North America the exploitation of child harpists was so conspicuous that 'little slaves of the harp' became a stock journalistic phrase for all underage Italian street musicians.

London, with its immense population and selective great wealth, was of course the principal magnet for all continental migrants. For reasons of economy and sociability most Italians lived packed together in one small area of Holburn, a warren of slum streets (now mostly demolished) situated conveniently close to some of the most fashionable residential and commercial districts in the city. Known to better-off Italians elsewhere in the city as 'Abyssinia', it was famed for its squalor and overcrowding and with far less justification shunned as a den of vice. (The Soho colony of mainly shopkeepers and caterers sprang up only toward the end of the century.)

Companies of wandering musicians and animal exhibitors periodically explored the potential of neighbouring towns and south coast resorts, or set out on long-distance tours to remoter corners of the kingdom where their presence would be more of a novelty. I have detected none in the North-East census returns before 1861, but that they were roaming the north from a much earlier date is evident from the case of an Italian convicted for fatally stabbing a local man when provoked into a fight in a quayside pub in Newcastle in February

1833. Giuseppe Sidoli, one of a five-man troupe of travelling musicians with dancing bears who informed the authorities he was a citizen of the Duchy of Parma and had been eight years in Britain fits the standard profile of a Val Taro itinerant. A couple of days earlier the party had been sighted in Houghton-le-Spring, some eight miles short of Newcastle.

'STABBED BY AN ITALIAN'

It was stated in our last paper, that during an affray which took place in The Shades public house, Grindon Chare, on Wednesday night week, an Irishman, named Ross, had been stabbed in the abdomen by an Italian. The wounded man was shortly afterwards conveyed to the Infirmary, where, though hopes were first entertained of his recovery, he lingered until Monday last, when he suddenly expired in the presence of the authorities who had attended to receive his deposition. His assailant, who was taken into custody on the night of the outrage, is a travelling musician, named Giuseppe Sidoli, a native of Parma, in Italy, and has been in this country about eight years. He came to Newcastle a few days ago, along with four other musicians and exhibitors of dancing bears. He was identified by the deceased before his death, and was present during the inquest, when he conducted himself with much propriety....'
(*Newcastle Courant*, February 23rd 1833: 'Coroner's Inquest on Hugh Ross')

At the trial, the jury of six Englishmen and six foreigners found Sidoli had acted in self-defence, and therefore returned a verdict of manslaughter. Sentencing him to seven years transportation to Australia, the judge emphasised that had he been an Englishman he would have got life for using a knife, 'but the custom was different in the country to which the prisoner belonged.' Readiness to pull a knife was held to be typical of Italians, and during the later public campaigns against the street musicians was routinely deplored by those who cried up their supposed depravity and criminal tendencies. At the Newcastle trial there was much fascination with this fact of the knife, most vividly evoked by a fourteen-year-old lad who had nipped into the pub to watch the brawl: "I saw the Italian draw something from his left side and heard him say, scringing his teeth, 'One, two, tree men to one, I finish one'. He then darted the thing into Ross's belly, and when it was in he shoved it three times, and then gave it a screw and fetched it out". Other witnesses credited the Italian with more fluency in English, asserting variously that his actual words were "You bugger, I'll stick you!" or "You bugger, I'll rip you up!" A female witness described the murder weapon as 'three-cornered like' and glittering. A reminder incidentally that crimes against the person were treated more leniently than those against private property is the fate two years earlier of Antonio Salvio, an Italian boy of only 14, who was sentenced to death for being an accomplice to stealing 'six silver spoons, apparel etc' from a grand house in Durham, though this was subsequently commuted to seven years on Van Diemen's Island.

By 1861 two groups of Italian street musicians, both from the central Apennines[2], were well ensconced in Newcastle under their respective *padroni* in a crowded labouring quarter on the edge of Pandon Dene. The smaller company had been around longest. Sharing premises with the families of a local bricklayer, a cow-keeper and a potter, they all lodged at 1 Pandon Place with their boss, thirty-seven-year-old Angelo Carpena, described in the census as a musical instrument player with eight 'servants', all of them unmarried Italian males between the ages of 20 and 35. Angelo will have concurred in defining his workers as 'servants' in conformity with the Italian *servo*, used for any person contracted by a *padrone*. Unusually, they included no children. Given the high average age of the company (28), most must have had long experience in the trade and could have been working the streets of the city for some time. Though its make-up constantly changed, the typical barrel-organ troupe was tightly organised, alternating pitches and beats between individuals all over town so as to vary faces and tunes. *Padrone* Carpena, if his system conformed to the norm, collected half his men's takings in exchange for board and lodging and for providing and maintaining the costly instruments. (A standard ten-tune barrel-organ cost upwards of £18, well over £1,000 in today's money).

The dominant figure in the younger and larger Newcastle company was 26-year-old Giambattista Lertoria who with his wife Antonina had turned part of their Matford's Entry tenement into an all-Italian lodging-house. This street music company, that is their fifteen 'lodgers' all listed as musical instrument players, was much more typical in its age differentiation, with six members under eighteen, including Giovanni, 13, and Ferdinando, 12. Children, the younger the better, were a precious asset in this trade so finely balanced between providing rudimentary musical entertainment and plucking the heartstrings of householders and passers-by. The Lertoria's own two children, still babies, had been born in Sheffield, so certainly the family and probably most of the troupe were very recent arrivals on Tyneside.

On the street there must have been plenty of rivalry between the *servi* of these two Italian teams competing for Geordie farthings, yet it seems relations between the *padroni* may have been quite cordial. For instance, when Francesco Viviani, the senior figure in the Lertoria company, had his first child baptised in 1863 his chosen godparents were Antonina Lertoria and Angelo Carpena. Perhaps such a public demonstration of solidarity merely marked a truce, but it is more likely that in the still very small world of Italians on Tyneside ties of provenance and custom were at least as strong as professional jealousies. The registers of baptisms and marriages at St. Andrews RC church for this period show that along with Federigo Lundi and Daniele Stacchini, the longest established Tuscan *figurinai*, the most influential personalities in the Italian community were our two *padroni*. Angelo Carpena was the favoured witness at five Italian marriages at St. Andrew's between 1864 and 1871, and Giambattista and/or Antonina Lertoria sponsored eleven Italian christenings outside their family circle between 1863 and 1873. Most of the young grooms and fathers were assuredly their respective *servi*.

Giambattista Lertoria, and his wife Antonina, pioneers of Italian street music and 'penny lick' ice cream on Tyneside. Giambattista first experienced Britain as a 10-year- old street musician.
(Photos: Fr David Milburn, a Lertoria descendant).

'Old Man Friday': Francesco Viviani, who died in 1901, was for long one of Newcastle's most familiar street characters. Usually accompanied by a pet monkey on his organ rounds, he began his Tyneside career in his mid-twenties in 1860 as the leading 'servant' in padrone *Lertoria's company of organ-grinders. Born in Borghetto di Vara (province of La Spezia), Francesco married twice within the Newcastle Italian circle. Despite the blander interpretation suggested by illustration 1 on page 87, Francesco's Geordie soubriquet was more likely a play on Robinson Crusoe's 'Man Friday' owing to his skin colour and his 'savage' appearance. (Newcastle Central Library).*

Two dozen full-time Italian street musicians – in addition to assorted local bands and buskers, Scots pipers, Irish vocalists, 'nigger' minstrels, German brass bands etc – serenading little old Newcastle and environs may seem close to overkill but it was nothing next to what was to come, and nothing to what Londoners had to face already. Perhaps not fortuitously, the arrival of Carpena and Lertoria's men and boys on Tyneside coincided with the intensification of a long-running public campaign to rid London of assorted 'street nuisances', foremost among them the Italian organ-grinders. I have found nothing to show it was a big issue in the north, where the Italians seem to have been considered at worst a minor annoyance and soft targets for harassment and bullying, but down in the Big Smoke feelings in the middle classes ran very high. Eminent composers and professors of music, well-to-do parents with piano-playing progeny, prominent literary figures like Dickens and Tennyson, men of the cloth driven out of their wits while trying to pen their Sunday sermons, even the personal harpist to Her Majesty the Queen, signed petitions to parliament and fired off irate letters to the *Times* deploring the 'instruments of torture' and their 'ruffianly' operators, and were rewarded with equally ill-tempered, even apocalyptic, editorials on 'this evil which threatens to make London uninhabitable'.

The foremost campaigners were Michael Bass MP, owner of the great brewery, and the mathematician Charles Babbage, inventor of an 'analytical engine' which is now the acknowledged grandfather of the computer. Both wrote tracts against street music. Babbage's exhaustive research in the field concluded that the torturers' supporters belonged 'chiefly to the lower classes of society', in particular frequenters of pubs and gin-shops, much to the profit of the proprietors: 'The worst and the most noisy kinds of music not infrequently give rise to a dance by ragged urchins, and sometimes by half-intoxicated men, who occasionally accompany the noise with their own discordant voices.' Servants and children and all others with 'minds entirely unoccupied' were invariably soppy enthusiasts, he reported, not least 'ladies of elastic virtue and cosmopolitan tendencies to whom it affords a decent excuse for displaying their fascinations at their own windows.'

Michael Bass MP, for his part, sought to aid the passage of his 1864 private members' bill by concurrently publishing a booklet packed with prestigious testimonies and newspaper articles proving how drastically street music obstructed 'the progress of art, science, and literature, and what torments are afflicted on the studious, the sensitive, and the afflicted.' Some contributors were convinced that the police, being of lowly origin themselves, secretly sided with the offenders. Certainly magistrates tended to tolerate the organs as 'the amusement of the poor' or even as welcome edification for the musically deprived masses who would never otherwise be exposed to the genius of Rossini and Donizetti and Verdi.

Since parliament still favoured the long-standing liberal 'open door' policy toward foreigners there was no chance of Bass getting an outright ban on street music in London as had been achieved in some other European capitals. He did at least win the concession of on-the-spot arrest by the police if a player refused to move on after being requested to do so by a householder 'or his servant', but the maximum penalty still remained a forty-shilling fine which a good *padrone* could turn in a couple of days. The best proof of the inadequacy of 'Bass's law' is that the number of Italian 'players of musical instruments' in London and indeed all over Britain was set to increase exponentially. Harassment and hostility in the capital drove more and more to try the provinces, thus opening up new territory for settlement.

On the evidence of local census returns the Carpena and Lertoria companies had dissolved by 1871, when no more than seven Italian 'musicians' are found dispersed about other inner city addresses in Newcastle: four lone operators, and a group of three 'bagpipers', i.e. *zampognari*, who were probably transients. This chimes with findings from other centres of population which show that street music's dominance by Italians from central Italy was drawing to a close. But new blood was on the way.

THREE VIEWS OF THE 'WANDERING MINSTRELS'

THE ORGAN-GRINDER.

The children always come to the window to listen to the street organ. They call this man "Friday," because he always plays in their street on that day. He is far away from his Italian home, and he often feels sad; but when English boys and girls are kind to him he smiles on them and thanks them very much.

(Above) The benign view, from a Victorian children's primer. (Beamish Museum).

(Below) The other view: 'Three Cheers for Bass and his Barrel of Beer, and Out with the Foreign Ruffian and his Barrel-Organ!' by John Leech, from Punch, 28 May 1864. Leech, who supplied Punch with a string of xenophobic cartoons on this theme, died this same year, though not before attributing his untimely end to the hated foreign ruffians and their 'instruments of torture'.

'A Foreign Invasion', by Henry Hetherington Emmerson, painted among Cullercoats fisherfolk about 1870, now in the Laing Art Gallery, Newcastle. The hackneyed title is so at odds with the warmth of the scene (the lad at the back has been given a drink to quench his thirst) that this affectionate depiction of the candid reception of a young zampognaro and his two companions can surely be read as a humane riposte to the xenophobes. The boys' attire proves them to be from Ciociaria. (Tyne and Wear Archives and Museums).

Southern street musicians and organ-grinders

'Here in Newcastle the majority are from the south of Italy', reports vice-consul Rizzetto in his 1892 account of Italians on Tyne and Wear cited at the head of this chapter, after listing his reasons for deploring the best part of his fellow-countrymen. With the arrival of new migrants from the south, in particular from Ciociaria, the number of Italian street musicians in England and Wales had almost doubled over the preceding twenty years (852 in 1871, 1,441 in 1891), and was due to far exceed two thousand by the turn of the century. Back in 1881, amid the surviving Comasque artisans and shopkeepers, the still steady presence of Tuscan *figurinai*, and a scattering of central Italian street musicians, the census for Newcastle had recorded its first distinctively Ciociaria surnames – Di Marco, Capaldi, Forte, Battista – young men variously logged as organ-grinders or street sellers of ice cream in the service of figures from the old establishment, notably Giambattista Lertoria who as well as reviving his lodging house for Italians (this time in Trafalgar Street) had reinvented himself as the leading 'penny-ice' purveyor, a trade set to become an Italian speciality all over Britain.

Detail from 'Blaydon Races – A Study from Life' (1903) by William C. Irving (Shipley Art Gallery, Gateshead). The identities of these once-familiar Tyneside characters are all still known except, perhaps significantly, those of the black man and the pipe-smoking Italian humping his street-organ and monkey alongside Blind Bob of Scotswood and his dog. In the foreground is Ned White. The characters behind him (reading from left) are Nanny the Maser, Strolling Mike of Gateshead (the Punch and Judy man), and Billy Lauder, the piper. (Tyne and Wear Archives and Museums)

The reinvigoration of the hurdy-gurdy business on Tyneside was principally due to Nicola Dipreta, from Arpino in Ciociaria, who around 1882 set up a tenement in Carliol Street as a receiving station and hostel for numerous fellow southerners, all involved in the trade. By the time of the next census, 1891, now aged 39 and recently widowed, he was the master of a household of thirty-four Italians squeezed into the same address. Apart from twelve assorted infants and very young children, every other member of the nine families installed, from Nicola's eleven-year-old daughter Emilia to his own parents-in-law, both in their late sixties, was working the streets with a musical instrument or barrel-organ. Nicola's status as supreme *padrone* or affluent patron and business adviser of numerous young southerners in Newcastle in the last two decades of the nineteenth century is confirmed by the exceptional number of christenings he sponsored along with his first wife Addolorata Vagnone and her sister Nicolina whom he married after Addolorata's death: twenty-five godparenthoods for fifteen separate families between 1882 and 1902. Unlike the predominantly male migrants from central and northern Italy who preceded them and had generally married into the local English or Irish communities, in all these cases both parents were Italian. Some couples had met up within the Tyneside Italian circle, but most seem to have come directly or indirectly from Italy as hopeful newly-weds, presumably using part or all of the bride's small dowry to launch them into the unknown. Battista, Franchi, Melucci, and Andreucci (Andrucci now) were four of these young families working under Nicola's auspices who were to put down permanent roots on Tyneside where their surnames are still encountered today.

'TRY YOUR FORTUNE BY A LITTLE BIRD FOR THE SMALL PRICE OF 2d'. The girl with the feathered fortune-teller is Emilia Dipreta whose father Nicola was the leading Newcastle padrone in the last two decades of the 19th century. Despite the outcry about cruel masters all the evidence is that by this time almost all the 'poor little Italian children' put to work on the streets of Britain were actually living with their parents.

This picture of a mutually supportive family-centred community of migrants from the same small area of Italy confirms vice-consul Rizzetto's observation that they clung to their cultural identity by living together and not mixing with the English, but seems scant justification for his unrestrained contempt ('they do no honour to our nation') which was so evidently fuelled by the wretched spectacle he feared these bizarrely dressed foreign vagrants must present to the industrious English, all suitably coloured by a heavy hint of loose morals. A later comment in the same report confirms how deeply this well-off northern Italian gentleman dreaded being tainted by association: 'Italians are not the only street musicians, there are Germans too, but not as numerous as the Italians nor as conspicuous, for in looks and dress they are hard to tell apart from the English, and they do not have barrel organs and monkeys, but form brass bands or play the violin.'

Not only a vice-consul in Newcastle, but infinitely more illustrious representatives of the self-conscious new Kingdom of Italy in prestigious embassies as far-flung as St Petersburg, New York and Buenos Aires, expressed a similar horror at the demeaning occupations and appearance and excessive numbers of these seemingly aimless rolling stones whose lives and livelihood looked to them no better than blatant vagabondage. For centuries Italians in general had been typified by northern Europeans as wily scroungers and *dolce far niente* layabouts, and for as long as this ragged army of toilers in the art of scraping a living haunted respectable neighbourhoods in the world's most advanced countries it would look as though the inspiring tale of once-wretched Italy's moral and political regeneration – Garibaldi, Victor Emanuel et al – which abroad had aroused the sort of wholehearted enthusiasm explored here in chapter 3 was not quite the whole story. The Risorgimento, the invention of a nation, was a victory for the patriotic upper social strata, not for the mass of people with their more immediate concerns of bread and debts. These seemingly rootless illiterate peasants were the all-too-visible face of the most intractable problem that vice-consul Rizzetto and other beneficiaries of the new regime had inherited along with their comfortable jobs: the alien reality of the southern poor. Even the democrat Mazzini, the great 'apostle of the people', had been careful to distinguish between *popolo*, the educated minority capable of sharing his vision of national redemption, and *gente*, the intractable 'common folk' or rabble who were a law unto themselves. After the unification of Italy this class-based view became more markedly ethnocentric: the middle classes of the north and centre identified European, viewing most southerners as a primitive separate race of exotic or savage 'Arabs' or 'Africans'.

THREE OPINIONS OF SOUTHERN ITALIAN MIGRANTS IN BRITAIN

'INERADICABLY BAD'

London, and many of our large provincial cities, are crowded with a class of Italians, who are, for the most part, non-producers. Abhorring agriculture, and in fact any settled occupation or trade, they cling to our large centres of population, and eke out an existence by means of the most degrading pursuits... They are, for the most part, the idle, the vicious, the destitute, the off-scouring of their own country, who, forbidden or hampered by the drastic laws now enforced in Italy against vagrancy and mendicancy, drift over to England, and here endeavour to pursue their nefarious mode of life which is denied them in the land of their birth... They mostly come from Naples and the vicinity, where they live in pauperism, filth and vice, with no higher ambition than to get cheap food enough to keep them alive. Uneducated and slovenly when they come, they never improve, and despite all efforts to restrain them, they persist in following here the same mode of living which they practised at home. They are ineradicably bad, and only the fear of the law's punishment, of which they have a lively dread, keeps them in any way disciplined. The degraded habits of this class of immigrants, innate and lasting as they are, stamp them as a most undesirable set, whose affiliation with our own people must in time work great injury.
(William Wilkins, 'The Italian Aspect', from Arnold White, *The Destitute Alien in Great Britain*, 1892)

'AN INFERIOR AND DEGENERATE RACE'

The foremost characteristic of the lowest social strata of the peoples of the south of Italy, stronger I believe even than the longing for home, is unquestionably the perpetual need for a change of air and sky, not in order to settle down in another land, but solely in response to this nomadic instinct which relentlessly drives them on, the same indeed which typifies the entire gypsy race, and which we see so strongly entrenched in this section of our population.

Poverty is a prime motive, but not the only one. The Irishman, too, finds no means of sustenance in his devastated country and emigrates to a more benign land, but not in order to take up degrading itinerant occupations. These, sadly, are entirely our preserve, the ignominious legacy of the pariahs of the human race; and we need fear no competition, for no one seeks to contest our easy monopoly.

These nomadic classes of vagrants constitute, for the sociologist, an important phenomenon in the natural history of mankind, not least in view of their threat to society... The ceaseless inner drive, the Wandering Jew's impulse to obey the imperious command to keep walking, inevitably draws on almost all their blood supply for physical exertion so that the muscles are fortified at the expense of the brain and their animal development is accomplished at the expense of their mental development. Thus is born an inferior and degenerate race whose characteristics may easily be verified in its representatives in this country. My own research conducted in England has clearly proved to me the truth of the axiom that whoever by inclination takes up a vagrant pursuit is invariably a degenerate, a delinquent in the making, or, to borrow a term from Lombroso's new school of thought[3], a veritable criminaloid...

The prime feature of this human type is repugnance for a steady job, all vagabonds abhor it, not on account of the physical effort required so much as their extreme aversion to the tedious repetition of muscular movements to which the division of labour in larger factories condemns the worker... Another cause of this obduracy is the love of idleness, no thought for the morrow, a total negation of the concept of thrift... Precocious sexual perversion is another characteristic, a consequence both of their living conditions and the fact that the men have no notion of respect and honour, and the women scant notion of modesty... Their chief passions are gambling and alcohol, and if they do not have the wherewithal to indulge them they resort to theft, a natural tendency for all nomadic races...

Criminal anthropology possesses a vast and wondrous field for observation in these people. Their anthropometric measurements, the atypical morbid cranial anomalies of these vagabonds, would more than suffice to found a separate branch of lengthy and demanding specialised studies which I can do no more than hint at in these pages, leaving to others a task too arduous for my powers.

Even the most superficial observer could not fail to note the prevalence in these wandering peoples of broad cheek bones, over-developed lower jaws, thick hair, abnormally long arms, the surly look in their eyes. I have also found an exceptional frequency of tattooing, which, although for other reasons common among sailors and soldiers, is nevertheless a pronounced characteristic of primitive nomadic man in the wild...
(Roberto Paulucci di Calboli, *I girovaghi italiani in Inghilterra e i suonatori ambulanti*, 1893)

'QUIET AND INOFFENSIVE'

If these improvements are made... I see no reason why the whole site should be razed and the Italians expelled from the district. They are very cleanly and healthy in their persons, quiet and inoffensive in their conduct, just and honest in their dealings, and punctual in paying their debts. It is astonishing how little illness there is among them, in spite of the stinks that are generated by their foreign habits and customs.
(From a report by Dr. Septimus Gibbon, Medical Officer of Health, Holborn district of London, 1887, for whom the worst 'stinks' in the Italian quarter came from cooking with garlic and the sweat of men in goatskins, a standard weatherproof for country people in southern Italy. There had been repeated calls in the local press for demolition of the whole quarter.)

Extreme traits of anti-immigrant discourse in our own time are easily recognised in the first two views printed above, and they were indeed among the shrillest voices in the chorus, but of greater interest is the fact that the second writer is not British but Italian. William Wilkins was the secretary of the Society for Preventing the Immigration of Destitute Aliens, an influential pressure group formed to oppose the sudden mass arrival of impoverished Jews fleeing persecution in Poland and Russia, and he unhesitatingly included 'the Italian proletariat' as equally candidates for exclusion in the quite mistaken belief that they too were mostly 'paupers or persons likely to become a public charge.' Nothing surprising about an alien-bashing Englishman banging on about slovenly filthy foreigners, but Paulucci di Calboli was an Italian official in London who rather than considering these people's needs saw it as his patriotic duty to denigrate them for giving Italy a bad name. So this northern Italian nobleman (he was a marquis) strong in his sense of belonging to a superior caste and culture invokes pseudo science to prove these embarrassing compatriots are nothing more than prize specimens of a primitive 'nomadic' criminal species as alien to civilised Italians as they are to decent British people. His damning study of itinerant Italian street musicians in England was published in the hope of hastening their total extirpation and widely applauded by his colleagues.

Clearly such visceral loathing does nothing to further our understanding of the marquis's 'nomads' whose values and conduct abroad were generally very far from his slanderous caricature. Even so, one allegation made by well-meaning Italians as well as Britons throughout the nineteenth century has to be examined seriously. The claim they routinely practised a 'white slave traffic' in young children.

'Slavery, or worse than slavery'

Probably but few persons are aware that year by year numbers of children, little older than infants, are leased from their parents in Italy, brought over to England, and treated as the property, to be bought and sold, of scoundrels who draw comfortable incomes from the earnings of their youthful victims in paths of degradation and crime. That such a state of slavery, or worse than slavery should exist within the bounds of liberty-loving England may well make philanthropists start; we have been trained in the idea that no sooner does a slave land on our shores than he becomes a freedman; and it amounts to almost a shock on our national honour to learn that children are imported for the express purpose of slavery. Were it not that we are assured that the present law is adequate to the emergency we should be inclined to demand instant legislation. But by a recent deliverance of the Home Secretary we are led to believe that a great deal may be done by enforcing the existing law. The School Boards have the power of catching up these foreign waifs and placing them in Industrial Schools, where out of the reach of oppression they may learn to live for something nobler and better than mendicancy; while under the Vagrant Act a person convicted repeatedly of causing children to beg is liable to a year's imprisonment and, if a male, to a taste of the warder's "cat". The vigorous enforcement of such provisions ought to go a long way towards destroying the trade of the wretches who import Italian juveniles in order to fatten on their earnings. We are glad, therefore, to note that the Middlesbrough School Board are inclined to apply their powers in this respect, and to rescue from the hands of their taskmasters the little foreigners who may occasionally be seen performing their primitive antics in our streets.

(The Middlesbrough News and Cleveland Advertiser, 4 August 1877.)

This somewhat apprehensive editorial was prompted by the arrest in Middlesbrough of 'a little Italian boy' called Antonio Curcio along with an older companion called Vincenzo Nicoli. According to a policing notice in the same edition ('Italian Beggar Nuisance') the boys had been apprehended outside the Middlesbrough Hotel where, clutching violin and harp, they had been observed entering in the hope of custom. Both were charged with 'going about playing the instruments with the purpose of begging'. In their testimony given through an interpreter at the hearing it emerged they had arrived in Middlesbrough after a week working Redcar and were in the employment of one Giacomo Derazzo, 'an elderly man' who had hired little Antonio for £7 a year. *Padrone* Derazzo was fetched from his lodgings. As almost always in similar cases, out of fear or loyalty Vincenzo tried to protect this old man with a different surname by claiming he was no less than his own elder brother and the little boy's father, but all in vain as Derazzo was severely cautioned by the magistrate and ordered to pay the cost of having Antonio accompanied to the Italian Consulate in Liverpool and repatriated to Italy. Since Vincenzo was released with a caution he must have convinced the court he was over 14 and therefore, in the eyes of the law, no longer a child. He and his 'brother' no doubt trekked on to Stockton, the old man bemoaning his depleted earnings and wondering where he was going to find a replacement for his young harpist in the middle of the season.

Cases such as this – and occasionally much more sensational – served to remind the reading public of the most disturbing feature of the Italian street music trade: the long-standing custom for families in the home villages to contract out their children to *padroni* on whom they would be wholly dependent while abroad, potentially making them easy prey for exploitation and abuse. The practice purposely exploited the poignant appeal of children within the busking industry, but was it slavery? For those actually in the trade the children were neither slaves nor beggars but workers, juvenile producers of music to generate pennies, and child workers were the norm all over Europe, not least in 'liberty-loving England' where they were used as cheap labour in almost every branch of agriculture and industry, not to mention Her Majesty's army and navy. The campaign to outlaw child labour had scarcely got under way[4], so the only reason the public at large should care about these 'foreign waifs' any more than their British equivalents slaving in mines and factories was that almost every mention of them by charities or the press came packaged in claims of horrifying maltreatment, all backed up by a whole sub-genre of tear-jerking Victorian fiction and theatre.

That the monstrous padrone was more than just a stock character is clear from some rare but truly horrific actual cases of vicious abuse, neglect, and even murder, which were widely disseminated in the press mostly during the 1850s and 60s when the trade was still dominated by itinerants from the Duchy of Parma and Piacenza. The Ciociaria *padroni*, though, also seem to have withheld food and used corporal punishment to 'school' their young *servi*, practices which like it or not have been used everywhere since time immemorial to maintain power over children. In the Middlesbrough case, despite the much-vamped 'slavery' theme, there is no suggestion of maltreatment, in fact master and boy seem to have colluded against the foreign authorities. All the Italians here knew there was no law against street music and that a conviction could only be secured by invoking the Vagrant Act and proving a child had been caught begging or procured for the purpose. In most cases wandering bands of Italians who were felt to be a nuisance were simply ordered to leave town. More feared, and more successful, was the Elementary Education Act which from 1870 made schooling compulsory for children under twelve and empowered local authorities to pursue truants.

To even the most well-meaning Victorian philanthropist the 'useless' poor belonged in prison or the workhouse or the Board School. Therefore the most effective strategy for the Italian Benevolent Society, the activist arm of the Italian embassy's long campaign to rid the streets of what the good marquis called 'the pariahs of the human race' was to convince police and magistrates and even the most charitable charities that Italy's 'wandering minstrels' were all a criminal fraternity of barely disguised beggars or worse.

The Middlesbrough case coincided with the appearance of a well publicised report by the Charity Organisation Society (C.O.S.), chaired by Sir Charles Trevelyan of Wallington Hall, Northumberland, entitled 'The Employment of Italian Children for Mendicant and Immoral Purposes'. Despite the sensational title it offered no actual evidence of employment for immoral purposes (never defined, but presumably theft, sexual abuse, and prostitution) but did provide ample testimony from police and local authorities all over Britain that children of both sexes in the employ of adults wandered from town to town making some kind of music to activate the charity of the natives. However in almost all cases the children were found to be accompanied by relatives, generally their own parents. The few who were not were unhesitatingly presumed to be at the mercy of unscrupulous adults connected with 'a comprehensive, organised criminal system' based in London's Italian quarter but running a network of child 'depots' in nine towns outside the capital from Brighton to Glasgow (none were mentioned in the North East). It is impossible today to determine how true this was, but since even the Italian Benevolent Society did not pick up on the claim it seems the C.O.S. was speculating wildly in order to reinforce its case. The fearsome depots were probably nothing more than all-Italian lodging houses such as Dipreta's in Newcastle where wandering bands of *padroni* and *servi*, usually from the same area of Italy, could socialise, exchange information, and do business. In the process child workers might well change masters, though most often along with their own parents.

Cruelty to minors was certainly not unknown in the Italian street music business, but that the North Shields case printed below was still a sordid exception seems clear from the fact that of the 108 reports submitted to the C.O.S. from all over the British Isles this was the one lone case of actual proven abuse.

THE WANDERING MINSTRELS AT NORTH SHIELDS

Yesterday, at the North Shields Police Court, Johanne Mark, an Italian, was charged with ill-treating two young children named Marianna Framepta and Marcolata Crola, two street musicians, who, as reported in yesterday's Chronicle, had been bought by the prisoner, and whom he was in the habit of ill-using. Bridget Smith, servant with Mrs. McGill, lodging-house keeper, Causey Bank, detailed the circumstances of the case as reported yesterday. The evidence of the girls was that they had been bought from their parents for £10 a year, and were sent out begging daily, sometimes from early morning until late at night. They made as much as 8s. to 15s. daily, and unless they brought in about 10s. the prisoner used to stop their food and beat them. Last Saturday night they stopped out very late, being afraid to return to their master, and, on Sunday morning, he took them out into a field and beat them with a stick. When they got back to the lodging-house they were examined by Mrs. Smith who found them covered with bruises. In consequence of this, Mrs. Smith reported the matter to Supt. Stewart, and took the children to the court on Wednesday. They were in a filthy condition, and were ordered by the magistrates to be sent to the workhouse, where they were properly cared for. When the prisoner was apprehended he had £27 10s. and a splendid watch in his possession. It transpired during the inquiry that no less than six children (boys and girls) had been engaged by the prisoner, and sent out for the purpose of begging, no matter what kind of weather it might be, and unless they brought him as much as 10s. per day he stopped their food and beat them. It also transpired that one boy was lying ill of fever in Newcastle Infirmary. – Mr. Adamson, in sentencing the prisoner, said he was one of the ruffians who preyed upon children, and it seemed to the Bench surprising that, notwithstanding all the warnings the public got, they should ever give these children money. It was not for their benefit but to keep such scoundrels as the prisoner. The children would be sent to the workhouse until the Italian consul was communicated with with a view to their being sent home. The prisoner would be committed to Morpeth gaol for six months, with hard labour, and unless he paid the costs of the prosecution he would have to undergo an additional month's incarceration at the expiration of that term. The magistrates also expressed a hope that the press would give publicity to these facts, and that they would tend to put down mendicity. (Newcastle Daily Chronicle, 24 July 1874)

The correct spelling of the Italian names was probably Giovanni Di Marco, Marianna Frammenta, and Immacolata Crolla, all recognisably surnames from the Ciocaria area. It is not known what happened to the other four children, but as to these two unfortunates the Charity Organisation Society reported that one girl was claimed by an uncle in London and the other repatriated to Italy, presumably through the agency of vice-consul Enrico Stella in Newcastle and paid for by the Italian Benevolent Society. The previous day's *Chronicle* had given the girls' ages as 11 and 14, reporting that Marchi had got them in London with promises of 'plenty of meat and clothes'. The girls, who had a single concertina between them, said they were nearing the end of a twelve month contract and had fled to North Shields from Sunderland on the Saturday (when earnings should have been best for the week) because they feared the consequences of not reaching their master's target. On the second day of the hearing (reported above) they appear to have sought to strengthen their case by considerably upping their master's expectations of earnings, as in their first deposition they had claimed the most they earned on a weekday was 3 shillings and 15 shillings was Marchi's minimum weekly requirement. This accords closely with *padrone* Tascarino's 'new regulations for the boys' detailed in the following extract from *Wandering Minstrel*, the autobiography of a former child *servo*.

There is an immense literature in many languages concerning the plight of 'the little Italian boys', but this memoir in English by 'Cagliardo Coraggioso' largely concerning his childhood as an itinerant musician in Britain is the only account ever written from the inside. The author, actually Eugenio D'Agostino from near Picinisco, arrived in 'England, the land of prosperity' in about 1897 when he was ten and the youngest in a 'company' consisting of two other boys and nine adult barrel organ and accordion players, both men and women. Some elements of the plot are plainly fictionalised for dramatic effect, but in the main the book documents an education within the music and ice cream trades which must reflect the experiences of numerous forebears of today's 'original Italian' families in the North East and elsewhere in Britain.

A BOY 'WANDERING MINSTREL' IN DURHAM

It was the same thing every day – nothing but tramp, tramp, tramp, all the time, playing the accordion and begging for food and money, sleeping in different, filthy beds almost every night… Almost every day, wherever I went, the boys and girls followed me in large numbers, laughing at me, throwing stones, shouting, and making a fool of me...

About twelve months after, my father became ill; he had rheumatism all over his body and could hardly move his legs at all. No wonder! For years he had been sleeping out – behind hedges and by the roadside – in all kinds of weather. He was advised by doctors that if he wanted to live a little longer he must return to Italy. He therefore squared up with his partner and went home. The company was now left in charge of his partner, the man called Cesare Tascarino, whose nickname was Catenaccio ['Bolt']. He was a beast of a man, with no heart, no soul, no conscience, no education, and no religion. His name should have been 'Poison'. The only thing he believed in was making money, which was his God.

It was then that the real trouble started with all of us. A few months later, having made his rules and regulations, he gave me and the other two boys a small pocket-book which contained the following, in writing:

STRICT REGULATIONS FOR THE BOYS

Rule 1. If any of the boys went back at night to the lodgings with less than 2s.6d, he had to go to bed without supper.

Rule 2. If less than 2s., no supper and no bed.

Rule 3. If less than 1s., no supper, no bed, and three strokes on the bare skin with the end of his strap, which had a large buckle at the end of it.

Rule 4. The boss would spy on the boys all day and if any one bought even a halfpennyworth of anything, he would be punished accordingly.

Rule 5. Everything we got from kind people must be brought home, especially foodstuffs; no one must eat anything. Those who had nothing to bring got nothing to eat, and were not allowed to receive any food from others of the company.

We were all treated like slaves, and none could run away because all were under a three years' contract. Tascarino told us that if anyone tried to run away he would be arrested and sent back, and was liable to pay a sum of money from his wages as a punishment. Every night before going to bed we were all searched to make sure that no one kept any money. The wages were paid once every six months and had to be put into the post office and Tascarino kept all the books. (The wages were 10s. per month). I was the only one not under contract, but I was too young to be able to understand and to do anything. He hated me most of all.

The first day I got my book of rules I was very lucky. I happened to be at a mining village near Durham. I started to play one or two of the latest tunes, such as 'A Bicycle Made for Two', but the most popular of all was 'Two Lovely Black Eyes'. Wherever I went I was asked to play it.

When I was playing in one of the village streets, I saw a house full of happy people. I started to play 'Two Lovely Black Eyes'. A man came out; he was very angry and made me stop playing that tune. I looked at his face. He had two of the blackest eyes I had ever seen. I came to the conclusion that he had been fighting, and there he was with a couple of beauties! Another man came out and insisted on my playing the tune, in spite of the other man's protest. One wanted me to play it, the other one didn't. At last they started to fight. The other people in the house came out and took me inside and made me play 'Two Lovely Black Eyes' again and again. They all began to make a fool of the man with the two black eyes and started to sing and dance. I discovered that someone had been married. They made me play all kinds of music and I was there about four hours. They went round with the hat several times and the collection amounted to about 6s. altogether. I didn't play again that day. I went back to Durham and *passed the rest of the day looking at shop windows. I went back to the lodging-house at night with a pocketful of money and the only person pleased to see all the money was the boss. The others had long faces; especially the two boys; one was short of his rule money and was being punished. If I had known I would have given him some money on the quiet, but it was now too late.*

It was winter-time. Every day it had snowed or rained, or both. There was a cold wind and frost all the rest of the time. It was very hard to earn any money. That night I worked late and wished to make up the 2s. and 6d.; in fact, I never went back to the lodgings until I had made the right amount of money. It had been snowing for days and I could not earn anything, owing to the snow coming down all the time, but that day I managed to make 1s.; all the others more or less had done the same. The boss began to curse and swear and said that this was the kind of weather in which to earn money, because people would take pity on us – and, instead, we had made less. He said he would make an example of us. The other two boys and I were beaten with the strap. This was the first time in my life I had got the strap. I was struck on the face, and kicked. The other two boys got more or less the same, and we all had to go to bed without any food.

The food we got from the boss was not fit to be eaten. He never bought tea, sugar, bread, or butter. We ate if we had been successful during the day; if not, we did not eat. Whenever we went into a lodging-house, the first thing he did was to collect all the teapots and take out the old tea-leaves and put them into a large kettle with a pinch of fresh tea which we begged from grocers; this is how our tea was made. One pennyworth of milk went round the whole company. Milk was the only thing he bought. All the other things we begged from grocers – bread, tea, sugar, old pieces of cheese, small scraps of bacon, and sometimes a red herring or a kipper (divided between two of us and toasted in front of the fire). Sometimes he gathered big turnips from the fields, boiled and mashed them, and mixed them with a spoonful of grease and onions. This was our food practically every night. Sunday was our resting day, because the authorities did not allow us to play our instruments that day. So it was our great feast-day – plenty of food and rest. On the Saturday night he bought the whole head of a cow, or six sheep heads, and made a large pot of soup, into which he would put a handful of rice. He collected all the old pieces of bread lying about the house and mixed them with the soup, and this was our great Sunday dinner. He scraped all the meat off the bones and kept this for himself for the next day whilst we were out.

(*Wandering Minstrel, The Life Story of Cagliardo Coraggioso Written by Himself*, London, 1938).

Not until he was thirteen was 'Coraggioso' able to escape the ever more tyrannical Tascarino and return to Italy. At fifteen he came back to form an ice cream partnership with a cousin in West Hartlepool and with the proceeds bought his own barrel-organ, taking to the road again for several years in partnership with an older man, Antonio Cellini from Arpino. In his early twenties he married an English girl and after various failed business ventures the couple settled in Leith to raise a family and run a very successful ice cream parlour.

For all the ugly parallels with the North Shields case of abuse, it must again be stressed that although life for the 'wandering minstrels' was tough, particularly for the youngest, cruelty to children was not the norm. Coraggioso's ill-treatment begins only after the departure of his admired father, the group's original *padrone*. In fact the arduous but adventurous life of the travelling musician was a proud tradition in this family for whom it had previously brought considerable financial rewards and even, if we believe the author, a personal invitation to his grandfather's team of *zampognari* to perform for Queen Victoria.

In a culture where children customarily worked alongside adults in almost every occupation and enterprise, the indenture of these young people was a well-tried rudimentary apprentice scheme little different to that applying in the other Italian wandering trades, including those described in chapter 2. The sons, and occasionally daughters, of the poor were contracted out by hopeful or desperate parents to a reputable local *padrone* with impressive experience of making money by journeying abroad with youngsters he supplied with a musical instrument or street-organ or performing animal, and lodged and fed and schooled in the ways and tricks of the profession. When older, with such invaluable experience behind them, who knows what wondrous ways of enriching themselves and their families might result. The written or more often verbal contract between parent and *padrone*, normally valid for three years as in Coraggioso's case, covered both the child's welfare (food and clothing, and medical expenses if ill) and discipline (fixed fines for breaking an instrument or absconding). Some also included a heavy financial penalty if the master should mistreat the child or fail to return to Italy with him. As for corporal punishment, it was no doubt taken for granted, if merited, for parents hardly expected their offspring to be more tenderly treated than at home but rather to receive a rigorous education in ways of survival in a harsh world. And that ought to be no shock when until so very recently it was the norm to clout and spank children in our homes and cane and strap them in our schools.

That the *padrone* system was a very useful family investment in its own future is shown by the fact that so many of the boys and young men who grew up within the trade became seasoned independent masters abroad in their own turn. As we saw in the case of Nicola Dipreta's enterprise in Newcastle, this was most commonly at the head of a family concern with various dependent 'servants' attached, not infrequently themselves with young families to support.

The North East's evolving Italian communities and the move into ice cream

'There were the Giordanos at number 30 Trafalgar Street, Matilda and the daughter Maria, and the two boys. They had a round freezer outside the front door and we used to take our cups and get a pennyworth of ice cream, or you took a bowl for all the family. Living in the same house, at the bottom, was Mr and Mrs Cavazzi, Matilda's old mother and father, and they went round selling hot chestnuts and roast potatoes. He was a character, only a tiny little thing, and he was the colour of mahogany, with

Newcastle, about 1885: Giambattista Lertoria, former doyen of the Newcastle barrel-organists, is now the city's leading purveyor of street ice cream. The figure on the right may be his son Charles. (Photo: Fr. David Milburn.)

a great big moustache hanging right over, and he used to wear this funny little trilby turned up all the way round. You used to see him pushing the barrow thing with the roast potatoes. The Lertorias were in Trafalgar Street too, on the same side as the railway yard, and they used to sell ice cream too, a nice family, seven lads and one girl. Then there were the Nicolettis who lived nearby on Carliol Square, three girls and three lads, hawkers I think. Mark Toney's had an ice cream place along by the Tanners Arms, and after Mr Cavazzi died we used to go along there on a Sunday with a basin. Then my mother always used to tell us about this Italian chap who had a bear on a chain and it used to dance on the street, and there were always crowds around.'

(Mrs Josephine Bracegirdle, born 1919, remembering the Italians of her childhood round Carliol Square, Newcastle.)

By 1900, relatively small but very evident concentrations of Italians were present in all the main urban centres of the North East, in the Manors district in Newcastle, in Sunderland's East End, and in the Cannon Street area of Middlesbrough, all zones where housing was cheap and more could be saved by crowding families and bands of *servi* into as few rooms as possible.

As vice-consul Rizzetto noted in his 1892 report quoted at the start of this chapter, the Italian 'aristocracy' within the entire region was miniscule. At its head, besides himself, were the Newcastle coal brokers Pietro Maria Rapetti, a partner in De Lorial & Co., and Vittorio Amedeo Montaldi, who was to become Rizzetto's consular successor. The two restaurant owners, both with establishments sited prominently in the city centre, were Gustavo Barawitzka at 1, Market Street (the famous 'Criterion', see page 269), and Francesco Marini, a ship broker and foodstuffs importer, at 49 Grainger Street. The three fancy goods shops were in the hands of remnants of the old Comasque colony: Antonio Bernasconi (Caxton House, Charlotte Square), Angelo Sereno Rizzi (59 Grainger St) and Mosé Antonio Molteni (49 Grainger Street, in the same building as Marini's). The proprietor of the food and wine store was none other than Angelo Carpena, the pioneering *padrone* of street musicians, who as far back as 1865 had abandoned his original métier to open his shop at 23 Carliol Street in the heart of the 'Italian' district. He kept it going well into his eighties (1901 census), and surely stocked Italian produce for a lot of his regular customers. The shop in Sunderland belonged to the second-generation Bergna brothers, jewellery and toy dealers, while the two North Shields ship brokers were Nicola Bruna and the aforementioned enterprising Francesco Marini who were among the very last of the once thriving Italian maritime community at the mouth of the Tyne reviewed in chapter 3.

Given his distaste for all their kind, vice-consul Rizzetto might have been expected to overestimate the numbers of street musicians who 'in certain seasons of the year switch to peddling ice cream', but measured against the previous year's census returns his figures look rather low, perhaps because he knew very little about these people and their actual lives. There were in fact at least 50 street musicians/ice cream hawkers in Newcastle in 1891, and not 5 but 20 in Sunderland. At least two of the leading Sunderland *padroni* had close ties with Newcastle's Nicola Dipreta, suggesting it was to him they looked for replacement *servi* and possibly to him that they owed their own training.

Ten years later, at the start of the new century and reflecting the sharp rise in immigration from Ciociaria, consular agent V.A. Montaldi[5] estimated that some 750 adult Italians (with several hundred children) were present within his jurisdiction (which then included Yorkshire North Riding), the vast majority in street trading and street music, and overwhelmingly from southern Italy. Italy's new man in the North East was again a northerner (from Garibaldi's home town of Nice) but a far more sympathetic observer – one cannot imagine Rizzetto wanting to start up a school – who clearly had the southerners' welfare at heart for all their cussedness and was even ready to declare the level of their morality 'good'. He calculated 500 adults on Tyneside, of which as many as 200 were women, plus another 250 dispersed southwards between Sunderland and Scarborough. These very approximate figures are considerably higher than the 1901 census disclosed (332 Italians on Tyneside, for instance), but Montaldi strenuously argued that the many names accumulating in his registry supported his own estimates which would have meant the

Italians were the largest foreign group in the region. He may well have been right, for no census can track the movements of itinerants and seasonal workers in and out of the same area.

Given the old hue and cry about 'slavery', and the recent introduction of the Child Protection Act, it is notable that neither Rizzetto nor Montaldi raises the issue of the exploitation of minors. In fact in no census return from 1871 onward have I found any record that Italian children in our region were living with persons other than their own family. All the same, as the following extract from Montaldi's full 1902 report makes plain, in other respects the padrone system was still very much alive.

THE NORTH-EAST 'ITALIAN COLONY' IN 1902

The great majority of the colony comes from the south of Italy. My register contains the names of about 500 [on Tyneside], of whom some 300 are male, but to these should be added the children, about 305 in number, few of whom however are registered despite my efforts to encourage this, even in the case of children attending the Italian School which I set up in this city in November 1901.

Our nationals for the most part practise the occupations of ice cream sellers, statuette makers (from the province of Lucca), and itinerant barrel-organ players.

About twenty are the so-called padroni, *men of some affluence; the others are the garzoni [apprentices] or servi [servants] whom they have persuaded to expatriate with all manner of inducements and promises which in effect come down to no more than board and lodging and a miserable recompense of fifteen or twenty liras a month [well under £1], which is frequently unpaid due to the absence of a proper contract!*

I continue to do what I can to restrain the greed of some padroni, *and in several instances have found permanent work in local firms for various nationals but unfortunately, with rare exceptions, as soon as they have put by a little money they have quit the job in order to resume the occupation of street musician, now in their own right, sometimes outdoing their former bosses in the tyranny they exercise over their newly-arrived compatriots recruited by them directly or indirectly from Italy. It should not be hard to remedy these excesses simply by obliging the* padroni, *on pain of legal proceedings or a fine, to deposit copies of all contracts drawn up in the home villages with the* garzoni *whom they have summoned or accompanied here.*

I say this because in the main the sort of written contract made in Italy prior to departure remains in the padrone's *keeping as warrant of the work expected of the emigrant, and so if a dispute arises this single wretched document is declared lost or stolen! I have quite often had cause to complain of such occurrences. Apart from these misdemeanours, common to other colonies of Italians dispersed among the larger cities of the United Kingdom, the personal conduct of our nationals is generally speaking good, and gives no cause for complaint.* (From an official report by V.A. Montaldi, Italian consular agent in Newcastle, 1902.)

It was a hard school, the old Italian padrone system, endured because at least it housed and fed and clothed a man (it is sad to note that not a few *garzoni* or *servi* bound to *padroni* in our region were lone married men in their forties and even fifties), and tolerated by the more ambitious for just as long as they could sustain the dream of one day becoming masters themselves. By liberating some of these grossly ill-paid subordinates from 'tyranny' Montaldi was unintentionally providing both the opportunity and means to hasten that day.

By now the old hurdy-gurdy *padroni* were discovering how lucrative could be the making and hawking of ice cream, at least in the warmer months. Consular staff all over Britain noted with relief this switch to 'a more stable, decorous and profitable' métier (Liverpool consul-general) than street music which they had never seen as anything other than shaming and shameless mendicancy. Now at last, they thankfully reported to Rome, the southern 'nomads' were selling something other than noise in the streets, and what is more some were even settling into the respectable role of 'confectioner', trading in ice cream and sweets and other treats from small shops with their own names in big letters above the door.

The early history of ice cream in Britain as a whole will be sketched in the next chapter. Here in the North East, to judge from the decennial census returns for Italians and their occupations[6], the switch to making a living off *la crema* (as Italians in Britain spoke of it) occurred very slowly. It seems in fact to have taken as much as thirty years to wean the bulk of the immigrant population away from the old reliance on street music or casual labouring jobs.

The first linkage between Italians and ice cream in our region occurs in the 1871 census when the sole operatives I have found were two men in their twenties based in Newcastle: Giulio and Teodoro Reggi, 'ice cream manufacturers' at 2, Back Pandon Street. They were presumably brothers and almost certainly from Bardi in the Val Ceno where their surname is quite common. Ten years later, still only two Italians were recorded as pursuing the trade in Newcastle, though now with assistants: 28-year-old Paolo Castelli in Percy Place, off Percy Street, employing two brothers from Ciociaria as street hawkers; and the familiar figure of *padrone* Giambattista Lertoria, now 43 and heading up a lodging house in Trafalgar Street. He was in ice cream with his eldest son Joseph and four of his many 'boarders', two of whom were likewise from Ciociaria. But even in this ice-creaming household accommodating no less than 30 Italians of all ages every other adult male was engaged in organ-grinding. Evidently the Geordies were not yet sufficiently hooked on *la crema*. The only others I have found pursuing the same line in our region in 1881 were in Mill Street in the heart of Sunderland's East End: 40-year-old Giuseppe Geraldi, 'ice cream maker', with six 'lodgers' from his same area of the Tuscan-Emilian Apennines, all assuredly employed as his helpers and hawkers. These few ice-cream entrepreneurs on Tyne and Wear were all from central Italy though evidently not above taking on willing southerners now that men from their own region were becoming thin on the ground. The even more drastic alternative, to take on British workers, would remain unthinkable for many years to come.

In 1891, a decade later and twenty years at least after the Reggi brothers first experimented with ice cream, in all Newcastle apart from Lertoria there were still no more than three ice cream 'merchants' and only a half-dozen 'vendors' against a total of thirty-eight 'musicians'. The census, though, was as usual collected in early April and some of the latter would assuredly switch to peddling ice cream for their respective *padroni* or even on their own account as the weather warmed up, as vice-consul Rizzetto reported was general practice by this time. Gaetano Papeschi, for example, 'ice cream maker and lodging-house keeper' in Lisle Street, had at his disposal two long-established organ-grinding families lodging with him. The new personalities in ice cream are all southerners now: Papeschi himself, Giacomo Jaconelli, soon to become a major employer as both ice cream dealer and wafer manufacturer, and Gaetano Andreucci, a former organ-grinder from the Dipreta stable who was seemingly the first Italian to set up as a confectioner in the city (in Stowell Street, near Jaconelli). Anticipating a trend to come, all three men were settled in better class neighbourhoods at some distance from the old Italian quarter around Carliol Square, hoping presumably to prosper on territory less densely patrolled by men in the pay of Lertoria and Dipreta.

Sunderland in the early 1890s already boasted three Italian confectioners, all in the East End, and all dealing in ice cream. Paolo Ciarella had enough work for his son and several *garzoni* in his well-situated shop on the High Street at n.18; Vittorio Melucci, one of Geraldi's former *servi* who later relocated to Newcastle, ran a corner shop in Robinson's Lane, a teeming back alley where many Italians first lodged; Pasquale Franciosi, the son of a street music family from Scapoli, headed a confectioner's plus horse-and-cart ice cream concern in Hartley Street. In short, in Sunderland the move into both ice cream and shop-keeping seems to have been more concerted than in Newcastle, indeed the 1891 census suggests that only two street musicians were still resident in the city, and both well on in years.

Middlesbrough, the region's third largest town, now finally had its own first batch of Italian settlers. Making a living by peddling both ice cream and street music, a team of a dozen young men and women headed by Antonio Defelice lived packed into a two-storey terrace house in Suffield Street. From this very modest nucleus was to spring the considerable network of Italian family ice cream concerns scattered all over Teesside by the start of the First World War. The Suffield Street workers already numbered Giuseppe Caira and Pietro Di Duca who were to be the first Italians to set up in ice cream in Stockton, and Francesca Scappaticci whose brother or cousin Francesco was destined to reign long in Middlesbrough as ice cream *padrone* supreme and chief conduit between Ciociaria and Teesside for many more aspiring young workers and their families. Most of the shopkeepers who went on to colonise Middlesbrough's densely populated Cannon Street district over the next fifteen years – Di Luoffo, Jaffrate, Martino, Ranaldi, Colletta, Angelo Rea, Minchella, each employing from two to five *servi* – served their English 'apprenticeship' under either Defelice or Scappaticci in Suffield Street.

Hartlepool's earliest Italians, all again from Ciociaria, also arrived in the 1890s. By the 1901 census they numbered about thirty, some married with small children but all dependent on just three *padroni*. It is significant for subsequent developments that the two oldest bosses, 56-year-old Raffaele Terribile (sic!) and Luigi Soave, 48, who had grown up in the United States, put their teams to work in both organ-grinding and ice cream, whereas their younger colleague 26-year-old Luca Bianco and his band lived entirely by peddling *la crema*. All Hartlepool's best-known ice families – Bianco, Facchini, Amerigo (D'Americo), and Di Duca, the junior branch of Stockton's Di Duca – began their local careers before 1905.

By 1900 the shift from organ-grinding to ice-creaming was apparent everywhere. The 1901 census shows that even *padrone* Nicola Dipreta's entire Newcastle street-music enterprise had finally gone over to ice-cream vending, and several families and individuals who had worked for him in the past now made a living in the same way. It was still only early April, but now just 26 Italian 'musicians' were recorded in the whole of Newcastle against 64 in ice cream. The balance in favour of *la crema* was in reality probably even greater, for some of these street musicians look like itinerants travelling all over the country – a four-man team of Emilians, and a father and his 15-year-old son lodging that night with the Lertorias. Aside from *padrone* Alfonso Valentini's large team of ten newly arrived on Tyneside, the regular street musicians in town were a pale reflection of former times: two *padroni* in their mid-thirties, each with only one *servo* of a similar age, two lone widows of deceased street musicians, and three self-employed elderly males, including the 65-year-old veteran grinder Francesco Viviani ('Old Man Friday', see illustration on page 85) who would not live to see the year out. In addition, some among the score of other Italians who figure as labourers in local factories and shipyards in the April census would certainly be hoping to drop tools or put in extra hours for the ice cream bosses come the summer.

Italians all over the region were thus now predominantly engaged in ice cream making

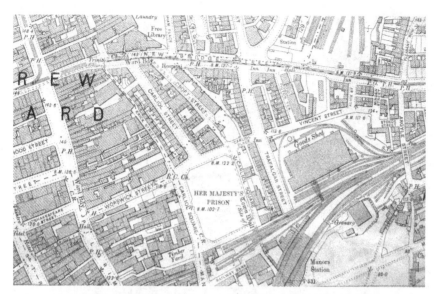

Manors district of inner Newcastle, showing the low-rent terraced streets to the east of Pilgrim Street traditionally favoured by the city's Italian community.

Daniele Stacchini's granddaughter Rosanna Batey outside the old family shop in the Manors, just off Carliol Square, 1934. (Photo: Bernadette Reddecliffe)

and vending, clearly very good business at least for the *padroni* and the self-employed, and still without native rivals. Besides attracting new enterprises into the area, the high returns were encouraging individuals and young families to break away from the all-controlling bosses and strike up on their own. Disaffected *servi* could be poached in the process.

Though their numbers were growing, the Italian presence in any one location still remained

R. RICHARDSON · 105 NORTHUMBERLAND ST · NEWCASTLE-ON-TYNE

When Vincenzo Battista (above) died of pneumonia in 1900 at only 47, Newcastle's Italian community lost a good man. Few compatriots can have been missing at the funeral which consular agent Montaldi reported was attended 'by no less than 300 persons, English and Italian'. In consoling his Newcastle-born widow Mary-Jane, Montaldi praised her husband as the 'connecting link of union' between the Italian colony and the consulate: 'He has since 1874, although in but a humble position, been spokesman and guide to every one of our compatriots who applied to him for assistance or counsel.' Vincenzo and his elder brother Giovanni, both trained tailors, were among the very first southerners to settle in the North East and must consequently have been instrumental in promoting the region's potential for many future immigrants from their home town of Cassino. In 1890 they were joined by their younger brother Antonio, a cobbler. All three, unusually, were literate. Giovanni and Vincenzo helped Giambattista Lertoria in his pioneering ice cream business and also grew to be close friends and associates of the organ-grinders' boss, Nicola Dipreta, for whom Antonio worked for a time. Vincenzo and Mary-Jane finally set up a confectionery shop in Gallowgate, Newcastle, while Giovanni formed his own street music business which eventually evolved into a large penny-ice concern in Tynemouth. All three brothers had numerous children, making Battista one of the largest clans of Italian descent on Tyneside today.

relatively small. Probably the only urban acres to merit the 'Little Italy' attribution lay in the Manors district of Newcastle in the few streets and back alleys bounded by the Town Jail and Carliol Square to the south and New Bridge Street to the north. Here in 1900 resided some 200 first and second generation Italians, either crowded into just three neighbouring tenements in the square itself facing the forbidding jail walls or at scattered addresses in the surrounding streets: principally Carliol Street, Trafalgar Street, Picton Terrace, and Erick Street. This lively and industrious community of diverse provenance and one religion worshipped at St Andrew's in nearby Worswick Street where their children attended the attached school, and shopped at Angelo Carpena's store in Carliol Street or Batey's corner shop on Manors run by old Daniele Stacchini's widowed daughter who had married a Geordie. Stacchini's in Carliol Street, and Lertoria's in Trafalgar Street, were still the main lodging houses used by Italians, though most other families also augmented their income by taking in compatriots as boarders and fellow-workers. Immigrants from Ciociaria now easily predominated amid such families as the Cavazzi and Bardetti in Trafalgar Street from the province of Piacenza, and a sprinkling of Tuscan *figurinai* who at the time of the 1901 census included a six-man company from Barga. Here too lived and thrived the biggest southern *padroni*, all fully committed to ice cream by now. There was the veteran Nicola Dipreta, now 50, with no less than 22 *servi* at 5-6 Carliol Street, while in the all-Italian tenements in Carliol Square resided Nicola's former underlings the brothers Luigi and Domenico Andreucci and their families with nine live-in *servi,* and also the relative newcomer, *padrone* Giovanni Marcantonio with another 15 *servi* including his teenage son Antonio, the future founder of the renowned 'Mark Toney' Newcastle ice cream firm. This was the moment of maximum density of Italians in the neighbourhood they had favoured for almost a hundred years, for in the course of the next ten years or so many dispersed to elsewhere in the city and its suburbs as competition for custom drove ice-cream dealers and shopkeepers to seek out new neighbourhoods. All the same, right up until the Second World War a distinct Italian presence could be felt in the Manors district, particularly around Carliol Square and Argyle Place, and to some extent also further to the west in Friars, where a close-knit community of southerners had formed around the original Italian businesses in Stowell Street and Blandford Street.

Sunderland by 1900 was also proving to be an ice creamers' paradise. The principal shopkeepers were Pasquale Franciosi and his brother Michele who now occupied Ciarella's ice cream shop on High Street East; Antonio Valente who had stepped into Franciosi's shoes at the Hartley Street shop; and Vincenzo ('Vengeance'!) Pompa, who with his brother-in-law Giovanni Amerigo kept another shop further along Hartley Street, a big step up from their former life as organ grinders based in the Robinson's Lane slum. Scattered over other streets and back alleys in the East End were some fifty more Italian males, a few with families making and selling their own ice cream but most employed as street vendors for Valente, Pompa, or Franciosi, or for two other ice cream *padroni* also operating in the High Street: Andrea Palumbo at number 79, and Giuseppe Valente, the younger brother of Hartley Street's Antonio Valente, at number 94. No less than twenty-three Valente men, women and children, were resident in Sunderland at the time of the 1901 census. This cluster of more or less closely related families from Cassino, at that time composed of five families and five single men, all employed as ice cream workers, seems to have drifted over here piecemeal from about 1890 in the wake of Antonia Valente's marriage to the widowed Domenico Rossi, a former wandering street musician who had became one of Franciosi's closest associates. As was the custom, the Valentes also brought over other *paesani* (fellow villagers) whom they housed and fed alongside their own families and put to work hawking their homemade ice creams around the city streets and out into the nearby collieries. Today's Valente descendants are found from Tyneside to Scarborough.

Outside central Newcastle, our region's 'Little Italies' were really no more than these scattered all-Italian households, dormitories-cum-canteens in effect, incorporating not only single workers and their bosses but several families, often with very young children, and providing security of numbers, language, and expense, as well as familiar food, a social life, and acknowledged leadership. One striking example is Annie Harrison's lodging-house at 10, Framwellgate, Durham City, which regularly took in Italian itinerants. In the spring of 1901 it slept 26 Italians. Presided over by the ice-cream brothers Salvatore and Vincenzo Dimambro, both with young families, the entire company had recently arrived from Scotland, or had swelled its numbers en route. The brothers shared eleven adult *servi* who worked as ice cream hawkers, while their older unmarried brother Giuseppe, their brother-in-law Domenico Pacitto and his 16-year-old daughter plus another *servo* made up a small hurdy-gurdy team. Five years before, placing all their faith in 'uncle Serafino' in Hull, the Dimambro party had walked the whole way from Italy. Serafino sent them on to a contact in Aberdeen who evidently proved unsatisfactory, for after a few months they all moved down to Dundee for a while before hitting the road again. Durham, much-visited but still unsettled by Italians, turned out to be their last port of call, for business proved promising enough to convince them to stay. By the First World War the Dimambros had several shops around the city, the start of a little business empire which went on to take in Langley Park, Sacriston, and Houghton-le-Spring, with further family outlets in Leadgate and Consett.

One wonders what such people would have made of marquis Paulucci di Calboli's claims that they and their 'nomad' kind had no notion of respect and honour and their sole creed was 'the love of idleness, no thought for the morrow, a total negation of the concept of thrift'. The late Joe Greco once put it to me rather differently, when speaking of that entire generation of adventurous pioneers: 'They were the backbone of the Italians, penniless. Dad was eight years of age when he came. He knew all the Italians who walked it from Italy. Suffering was like tempering them. The third generation, we were with silver spoons compared to them'.

By 1900 even the smallest towns in the North East were well accustomed to the sight of colourful bands of Italians peddling their ice cream round the streets in summer, and chestnuts in winter, and it would not be so long before their gaily painted horse-drawn carts and hand barrows and little confectionery shops and cafés were as familiar in the remotest villages too. Though families continued to open new shops well into the 1920s, and sporadically long after, the forty-year process of settlement throughout the North East was more or less completed by the time the First World War put a brake on further expansion.

This chapter has concerned the lives of the first Italian migrants to reach the North East in considerable numbers in modern times, those whom their descendants now collectively term with some pride 'the original Italians'. In their day they got a pretty poor press, like every fresh immigrant ethnic group before and after them. But no matter what anyone wrote or said or thought about them, later generations of Anglo-Italians do indeed have good reason to be proud, and thankful too, when they consider how much their ancestors achieved and against what odds, with no money, no education, no English, and no favours.

THE LAST ITALIAN STREET ENTERTAINERS OF NEWCASTLE

All about that way where the old prison was it was full of Italians. There was Marcucc' living on Argyle Street, next to Jaffrate, and he went all over, all the rough streets and that, right out to Gosforth, hauling the barrow with the heavy organ. He would sing and entertain, with all the hands and broken English, not a very good singer but he could get by. An Italian woman, Di Palma, used to go about with him, a stout woman and dressed real Italian still, red scarf and all gay colours. When they'd finished the organ she used to go round the pubs with a lovebird in a cage, and it would tell you your fortune, picking the message out for a penny.

There was another old Italian with a beard, and he left a fortune. He knew exactly where to go. He had like a pram with a little organ on it and he did the better-class places, the picture houses, and round Jesmond. He never mixed. He had a dog, his special corgi trained to sit up and hold this little pail in its mouth like the kids used to take to Whitley Bay to put the sand in, and the bairns was always stopping for the dog, stopping their mothers.

'Dad-oh,' Stockton's last Italian organ-grinder, lodged with the Sperduti family and died in the 1920s.

Everyone was so sympathetic for the dog and so sorry for him, because he was such an old man and shabbily dressed – and I tell you when he died he had thousands, for them days! Mind, he'd always make sure there wouldn't be too much in the tin, always emptying it out to leave a bare copper in the bottom. And then he would go home to the best of food, the best of everything. And of course the dog would be more than well catered for.

There was also an English woman who went round with all the Italians. Everyone knew her: Meggie Lockie, and she used to go with the organs. She spoke fluent Italian and she lived years and years with Prosperini, the original Prosperini. He'd always keep saying, 'I'll marry you at Christmas, I'll marry you at Easter'. And of course he never did, and in the end it drove her to drink. But she never forgot him. She kept all the songs, all the tune sheets for the organ, even the receipts, and treasured them right till she died.

(Jackie Moore, born 1911, looking back in 1991)

BOOKS AND SOURCES

The extracts from consular reports for the North East are translated from *Emigrazione e Colonie: Rapporti dei RR. agenti diplomatici e consolari*, published by the Commissariato Generale dell'Emigrazione (Rome 1893 and 1903). Though it does not consider the North East, Lucio Sponza's *Italian Immigrants in Nineteenth-Century Britain: Realities and Images* (1988) is a fundamental resource for all the main themes treated in this chapter.

The era of mass migration. There are many admirable studies of this central feature of Italian history but still essential are the classic early accounts: Francesco Colletti:'*Dell'emigrazione italiana*' (in *Cinquant'anni di storia italiana*, vol 3, Milan 1911), and Robert Foerster, *The Italian Emigration of Our Times* (Harvard 1919). The best recent study is *Storia dell'emigrazione italiana* (2 vols, 2008), edited by P. Beviliacqua, with contributions from many specialists. A superb overview of European migration both within and beyond the continent is Klaus Bade, *Migration in European History* (2003). For more on social conditions in Italy: J.A.Davis, *Conflict and Control: Law and Order in Nineteenth Century Italy* (1988). For the realities of rural life and the effect of mass emigration on the main 'sending communities' linked to Britain: G.Mortali and C.Trufelli, *Per procacciarsi la vita: L'emigrazione del Taro e del Ceno dall'ancien regime al Regno d'Italia* (Reggio Emilia 2005), R.M. Bell, *Fate, Honour, Family and Village: Demographic and Cultural Change in Rural Italy since 1800* (1979), and R.Sarti, *Long Live the Strong: A History of Rural Society in the Apennine Mountains* (1985).

Early street entertainers. Pausanio's correspondence was kindly shown to me by Antonio Maldini of Barga. The Sidoli case was brought to my notice by Barry Redfern. For the boy Antonio Salvio, see *Durham Advertiser* 25 February 1831. The classic texts of the movement to suppress 'the organ nuisance' in London are M.T.Bass, *Street Music in the Metropolis* (1864), and Charles Babbage, 'A Chapter on Street Nuisances' in his *Passages from the Life of a Philosopher* (1864). A refreshing contrast is Henry Mayhew's great work, *London Labour and the London Poor* (1862) which includes several strikingly sympathetic encounters with Italian street entertainers.

Southern street musicians and organ-grinders. R. Paulucci di Calboli, *I girovaghi italiani in Inghilterra e i suonatori ambulanti* (Città di Castello,1893). Equally vitriolic about Italian itinerants in Britain, not sparing even the *figurinai* and the artists' models, is Giuseppe Prato, *Gli italiani in Inghilterra*, (*La riforma sociale*, vol. 10, 1899, and vol. 11, 1900).

'Slavery, or worse than slavery'. J.E.Zucchi, *The Little Slaves of the Harp: Italian Child Street Musicians in Nineteenth-Century Paris, London, and New York* (1992). Cagliardo Corraggioso, *Wandering Minstrel* (1938). The Middlesbrough case was brought to my attention by Dr Malcolm Chase.

The North East's evolving Italian communities and the move into ice cream. This account draws on family memories, trade directories, the decennial census returns, and the registers of the Roman Catholic churches most favoured by the principal communities: St Andrew's and St Mary's Cathedral in Newcastle, St Patrick's in Sunderland, and St Mary's in Middlesbrough. Mrs Bracegirdle's reminiscences were recorded by Barry Redfern.

FROM EMIGRANTS TO EMINENCE

The Dimambro brothers Vincenzo (left), Giuseppe (centre, unmarried), and Salvatore (right) pose with family members shortly after their arrival in Durham by way of Scotland in 1900.

Salvatore's son Andrew (right) with Terry Martin at the door of the Dimambro 'Ice Cream and Soda Fountain' parlour on Elvet Bridge, Durham, in the 1930s. Other notable Italian businesses in Durham City by this time were Valente's 'Savoy' and Gallone's 'Vaudeville', both in North Road.

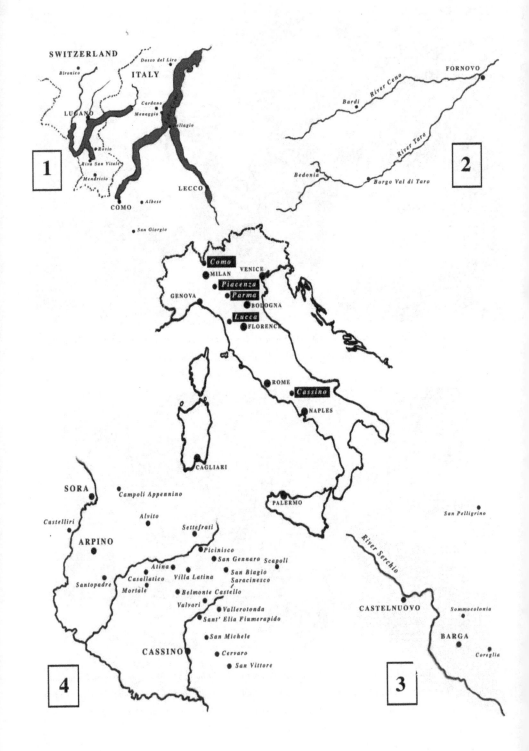

WHERE THEY BELONGED

Home Territories of the North East's 'Original Italians'

Up to the Second World War, four relatively small areas of Italy were the home territories of most Italian migrants in Britain. These distinct origins are still reflected in surnames in the North East inherited from Italian forebears who settled here during the nineteenth century and the early decades of the twentieth. Though geographically separate and therefore different in speech and allegiance, all four areas have in common a history of large families struggling to make a living in rugged upland terrain as peasant farmers, field labourers, shepherds, or artisans. Temporary or permanent emigration was a pragmatic response to poverty and chronic underemployment.

Moving from north to south, the four areas are:

1) The zone of Lake Como on the edge of the Italian-Swiss Alps, home territory of the *barometai*, the itinerant barometer makers and picture framers who first appeared in the North East in the last decade of the eighteenth century. (The map also shows the home towns of the principal Swiss *stuccatori* operating in the North East in the mid-eighteenth century.)

2) The Val Taro and the Val Ceno (Taro and Ceno river valleys) on the eastern slopes of the Tuscan-Emilian Apennine mountains in the former Duchy of Parma, now shared between the provinces of Parma and Piacenza, home territory of the animal exhibitors and the first wave of street musicians who though present from the early nineteenth century did not settle in the North East until after 1850.

3) The area of Barga, some sixty miles south of the Val Taro, in the higher reaches of the Serchio river valley on the Tuscan side of the Apennines, province of Lucca, home to the *figurinai*, the itinerant makers and vendors of plaster statuettes, present in the North East from around 1800.

4) The Ciociaria area (also known as the Val Comino), formerly province of Caserta, now province of Frosinone, extending along the western slopes of the southern Apennines midway between Rome and Naples, home to the many street musicians and organ-grinders who found their way to the North East mostly after 1870. Here the largest town is Cassino.

Owing to the cohesion and relative isolation of most rural communities in Italy in earlier times, an individual's surname is generally a reliable clue to the locality in which the family originated. All surnames listed on the next pages have had connections with the North East at one time or another, and many are still found here today. For areas 3 and 4 the name of the town or village of origin is printed first. Unfortunately I do not have sufficient information to provide the same breakdown for areas 1 and 2.

1. Surnames from the Lake Como area

Arnoldi, Bernasconi, Bergna, Bianchi, Bregazzi, Falla, Giobi, Grassi, Lazzari, Mastaglio, Molteni, Origoni, Patriarca, Paulucci, Rampoldi, Rizzi, Tacchi, Tarelli, Taroni.

Lake Como: looking towards Menaggio and Cardano, and the Swiss Alps

2. Surnames from the Val Taro and Val Ceno area

Bardetti, Beccarelli, Bernardi, Bertorelli, Bracchi, Carpena, Cavazzi, Corvi, Costella, Gasparini, Fecci, Geraldi, Giacopazzi, Longino, Longinotti, Questa, Reggi, Resteghini, Rossi, Sassi, Seghini, Signorini, Sivori.

(From localities closer to Chiavari, on the Ligurian side of the same mountain range: Giacinto, Rissetto, Viviani, Lertoria.)

Bedonia, Val Taro   *Bardi, Val Ceno*

3. Surnames from the Barga area

BARGA: Arrighi, Bacci, Bernardi, Biagioni, Bonaccorsi, Brucciani, Castelvecchi, Conti, Corrieri, Cosimini, Ferri, Funai, Giuliani, Groppi, Guidi, Lunatici, Mazzolini, Nardini, Piacentini, Pieri, Rigali, Rinaldi, Santi, Serafini, Tognieri, Torre, Turicchi.

CASTELNUOVO: Bimbi, Brunini, Donnini, Fiori, Riani

COREGLIA: Santi

SAN PELLEGRINO: Lonardi

SOMMOCOLONIA: Badiali, Marchetti, Massaglia, Moscardini, Passerotti, Pieroni, Rinaldi, Vincenti

Barga

4. Surnames from the Ciociaria (Cassino) area

ARPINO: Bellezza, Borsumato, Borzamato, Bove, Citrone, Di Luoffo, Di Palma, Dipreta, Dragone, Gabriele, Greco, Ranaldi, Rea, Reale, Rovardi, Stefani, Tomaselli, Villa, Zaira

ALVITO: Jaffrate

ATINA: Caira, Coppola, Di Luca, Di Paolo, Evangelista, Fusco, Jannarelli, Parisella

BELMONTE CASTELLO: Jannetta, Soave, Visocchi

CASALATTICO: Gallone, Rosselli

Picinisco

CASSINO: Battista, Cassanelli, Colella, Dimambro, Fionda, Nardone, Pacitto, Pontone, Risi, Sacco, Someo, Tomassi, Valente, Varlese

CASTELLIRI: Quadrini

CERVARO: Bianco, Ciaraldi (Giraldi), Colletta, Fascia, Margiotta, Pucci, Vettese

MORTALE (MONFORTE): Forte

PICINISCO: Amerigo (D'Americo), Arcari, Briganti, Capaldi, Capocci, Cellini (Selini), Ciarella, Crolla, D'Agostino, Lanni, Mancini, Marcantonio, Pacitti, Pelosi, Perella

SAN BIAGIO SARACINESCO: Cocozza, Coia, Jaconelli

SAN GENNARO: D'Ambrosio

SAN MICHELE: Minchella, Minghella

SAN VITTORE: Paolozzi, Sebastianelli, Vanitelli

SANTOPADRE: Martino, Quaglieri, Scappaticci

SANT'ELIA FIUMERAPIDO: Dimanno, Palombo, Santi

SETTEFRATI: Buzzeo, Colarossi, Fanone, Massarella, Vagnone

SCAPOLI: Franciosi

Valvori

SORA: Antonini, Baldasera, Casinelli, Di Cosimo, Di Passio, Di Stefano, Evangelista, Facchini, Figliolini, Giannandrea, Martino, Palleschi (Paleschi), Panicca (Panicchia), Panico, Porretta, Prenelle, Sperduti

VALLEROTONDA: Todisco

VALVORI: Di Mascio, Di Meo, Fella, Notarianni, Rossi, Verrecchia

VILLA LATINA: Franchi, Marcangelo

Montecassino, looking towards Valvori and San Biagio Saracenesco. (Photo: Michael Jaconelli).

5

THE ICE AGE

Jackie was eighty-one when I visited him more than twenty years ago in his tiny flat near the top of a high rise in Gateshead where we had to converse against the din of traffic on the A167 flyover. A small, vital, soft-spoken man with a boundless enthusiasm for the Italians born of long and close acquaintance, he gave me a vivid sense of the way of life in the epic years when ice cream was the basis of the prosperity of so many of the North East's Italians. While still a boy, simply because he loved following the barrows, he was more or less adopted by the Reale family of Newcastle and he went on to work with them for sixty years – a big foreign family that took him in and gave him a tough but fascinating living,

Jackie Moore, Gateshead, 1991: *'We worked hard all our lives – these modern ones they don't know of it, this modern age it's all been press-buttoned, they've never known the ice age.'*

bringing him up in their ways and moods and even passing on their dialect. At dawn on summer mornings he helped haul home great blocks of ice from Robinson's ice factory on the Quayside, in winter he cut ice with them on Paddy Freeman's Pond, and 'hail, rain, snow or blow' was out there every day pushing a 'J.Riale' ice-cream cart with its big freezer packed with salt and ice. Jackie talked of the personalities and the families, the rivalries and alliances, the hard workers and the hard drinkers, the savers and the gamblers, the big-hearted and the stingy, the plain rough and the plain snobby, all of whom, he insisted, no matter what their later achievements had begun their England adventure as 'poor peasant people living packed together in a couple of rooms'. He spoke also of what big profits were to be made off ice cream 'in them days', with the barrows as much as the parlours, all those pennies and sixpences squirreled away in biscuit tins, and how when everything was over and done what a big welcome awaited them on the annual winter break back in the family home in Arpino, 'when they brought accordions and food from each outlying farm'. With cousin Ester, there were ten children in the family, and you had to listen very closely to guess which of all the girls he was fondest of. But now here is Jackie on his employers, Vincenzo and Rosalinda Reale – Jimmy and Hannah Riley to the Geordies – who when they arrived here could not write their own names and yet together built up one of the most efficient and effective Italian enterprises in town: 'They made a marvellous pair. They never went out, too hardworking. He was such a good man, and she was a lovely woman too. Just think, a family of nine kids *and* work! Up every morning at five to start the machines away, smashing ice by hand, boiling the milk, then putting it through a strainer into the pails and letting them cool for the next day. And giving us all our dinner at half-ten, a good meal, so we'd be away by eleven – never a minute after eleven, and not back till night. And then she'd load up and come out and go ice-creaming.'

A scoop of history

Ask any Italian connected with the trade who invented ice cream and he'll tell you nobody knows but it was definitely an Italian, or if feeling more magnanimous toward the rest of the world that its universal popularity today is down to one Italian: Marco Polo who brought the recipe back from his travels in China.[1] Sadly for Marco and everyone else born too early, at least another three centuries had to pass before the irresistible concoction made its obscure European debut. Summer drinks were cooled with natural ice stored underground in antiquity, and sweetened cordials and aromatic Turkish-style 'sherbets' chilled in the same way were popular in southern Europe from at least Renaissance times. But the actual freezing of flavoured waters and creams had to wait for the

Making ice cream the old way: three generations of the Forte family in their backyard ice cream factory, Washington, about 1920. The freezer, a metal can containing the ice cream mix, sits inside a wooden tub packed with the freezing agent, a mixture of ice and salt. The long paddle or spatula has two functions: to scrape the hard film of mix from the side of the can as it freezes and to keep the mix smooth by whisking in air to prevent ice crystals forming.

discovery, supposedly first made in India, that when ice or snow are melted by adding salt the temperature of the resulting brine remains for long below zero, and consequently a liquid inside a vessel packed round with ice and salt will freeze. This natural phenomenon served most ice cream makers long after the advent of ammonia compressors and electric freezers in the early twentieth century.

GETTING IT TO THE CUSTOMER

(Left) Pietro Rea (see pages 122-23) with his father's handcart, Middlesbrough about 1912.

(Below Left) Atti Bianco with 'Stop Me' cart in 1930s Hartlepool.

(Below Right) It takes two: Frances and Domenic Dragone loading a freezer outside the family's backyard factory in Felling in the 1930s.

(Above) Leonard Risi with tricycle freezer in 1930s Jarrow.

(Left) Lizzie Valente selling from a handcart in Sunderland's East End in the 1930s.

Joe Valente with horse and cart, Sunderland, 1938.

*Liberato Greco with motor-cycle and side-car,
Middlesbrough, 1926.*

*Louis Donnini with the family's purpose-built bullnose Morris
ice-cream van, Easington Colliery, about 1930.*

*Antonio Ranaldi (right) with his children and brother-in-law, and specially adapted van, Shildon in the 1920s.
Antonio, who later moved his business to Redcar and Middlesbrough, was lost in the Arandora Star disaster in
1940.*

Ice cream came late to Britain. King Charles II reportedly relished 'iced creame' prepared by his Italo-French chef, but this continental delicacy long brought to perfection by Sicilian and Neapolitan confectioners was not generally available even to well-to-do Londoners until the opening of Domenico Negri's shop in Berkeley Square in 1769. Its diffusion as a cheap delight for all classes had to wait for Carlo Gatti and his 'penny ice' stands at Hungerford Market near Charing Cross a whole century later.

Gatti was an Italian Swiss who at the height of his success in London in the 1860s and 70s owned a string of confectionery shops and restaurants and a fleet of ships to bring in natural ice from Norway. Apparently Gatti's specially imported assistants would tempt passers-by to taste a sample by calling out, 'Ecco un poco!' – 'Here's a little bit' – and so in time a street-bought ice became 'hokey-pokey' to the English, and its quaint-speaking foreign vendor 'the hokey-pokey man'. Louis Ciaraldi, a Sunderland ice cream man who loved retelling the stories he heard as a boy within the old Italian community, used to give a more phonically plausible explanation. Down London they had no halfpenny ices, he'd say, so there they'd shout, 'O che poco, per un sold'!' Roughly: 'Look how cheap, just a penny!'

The standard penny-ice mix was a frozen flavoured custard made with fresh milk, eggs, sugar, cornflower, and a stick of vanilla. Customers paid very little but since the ingredients were inexpensive and all utensils reusable the profit margin was high. Gatti had started out around 1845 producing and selling it as just one more hopeful migrant hawking snacks in the streets of London. Twenty years later hundreds of Italians were capitalising on his extraordinary success. The Ice Age had begun.

By the turn of the century probably as many as four thousand Italians all over Britain were involved in one way or another in making and selling ice cream. Of course it was never the only occupation of Italians here, in fact the 1901 census found three times as many working in other ways. There were still more than seven hundred organ-grinders, a couple of hundred terrazzo workers in what was another Italian monopoly, and many a road worker or specialist 'asphalter' willing to do hideously hot and filthy work that otherwise none but the Irish would contemplate, plus a very few merchants and manufacturers, priests and professors, rather more professional musicians and singers, artists and artists' models, many more restaurateurs and confectioners, shopkeepers, tailors, hairdressers, bakers, cabinet-makers, boot makers, and over two thousand waiters and domestics.

Consular officials felt obliged to explain to their perplexed masters in Rome why so few laboured in Britain's mighty industries. Vice-consul Rizzetto reported from Newcastle in 1892 that there were none at all in the North East's many shipyards and collieries and factories, citing abundant native manpower and intense trade union hostility to foreign workers as explanations for their absence. In fact it was general practice, certainly in our region, for Italian males to seek casual employment as unskilled labourers, particularly when times were hard, which for the ice man could mean all through the wintry months when demand for his cold comfort diminished. In the rest of the year too, as with farm work back home, earnings from la crema would fluctuate unpredictably according to the weather.

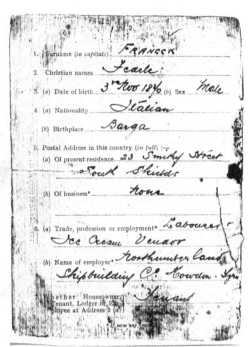

11. PERSONAL DESCRIPTION. *(To be filled in by Police, not by applicant.)*

Height _5_ feet _5½_ inches.

Build _Stout._

Hair, Beard, etc. _D.B. hair. Auburn Mische_

Distinctive Marks _Cut scar left side_
neck. deformed nail left
thumb

Signature of applicant: _Fedele Turicchi_

Left Thumb Print
(if unable to
sign name in
English Characters)

Photograph
(to be affixed by applicant)

---

1. Surname *(in capitals)* _FRANCHI_

2. Christian names _Fedele_

3. (a) Date of birth _3rd Nov 1870_ (b) Sex _Male_

4. (a) Nationality _Italian_

   (b) Birthplace _Barga_

5. Postal Address in this country *(in full)* :—
   (a) Of present residence _23 Smithy Street_
     South Shields

   (b) Of business _none_

6. (a) Trade, profession or employment _Labourer_
   Ice Cream Vendor

   (b) Name of employer _Northumberland_
   Shipbuilding Co. Howdon. Tyne

7. Whether Houseowner,
   Tenant, Lodger or Em-
   ployee at Address 5 (a)
     If none say

'Labourer and ice cream vendor'. Two pages from the Alien's Registration book for Fedele Turicchi, better known as Franchi, issued at South Shields in 1916. Franchi and his wife Emilia Piacentini, both from Barga, seem to have been the earliest ice creamers to settle in South Shields (1898). Every winter 'Frankie' found employment with the Northumberland Shipbuilding Company, and in return for time-off in summer worked throughout the year as knocker-up for his shipyard bosses. The couple's first ventures were a sweet stall in the market all year round and an ice-cream stand on the sands in summer. Their business operations eventually included two big cafe-kiosks on the North and South beaches and several fish and chips outlets in town. Direct descendants run the award-winning Colman's fish restaurant in Ocean Road today.

'Frankie's Golden Beach Dairy' on South Shields sands in the 1920s.

Pietro Rea, from Middlesbrough, at the Italian front circa 1916.

Pietro with his sweetheart Angelina Reale in a photographer's studio after his safe return. Almost every day he served in his Alpine regiment Pietro sent a loving postcard to Angelina at Buckingham Street, Newcastle ('Neccaslle, Bunghengliam Stretto N.110, England') where she had lived since coming from Italy at the age of 13 with her elder sister to help mind their aunt Rosalinda Reale's children (see introduction to this chapter and photo on page 205). The couple married as soon as they were reunited and worked side by side in the ice cream trade in Middlesbrough before moving to Newcastle where they built up a thriving café business in Barrack Road with a fleet of ice cream carts.

Pietro's Buona Pasqua ('Happy Easter') card to Angelina dated March 1917 reports he is no longer at the front but in a military hospital in Cuneo with a bad ear infection, but not to worry because he is 'better off here than where the others are'. Able to write little more than his name, Pietro relied on a comrade to pen this card.

Our climate was not the only threat to the ice men's livelihood. The bewilderingly diverse Sunday trading bylaws (the Sabbath was the ice cream man's best day) were a constant challenge, and not only Protestant bigots but other shopkeepers resented 'Maccaroni' Catholics making money on everyone else's compulsory day of rest. More drastically, the Aliens Act of 1905 put an end to Britain's liberal open-door policy which had always permitted free entry to all in the Italian wandering trades, with or without a passport. This first legislative victory for the growing 'bloody foreigners' lobby reduced to a trickle the flow of more or less penniless migrants entering the country to pick up casual work as organ-grinders or ice cream vendors. Besides satisfying the immigration officer he was not 'a lunatic, idiot or mentally deficient' a new arrival now had to prove he was able to support himself and any dependents, a stipulation which put yet more pressure on Italians already established here to guarantee work for needy relatives and fellow-villagers. The total of Italians in Britain, after more than doubling in the decade 1891-1901, barely increased at all in the years following the 1905 Act.[2]

But the worst of the ice men's troubles were of their own making. The primitive conditions in which so many produced *la crema* became an issue of both official and public concern for fifty years and more after an outbreak of typhoid in the capital in 1879 caused the medical journal *The Lancet* to investigate the Italian quarter. Despite deploring its poor sanitation and gross overcrowding the report found no actual evidence for the rapid spread of disease, in fact even commended the 'abstemious and frugal' habits of the colony, while still concluding the area would 'soon become a standing menace to the public health of London'. Thereafter the least hint of an epidemic would lead to scares about infected ice cream and renewed demands for the flattening of the whole Italian quarter. Things came to a head in 1898 when the death of a London child was again blamed on unclean ice cream, causing the *Daily Telegraph* to describe the by now substantially improved neighbourhood as 'a huge plague factory' infested by 'a horde of unwashed, illiterate, semi-barbarous foreigners, who treat the lives of British children as if they were as valueless as their own.' Following the general outcry, at the start of the new century London became the first authority to introduce controls on the manufacture, storage, and sale of ice cream

In the end the pressure to clean up its act was also healthy for the ice cream trade itself. Though it took many more years[3] for all small producers' premises to have to be licensed and regularly inspected by district health officers, the publicity given to the clean-up process finally made ice cream far more acceptable to adults and the 'better class' of people. And unquestionably its best practitioners prospered, laying the foundations for family businesses which would flourish for sixty years and more.

In 1915-18, for entirely new reasons, there took place an unprecedentedly high incidence of 'return migration': over 8,000 Italian-born men resident in Britain left for Italy to serve their country in the common struggle against Germany and Austria in the Great War. As they gathered round the national flag in their hundreds at stations and ports to join the Allied cause the population warmed to the Italians in their midst.

Italy had prudently kept out of the European conflict until May 1915, but once the die was cast general mobilisation was immediate and residence abroad gave no exemption. As well as incalculable heartache it precipitated financial crisis in self-supporting households that lost their breadwinners to conscription. Call-up notices and medical inspections for males aged 18-39 were managed by the Italian consular service here, while local constabularies obligingly rounded up recalcitrants as 'deserters', a move which was considerably resented since there was as yet no conscription in Britain. In three and a half miserable years of war in horrendous conditions on Italy's mountain frontier with Austria more than half a million Italian lives were lost. No one knows how many of the fallen came from Britain. A memorial in St. Peter's, the Italian church in London's old Italian quarter, lists 175 members of the local community.

Not all served in Italy. Naturalised Britons like Angelo Baldasera (Wheatley Hill), Angelo Rea (Willington) and Attiglio Giacinto (Shildon) served of course in the British forces, yet so intense was the war fever in Britain after August 1914 that a good number of young Italian residents also responded by enlisting for this country. Among the volunteers were Antonio Prenelle (Sunderland), Manlio Panzieri (Bishop Auckland), and Tommaso Sacco (Langley Park). Tommaso apparently died in France, while the other men were transferred to the Italian front after the country of their birth joined the Allied cause. More impressive still is the fact that others like Giuseppe Minchella (Boldon), Domenico Pontone (Horden), Paolo Martino (Middlesbrough), Remigio Battista and 'Jack' Pecconi (Newcastle) despite having the option of fighting for Italy chose to serve out the entire war in the British Army.

World War I put an end to Italian mass migration. Its resumption immediately after the war was soon checked by the US Immigration Restriction Acts of 1920 and 1924 which had already been preceded by the Literary Test introduced in 1917 expressly to curb the huge influx of uneducated southern Italian peasants. Comparable measures in Brazil and Argentina drove prospective emigrants to Canada and Australia for the first time but diverted many more to Europe, and might have produced an increase of Italians in Britain had not entry restrictions been tightened here too. The 1920 Aliens Act, or 'Anti-Aliens Act' for its opponents, was a refinement on the Aliens Restriction Order rushed out in 1914 to control the movements of German 'enemy aliens' in Britain. All resident aliens now had to register with the police, while new entrants were required to exhibit a Ministry of Labour work permit which itself could only be released in cases where no local person had come forward to fill the relevant job. This put considerable strain on the Italians' customary practice of bringing in family members and *paesani* to refresh the labour pool, compelling many to employ native workers for the first time. Two common ways round the law were to bring over relatives while still under working age (14) and to procure marriageable workmates from home for one's offspring, since these categories were still unaffected by the new restrictions.

In 1926, embarrassment at this global opposition to the mass movement of unskilled Italian labour compelled the new fascist regime in Italy to reverse the long-standing policy of state backing for emigration. The special red emigrant passport was scrapped and fresh passports were issued only to skilled workers and professionals who would not risk tainting Italy's image abroad. By this time some 60,000 people had already fled the country as the regime tightened its repression of all opponents it defined as 'anti-fascists'. Around 10,000 of these political fugitives settled in France but only a few score in Britain, where instead Italian fascism found comparatively fertile soil among the established immigrant population (see next chapter).

For most Italians already here the twenty inter-war years were therefore a time of consolidation of hard-won achievements and long-term commitment to a future in a country where they had begun to find a measure of prosperity and social acceptance. Growing numbers naturalised. Despite the long economic depression the statistics imply that the majority of resident Italians still felt their best chance lay with Britain: by 1931 numbers had declined by less than ten percent from a peak of around 24,000 in 1921, and even with growing fears in the later 1930s that Italy and Britain might be on opposite sides in an eventual war there was no mass exodus. Apart from the tightened entry restrictions, the decrease was largely due to first generation pioneers opting to live out their last years back home in Italy.

Even so, times were hard for many an Italian-owned small catering business, and nowhere more than in the North East's shipyard towns and colliery villages. Not all managed to weather the long lean years of mass unemployment. Some shut up shop and went off to work with relatives or *paesani* in less improvident areas of the country, while a few threw in the towel altogether and returned to Italy where it is probable they fared little better. Patriotic fund-raising events and a special charity to assist indigent members of the community were organised by Nestore Tognoli, the energetic vice-consul in Newcastle during all the years running up to the war. *L'Italia nostra*, the Italian-language weekly and official voice of the Italian fascist party in Britain, sometimes gave space to his efforts. In the grim winter of 1928 'providential woollen garments' were presented to the most needy children at the Christmas Tree *festa*; the following year the consul's welfare fund netted £49 7s 3d at the annual November banquet; and after the 1932 Fascist Twelfth Night party kids from the poorest families were sent home not just with the usual bags of sweets and fruit but 'good thick socks'. 'Italians must help Italians', proclaimed the paper, reinforcing its message of communal solidarity both social and political.

While life was indeed tough for the typical small family-run Italian confectioners and cafés reliant on a small but steady turnover in the hard-hit pit villages, there was still a lot of money to be made out of ice cream by larger operators in town who could reach a potentially vast population and could hire and fire according to demand. As with mass enthusiasm for the movies (ice cream sold exceptionally well in cinemas), there appears to have been a close correlation between sweet needs and dark times. In 1935, barely emerging from the worst of the Depression, the secretary of the Ice Cream Federation, Achille Pompa, was able to congratulate his fellow traders: 'ice cream now sells to the tune of something like 60,000,000 gallons per annum, instead of only 20 or 25 millions a few years ago.'

The Ice Cream Federation or *Associazione dei gelatieri* had been founded in the Mazzini Garibaldi Club in London in early 1918 not out of some sudden surge of optimism at the prospect of hundreds of young ice men returning from the trenches to swell the depleted ranks, but because in the last days of 1917 to protect sugar and milk reserves the government had delivered a bombshell in the shape of a total ban on the manufacture and sale of *la crema*, leaving men too old or unfit for call-up suddenly compelled to combine forces to fight for their own survival. 'Frostine' was the ersatz secret weapon some canny old-timers in the Federation came up with, a flavoured flour and water ice so cheap and easy to make that its immediate mass production dwarfed all previous records for sales of the real thing. Within months Ice Cream Federation branches, with 90% Italian membership, had sprung up everywhere. The Northumberland and Durham branch (president: Cecil Di Duca of Darlington, secretary: Vittorio Banfi of Gateshead) was immediately several hundred strong, and when the hated ban was lifted within only months of the end of the larger war the committee successfully negotiated mutually advantageous discounts with local suppliers of sugar and milk and cream. 'Final victory', *la vittoria finale*, was celebrated by the entire ice cream army in December 1919 when the legal hour for evening sales was raised from 8 pm to 10 pm, excluding Sundays, a breakthrough it attributed entirely to its own bold campaigning. Risi's of Newcastle, claiming to be first in the north to produce water ices in the war, certainly found plenty to cheer about.

> *Ever ready, always fresh,*
> *Soothing, pleasing, proved the best,*
> *Stood the strain of war's restrictions,*
> *Satisfied all jurisdiction,*
> *Brought relief in many a crisis,*
> *Sold all over – RISI'S ICES!*

But was such jubilation overhasty? At this very time territory which up to now had been almost exclusively Italian was being invaded by troops of demobbed *inglesi* who had noticed the easy profits to be made, and even more threateningly big guns were massing in the form of national food companies equipped with vast capital and the latest machinery and slick promotional ideas and novelties from America where ice cream was booming as never before. The big three were Walls, Lyons, and Eldorado. The Italians were well used to treacherous rivalry between each other, but now ageing barrow-men on time-honoured pitches and old-style *padroni* who paid their *garzoni* 25 shillings a month for a 16-hour day were having to contend with legions of 'Stop Me And Buy One' trikes pedalled by desperate-for-work natives paid as much as 3s 6d a day, plus 2s in the pound commission on sales. 'More than

'Proved the best': Risi's Quayside stall in the 1920s.

127

thirty Jewish firms', *L'Italia nostra* noted with vague but snide alarm in November 1924, were aleady gearing up to wheel out next season even more battalions of these accursed new tricycles which 'specialise in parking in front of our shops and right beside our barrows.' All Italians, it proclaimed, must forthwith overcome the age-old vice of loathing one another's guts unless from the same region, not to say parish, and once more band together as they had shown they could 'in Manchester, Newcastle, Cardiff, and London' during the great crisis precipitated by the 1917 ban, if ever there was to be hope again of winning a crust for their families...

But these fresh challenges, like the health scares, probably did the Italians more good than harm in the long run. Many settled for an inferior product (most commonly by watering down the milk), but others tightened up their act and tried to reassert their unique expertise (those much-vaunted 'secret recipes') while still investing in time-saving new-fangled gadgets and attractions like iceless freezers, homogenisers, viscolizers, choc bar machines, and fancy American soda fountains. And in time to their rescue even rode the dreaded health inspectors with their obsessive bacteria counts and norms for a minimum of milk fat but also with very promising signs of finally listening to the ice cream lobby's 'scientific' evidence that their product should be officially recognised, as in America, as not just a treat for kids but a supremely healthy *food* for all. Although this view was doomed never to win official endorsement its forceful promotion between the wars helped to make ice cream an all-year-round desirable and hasten its adoption as probably Britain's favourite dessert. 'It *appeals* to the human stomach,' insisted Achille Pompa in 1934, in one of his many vigorous claims for the product's dietary virtues, 'and is therefore more easily digested and assimilated. It is an ideal food from the point of view of a perfectly clean and healthy alimentary canal. It tones up the system towards perfect health, feeds the bones, teeth, hair, skin, etc., makes one feel well and happy instead of sluggish and despondent, and keeps the complexion in a healthy colour.' And he was able to round off his celebration of this virtual panacea by citing an extraordinary reversal of the oldest prejudice of all: 'American doctors have, for many years, prescribed ice cream (and nothing else but ice cream) for typhoid patients for the first five or six days of their illness...'

Like organ-grinding, the humiliations of the old hokey-pokey days were receding into the past. Only 97 hurdy-gurdy players were recorded in the whole country in 1931, while who could count the numbers of their well-dressed compatriots, not to say former colleagues, who were now respectable traders and shopkeepers with immaculate premises in the best working-class districts in town, and even right on the High Street?

In very little time the Ice Cream Federation had swelled into the Ice Cream and Temperance Refreshment Traders Federation of Great Britain and Northern Ireland, and had even spawned a rival, the Ice Cream Association. Its motto 'Cleanliness, Quality, Progress' speaks not only of determination to raise standards within a trade that had for long been looked upon as dodgy, even toxic, it proclaims the improved status and well-being of the Italians themselves within the population at large. So many illustrations in this chapter testify to this sense of significant achievement, a hard-won transformation in their fortunes.

B. COIA

(Successor to M. COIA)   ESTABLISHED 1887.

INSIST ON EATING

OUR ICES

You are then sure of value for your money,

Not Quantity but Quality

SAEFTY FIRST

The Ices which have once again scored a huge success.
GOLD MEDAL AND DIPLOMA AWARDED.
CENTENARY EXHIBITION ROME JUNE 1925.

Volume for Volume

COIA'S ICE CREAM

Is far more valuable food than meat, fish or Vegetables.
Children who eat a lot of Ice Cream are invarialy fat and
strong. The fact that our Ice Cream is made from Milk,
which is boiled before being frozen and Cream, Sugar and
Eggs' makes it not only Hygienic Food but a very
powerful body builder.

Our ICES are GUARANTEED PURE and
Manufactured in a hygienic factory under
EXPERT SUPERVISION.

NOTE ADDRESS—

5 Cheapside & 4 Weardale Chambers

Spennymoor.

Wholesale and Retail Confectioner and Tobacconist.

Advert for Coia's ice cream, Spennymoor, about 1930. Biagio ('Jimmy') Coia was the energetic secretary of the Durham and Northumberland Ice Cream Federation. His father Massimino, from the remote southern Apennine village of San Biagio Saracinesco, had roamed as a young itinerant musician through Greece, Turkey, Montenegro and Austria before settling in Paisley, Scotland. He moved his family to Spennymoor in 1904. See also page 294.

The street traders

Achille Pompa, the ice cream trade's genial memoirist and lifelong champion of the 'small maker', used to love to recall lying in bed as a boy in the early morning 'inhaling the aroma of vanilla and eggs then in process of boiling: even now I can conjure in my imagination that delicious odour, and with it many of the pleasures of childhood'. Born into the business, he had vivid recollections of London's old Italian quarter 'when as many as 900 barrows were housed every night in yards, passages, alleys and even front rooms, and where pandemonium reigned every summer for at least 20 hours per day.' In his later years he wrote many articles for the *Ice Cream Industry* recalling former times and marvelling at the changes he had lived through: from ice cream laboriously prepared by hand in back-kitchens and backyards to immaculate bacteria-free purpose-built 'factories' where everything was mechanised; from horse-and-cart hawking to fully equipped motorised vans; from makeshift front-room shops to luxurious ice cream parlours and 'saloons' replete with abundant uniformed staff, and with always an emphasis on improved hygiene,

Saverio ('Sammy') Risi, Newcastle, about 1910. For Sammy's career see page 158.

presentation, efficiency, machinery. Though ever careful to insist there had been no lack of 'good, honest and religious families who treated all their workmen as members of the family, giving them the best of everything,' he also loved to relay many a wry tale of the meanness and greed of the bullying *padroni* of old, 'the scanty wages (when paid!) and the ill-treatment accorded to the poor, illiterate and ignorant *garzoni*'.

For of course the making and hawking of ice cream was simply a continuation of the same padrone system which had controlled the street music trade, and out of which it grew. The average 'ice cream jack' or 'Tony', the hokey-men and youths in charge of the barrows, continued for a long time to be for the most part assistants engaged from Italy and provided with board and lodging, clothing and laundering, and a meagre wage of no more than £12 to £16 a year. New protégés had to work off whatever the *padrone* had advanced for their travel expenses from Italy, and of course had to hand back immediately the five pound note they were customarily loaned to produce on disembarkation to prove they were not the undesirable alien paupers it was the immigration officer's job to reject.

Unlike the music business, ice cream had the great drawback of being essentially a seasonal trade, although it is interesting to find Pompa maintaining that 'before the Boer war' it sold well in winter as well as summer, at least on Saturdays and Sundays, and oddly enough in the north of England in particular. 'Even in the winter there was a bit money with the ice cream on a Sunday', confirmed Jackie Moore about later times, though I'm also told it was a Reale family saying that you never sold much ice cream until Newcastle's Race Week in June. If not sent back to Italy, the principal winter work of the *garzoni* ('garzons' in Anglo-Italian jargon) was to resume organ grinding or go out selling roast chestnuts on their customary ice-cream pitches at street corners and outside pubs, picture houses and sports grounds, sometimes switching to hot potatoes right up to closing time for the pubs. Street sales of baked potatoes go back to at least the eighteenth century, but the roast chestnut alternative was more an Italian speciality since so many who emigrated to Britain had grown up among Apennine forests where chestnuts were a vital food resource. Some turned to importing the raw material for the trade.

When the cold set in the most affluent employers would take a long break back in Italy, using the time to engage fresh workers to replace those who had quit, and finally (once the days of legging it were over) making the three-day journey back by train with their recruits around Easter in good time to prepare for the next season. An extra reason for returning home was that a lot of the old timers were plagued with rheumatism, an occupational hazard for people who worked outdoors in all weathers and habitually handled ice and salt. 'The Italian sunshine, and occasionally treatment at one of the many spas,' claimed Pompa, 'did wonders to the sufferers.'

Street-vending operators who could not afford the return rail ticket (at least £50 from the North East for the average family in the 1920s) might pay off their two or three assistants at the end of the season and seek alternative employment labouring in an Italian terrazzo company. Docks and shipyards and foundries presented other job options, providing employers were prepared to risk union wrath by taking on a foreigner. In the tough winter of 1926-7 Antonio Prenelle, a Sunderland confectioner, signed on as stoker on Italian steamships trading between the North East and Genoa and Venice. Underground work, so plentiful in the region, held scant attraction. Raffaele Bove worked at a Spennymoor pit before opening a temperance bar in the colliery village of South Moor, but then he and his father (who lost his life in the process) had already worked as miners in the United States. When I asked Louis Ciaraldi whether his formidable memory retained details of Italians working in the pits in the difficult interwar years he could only come up with one instance: a Venditelli from Blyth. In 1924 *L'Italia nostra* reported an unspecified number of Italian miners working at Easington, but they had been recruited by the owner direct from Italy, and about them I have discovered no more than this bare fact. The earlier case of lead miners at Nenthead, similarly recruited, is more fully documented (see over).

With time, an ambitious 'garzon' who had endured the tough regime of long hours and poor pay would grow older and considerably wiser and would start laying plans to use his earnings (and whatever else he had been able to secrete from his master's eagle eye) to somehow set up on his own. An eligible bachelor now, with some savings and much valuable experience, he would as a rule marry within the British Italian community or use his own family connections to secure a wife from home who was known not to be workshy. And so ice-creaming would pass to another generation as even more of a family operation, with all members working at making and vending: the wife and even the youngest children, and in time *their* sons and daughters and spouses too. The old authoritarian padrone system might be on the wane but the mentality it fostered had scarcely altered. The *padroni* were the patriarchal fathers now, running the family as a business operation, strict with their offspring and reliant on dedicated hard-working wives committed to raising a large brood who from a very early age had to learn to pull their weight in the family concern. The peasant survival ethos prevailed undimmed: self-reliance, hard work, frugality. A fiercely self-sufficient family like the Reales of Newcastle built and painted its own carts, shoed its own horses, made its own wafers and cornets, and set the children working long before they left school.

ITALIAN MINERS AT NENTHEAD

Italians are among this group of miners at Nenthead photographed about 1900. (Photo: Nenthead Mines Hertitage Centre)

This 'Italian hut door' carved with residents' names and initials is displayed at the Centre. 'A.Reich' was likely one of a number of young men recruited from the Trento region on the Austrian border. Pietro Rolando, whose last name figures so prominently, died of exposure on the Carrshield road one freezing night in March 1907, aged 53. A comrade, Basilio Corsi, lost his life in an accident at the mine the following year, aged only seventeen.

The many miles of old mine workings at Nenthead have recently been opened up to visitors and explorers. In 1896 the Vieille Montagne Zinc Company of Belgium, which also owned mines in Sicily and Sardinia, acquired the lease from the Nenthead and Tyneside Lead and Zinc Company. Over the next twenty years, some 300 Italians and lesser numbers of other 'alien competitors' (*Hexham Herald*) toiled alongside the local workforce. The foreign workers' huts or 'barracks' were at Nenthead and Carrshield. One newly arrived batch of 13 Italians in 1904 was hailed by the same local paper as a 'robust, active, athletic class of men, similar to the men in agricultural districts of Northumberland'. Even so, 'a strong undercurrent of bitter feeling by the English against the Italian element' (*Hexham Courant*) was a constant feature, particularly when the element rose to as many as sixty. On Christmas Day 1903, and again in October 1905, fighting broke out between local men and the Italians, the latter incident leading to charges of 'riotous assembly' against the Italians. Seven landed in Carlisle jail. Though their numbers dipped thereafter, Italians continued to be employed until June 1915 when the *Courant* reported the last fifteen had departed 'in quite a happy mood' to soldier in Italy, having marched to Alston station 'singing what appeared to be one of their national songs'.

A week of hard frost, even a good snowfall, was a way of saving on ice, as Giulio Zair of Bishop Auckland once explained to me. 'Coraggioso' in *Wandering Minstrel* (see pages 95-97) relates how he and his cousin and other ice cream men in West Hartlepool combined to turn a large cellar in their back yard into an ice house. 'It was the custom in the winter-time, when all the surrounding small lakes were frozen, for us all to get together, hire a couple of horses and lorries, and, armed with picks and shovels and hammers, go to the lakes. First of all we broke the ice, then loaded the lorries, and in a few weeks' time that enormous cellar was packed with ice and covered with sawdust. Before long it became one solid block and kept us all going during the summer-time.' I'm told some Middlesbrough and Newcastle ice creaming families would take their horses and carts as far away as the Lake District to stock up on great quantities of free ice.

Another winter task was the making and storing of that other essential of the trade, the wafer. Its use only became widespread in the wake of the official onslaught on unhygienic practices which had so tarnished the reputation of the trade around the turn of the century, and in particular damaged street sales. Until then ice cream was scooped from the tub with a wooden spoon and dished out onto white paper, even newspaper, or into small conical 'penny-lick' glasses which were rinsed in the same water and used again and again. Zeller wafers, reports Pompa, were the first ice biscuit, tubular in shape, to be followed by the more convenient and ever-popular cone or 'twist' which after all is just a glass in edible form.

Some Italian biscuit makers became outstandingly successful, employing scores of travellers to promote and deliver their wares up and down the country: wafers, cones, cups, 'boats' and other fancifully shaped biscuits. The myriad ice cream carts on Britain's streets made perfect publicity floats for big firms like Zaccardelli & Cervi, Valvona, Antonelli, Askey (actually Tedeschi, but that was hardly suitable in times of acute Germanophobia), who all freely supplied big colourful tins to preserve their wares in all weathers. Intense competition between them brought prices down so much it was scarcely worth making one's own, though even as late as 1935 Pompa still claimed to know of some thirty manufacturers of wafers and cones, most of them unknown outside their own town or district, where 'a small room or two would be fitted up with benches, gas-rings, moulds or "tongs", and husband, wife, children and all and sundry would spend most of their time in the winter months making up stocks for the summer demand.' From such humble beginnings the Jaconelli family of Newcastle, Mark Rea ('Reay') of Benwell, and Petrozzi in South Shields built up strong wholesale businesses between the wars, as did the three Greco brothers in Middlesbrough whose descendants run the only North-East Italian biscuit firm still going today. Another significant employer was Percy Brown's Variety Wafer Biscuit Company in Chester-le-Street. Though not Italian, Brown was a friend and champion of his many Italian customers, a role he fulfilled admirably in the hard years for Italians during World War II.

As always, ice cream's best customers were children, and apart from touring all the back alleys after school hours and at weekends the best pitch was of course right at the school gates, despite the risk of a fine for causing an obstruction. Kids didn't get much pocket money in those days but a couple of coppers could buy a lot of ice cream. No doubt few lashed out on Joe Dimambro's threepenny 'fancy', but an ice cream sandwich from his roving cart round Sacriston and Stanley in the 1920s was only a penny or tuppence depending on size, and a cornet just a halfpenny. 'It took a lot of pennies to make two-three pound in a day', Jackie

Moore recalled, 'in fact if you made £3 you'd done well. There were no cartons or nowt like that in them days. Everybody brought their own cups for a pennyworth, two-pennyworth in each cup.' Some readers might need reminding that to accumulate three pounds you'd need to take no less than 720 pennies.

The barrow lads and the vendors working with horse-drawn carts generally announced their arrival by blowing a whistle, even a bugle, and of course by honking the horn when some began to get mechanised. Just as with street music in earlier days, and indeed when van chimes were first introduced in the 1960s, in the posher residential areas objections were plentiful to this old-time cacophony of whistles and horns and even snatches of Italian opera, or just a great human wail of 'Iceeeee!' Persistent offenders landed in court, particularly for disturbing the peace on the Sabbath, on occasions right outside a church. In 1932, for instance, Pietro Someo of Sunderland was fined 10 shillings for tooting his trumpet on the Lord's Day. That same summer an exasperated Billingham District Council declared it wanted nothing less than 'a war' waged on offenders.

Naturally street trading was also plagued with considerable hygiene problems, most dauntingly in the shape of the local Medical Officer for Health. A strong advocate of the 'more hygienic system of ice cream bricks' was the MOH for Sunderland, Dr A.S. Hebblethwaite, a persistent hounder of small manufacturers and traders with unclean premises, not to mention street salesmen still guilty of 'the more objectionable methods of the sandwich and of retailing ice cream in the open'.

When for these same reasons right at the start of the 1933 season Newcastle's MOH threatened to shut down Risi's and Mark Toney's very profitable stalls in the Bigg Market, the two bitter rivals hastily joined forces and even won their case by pleading philanthropic motives reminiscent of the London magistrates' old argument in favour of street music for the masses: 'that they serve large quantities of pure and in every way satisfactory ice cream to the crowds which frequent the market, working class people who cannot afford the higher prices charged

Making wafers the old way: Greco's factory in Middlesbrough. By the 1930s the firm was advertising as 'the biggest biscuit manufacturer in the North of England'.

in better class shops and restaurants'. Other common brushes with the law for 'outside traders' arose from the obligation for those without a licensed pitch to keep moving and not cause an obstruction (hence 'Stop Me And Buy One'), and also contravention of the Sunday trading restrictions which could frequently change even within the same council according to which faction predominated, the church-minded or the secular. In Blyth, where all caterers were permitted to work seven days a week, the parish council resorted to the old argument that ice cream is not a food in order to halt the proliferation of ice cream stands on Sundays. When Middlesbrough banned Sunday street sales outright the ice cream lads were forced out to South Bank and beyond in the hope of eluding a fine.

Traders with horse and cart, or even just with hand barrows, roamed far and wide for custom. Joe Rea of Newcastle, the youngest son of Pietro and Angelina pictured on page 122, remembered as a boy of ten pushing his handcart from the family base near Leazes Park right across town to a pitch near Scotswood bridge to pick up custom outside the Armstrong works; only two years later he was already touring his parents' horse and cart round all the pit villages immediately to the north: Wylam, Wideopen, Dudley, Seghill. Camillo Rea's horses and carts in Middlesbrough made regular circuits as far as Stokesley, Ayton and Guisborough. Those with horse power, and of course motor power even more, often clashed with humbler vendors on two legs who couldn't be everywhere at once. The new motorised vans could cover most 'fair grounds, race courses, farm sales, gymkhanas, dog tracks and fêtes', enthused *The Ice Cream Industry*. Big local days out like the Yorkshire show, the Durham Miners' Gala, and the Northumberland Picnic were chances to amass many sovereigns with *la crema*.

The barrow lads, particularly if they had little English, could get a hard time from some elements of the public. No one dared mess with old 'Santopadre' Quaglieri of Newcastle, Jackie Moore told me, because it was known he kept 'a big long knife' in his barrow. The Tomassi and Dimambro children of Durham however were brought up on tales of the bother their parents and grandparents had to face. The men of the family and their many assistants (the Dimambros had 15 *servi* at the time of the 1911 census) would push piano organs and ice cream carts four or five miles out to the surrounding pit villages, and coming back at night could encounter strong opposition on the edge of town. On one occasion, 'when the women of the family heard the men had been held back again at the top of North Road from coming into Durham they grabbed anything they could, shovels and spades to do battle, and that's how they got them through.' Louis Ciaraldi had a fund of such stories in which his father invariably figured as saviour. The lads, he said, who on the morning had walked their barrows out from their Sunderland East End bases as far as Murton, Easington, and even Seaham, would congregate at dusk at the Toll Bar waiting for Big Louis who was all of six-foot-seven to show up with his own cart and escort them home. 'Because,' explained his son, 'even the biggest of them was only about five-foot-six, and in Grangetown they were often waylaid and robbed of the takings and had all sorts thrown into their tubs, or had their barrows tipped over'.

No matter how troublesome the aggro or the weather, road sales were the mainstay of every ice cream enterprise, large or small. But right from earliest times some had seen the benefits of opening up a 'shop' to extend the scope for business. Despite the overheads, a café or confectioner's offered the steadier returns and greater security of an all-year-round trade – indeed, as we shall see, most Italian-owned premises were open for custom every day of the year, every hour of the day, and well into the night.

Family members gathered outside Pasquale Ciarella's shop on Prospect Row, Sunderland, about 1920. Most Italian businesses, as is evident here, combined shop-keeping with street trading in homemade ice cream.

The Gaiety Temperance Bar in Houghton-le-Spring. Colombo Riani (see page 216) moved his family and business the few miles from Newbottle village to the centre of Houghton when this prime location opposite the Gaiety Theatre came up. 'It was a great time, all the actors used to come into the café ,' recalled his son Furio when the premises closed in 1986.

Luigi Maggiore at the door of his Ryhope shop, with behind him 'Jock' Tricchi who took over when the family moved to Sunderland. Luigi's name lives on in the popular 'Louis Cafe' in Park Lane, the last surviving old Italian business in Sunderland.

Carlo Arrighi in about 1930 outside his Crescent Cafe, Seaton Deleval, another rare survivor now into the fourth generation. 'I tend to find interest in display, a good shop window well displayed, and all the interior spotless, scintillating, bags of light, everything neatly arranged, good prices, easy access, all those sorts of things' (Aris Baldasera, Wheatley Hill).

Interior of Rossi's 'Central Café', Consett, installed in the 1930s and now re-erected at Beamish Open Air Museum. (Photo: Beamish Museum)

Luisa Bove and son Domenic outside their South Moor temperance bar in the late 1930s.

The 'shops'

Progressing from the customary combination of back-kitchen 'factory' and street sales, all over the North East more and more family ice cream concerns started fitting out their front rooms as rudimentary shops selling sweets and soft drinks, and sometimes also fruit and vegetables, or took the bigger step of setting up as tobacconists and confectioners in regular premises which in time might be adapted into 'sitting-down shops' dispensing hot and cold drinks and sandwiches as well as homemade ice cream. If things went well, and with a lot more hard work, the family could be on its way to opening a grander 'parlour' elsewhere in town patronised by the kind of customers who would not be seen eating ice cream on the street.

Back in Italy, these peasant families had seen shopkeepers and café proprietors as well as artisans and even some itinerant vendors managing to get by all year without needing to dig the stubborn earth or tend dumb sheep. Here in England ice cream production with street sales run from a shop-cum-café combined all four more agreeable ways of making a living, and turned out to be a winning formula. Almost everyone in the surrounding streets and lanes could afford some little luxury on offer. Once again, as with street entertainment and street music, the Italians had contrived to carve out a small economic niche for themselves within the wider society.

The phenomenon was general all over Britain. By 1930 some 700 London cafés and restaurants were in the hands of Italians, a considerable achievement which even so was dwarfed by the situation in Scotland where *L'Italia nostra* in that same year found 90% of the mere 6,500 resident Italians were working in catering, and of these precisely 1,774 were proprietors of ice cream or fish and chip shops. A chippie offered a nourishing hot dinner on the cheap, but no one has yet quite explained why northerners took so wholeheartedly to frozen custard. The 'Tallies' with their chippies and ice cream parlours, concentrated in Edinburgh and above all on Clydeside, spread all over Scotland in the space of a generation, right to the Outer Hebrides. At the same time the Irish experienced a similar 'Roman' conquest.

As for our own northerly region, we saw in the last chapter how following its introduction by a few pioneers from central Italy the bulk of the *crema* trade passed into the hands of ever-growing numbers of immigrants from Ciociaria, some of whom had already opened 'shops' by the 1890s. As elsewhere they multiplied fast. The quantity and spread of these hard-working small family businesses is documented in the Appendix. By their peak in the 1920s and 30s there must have been some three hundred within our region. No fair-sized pit village was without at least one. Wingate in County Durham had three, Stanley had six, Ashington in Northumbria boasted at least a dozen.

Some of our region's best-known names in ice cream – Rossi, Jaconelli, Notarianni, Fella, Gallone, Coia – gained experience of street music and then ice-creaming and shop-keeping first of all in Scotland. When saturation there drove these and other families to move south of the border they tended not to head for the cities where competition was as fierce as anything they had left behind but settled instead for smaller centres and colliery towns: Consett, Bishop Auckland, Houghton-le-Spring, Spennymoor, Wingate. The bearers of each of these six family surnames and the relatives and assistants they brought with them hailed exclusively from Valvori and San Biagio Saracinesco, two small hamlets linked by muletrack high in the hills above Cassino.[4]

Choosing a good location for your shop was crucial for business, just as it was for where you leased an ice cream stand or parked your barrow: front streets in the villages; high streets, market places, and principal intersections in the towns; best of all a busy shopping district close to at least one of the many cinemas, theatres, dance halls and music halls then to be found all over. The small Durham pit village of Wheatley Hill, in uncontested Baldasera territory, had two cinemas and a dance hall until the 1950s, while the venerable town of Stockton which has not one cinema today possessed six picture palaces as well as the Empire Theatre next to which snuggled Rossi's celebrated ice cream parlour, itself destined for oblivion when 1960s 'development' flattened every building on that side of the street.

In bygone times when no pub was considered wholly respectable the Italian parlours, cafés, and 'temperance bars' were hugely popular places for meeting up and socialising. Joe Dragone spoke fondly and proudly of how the family café in Felling Square 'became a legend': 'We had the Corona picture hall right across and the other called the Palais, so we had people coming in for teas or coffees or ice cream, and then off they used to go to the pictures. The second house pictures started about half past eight, quarter to nine, so then we used to get the rush of the people moving in for the second house films and the other cinemas coming out. So the young people from Felling were there most nights; they met their girls, they got married, and these memories have always been with the Felling people, how they met their wives in Dragone's coffee shop'.

As well as ice cream Dragone's made its own cordials and sodas. Along with the sundaes and cones and sliders and '99's all the Italian cafés and temperance bars sold not just teas and coffees but hot drinks like Bovril and Oxo and Horlicks, and beverages long forgotten such as Vitamin Nog, Milk Possett, Savon Whey, Rumto, Vimto, Hot Tom. 'The profit wasn't in it like now, so you worked all hours', explained Domenic Bove of South Moor whose temperance bar started by his father and mother in the 1920s only closed a couple of years ago under his sons' management, the very last cafe of Italian origin in all County Durham's many former colliery villages. 'We had our temperance licence from Durham to serve non-alcoholic drinks and to keep open certain times. People used to come in and get a coffee, an Oxo, a sandwich, and sit and joke and that. It was a social meeting place. We had two cinemas here, with two separate houses, so it was always busy at night. We did well with the cricketers too, and when people came out of the pub, and after church on Sunday. The colliery offices at South Moor paid wages out for all the pits in the area, so on a Friday night it was just the same as Newcastle. It used to be a pleasure in them days to be in business. The people were more sociable, you had the stuff to give them, they weren't as grumpy, they respected you more. Everyone would go in for the raffles, for the money or cigarettes or a box of sweets, and take it home for the family. It was nothing like it is now, it was different then, it was homemade fun. At Easter time Father used to boil and colour the eggs for jarping and they used to stand outside the shop till 2 in the morning – outside the shop used to be all eggshells! Now it's Bingo took over, there's no picture houses, and TV keeps people at home.'

The canny 'temperance bar' designation was adopted by this Catholic ethnic minority predominantly in Kirk-dominated Scotland and in non-conformist Wales and the North East, territories in which the Temperance and Sabbatarian movements commanded huge support in the very years the Italian 'shops' began proliferating. Besides emphasising that drinks at the 'bar' were safely non-alcoholic the appellation promised blamelessly respectable public premises suitable for both genders and all ages, harmless haunts even on a Sunday. Tactically it was a shrewd move in an alien culture where a large and very vocal section of the population was opposed not only to the demon drink but to *any* trading on the Lord's Day, though it did risk sounding especially smug in Wales and Scotland where the main competition, the pubs, could not even open on the Sabbath. In the North East local sensibilities tended to be respected in this way most of all in the smaller towns and villages where the Wesleyan chapel next door or the Congregationalist church up the road were formidable social forces to be reckoned with. So we find Riani's 'Gaiety Temperance Bar' in Houghton-le-Spring doing good business right opposite the Gaiety Theatre, Rossi's 'Temperance Bar' in Bishop Auckland chastely installed inside the former Waterloo public house, and – absolutely no contradiction in terms – Mazzolini's 'Miners' Temperance Bar' on the main street of the bustling pit village of Ashington. That the appellation could sometimes be 'rather ironic' was fully recognised by Bernard Moscardini in his recently published family memoir, *La vacanza,* 'bearing in mind that my father was a copious drinker and he frequently returned home quite inebriated after a night out in one of the local public houses'. Their particular teetotal 'bar' was at Bedlington Station in Northumberland.

Apart from the classiest chocolate boxes nothing on offer cost more than a few pennies. The typical Italian caff in the North East was a mixture between a snack bar, a sweet shop, and a tobacconist's, always with a big window or two out front stacked with enticing specimens of the temptations on offer inside. The Bove shop window was redressed every week. 'The main firms – Cadbury's, Fry's, Terry's – used to send dressers out: different coloured crepe papers in fancy patterns and that, fancy chocolates in the centre, all in boxes, jars, or baskets, showing it out.' To local Hansels and Gretels the interior was even more bewitching: 'We sold orchid creams, Brazil nuts, roasted almond nuts, all the exotic chocolates in these nice fancy jars behind the counter, with a glass mirror behind the jars. Christmas boxes were terrific then, and Easter eggs'.

As for the seating, even the very smallest premises were generally fitted out with two or three wooden panelled cubicles with cut glass mirrors and marble-topped tables. In the grandest seaside parlours where ice cream was served by platoons of waitresses in sanitary white and consumed with a tiny spoon out of a polished metal dish presented on a saucer, cane furniture was favoured, with tables set far apart as in a superior hotel dining-room.

Starting-up costs in the inter-war years when few in work were earning more than thirty shillings a week could be considerable, ranging from £65 for the purchase of a small street-trading business from a fellow Italian in Seaham Harbour (paid off in five-shilling weekly instalments) to £375 for a soda fountain bar complete with all its elaborate fittings and serving utensils. A fully up-to-date ice cream plant could set you back £300. Hire purchase rates were offered by firms supplying such things, along with regular maintenance visits.

Nearly all proprietors with a shop to keep also ran street sales, using younger family members or Italian assistants to get the wares out, or at last taking on English lads when there were not enough hands available. In a very small concern like the Bove's the husband went out with the horse and cart leaving his wife to mind the shop after she too had risen early to help prepare the day's ice cream supply. When September came round road sales would fall and most such self-employed men would not go out ice-creaming again till Easter, which meant leaner months ahead.

To attract and retain custom Italian shops especially in smaller centres would put a snooker table or two in a corner or in the back room. Some, like Moscardini's in Bedlington Station, built on substantial billiard halls. Even in the midst of the Depression, writes Bernard

Moscardini, 'business boomed right from the start. A game of billiards or snooker or pool cost only a penny and this was just the perfect form of entertainment for men who could afford little else. In the billiard hall there was also a kiosk which sold soft drinks (by the glass), ice cream, sweets and tobacco products. By law, the billiard hall could not open on Sundays, which was ideal because Sunday was the busiest day of the week for the temperance bar'. The most ambitious Italian billiards enterprise between the wars was the partnership developed by Carmine Rossi of Consett and Biagio Coia of Spennymoor who between them opened saloons in Thornaby, Bishop Auckland, Ferryhill, Chester-le-Street, Annfield Plain, and Ashington, as well as on their own patches. Here you could buy a cup of tea and play all day.

Since the takings were small the hours were long. The Bove shop would open at five in the morning to catch the first shift of pitmen on the way to work 'wanting a packet of Woodbines' and wouldn't shut again until after midnight long after the pubs had closed and the last cinema had emptied. Larger businesses in town could afford the luxury of shutting their doors before the pubs closed and so avoid the worst trouble, yet that was when you got some of your best trade. 'The likes of us depended on that night-time money', confirmed Jackie Moore. Everyone I have spoken to has vivid anecdotes of occasional violence, but all learned to deal with it without summoning the law.

The proprietors sometimes fell foul of the law themselves, most often for selling ice cream and tobacco after hours, but also for overworking assistants. In November 1931, Camillo Rea of Middlesbrough was fined 40 shillings for working a girl an average of 85 hours a week and with no statutory half-holiday. She was on duty from 10.30 in the morning to 11.30 at night, she stated, and had all meals in the shop. In 1935, a year after the Shops Act set 52 hours as the weekly maximum, Margaret Risi of Newcastle was fined for working a 15-year-old girl from 10 a.m. to 9 p.m. six days a week. 'It was a short season,' explained Tony Tomassi. 'They just had to work all the time, but nobody thought there was anything wrong with this, because it was matched by the proprietor and his family.'

Before our present age of 'live sport' in family-friendly pubs, never mind the conflicting lures of binge-drinking or TV couch-potatoeing, the numerous Italian ice cream parlours and temperance bars were an indispensable and enormously popular leisure time facility in our towns, and most especially our villages, since apart from the pub (where children were banned by law and no respectable woman would set foot) there was often nowhere else for young people to meet up and sit round a table together in pleasant surroundings presided over by genial foreigners who had long grown to be local characters in their own right. 'These were pit villages,' my friend Johnny Dent, a baker's delivery boy in those far-off days, used to say, 'everything was grime, was black dust. But when you walked into the Italian café it was spotless, everything was so nipping clean. I always remember that gleaming coffee machine, it stood out to me. It all set you back a bit in comparison to the surroundings.'

Deeply and affectionately assimilated into local life and parlance, those comfortable and stylish establishments are almost all gone now: Guy-o-vanny's in Spennymoor (Giovannone), Diplo's and Atty Richard's in Darlington (Di Paolo and Antonio Rizzetto), Notriannie's in Sunderland (Notarianni), Rizzy's and Ree's in Newcastle (Risi and Rea), and the famous quartet of 'Ross-Eyes' on the busiest shopping streets in Stockton, Bishop Auckland, Consett and Annfield Plain, whose Valvori-born proprietors were all descended from the seven sons of Giuseppe Rossi.

The coast and the collieries

Summers here may be all too short and none too warm, but until the irresistible temptation of cheap package holidays abroad under a Mediterranean sun trade boomed for all who lived off the universal craze for day trips and family holidays on the coast. Photos taken a century ago of huge crowds bathing or promenading at South Shields or Roker or Redcar on summer weekends testify to the liberating effects of the novelties of a Saturday half-holiday for most workers, summer fortnight breaks on full pay, and cheap and plentiful public transport. Itinerant Italians with their hurdy-gurdies and performing animals, ice cream barrows and Punch and Judy shows,[5] were present in small numbers everywhere, wandering from resort to resort, or dispatched by *padroni* from permanent bases in nearby towns. Some settled by the sea for good.

Alberto Mancini's ice cream parlour in Ocean Road, South Shields, in 1939, perfectly situated for both holiday crowds and cinema-goers. At the turn of the century his father Pietro Mancini (inset), from Picinisco, had toiled as a servo in a street-hawking venture run by padrone Antonio Valentini out of Reed Street in North Shields. After setting up independently in neighbouring Bird Street, Pietro laid the foundations of the family fortune by taking his own ice cream round the neighbourhood with horse and cart.

The Northumbrian resorts and ports were settled predominantly by families from both sides of the Tuscan-Emilian Apennines: Corvi and Signorini in Berwick, Seghini and Giacopazzi in Blyth, the three Bertorelli brothers at Newbiggin and Whitley Bay and Tynemouth, Torre also at Whitley Bay, Longino and Rinaldi in North Shields, and Resteghini at Morpeth, just a little inland and not so very far from the many Tuscan families thriving in Ashington. Further south the regional provenance of Italians was quite different. Although as many as one in three Italian shops in Sunderland between the wars was in the hands of an immigrant from Barga, and the nearby coastal colliery district round Easington was an all-Barga preserve, the whole of the rest of the Durham and North Yorkshire coastline from South Shields right down to Redcar and Scarborough was colonised by immigrants from Ciociaria. The dozen families in Hartlepool were without exception from Ciociaria. The same goes for all of Teesside.

Ice cream concerns which had done well elsewhere soon opened up outlets on the ever more popular sands and esplanades. Risi's of Newcastle ran a kiosk on the promenade at Whitley Bay, and both Notarianni and Guidi of Sunderland opened very handsome parlours in the nearby village of Seaburn as soon as it became a popular resort in the early 1930s. Ice cream and Bertorelli grew to be synonymous in South Northumberland as Celeste, Lodovico and Beniamino Bertorelli, sons of a Val Ceno piano organ builder and repairer in London's Italian quarter, built up an extensive network of parlours and outdoor trade all along that part of the coast. Smaller businesses extended too. Dragone's of Felling had a regular pitch on the beach at Cullercoats, and the Gasparini family of Hexham maintained a branch in Seahouses all through the summer. Further south, Gallone of Wingate, Rea of Middlesbrough, and Pacitto of Stockton all ran lucrative ice cream outlets on Redcar promenade.

Others ventured much farther afield in search of the holiday trade, particularly as the Depression began to bite. In partnership with Pacitto's, the Tomassi family in the Durham colliery village of Langley Park sold up and went south to manage an ice cream parlour in Southend entirely staffed by girls from the North East. Rossi in Bishop Auckland, again in partnership to spread costs, took a lease on a parlour in Southport, splitting the family between the two locations for long stretches of the year. Five of the seven enterprising Notarianni brothers left the region altogether to open new businesses, mostly in leading seaside resorts.

The Italians very soon found that a good living could also be made among the Northumberland and Durham miners. Penetration of the coalfield communities began around 1900 and developed rapidly right up to the First World War during the years of the industry's maximum expansion when the army of pitmen in County Durham alone soared from 85,000 to 165,000. Miners were a little better paid than other manual workers, particularly once coal came under government control during and immediately after the war, and right up to the great crisis of the latter 1920s. The subsequent long depression caused by falling world demand for British coal naturally affected local shopkeepers too until full employment returned with the Second World War and under post-war nationalisation. 'They were all good spenders', Raffaele Moscardini commented when asked about his memories of his parents' temperance bar in the mining town of Stanley, North Durham. 'They worked hard and they played hard. It was a dirty job, but they made their money and they spent their money'

Raffaele's parents Federigo and Fernanda Moscardini were both born in the hilltop village of Sommocolonia, the 'summit settlement', perched high above Barga in the Tuscan Apennines. This remote hamlet accessible only by a three-mile mule track through dense forest and with never more than 700 inhabitants was home to many others who set up shop in our region's pit villages. Antonio Pieroni, who is thought to have gained his adventurous spirit from travelling through central Europe as a boy with his *figurinaio* father, was by all accounts the first 'Sommocolonese' to find his way here in circumstances lost to memory. Around 1903 he opened a confectionery shop in Stanley, itself little more than a hilltop village but with six thriving collieries within its parish. In synchrony with its growing population and prosperity he was soon able to add more businesses to his name, a general dealer's and a pop factory run in partnership with his brothers-in-law Pietro and Ernesto Vincenti who had been summoned to join him. Valentino, his youngest brother-in-law, followed in 1912 at the age of fourteen and had to work his way up like any other shop lad. All Pieroni's *garzoni* were drawn from the village at a similar age. Federigo Moscardini, Raffaele's father, was likewise only fourteen

Antonio Pieroni, the first of many kinsmen from the remote Tuscan village of Sommocolonia to setttle in North Durham and Northumberland. 'Zio Tonio always looked majestic to me as a kid,' recalls his nephew Ron Vincenti, 'always immaculate in his dress: gold cuff links, rings, watch, white handkerchief, sometimes spats, and always a titfer on his head'

when he made the long journey in 1907. He was immediately set to work 'without a day off for three years for very little money' according to his daughter Virginia, who also reported his puny wage packet was docked 'for ages' to pay off his travel expenses.

By the time Pieroni chose to retire soon after the First World War, still only in his early forties, his good fortune had set in motion a chain reaction which triggered the proliferation of many more similar small enterprises over here. As soon as the Vincenti brothers split their several Stanley concerns between all partners, by now including Federigo Moscardini, it fell to Federigo to do his own nearest relatives a good turn. After working for him each went off to try his luck in other mining communities. To Northumberland went brother Giuseppe to open the Bedlington Station temperance bar mentioned earlier, to Easington on the North Durham coast went brother Mansueto to run another shop and billiard hall, while cousin Vittorio settled among the miners and farmers of Weardale with first a shop in Willington, then a fish and chip shop and an ice cream parlour in Crook. And so it went on. Once Vittorio was faring well it was his turn to organise a North-East future for his two sisters and their Sommocolonese husbands. Maria and Ernesto Vincenti opened an ice cream parlour near Vittorio's in Crook before returning to the family base in Stanley to run a fish restaurant, while Vittoria and Ivo Pieroni took a lease on a sub-post office and general dealers in Blackhall Rock.

Just three pits at Ashington, 20 miles north of Stanley, once provided employment for 5,000. The first Italian settlers to explore the potential of 'the biggest mining village in the world' were also from Sommocolonia. In 1910 the brothers Giuseppe and Alfredo Marchetti, who had both worked as young *figurinai* in the streets of Chicago and Detroit, took a greengrocer's in Station Road next to the Buffalo cinema and transformed it into the Station Temperance Bar, complete with an American-style soda fountain. Their prospering enterprise produced another textbook story of kith-and-kin migration in the wake of successful pioneers. With a third brother they opened a fish and chip shop and a second café in Station Road, the expanding village's main thoroughfare, and soon enough in their wake as sure as flies follow ice cream came a stream of *paesani* from Sommocolonia and Barga – Arrighi, Badiali, Cecchini, Cosimini, Marchi, Mazzolini, Nardini, Rossi, Sassetti, Tognieri, are among those who stayed and made a local name for themselves – all working first for fellow villagers then setting up their own concerns elsewhere in town and in nearby localities or on the coast. It seems likely that the very first link in this chain was once again Antonio Pieroni, since he was not only married to a Marchetti but regularly employed lads of that name in his Stanley shops, and in fact the 1911 census already shows further Marchetti shopkeepers installed in Willington and Blaydon. If so, the circle was completed in 1937 when the former hard taskmaster's savings dried up and he had to leave the big villa he had built himself in Barga. In partnership with his one-time 'garzon' Federigo Moscardini, Antonio Pieroni began selling to the English all over again, this time in Ashington.

A good tarmac road now links Barga to Sommocolonia but it is a ghost village today, deserted by almost all but a few summer vacationers. England and America have taken its life and its population. As for Stanley and Ashington, just like the mighty pits themselves it is hard now to find a trace of that Italian mini-gold rush. The lone survival is Mario's in Station Road, Ashington, whose present proprietor is Alfredo Marchetti. He shares his name with his grandfather who first opened for business on this very spot just over a century ago.

'A SHREWD BUSINESSMAN, VERY AMBITIOUS'

West Hartlepool, 1903: wedding photo of Angelo Baldasera, from Carnello near Sora, with his bride Erminia Vincenzo. The couple met while Angelo was doubling as organ grinder and ice cream vendor with four other servi including Erminia's father and mother (seated to left and right of the wedding couple). Their boss was Angelo's maternal uncle, a Hartlepool padrone with the awesome name of Raffaele Terribile.

Angelo, who in the interim had naturalised, served proudly in the British army in World War I while his second wife Rosaria kept the Wheatley Hill shop running. His other five businesses had to be closed when the Italian assistants he had installed received their call-up papers from Italy in 1915.

In remembrance of an enterprising immigrant called Angel: Angelo's tomb in Carrara marble in Wheatley Hill cemetery, with the pithead clearly visible in the background. Five of Angelo's ten children by Erminia and Rosaria spent their working lives maintaining the cafés and the extensive ice cream retail business their father had built in the colliery villages of East Durham. The story of how it all began is told below by Angelo's fourth son Ersilio ('Aris') Baldasera, who inherited the family shop in Wheatley Hill.

'It would be about 1898, and things were not good at all in Italy. My father managed to save up, somehow eke out his fare, and he landed in Hartlepool to an uncle who was a very hard case, a hard businessman, and of course that type jumped at the opportunity of having cheap labour at his disposal. He sold ice cream around the streets of Hartlepool and had to submit back fifty per cent of everything he took. Then, as a shrewd businessman himself, very ambitious, he managed to buy his own barrow and started to buy his ice cream off another Italian family called Vincenzo. Eventually he married one of the Vincenzo daughters and they opened a shop together in Musgrave Street.

There were a lot of pits round this area. There was a pit at Wheatley Hill, there was a pit at Thornley, a pit at Shotton, a pit at Easington, pits all over, barely three miles from each other. And the pits were doing well. They had what is called the marra system, where six or seven or eight men grouped together and made a contract with the employer on an agreed payment system. They did very well, and the wages were very high. Now my father knew that, and he knew that in Hartlepool in its present state there was no future. So he used to put his hand barrow on the train and get off at Thornley station and push his barrow to Wheatley Hill and Thornley, sell his ice cream there. And the demand and the cash flow were so good that he used to come practically every day. So he became more ambitious and he opened a shop, a very small shop, in Wheatley Hill, which did well. Then he opened another at Thornley, in Hartlepool Street. As time went on he opened four more, at Trimdon, Haswell, Wingate, and Coxhoe. In the end he had six shops altogether, all run by Italians he had sponsored to come into England.'

The family thing

'You can make quite a bit of money, but it's a tiring hard job working when others are enjoying themselves,' Mario Dimambro once remarked to me, and it brought home once again what so many second and third generation Italians mean by saying that in order to understand how it was to be Italians in England in earlier days one need only look at the Pakistanis, 'We were the Pakistanis of our time,' I have heard it said again and again. They are thinking of course of shop-keeping as a favoured route to relative prosperity, and no doubt too of the casual racism any such outsider group comes to expect

Adelina and Diamante Jaconelli (centre) among family on their Golden Wedding day, Houghton-le-Spring, 1974. The couple, from Valvori, began their working life together in Easington Lane in 1925. Both daughters, Dolores and Sylvia (seated left and right), married within the North East Italian community.

from some of the public they serve, but the closest parallel most have in mind is how tightly entwined were the twin priorities of family and business: the family instinct and ethos as primary principle and resource, and the family-run business as the best means of mobilising and exploiting these loyalties. Like the first wave of Pakistanis, the first generation of Italians were on the whole country people with strong cultural traditions but little or no schooling, resistant to integration, wary of any but their own kind, here to make money, quite literally happiest when left to mind their own business.

As if still working its own smallholding, each family was a determinedly self-reliant unit therefore, and yet with connections everywhere. Connections first of all reaching back to the home village, *il paese,* the dreamed-of place of origin and eventual return, source of cheap labour for menial workers in the business, source of fresh blood for the family to renew itself through marriage and the children who would follow. Connections too all over the United Kingdom, due to the extremely localised history of immigration from Italy. When a descendant of our 'original Italians' uses pen and paper to explain the family tree you see a pattern of almost Lindisfarne Gospel intricacy emerge, its interweaving branches mostly stemming from a common stock of other families of similar provenance also long established here. Alfie Forte, of the Berwick-on-Tweed café of that name founded over 90 years ago by his father and mother, both of them Fortes, could at one time count twenty-four close cousins in England and Scotland and numerous others 'only slightly more distant' either over here or back in the *paese* (Mortale, the remote Forte stronghold in Ciociaria).

The old families were large, with seldom less than six children and often as many as ten. Brothers, sisters, cousins, in-laws, if they did not all come over together, soon followed once a family began to gain a little prosperity. *La famiglia è famiglia,* family is family: we stick together, and we stick by each other. Because who else cares about us, who else can we trust? In the villages cousin marriages were frequent, and it was the norm to have a widowed spouse remarried to one of the late partner's siblings, particularly if there were children and an imperilled inheritance to safeguard. Thus Antonio Quadrini came over to marry Pasqua Quadrini of Witton Park after his brother's early death left her with three small children to care for. Double weddings were cause for special celebration, more than ever if siblings in one family were paired with siblings from another. Two Jaconelli brothers married two Gallone sisters, both families in Britain, both from the same village of Valvori. Exceptionally, two Valente daughters married 'out' to two brothers from Monkwearmouth, both pit lads, though the risk of family rupture was avoided by taking the foreign spouses into the business. Yet what a perilous leap into the unknown, and twice over!

'Wives and oxen from your own neck of the woods' (*mogli e buoi dai paesi tuoi*) was the good old peasant saying and sentiment. After all, when you know what you're getting there's less chance of being cheated, not to mention that the best wife works like an uncomplaining ox. 'These were not arranged marriages as such,' Bernard Moscardini writes in *La vacanza*, 'but they all knew what was expected of them. I gather that Mother had in her late teens fallen in love with an Englishman. Because of the long established tradition of marrying within the strict boundaries of the Italian community she had had to suppress her strong feelings in this matter. And that was how she came to marry Father.'

When Angelo Baldasera's first wife Erminia (see end of previous section) died of pneumonia leaving him with four young children 'that was devastating for my dad because he had a family and he had a business which he had to run,' his son Aris explained. 'So he went back to Italy, back to Sora to marry again, to pick a wife. That's what the Italians did in those days, there was no element of courtship, there was more or less like a bargain with the old man and his daughter had her dowry paid.' A successful emigrant was a good catch whatever his age, an investment promising dividends not just for the girl but all her family. 'I had plenty of boys after me, I'll say that,' reminisced Rosina Staffieri, the third of eight children brought up on the small family farm near Arpino, too poor for their parents to send them to school 'because you had to buy a little book and a pen'. 'But my father would say, "That one hasn't got a house, that one hasn't got a job, that one's gone bankrupt" – so I had to get one suitable for the family'. The suitable candidate was Francesco Citrone, her first husband, already doing well in England, who came back to collect Rosina and settled down with her in Chester-le-Street where their grandson still runs the Front Street café that they founded together.

Though restrictions were harsher for girls, who all report fathers in particular kept a strict eye on their movements, the marriage issue was ultimately no different for the boys. 'We weren't forced to,' explained Domenic Bove, 'it was just the environment we got into. I left Italy when I was two. Our parents preferred us marrying in our own circle for the business. Our type of business was long hours and hard work, and if you married one of your own they knew the business. Others they wouldn't stand it. Just like a gypsy marrying a gypsy.'

Sylvia Dimambro, daughter of one of the Jaconelli-Gallone unions, stressed another aspect of the 'environmental' pressures over here: 'Like the Pakistanis and Chinese, it was expected that you married an Italian. You weren't accepted here then, you were scoffed at, you were "eating worms". So there was a lot going for you if you married someone of the same background, the same religion.'

The second generation, whose voices we have been hearing, did as a rule marry someone of the same background, but having grown up in England very often retaining little Italian into adulthood they were on the whole far more flexible when it came to their own children's choice of partner. The deeply ingrained ethic of endogamy had ruled their own younger lives, and some had suffered for it in ways they would not want their offspring to go through. Also in their day the old peasant certitudes had been reinforced by the principles of Italian distinctiveness and togetherness preached by all Italian males in positions of authority in Britain during the years in which not a few sons born here were baptised Benito or Romano. With the Second World War, and the profound heart-searching round the old identities and allegiances after the discrediting of Italian fascism, came a craving for greater integration, even the full disguise of 'assimilation', which in the older generation took the form of taking out naturalisation papers and in the younger could go as far as obliterating their origins altogether by Englishing their surnames. 'The Italian fraternity just fell apart', as Domenic Bove summed up those traumatic times he lived through as a boy.

But in the pre-war years covered by this chapter and the next any infringement of the paternal will was seen as rank disloyalty. I have heard of many instances of families torn apart over the marriage issue, even after the war. In extreme cases, errant offspring were disinherited. Such was the fate of Alberto Iannarelli who fell out with his father for marrying a Darlington lass and was permitted no further part in the family business.

Marriage considerations and business calculations were inextricable. A father with multiple shops would typically pass one on, or part of one, as a dowry for his daughter. When Pasquale Tomassi married Salvatore Dimambro's eldest daughter Marianna her dowry brought him a half-share in the shop her father owned in Langley Park, but he still had to work to buy the other half from her father.

In such settlements there was commonly no written contract, no recourse to a solicitor. Deals were done with a promise and a handshake, for a man's word is worth infinitely more than a scrap of paper. Lawyers, doctors, bankers, taxmen – have as little to do with them as possible, they're only after your money. Why give the state what it never sweated to earn? What use is a bank? 'You put it there, then you have to go back and get it out again', is how Madeleine Taylor (née Sperduti) of Stockton explained her father saw it.

In addition to their age and status filial respect was due to the founding fathers for the formidable sacrifices they had undergone in their youth for the sake of the family's advancement. As he gained in years and prosperity a *pater familias* came to look more and more the part, most often advertising his improved social standing by cultivating a luxurious moustache. Nobody could eat until the head of the family, *il capofamiglia*, sat down to table. Some of the old patriarchs, peasant-style, never took their hats off even in the house. May Crolla spoke fondly of her grandfather 'Papa Santucc' (Santi Rea of Middlesbrough) as a 'wonderful character': 'All we girls had to wait on him hand and foot. He had a big tummy and he couldn't bend to get his shoes off – we had to take them off and put his slippers on, then run to the corner shop for his Walnut baccy.' Paul Risi too remembers how his grandmother Filumena, 'a great church-goer who spoke very little English', used to remove her husband Benedetto's shoes for him when he came home: 'He always wore black and was a bit of a tyrant, and she always called him "Signor". *Signor Risi, il cibo è pronto*: "Mr Risi, the meal is ready".'

But did every husband rule the roost? These families were not just patriarchal, they produced formidable matriarchs too. 'The brigand men are by no means fierce,' D.H. Lawrence wrote about the peasant people he lived among briefly in Picinisco in 1919, 'the women are the fierce half of the breed'. Although English census returns seldom recorded any occupation for an Italian immigrant's wife – a very few are described as 'musician', or 'assisting in the business' – the fact is most did everything that the men did and had the babies as well. So often I have heard sons and daughters of 'original Italians' pay warm tribute to their mothers, and especially their grandmothers: 'The hardest-working woman I ever knew' – 'My mother worked very, very hard for countless hours' – 'Nana was the greatest old lady there ever was' – 'Everyone was frightened of Lavinia Notarianni!' Because of the habit of work most never quite retired, even long after they were widowed. Celestina Niro was still going into her Stanley shop at 90, saying she was bored at home and needed to keep up with the gossip.

Not a few of the men, by contrast, are represented in family memory as more lightweight, and lighter with the money, while those few families saddled with gamblers, drinkers, womanisers, were of course especially reliant on the women to hold it together. But no matter how indomitable, every shopkeeper's wife had to accept she had also wedded the shop. 'Babies belonged upstairs,' Gemma Jaconelli recalled of her first years in England, 'downstairs was "money time". You had to work all the time, all the time, I mean from early in the morning till late at night. When I sat down a moment with the children my father-in-law used to say, "Downstairs! This is no nursery here – my wife had seven children and still worked!"

Since the family lived above or behind the shop the children grew up in the interface, confusingly caught between Italy and England. The importance of the family bond and bloodline was reinforced by giving firstborn boys and girls the Christian names of their paternal grandparents, and each successive child was cemented into the family's wider social circle by the careful choice of godparents, an honour sometimes given to a favoured uncle or aunt but more often to key individuals within the parents' support network, a former *padrone* who had stood by the family in the early years, or a prosperous business associate.

'If you want to know how they did it', says Nichol Citrone of Chester-le-Street, whose first assignment in the family café was doing the washing up, 'it was the children, we were *slaves*. It was straight back from school and straight into the business'. And Joe Dragone: 'As soon as we could change a pound note we were in the business – that was our A Levels!' And Raffaele Moscardini: 'There was no off at the weekends, I couldn't go to a football match. We were all in the shop, everybody worked, there was none of us liked it but we had to do it. That's how we spent our youth. They talk about unsocial hours now – they don't know what they are!' From the age of nine, every morning before school Milio Gabriele of Bishop Auckland had to fetch home a ten-gallon churn of milk which the farmer would send in on the bus. At eleven he was pushing an ice cream barrow round the streets at weekends. Strict, is the word all use to describe their upbringing.

Joe Risi of Newcastle has a remarkable anecdote from his boyhood: 'My grannie's front door was next to the factory, and she used to sit and watch us. One time she saw me she said, "Come here, Joe, come here – I want you to stand by this barrow and you can sell ice cream." She put a little top hat on us, and a little white jacket with a bow tie. It was sixty scoops to the gallon, at a halfpenny or a penny. "What a canny little lad," people would say, "selling ice cream!" I was under five.'

Of course there was no escape for the girls, every day after school hours and all weekend in the shop, although work outside could be freedom, as Pietro Rea's daughter Yolanda discovered: 'We had a very strict life, both Mam and Dad were very strict. I was twelve when I first went out with the horse and cart. Dad taught me how to drive, shouting his head off! At first I went round with him, and when I learned to drive I took his rounds: I loved it.' 'Did your age not matter?' I asked ingenuously. 'Oh no, I was making money, wasn't I!'

In other respects their unusual lives could feel quite privileged. Bernard Moscardini writes of how in stark contrast to other children in their pit village during the great depression he was 'always very well dressed and neatly turned out', and of course he could help himself to as many chocolates and sweets as he liked. Another exception for the children, if their families could find the money, were the holidays in Italy, though all seem to have experienced what little Bernard discovered very quickly: 'The children of the village would not play with me and I felt very much alone and really unhappy. Whenever I tried to join them they would have nothing to do with me and would say, *Va a casa* (go home) *inglesaccio bastardo!*' 'They all used to follow you around,' recalled May Crolla, Yolanda's cousin: '*Oh Ingles*'! – that's what you got all the time'. Most agree the local kids' taunts were open reflections of the jealousy and resentment their elders felt, who had never gone abroad.

'I suppose if we were Chinese we'd be called all sorts of names,' mused Raffaele Moscardini, speaking instead of his boyhood in Stanley. 'Even when we grew up, in the streets sometimes you'd get someone shouting at you. You got used to it, you weren't liked by some people. The thing was: 'Why should they have the money and us not have the money?' They thought us rich, but we were no more rich than anyone would have been if they'd worked.'

Such attitudes explain why Ray Pacitto says his parents in Stockton 'wanted the family to be as English as possible.' Eddie Rossi of Bishop Auckland put it more positively: 'My mother was a very moral and strong woman. She would not allow Italian to be spoken in the shop, no, because she always said, "You are in someone else's house, it's a discourtesy to speak Italian in front of your customers because you could say anything you wanted and they wouldn't understand." It was right, but really we suffered for it because the language was just dropped.' Most second generation sons and daughters came to regret this inevitable consequence, the crucial loss of language, though at the time it was of no concern to kids attending school and trying their best to fit in. Even so, their Italianness remained with them, not so much in a few dialect words and phrases retained from childhood but in their own distinctive looks, and the names handed down from the ancesters, even if long prudently Anglicised.

As for education, most first-generation parents had little or no schooling themselves and thought the best education was training for the business. 'Leave doctors' families to be doctors, the business is there for you', Mary Marcantonio – a very bright schoolgirl – was told when she confessed to her parents she was thinking of the medical profession. Alfredo Moscardini, a professor of mathematics today, considers his grandfather was exceptionally cruel to his three sons: Osvaldo wanted to be a musician and his father 'stamped on his violin,' Alfredo wanted to be a dentist but was forced into the shop, while Raffaele (whom we heard from earlier) was the only one of the three with a business head. 'Intelligence didn't count for much,' insisted Eddie Rossi. 'All of us went to Grammar School and came out and had to go in the shop. For my sister in particular it was an absolute tragedy because she had ten As at O level. She was brilliant, but it was the business, the business, the business...'

As always, there were exceptions. Eddie's cousins, the Rossis of Consett, received every encouragement from their father Carmine, all going on to boarding school or convent school after junior school. Only John and Lena, the eldest, went into the family shops; Celia, Virginia and Angela became teachers, Teresa a dentist, Joseph went into the priesthood and taught at Ushaw College, and Tony became a successful architect. Perhaps, as Lena suggested to me, what explains the difference is that both their parents could read and write.

More positive attitudes toward education inevitably appeared in the second generation who had had to suppress their talents, as in the exemplary case of Carmine Rossi's younger friend and business partner Biagio Coia who did everything to further his children's development (see page 294). Tony Dimambro, another second-generation Italian born into a County Durham ice cream family, explained his attitude this way: 'For us there was no way out, but it was different for our children. They'd all had to help out, they knew how it was – the long hours, the hard work – so I used to say to them: "Either you work hard at school and get your exams or this is what you do for the rest of your life." And of all six not one has had to carry on the business!'   But for as long as the founding fathers remained alive the links with the old ways and origins stayed strong. It was to Italy they turned not just for eager recruits as business grew, or

The Marcantonio villa in Picinisco, with 'Mark Toney' on the balcony with his wife and sister-in-law.

holidays for the affluent few, but for suitable brides and grooms, and sometimes for childbirth too: each time she fell pregnant Eufemia Risi of Newcastle returned home so the baby could be born Italian and be baptised in the same church in Cassino. Even the dead went home, if it was their last wish. Aleardo Rossi's headstone stands beside that of Giacomantonio Pacitto in a Stockton cemetery today but his body lies in the family mausoleum in Valvori. In *L'Italia nostra,* the Italian community paper, Albert France & Son, funeral directors, regularly advertised their expertise in 'sending bodies abroad'.

Money went home too, to support elderly parents or indigent relatives and to pay for the construction of an ostentatious villa to publicise the family's fortune-gathering in a distant land. Some of the most prosperous emigrants also put their savings into civic initiatives. Benedetto Notarianni and his brother Luciano were prime movers in the consortium that turned the muletrack between Valvori and the populous valley into a decent road, and they also helped to raise funds among other exile *paesani* to erect the first proper parish church and a monument to the hamlet's fallen of the Great War. Antonio Marcantonio of Newcastle displayed similar public largesse in his home village of Picinisco.

For the first generation the hope was almost always to return permanently to Italy at the end of their working lives. In the economically distressed Thirties a few went back early who could not make a sufficiently good living, but more typical was the experience of the Franchi family of South Shields who never got to spend their last years in the house in Barga they had been sinking their savings into. In any case, a handsome villa back home and extra acres of land might only be laying up trouble. Too often these new territories and great houses – a long broad avenue in Barga is lined with them – have fallen victim to Italy's inheritance laws whereby half the estate must be split equally between all siblings. Given the size of families, this was a recipe for futile infighting at the expense of the property itself which might well end up an abandoned ruin.

So far I have made no distinction between 'Toscans' and 'Napoletans', drawing on examples from both sides of the north/south divide because I find there is little to choose between the two when it comes to basic mindsets and typical responses to new ways in this country. All the same both factions felt they had nothing in common, and marriages across the divide were very rare. Vera Massagli of Ashington, whose mother Maria Marchetti's first husband was a Pontone from Horden, told me she couldn't understand how her mother ever got to meet her father 'because they didn't mix'. Jack Rea of Jarrow simply said he was brought up to think all Toscans were 'wicked people'. Similarly, Ron Vincenti says of his Tuscan family's attitude to their 'Napolitan' neighbours: 'They were there but we never bothered with them, although we all lived within a couple of hundred yards and used the same church. I thought it was odd, with their being Italians, but my mother said: "They come from the south." We all had thriving shops in Stanley, so it wasn't that we were losing out businesswise. Only towards the end of their days did we get to talk to each other.' When it came to their own kind, however, all pulled together, particularly in times of stress or bereavement. 'They were always in touch, always visiting. The Ashington ones came here, and we went there. We had relatives in Crook too, and they often stayed with each other. When they were short in the shop, or if my father was ill, they sent one of their daughters. The Pieroni girls came through to help out too.'

Since business hours were so very long there was little opportunity for wider socialising, but in any case, as Bernard Moscardini writes, 'in those days the Italian immigrants were a very close-knit community, and as such very rarely even attempted to integrate into the local population.' 'You used to meet in each other's houses,' explained his cousin Raffaele, 'because I suppose in a foreign country you kept together more.'

Some say their family never took a day off, or at best once a year, as was the case with the Rea cousins of North Ormesby and Middlesbrough who used to all get together on Redcar sands on August 15 for *la Madonna dell'Assunta*, the big feast day back home in Arpino. Others, I'm told, took a regular Wednesday or Thursday off and went visiting. 'Grandfather used to have a lot of his cronies come in,' recalls Ray Pacitto of Stockton. 'There'd probably be the Dimambros coming from Durham, and the Paleschi from Thornaby, and they'd get together at the back of the shop for a meal and a game of cards in the typical old Italian way.' May Crolla loved to remember how when relatives and friends came round all the men seemed to be able to play some sort of musical instrument: 'Uncle Andrew had a mandolin and a concertina and an accordion. They were all card players of course, or they'd play *bocce* along the roadside, my dad and all his brothers.' Men of a political turn of mind on Tyneside and Wearside gathered on Thursday evenings at the Pineapple Grill in Nelson Street, Newcastle, or at the *fascio* club in Saville Row.

Finally, at least for those who could afford it, there was the big annual patriotic November banquet at Newcastle's County Hotel under vice-consul Tognoli's auspices (see next chapter), and of course the Ice Cream Alliance divisional dances when prizes were distributed to the year's champion producers –at the Assembly rooms in Newcastle, the Walker hotel in Sunderland, or the Coatham hotel in Redcar, events always held in the winter (as they still are) because families were too busy selling *la crema* in summer. These were the rare moments when the dispersed and divided community actually got together, Napolitans with Toscans, and I like to imagine that towards the end of the evening when the formalities and speeches were over and the band was playing the atmosphere became almost like a village *festa* back home. 'The Ice Cream Alliance was open to anyone,' recalls Nichol Citrone, 'Italian and English, but the majority were Italian. There were very few strangers, outside the business. It was a little Italian society. And I think that's where everyone met their sweethearts, from one family to another.'

'ONCE AGAIN, IT'S THIS FAMILY THING'

Belmonte Castello, near Cassino, home town of the Soave family of Gateshead.

Dad was born in 1919 in a little village called Belmonte di Castello about thirteen kilometres from Cassino. Mam came from the same village, one of those villages up on the top of the hill, in the Appenines. In its heyday there would have been at the most 600 people, and most of them were probably interrelated in one form or another, second cousins or whatever. It's so noticeable that even five miles down the road another village has a totally different dialect. I think this must come about because they do sort of stick together.

In the village now you'd be lucky if there are 150 people left, and they're all old. The younger people want to be out into the towns, they don't want to stay in an old village where nothing happens. You go back and it's like going into a time warp. But we as kids loved it.

Most of the people from there are very poor, even now, although in some ways they are a lot better off than we are. The pace of life is so gentle, so easy. If they're of the older generation, still at the olden ways, they think very much more of the family. They will sacrifice their own life for the family. 'That's the trouble today', they say, 'there's not enough family life.'

My grandfather died in 1981 and I went across to Italy for the funeral. It's an incredible sight, they all gather on that day and it's huge – everyone's interrelated so the whole village comes out. Three of Grandad's daughters were there, but I was at the head of the family because I was the male. I came before the daughters, which I thought was crazy, but that's how the Italians do it. I was one of the coffin bearers and you had to walk up the long curving road, walk all the way up to the church carrying this coffin in the sweltering heat, and it was three o'clock in the afternoon, I thought I was going to pass out. But I looked back down the hill and all I could see was just people, all the way up the road.

Oh it was terribly moving, you're moved beyond words. And the support that Grandma got – everybody coming for food and the other women doing everything for her. Once again, it's this family thing.

(Mario Soave, reminiscing in 1990. His grandfather, a shepherd, had been a skilled bagpiper, or *zampognaro*, who though he never went abroad travelled widely in Italy with his pipes.

Ice cream dynasties in the North East

Today, with several outlets in prime sites around the city centre and a considerable wholesale trade to extend its name and visibility, the firm of Mark Toney proudly advertises its historic status as 'Newcastle's oldest and most famous ice cream company'. That may be so now, but back in the boom times of the Ice Age with any number of other well-established Italian concerns on main roads and back streets all producing their own ice cream and all renowned at least in their corner of the city there would have been many other claimants for the dual title. Even so, in the period between the two world wars Mark Toney emerged as one of the three leading Italian enterprises on Tyneside: Mark Toney, Risi, and Reale, the latter contributing later by marriage to the rise of Quadrini, a newcomer to the city if not to the region.

Mark Toney was the Geordie version of his name adopted in about 1910 by Antonio Marcantonio from Picinisco who had first lived the ice cream life in Newcastle before the turn of the century as a teenage street hawker for his father

Angela and Antonio Marcantonio in Newcastle with daughters Anita and Angela, the first of seven children all raised to work in the family business. Like other studio portraits preserved in family albums this was probably posed to mark the couple's achievements in a foreign land and to impress the extended family and fellow villagers back home. By this time the family was out of the Italian 'ghetto' in Manors and established in a small flat in Byker.

Giovanni, one of the biggest *padroni* in the Manors district, with over a dozen *servi* at his beck and call. Around 1904 Giovanni took his son and savings back to Picinisco to retire. Soon enough, and defying his father who wanted to keep him to work the land he had acquired, Antonio was back in Newcastle with a young wife to try his luck on his own account. Angela, too, had had to work with her family in Newcastle at a tender age. Like many other aspiring husband-and-wife teams around this time they were determined to be free of the slavish dependency on a *padrone*. Operating out of a couple of rooms in an alleyway off Carliol Square, Angela helped make the ice cream and Antonio sold it round the streets. Within only eighteen months, so family memory relates, the wayward son was able to prove his worth by sending home the princely sum of fifty gold sovereigns. A year or so later the couple were able to move out to a flat in Stepney Bank where they raised a family of seven and set up a small ice cream factory at the back. Bit by bit, penny by penny, profits from sales were channelled into first a small shop in Gateshead High Street, then after Antonio's return from the Great War a shop in Shields Road near Byker Bridge, two stalls in the Grainger Arcade, and finally a grand parlour in Percy Street. In addition, the family maintained very popular regular pitches in the Bigg Market, and down on the Quayside in summer ministering to the customary great Sunday morning crowds.

Like many another astute ice man in those years Antonio made a lot of money. He built himself a house beside Jesmond Dene and an imposing villa back in Picinisco (see illustraton on page 152) where as one of the town's most successful sons he was honoured with the title of 'cavaliere'. Cavaliere Marcantonio also grew to be a commanding figure in wider ice cream circles (his gold diplomas awarded in London and Paris are still on display in the Percy Street shop), and locally was a staunch backer of vice-consul Tognoli's efforts to politicise the North East's Italians and instil in them a pride in Mussolini's new Italy. His three sons and four daughters each followed one another into the expanding business on leaving school at fourteen. The fifth child, Mary, who never married, emerged as the main force in the firm during World War II when her father was interned and her brothers were in the forces. As all Mark Toney's most loyal customers will remember, George (Geraldo), the eldest son who died in 2000, was still watching the till at the Percy Street shop well into his eighties. Today the company is headed by George's son Anthony together with his wife Anne and sister Angela.

'THE CREAM OF ALL ICE CREAM'

Risi's factory in Wilfred Street, Byker. Saverio ('Sammy') Risi with his father Angelantonio on the left; his mother Eufemia and brother Giuseppe Angelo ('Joe') extreme right.

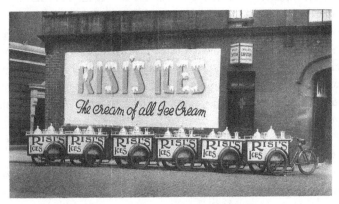

The firm's twin-tub tricyle fleet outside the factory.

Sammy Risi at the height of his success, in his Bean 11.9 two-seater.

A characteristically ornate Risi barrow.

Angelantonio Risi was Marcantonio's senior by some 25 years. Born in Cassino in 1861, he was already a professional baker with a family when, in 1898, presumably through contacts in the dense Cassinese network in Britain, he took to organ grinding and ice-creaming in Scarborough as a first step to a new life abroad. Within a year he was in Newcastle, soon settling for Byker, which was later also to be the Marcantonio family patch. Somehow he prospered, for the 1911 census finds Angelantonio and his second wife Eufemia, whom he had fetched from Cassino in 1902, employing numerous *servi* to maintain a thriving road sales business from their home in Conyers Road. By the 1920s, besides busy stalls within shouting distance of Mark Toney's rival stands in the Grainger Market, the Bigg Market and the Quayside, and on Whitley Bay promenade in summer, the firm possessed an imposing factory in Wilfred Street (a former warehouse still standing today) where a score of workers turned out 250 gallons a day of 'Risi's Frozen Joy' for hotels, restaurants, cafés, cinemas, shops, and big stores like Woolworths, as well as the firm's own outlets including three in the Shields Road. One of the latter was the swankiest ice cream parlour in town, a lavishly fitted 'Ice Cream Saloon and American Soda Bar' with terrazzo flooring and a big soda fountain, the showpiece creation of the flamboyant eldest son, Saverio, universally known as Sammy. In a brief unpublished memoir by his nephew Angelo he figures as 'the toast of the town, man of fashion, dapper, elegant, a sharp business brain with a limited wit but a likeable one, hobnobbing with the famous theatricals of his day' – for the Risi factory was right next to Byker's Grand Theatre. Sammy had a showman's flair for marketing but unfortunately also a playboy's way with money, and by the time of his death in 1934 when just forty-four he had vastly expanded and finally bankrupted the Risi empire. Within three years his milder younger brother Joe (Giuseppe Angelo), who had long fallen out with Sammy and stuck patiently to pushing his yellow barrow round the streets, got the business back on its feet with the aid of the indomitable Eufemia, by now a widow. Together mother and son won back the street custom and the wholesale side of the business, but the shops apart from the Grainger Market stall were all lost, and Risi's was never again the force it had been in Sammy's glory days.

The family name and tradition live on in Giuseppe Angelo's son Joe and his wife Betty who with their own sons Joe and Marco have shared a number of ice cream and catering enterprises and as a family have long been leading figures in the struggle to hold together the Tyneside Anglo-Italian community (see last chapter). Joe Jnr now runs the family's café and conference centre in Millfield House, Jesmond Dene, while Marco has renewed a Risi presence on the Quayside in the form of an Italianate parlour offering pasta and other dishes alongside his own handmade ice creams and sorbets. Its walls, as at Millfield House, are adorned with evocative pictures from the family archive, some reproduced here.

During the Great Ice Age the rivalry between Toney and Risi, the biggest ice cream companies in town, was legendary and played out daily in public. Besides competing stalls at opposite ends of the Grainger Arcade each firm habitually pitched wondrously ornate trailers (Sammy Risi called them portable saloons) in close proximity in the Bigg Market, and also on the Quayside. During the happy mayhem of Hoppings Week, remembered Jackie Moore, 'they had these beautiful ice cream trailers next to each other, all crowded together down the Town Moor, and they'd shout abuse at each other and bring up all the past. But it was all an act, a business act, a gimmick. And they made money – they made a fortune!'

Without wishing to start another ice cream war, I can hardly avoid the obvious question: is Mark Toney truly the oldest Italian ice cream business in town? 'Founded 1902', declares the well-known logo, and the centenary was celebrated with well-deserved fanfare in 2002. Yet Risi, who today promote their much reduced family business as only 'one of the oldest', claim to have been selling ice cream since 1898, and on Tyneside since 1899. I have to say the evidence suggests this is the case. So, yes, first prize in the antiquity stakes should really be Risi's. But even Mark Toney's '1902' claim is questionable, since in that year Antonio Marcantonio was barely seventeen and still dependent on his father Giovanni who was about to wind up his entire Newcastle concern and return to Italy. On the other hand, unless today's Mark Toney heirs understandably choose to regard all such hair-splitting as a load of wafers, they can always reassert their supremacy by claiming their true founder was actually great-grandpapa *padrone* Giovanni Marcantonio, which would back-date their origins to at least 1894!

'MORE LIKE AN OPERA'

The big show was on Saturday nights, and the stage was Newcastle's Bigg Market, filled with stalls offering everything from whelks to tray toffee and sarsaparilla. Naphtha flares, paraffin and gas lamps, gave the place a feeling of cosiness on a cold winter's night. The rival horse-drawn wagons of Toney and Risi would take up their positions glowering at each other, great gaudy Rococo monsters they were, their minders at the ready in lily-white aprons ('Our Motto Is Cleanliness') aching to plunge their wooden spoons into the ice-lined

The Risi and Mark Toney 'Rococo monsters' in the Bigg Market, Newcastle, in the 1930s. The Mark Toney stall is in the foreground (extreme right).

metal bins and scoop up dollops of delicious ice cream. Risi and his men vied with Toney to produce the most gargantuan ice cream sandwiches imaginable for the sum of three-halfpence, so high and wide some of them you could hardly get your fist round them. Chucked out of the pictures after the first house and practically skint, my mates and I would stand transfixed, torn between the warring factions trying to make up our minds. Was it to be Risi, who offered the thicker sandwich, or Toney, who charged a halfpenny more for an allegedly superior product which carried a seal of approval from the connoisseurs? The whole thing was staged for the benefit of the punters of course, with characteristic Italian flair, more like an opera.

(Richard Kelly recalling Newcastle in the 1930s, on Radio 4, November 1991)

Vincenzo and Rosalinda Reale with their first baby, Assunta, 1913.

J. Riale's horse and cart fleet outside the family's Lido Parlour in West Road, Benwell, about 1930. 'Old Vincenzo couldn't write himself, so he had this chap who used to sign write and he put an "I" instead of an "E", and they left it in – and by God it was a lucky name to him!' (Jackie Moore).

Vincenzo with daughters Assunta, Amelia, Marietta, Enrica. 'The first were all daughters with two years between each, and as one left school and went on the horse and cart the next went in the shop' (Jackie Moore).

The future 'driving force': Assunta at the wheel of her parents' van, about 1937. Perched behind is her eldest son Vincenzo Quadrini.

Quadrini stall at the Hoppings in the 1950s, with Tina De Laurentis (right) serving.

The Reale family of Newcastle, about whom Jackie Moore spoke so warmly, has its origins in Arpino, the home town of many 'original' Italians in the North East, not least the large Rea clan which is now spread all over the region. Vincenzo Reale was twenty when he stepped ashore at Dover in 1896 bound for Liverpool to purchase a cut-price emigrant's ticket to the United States like multitudes of his compatriots in those years of the great transatlantic adventure. Once in Liverpool however, presumably through the local Arpino grapevine he heard that in a place called Middlesbrough a lot of *paesani* were making good money out of ice cream, and on impulse took the train. There he acquired the essential know-how and also a bride, Rosalinda Di Luoffo, daughter of one of the many Italian confectioners in Cannon Street (see illustration on page 75). Around 1906 the couple moved to Trafalgar Street, Newcastle, in the heart of the Italian district, later relocating to Buckingham Street in the West End where they opened a small ice cream parlour as a base for an extensive street trade. As was customary, all nine children were brought up to work for the enterprise. Even though the first four were all daughters, at fourteen each went out trading with horse and cart under strict orders not to be back till the lamps were lit, which could be after nine in summer. At dusk Vincenzo would be waiting on the doorstep: young girls could be out all hours ice-creaming but not to go dancing.

The Reale-Quadrini connection, never a business merger, came about when the family elders agreed to pair off their firstborn. Tony Quadrini used to recount that when he first met his bride-to-be he left the Reale home still not sure which of the striking girls was his intended, but certain any would do. Assunta, the eldest, who came with a dowry of £600 for the couple to start up a shop, was a canny parental choice as she proved to have a formidable business head. Tony's mother Pasqua and his step-father Antonio ('Jack') Quadrini ran an ice cream business in Witton Park, then a thriving colliery village with a busy picture palace conveniently situated right opposite their shop. Jack, who kept working until he was 82, was reportedly the last ice cream vendor on Wearside to stick to horse and cart.

Between them, Assunta and Tony made Quadrini one of the biggest ice cream names in the north, with a fleet of thirty sales vans after the war and a showpiece state-of-the-art factory in Two Ball Lonnen. The business was sold in 1966. Their youngest son Michael, the North East's only home-grown tycoon of Italian extraction (see last chapter), attributes his own business head entirely to his mother whom after her death at 82 in 1989 he described to the press as the 'driving force'. Until they retired, his siblings Vincent and Angela were familiar friendly faces to all who patronised their always busy 'First Stop' café in the Eldon Square bus terminus. Rosalinda, named after her formidable grandmother, kept 'Quicks' café in St Mary's Place.

Sunderland's grandest ice cream parlour, and probably the most famous in the region, was Notarianni's on High Street West. Benedetto Notarianni, the eldest of seven brothers from Valvori, began his career here as a humble *garzone* working for an uncle in Glasgow. Called up in 1915, he returned to Scotland after the war with his young wife Lavinia and two of his brothers to manage shops for other Italians. With the arrival of the last four brothers all decamped to Wearside in 1925, setting up shop in Houghton-le-Spring and on Silksworth Row, Sunderland. Brother helped brother, and within little more than ten years 'Notarianni Bros' was one of the leading family ice cream empires in England, with handsome parlours not only in Sunderland, Seaburn, and South Shields, but in Bridlington, Blackpool, Eastbourne,

Hastings, Margate, Ramsgate, and London. As a boy, Claudio Gallone (see chapter 7) was often taken through to Benedetto Notarianni's High Street shop when his father had business to discuss with his Valvori *paesano*, and the numerous white-clad staff, the elegant decor, and Lavinia's ceaselessly ringing till convinced him that 'Uncle Benny' must be the richest man in the whole North East. A supportive counsellor for the many other *paesani* whom he helped to sponsor in our region, Benedetto also liked to share his flair for shop design and presentation, arts which did not come naturally to all.

There is a Notarianni connection in the Minchella family's rise to fame, a change of fortune which ultimately led to domination of the trade on South Tyneside where the cream and green Minchella kiosks are now such a familiar sight all along the coast. Giuseppe (Joe) Minchella started out in 1905 as a *servo* hawking ice cream round Sunderland for Giuseppe Valente's High Street business. His first venture after returning home to marry Maria Capaldi was in the pit village of Boldon, and next Murton, and finally Fencehouses where the couple settled after the Great War. The move to South Shields came only in 1937 when Giuseppe pooled resources with two other *paesani* to lease Luciano Notarianni's shop in King Street when Luciano decided to invest his money and hopes in a parlour in Eastbourne. The business connection became a family one when Giuseppe's son Toney married Luciano's daughter Alda. The King Street shop was bombed in the war, so when the D'Ambrosi family left ice cream to start up their celebrated fleet of taxis Minchella seized the chance to take over the venerable 'Roma' café in Ocean Road. The family's post-war expansion and diversification is owed to the three sons, Toney, Louis, and Freddy, and several of their children in their turn. The Ocean Road parlour and factory are today run by Freddy's son Michael, a former president of the Ice Cream Alliance whose great-grandfather on his mother's side chanced to be Giuseppe Minchella's original *padrone*, Giuseppe Valente, the wealthiest Italian in Sunderland in his day. With Pacitto's of Redcar, Minchella's is the last prominent coastal ice cream firm of Italian origin in the region.

The Notarianni brothers' first Sunderland shop on Silksworth Row, circa 1926: Benedetto (centre) with staff and children Gino and Eva. After the move to High Street West this shop passed to the Fella family, also from Valvori via Scotland. Fella's became the biggest wholesale ice cream manufacturer on Wearside.

Twelve years on: Benedetto now owns a grand parlour on the High Street, and another on Seaburn promenade.

Interior of the High Street West shop with Lavinia (second left) behind the counter, and Benedetto just visible through the hatch at the back.

Freddy Minchella (left) with Luciano and Giulietta Notarianni and staff outside Minchella's King Street shop, South Shields, about 1938.

Minchella's, Ocean Road, South Shields, decorated for the Queen's coronation, 1953.

THE ICE CREAM PARLOUR THAT MADE MARRIAGES AND MEMORIES

Notarianni's is closing down. On October 22, 1988, after 60 years, several million gallons of milk, inestimable mountains of corn flour, whole towers of ha'penny cornets, surely enough tuppenny sliders to girdle the earth a time or two, millions of malted milk shakes, one world war, two slumps, umpteen depressions, and a myriad romances broken and unbroken, the last dish of Italian ice cream will be served. And the lock will turn for the last time at 251 High Street West.

Interior of Notarianni's, custom built in 1938 with living accommodation above and a state of the art factory at the rear.

Notarianni's. Notriannies. Or Naughty Annie's, as we used to call it with adolescent wit as lighted tram-cars like great double-decked Venetian gondolas swayed past the window on the penny trip to Millfield... And as we lingered over our cups of hot chocolate and eyed the incoming girls, each a laughing mystery, bright-eyed and Dinky-curled, each putting on her own bravado for a Notriannies night, each – well almost each – a Lana Turner or a Rita Hayworth.

'Haven't you got a home to go to?' asked the waitress in her white overalls. 'No,' we chorused, assuming the air of teenage boulevardiers, snitching another sugar lump to scrunch, stretching out the glittering present in order to delay damp, unknown, unknowable tomorrow.

Notriannies...

A double row of horse boxes stretching back from the High Street night into the warmth and clatter. Screens of polished mahogany separating stall from stall and tribe from tribe. Each barrier inset with glittering panes of engraved glass. Boat-shaped dishes of ice cream on marble tables. And served by waitresses!

Before that, though, Notarianni's was where visiting aunts took you for a treat as ritual tribute to your parents for their bed and breakfast. You were sat on the oil cloth cover of the scullery table as the wicked button hook was used to skewer you into vile leather leggings. Hair wire-brushed. Ears inpected.

'Where shall we take you, luv?' said the adults. It was rude to answer, but you hoped.

'I know, let's go to Notriannies', one of them had to say.

And if the aunt was mildly prosperous there would be ice cream for all with bright red 'monkey's blood'. Which tasted a bit like that delicious medicine called Parish's Food. Or if she really wanted to impress, even chocolate flake, while she and the rest of the adults drank 'night starvation' Horlicks.

'Very nourishen... very nourishen,' they'd say to excuse themselves their self-indulgence.

But it was in calf-love days when Notriannies became Palm Court, the Café Royal Grill, the Paris Crillon, the temple of romance.

You ordered with as much nonchalance as a brilliantined 16-year-old could muster. And with as much money as your fire-watching pay – six bob a night – afforded. You hoped she would not notice that your trousers were too short or your blue serge suit too shiny. And you hesitated, dared, hesitated, dared, to advance your hand along the seat, and then touch fingers. The dream girl with her page-boy hair, her tea-dyed legs instead of stockings, her coat made from an army blanket.

Notriannies was the first place where anybody called me Sir.

In 1941 it was. I was 14, wearing my first long 'uns and in the company of a grown-up family friend with what, I thought at the time, was great sophistication and stunning looks.

She wore scent. I rather hoped I would be seen by class mates.

That didn't happen. But what did was that the nippie came up and took the order for the two wartime utility ice creams – from me and not from her. My companion pushed the coins to me from underneath the table top. And the waitress called me Sir, she did. She called me Sir.

I think I blushed a little. And I can tell you that moment was far more memorable to me than my first drinks in the Ritz Crillon, or the day I ordered jellied eels among the red plush and mirrors of the Café Royal.

For it is not just town halls and civic centres that make Sunderlands. Ice cream parlours can be institutions too. Moreover they may remain longer in affection.

Marriages, and a million memories were made at those marble tables installed by old Benedetto.

So sigh, my brothers and my sisters, sigh.

And 'ciao'.

(Frank Entwhistle, *Sunderland Echo*,17.10.1988, slightly abridged)

The boss: Francesco Scappaticci with his family in Middlesbrough, about 1905.

The successor: Camillo Rea, a cousin, was one of many young men brought over by Scappaticci. The cousins eventually went into partnership, Rea in his turn becoming a major importer of fellow townsmen.

'Pure Ice Creams': The Scappaticci-Rea shop and factory in Suffield Street, Middlesbrough: Francesco and his wife Ann Trainor in the doorway. Both Scappaticci and Rea married into local Catholic families.

Many a familiar Italian surname in the North East stems from the industrious organ-grinding and ice cream fraternity in Middlesbrough before the Great War when Francesco Scappaticci ruled as *padrone* supreme. Himself a former boy organ grinder, he hailed from the tiny village of Santopadre high in the Apennine foothills beneath which lies the small town of Arpino, a major source of migrants to our region. 'People couldn't just go to the North East', I've often heard said by familes from the same area, 'they had to go to Scappaticci in Middlesbrough'. The same is said of Camillo Rea, his cousin and business partner, and finally successor, who started out as one of Scappaticci's dozen and more young *servi* in 1897. For thirty years the Scappaticci-Rea ice cream shop and wafer business extending over two terrace houses in Suffield Street served as both workplace and dormitory for a succession of men, women, and lads brought over from Santopadre, Arpino, and neighbouring hamlets.

Neither boss could read or write but both must have been abundantly endowed with instinctive business acumen and people skills. Beside a host of Reas (nine of that name were living on the premises or housed across the street at the time of the 1901 census), the Suffield Street partnership is credited with bringing over an astonishing number of men whose later careers made them household names in many corners of our region, among them Alonsi, Amerigo (D'Americo), Biesi, Borsumato, Di Palma, Di Stefano, Greco, Lucantoni, Minchella (of Middlesbrough, not South Shields), Martino, Quadrini, Serra, Zaira (Zair). Though this steady flow of willing young labour from home of course served their business interests it was also a matter of personal obligation and honour for anyone well-established abroad to assist needy kinsmen and townsmen. Scappaticci apparently took this pragmatic altruism a step further by using part of the large fortune he took home after the First World War to found a biscuit factory also in Arpino. It was not just for personal gain, his grandson Francis Hyne insisted, it was to ensure that not so many of his townsmen would have to leave home to make a living.

Another influential Middlesbrough-based importer of *paesano* labour, this time from Cassino, was the ice factory owner Vittorio Pacitto who after wandering the north for some ten years settled in the town around 1898. The 1901 census found nine kith or kin from Cassino working for him, including his wife Antonia who bore him fourteen children, though just eight survived into adulthood. Among the many others who contributed to Pacitto's success as Middlesbrough's main artificial ice supplier were the Palleschi family, now Paleschi, who were to settle in Thornaby, and Vittorio's younger brother Giacomantonio who after a dozen years quit the family firm to compete very effectively against the half-dozen Italian ice cream businesses already operating in Stockton. Probably the most notable wedding ever between offspring of the North East's leading ice cream families was that of Giacomantonio's son Ernesto with Anita Marcantonio, the eldest daughter of Mark Toney's of Newcastle, which was celebrated in grand style at St Dominic's priory in that city. The couple went on to build a considerable ice cream empire in West London. In 1940, shortly before his internment as an enemy alien at the age of 70, Giacomantonio launched Pacitto's as a private company, splitting the numerous interests he had built up in Stockton, Redcar, and Scarborough between his sons Domenico, Alfonso, and Salvatore. His great-grandson Marco now runs Pacitto's in Dovecot Street, Stockton, the town's very last ice cream parlour and café of Italian origin.

Even after selling his 'Ice Wafer, Sugar Wafer and Twist' factory in Suffield Street to the Greco brothers, Camillo Rea remained one of Middlesbrough's leading Italian businessmen, employing a large staff to maintain his popular temperance bar in Linthorpe Road, his ice cream parlour in Saltburn, and a parlour and chippie on Redcar esplanade. His prominent role in the trade, and the patronage which went with it, passed to his sons Gaetano and Camillo (Camy), who after the war turned the Rea family concern into the largest ice cream enterprise on Teesside, with a chain of a dozen parlours and coffee bars, a special line in its own purpose-built ice cream vans, and a vast wholesale business trading as far as Manchester and Aberdeen.

As a young man Camillo Rea worked his passage to Australia and later voyaged to New York and even Panama in search of further adventure and work opportunities. After opting definitively for Middlesbrough he was absent from Teesside for another four years while serving his country in the Great War. Having survived all that, he was to perish at sea at the age of sixty-one in the tenth month of the next world war when forcibly embarked for deportation along with hundreds of other Italian men who had lived and worked in Britain most of their lives. How this could have occurred is the subject of the next two chapters.

BOOKS AND SOURCES

Information on the ice cream world in the North East is from census returns and trade directories, but above all from oral sources. Immense thanks are due to all the many informants who made this aspect of the book such a pleasure to research and illustrate. Apart from our own recorded interviews, mostly made in the early 1990s, I have drawn on several conducted by Rosemary Allan for Beamish Museum in 1991. *The Ice Cream Industry,* the journal of the Ice Cream Association of Great Britain and Ireland with its running reports on the ups and downs of ice cream, and particularly the many articles by Achille Pompa, was my main source for detailed information on the trade in its heyday. The global success story of ice cream is authoritatively traced and wonderfully illustrated in Pim Reinders, *Licks, Sticks and Bricks: A World History of Ice Cream,* published by Unilever in 1999. Elizabeth David's *Harvest of the Cold Months: The Social History of Ice and Ices* (1994) was put together from her papers after her death and was to have been followed by a history of ice cream parlours and soda fountains. Bernard Moscardini's *La vacanza* (2009, text in English) is a fascinating record of his boyhood years in wartime Sommocolonia with also some recollections of pre-war life among the Italians in the North East. Mike Kirkup's *The Biggest Mining Village in the World: A Social History of Ashington* (1993) has more details of the Ashington 'Italian connection'. Colin Hughes's *Lime, Lemon & Sarsaparilla: the Italian Community in South Wales 1881-1945* (1991) traces a similar story of chain migration (mostly from the Val Ceno) and penetration of the colliery towns. Many thanks to Peter Jackson and Dave McAnelly of the North Pennines Heritage Trust for help with information on the Nenthead miners.

ICE CREAM JUDGES

Class B
Ice Cream Judges
deciding the merits of this delicacy.
Mssrs L.MASSARELLA, A.POMPA AND C.FORTE

These judges at the 1938 National Dairy and Ice Cream Convention at London's Olympia were three heavyweights in the Italian ice cream world: Louis Massarella of Doncaster owned one of the biggest ice cream firms in the north; Achille Pompa was the indefatigable secretary of the Ice Cream Federation; Charles Forte, later Lord Forte, made a fortune out of his chain of milk bars. A diploma award, not to speak of a gold medal or the coveted Silver Cup, gained the winner prestige among his peers and the commercial benefit of guaranteeing the quality of his product. Judges apportioned points according to texture (40), general flavour (30), richness (15), and appearance (15). All the established North-East ice cream businesses competed for awards, and a few even competed at international level. (Ice Cream Industry cartoon, October 1938)

6

FROM FRIENDLY FOREIGNERS TO ENEMY ALIENS

In May 1915 Italy finally abandoned a position of uneasy neutrality and entered the war alongside Britain and France, opening an Alpine front against neighbouring Austria, her old enemy but for the past thirty years her partner with Germany in an anti-French 'Triple Alliance'. The switch of allegiance was bought by the secret Treaty of London which in the event of victory promised the young nation Austrian-controlled land beyond her north-eastern borders and vaguer concessions elsewhere round the Mediterranean. After the war, the reluctance of the wartime allies to honour the full terms of the treaty fanned nationalist resentment in Italy and fuelled popular support for fascist imperialism in the Mediterranean and Africa, a course which was bound to collide sooner or later with British overseas interests. However, at the heady moment of Italy's entry into the war, 24 May 1915, British citizens and Italian residents mingled in the streets to celebrate the common alliance for victory, with big turn-outs in London, Manchester and Glasgow, the cities with the largest concentrations of Italians.

Very different was the experience of Germans and Austro-Hungarians in Britain in the same month. Ten thousand males of military age from these communities had already been crammed into a huge internment camp on the Isle of Man following the start of hostilities in August 1914, and some German business premises had been spontaneously sacked, but in the days following the torpedoing of the *Lusitania* on 7 May 1915 with the loss of over one thousand passengers, a wave of xenophobia whipped on by the press caused such a frenzy that even dachshunds were not safe. Virtually every shop and business carrying a German-sounding name was wrecked and looted, its owner and family terrorised by mobs often numbering thousands. The North East was no exception, with mass violence in Newcastle, Gateshead, Sunderland, North and South Shields, and even in smaller centres like Hebburn and Crook. German pork butchers' shops were the favoured target, no matter whether their proprietors had been settled here for decades or had even naturalised. As a sop to the general hysteria the government stepped up harassment of 'enemy aliens' to the extent of interning another 20,000 over the following months.

No Italian chanting for victory alongside British friends and neighbours in May 1915 could have imagined that twenty-five years later the same fate awaited his own community.

Fascism in Italy and Britain

'THE FASCIST SALUTE at Eldon Square, Newcastle, today, where the party of Italian coal delegates visiting the North-East placed a wreath on the war memorial' (Newcastle Chronicle and Journal, 15 June 1934). Vice-consul Tognoli (centre), who arranged this tribute to the fallen of both countries in the common cause in the Great War, had accompanied these leading buyers of North-East coal and coke on a tour of the region's coalfields, and at the Lord Mayor's dinner in their honour spoke warmly of the historic tradition of Anglo-Italian friendship and commercial collaboration.

After a long and bitter war in which ultimately five British divisions had shared the rigours of the Italian front, solidarity between the two peoples seemed assured for all time. 'We fully recognise the great and immortal part Italy has played in this the world's greatest conflict, and we feel that Italian and British hearts are for ever interwoven to such a degree that nothing – please Almighty God – shall ever separate them.' That was the message marking the first anniversary of victory over Austria which the Pro-Italia Committee[1] for northern England asked the Italian consul-general in Liverpool to pass to 'the King and chief representatives of your glorious country'.

In Italy itself, as in other countries convulsed by the European conflict, the early post-war years were however not a time of national celebration and unity but widespread disaffection with conventional government as its war-wearied population struggled to cope with food shortages, runaway inflation and mass unemployment, particularly high among the five million demobilised servicemen. The ruling liberal government's decision to introduce proportional representation and give all males the vote in time for the 1919 elections fatally undermined its long hold on power by greatly strengthening two ideologically opposed mass parties, the Socialists and the Catholics, each with overwhelming backing among the discontented poorest classes: industrial workers in towns, peasant farmers and labourers in the countryside. Neither party was strong enough yet to unseat the old social order, a coalition of elitist interests that had ruled since unification, but outside parliament the air of crisis intensified as the non-arrival of promised reforms led to land grabs by peasant leagues and unparalleled workplace agitation. Fearful of a proletarian revolution like that in Russia, the propertied classes clamoured for decisive counter-action, but the administration, never doubting the loyalty of army and police in the final instance, patiently looked on, correctly calculating that the uncoordinated revolutionary fervour would eventually fizzle out if granted a few concessions.

The largest mass party of all, the National Fascist Party (PNF), with four million members at the start of the next world war, did not yet exist. Benito Mussolini's miniscule protest movement of young war veterans impatient with 'degenerate' parliamentary democracy derived its sudden growing appeal from its leader's aggressive nationalism and his long quarrel with the socialist party's refusal to back the country during 1915-18 in what it had denounced as a capitalist war. As the leftist revolutionary impulse lost its way in indecisive leadership and anarchic and sometimes murderous excess, Mussolini's incendiary rhetoric inspired armed gangs of 'patriotic' ex-servicemen and others (often abetted by police and army elements) to unleash a campaign of terror to crush 'red' militancy in its strongholds all over the wealthier north and centre of the country. Catholic peasant unions and cooperatives were not spared either. In his pursuit of power the former extremist revolutionary socialist was not only playing to middle class fears but repositioning himself to appeal to the left's most formidable traditional enemies who had everything to gain from authoritarian rule: the monarchy and the Vatican, big business and the big landowners, the very forces of reaction and capitalism which Mussolini had denounced only in 1919 when founding his black-shirted 'combat groups', or *fasci di combattimento*.[2]

By mid-1921, when the government called snap elections, fascism was a mass movement, especially strong in central Italy where it had seized administrative control of many towns and dragooned workers and peasants into its own labour syndicates. The Fascists only gained 35 seats out of more than 500, but in a virtually hung parliament and with parts of the country in the grip of his armed supporters Mussolini exerted disproportionate power. In October 1922, when thousands of fascists resolved to force the issue by staging a 'march on Rome' – with deliberate echoes of Garibaldi's patriotic attempts to seize the capital in the name of the people – government and king lost their nerve and Mussolini was asked to head a coalition government of national reconciliation. Within less than three years, having won over most conservative interests and outmanoeuvred the divided opposition, his position was strong enough to rewrite the parliamentary system and institute a one-party state. Leading opponents were jailed or fled the country.

In Britain, where to right-wing consternation the introduction of universal suffrage had won Labour unparalleled advances, Mussolini's suppression of socialism and his apparently successful experiment in nationalist dictatorship were viewed with favour by most conservatives, and by some with unqualified enthusiasm. One such was Alan Percy, duke of Northumberland, editor of the reactionary-imperialist paper *The Patriot*, another the Tyneside ship owner Lord Runciman, men with no love for democracy who saw the growing militancy of the working class as a sure prelude to red revolution.

The British Fascisti, founded in 1923, and their imitators the National Fascists, were early attempts to launch paramilitary fascist movements along Italian lines. Small branches existed for years in Newcastle and Sunderland. Though they won some limited support among working-class ex-servicemen and a few right-wing MPs and peers and senior military men, and of course hard-core anti-Semites, they were never more than a fringe curiosity, easily ridiculed for apeing funny foreign ways. The same goes for other slightly later fascist forerunners of the more successful British Union of Fascists in the hungry 1930s.

However, it was not the views of a few extremists that from early on gave credence to the notion that at least for 'backward and excitable' Italians fascism was an acceptable answer to labour unrest and national disunity, it was the generally very benign assessment of the new Italian regime regularly put out by the very influential Tory-controlled section of the press and many prominent politicians and intellectuals who were certainly not fascist. National figures like Lloyd George, Churchill, Austen Chamberlain and Neville Chamberlain, Rudyard Kipling and G.B.Shaw, at one time or another expressed wholehearted admiration for the 'Duce' (invariably found 'charming' by British visitors) and all he had 'done for Italy.' The *Times* and *Daily Telegraph* were almost always favourable, while the crusading anti-Bolshevik *Daily Mail* and *Sunday Despatch* were positively celebratory. Overall, the establishment's view is perfectly summed up in H.G.Wells's conclusion: 'Fascism indeed was not an altogether bad thing; it was a bad good thing; and Mussolini has left his mark on history.' This flip verdict, which still seemed to regard fascist totalitarianism (a term proudly coined by Mussolini) as an unexportable Italian phenomenon, was published the year Hitler came to power.

Mussolini did not have to wait long for British endorsement of his rule and methods at the very highest level. On a state visit to Rome only seven months after the 1922 coup, King George V bestowed the Knight's Grand Cross of the Order of the Bath on the Duce, and in his farewell speech spoke warmly of a national crisis overcome 'under the wise leadership of a powerful statesman.' This was equally a compliment to his Italian opposite number, King Victor Emanuel III, who had selected the saviour.

In 1929, when Mussolini and Pius XI signed the Lateran Agreements, or 'Conciliation', declaring the Vatican's territorial sovereignty and Catholicism as the state religion, the Pope himself, who had never disguised his sympathies, bestowed his incalculably influential blessing on the Duce by hailing him as the 'man sent by providence' to heal Italy's historic rift between church and state. Small wonder, then, that the ordinary Italian emigrant in Britain felt proud to be associated with the popular new order and joined in the activities of the national network of Italian fascist clubs sponsored by the consular authorities in all centres with sizeable communities of Italians.

TO THE YOUNG

The old remember the grim Calvary of days gone by. Not the young. They were born in the heady climate of the Fascist Revolution; almost the first thing they saw was the thrilling sight of massed tricolours; their hearts have known only noble surges of pride.

To all young people who turn to this book to learn about the character and spirit of that hard-working, great-hearted phalanx of Italians who have brought the long way here, to Great Britain, the strength of their vigorous arms and their intelligence and innate Italic virtues, this page is dedicated.

No need to go far back in time. The Red Passport – that stigma of poverty and inferiority borne by all Italians setting out to win their bread beyond the confines of the Motherland – lasted right up until the war.

Emigrants they were called, and they were legion. Thronging the frontier stations, the seaports, and the vast smoky basements of the Emigration Offices. Their destination the World. Desperately lonely, shouldering a few wretched belongings, they left to seek the bread that the land of Italy denied them. They left to till uncultivated lands, drain pestilential swamps, dig through the bowels of the earth, lay vast networks of railway tracks, raise infinite buildings to the sky.

They left to procure prosperity and ease for arrogant, ungrateful masters. With no word of comfort or encouragement, no help from those who stayed. They were Italy's ballast, the unproductive surplus to be jettisoned with a sigh of relief: 'Get out into the world, there's bread and jobs out there for everyone…'

How long did this leaching of our race's blood endure, the pitiful and painful exodus of millions of Italians? Twenty years? Thirty years? Forty? 'No corner of the world without the bleaching bones of some stout-hearted Italian.' Garibaldi's very words. Then came the War. The figures prove that for all their moral and material Calvary in their hearts the Emigrants still preserved intact the ties which bound them to the Motherland: from all over the world more than three hundred thousand returned… And they might have been more had not our Consular Offices, festering in indolence and fusty bureaucracy, hindered many from embarking.

They fought like heroes, and then silently went back to their adoptive countries. Asking for nothing. But with hearts full of gall: for at their backs, in the Peninsula, the Bolshevik tempest seemed bent on uprooting everything. Best be away again, they reasoned, than stay to see the end…

And that is why Fascism, the champion of their rights and duties, fearless defender of the moral and material qualities of the race, suddenly fired their imagination. Too long had the emigrants been despised and taunted by the foreigner to remain unmoved by the proud battle cry raised in every corner of the Peninsula. The hour was nigh for national resurgence, the moral and material vindication of the race.

And once again the emigrants were in the front line. They rallied to the black pennants. The Fascist sections abroad (fasci all'estero) multiplied, joined forces, formed a magnificent army. 47 martyrs fell to the enemies' blows, hundreds were wounded.

And the Duce who understood, who himself has known the inexpressible bitterness of life far from the Motherland, struck the first vigorous blow to erase the past. No longer Emigrant, no longer anonymous worker abandoned to the tender mercies of dishonest and brutal employers. A new name: Italian Abroad (Italiano all'Estero).

In the great metropolises, over boundless plains, and in remotest villages, an invigorating gust of

175

pride blows wherever beats an Italian heart. The consular authorities have transformed their spirit and functions: everywhere new initiatives arise, activities thrive, doubters are counselled, the weak defended. "WHEREVER IS AN ITALIAN LET THE MOTHERLAND BE, MAY THE TRICOLOUR FLY, MAY THE GOVERNMENT BE DEFENDED". Once more, the Duce's masculine voice commands redemption.

Now, as year XIV dawns, more than 800 fasci proudly raise their banners beneath eight hundred different skies, amid eight hundred different peoples. Every year more than 15,000 sons and daughters of Italians Abroad leave their countries in response to the maternal summons of the Summer Camps in the Homeland; thousands of workers are mobilised in Fascist organisations; every day the Welfare Agencies extend their work.

Ten million Italians abroad, no longer a footnote detached from the Mother Country, march securely and serenely under the aegis of the Roman standards. They are the Motherland herself, with her social guarantees, her norms for a new life, her renewed creative civilisation.

(Translated from the preface to the *Guida generale degli italiani in Gran Bretagna*, 1936. The *Guida* was both an alphabetical directory and a celebratory account of Italians in Britain issued by Edoardo Ercoli, London publisher of the fascist weekly *L'Italia nostra* (formerly *L'eco d'Italia*), the sole organ for Italians in Britain after 1924. The front cover of the *Guida* for 1939, year XVII of the Fascist Era ('E.F.'), pictured here, shades the British Isles as though they were an imperial possession on a par with Italy's colonies in Africa. Under the angelic figure of Fascist Peace (or Victory?) massed blackshirts salute Rome's 'civilising' world mission, mindful of the regime's manifold achievements celebrated in the marginal vignettes. Many families whose members suffered internment during the war blamed this meticulous listing of Britain's Italians and its accompanying articles steeped in fascist rhetoric for supplying the police with all the information they needed for the round-up of 10 June 1940, and for promoting the impression that every Italian in Britain was a dedicated fascist. In reality local police had for long kept records on all foreign residents under the Alien Certificate of Registration system.)

'Italians Abroad': The Fascist organisation of Italians in Britain

In December 1922, when as the new head of government Mussolini arrived in London for a conference of the wartime allies, reporters were intrigued to find black-shirted Italian residents lining the platform at Victoria Station to greet him with the 'Roman' salute and a band playing *Giovinezza* ('Youth'), the catchy fascist anthem. They were members of the London *fascio*, a new overseas branch of the National Fascist Party, the first in Britain.[3] It was soon destined to be emulated all over the country, to the extent that within a few years the *fasci* would become the sole power centres among the immigrants. Typically, a new *fascio* would arise at the instigation of a politically committed consular representative in collaboration with young patriotically minded veterans of the Great War and leading members of the local Italian business community already involved in organisation and welfare work among the immigrant population.

The annual November banquet for the North East Italian community, commemorating victory in the Great War and the birth of Fascism, County Hotel, Newcastle, circa 1936. Until about the time of this photograph relations between the two former wartime allies were unproblematic and Italians in Britain would have felt no particular division of loyalties. Indeed a portrait of King Edward VIII appears to hang on the wall alongside those of the three figureheads of institutional Italy, King Victor Emmanuel III, Pope Pius XI, and (centre) Mussolini. On these intensely patriotic occasions vice-consul Nestore Tognoli, representing the Fascist state, habitually proposed ceremonial toasts to the reigning monarchs of both Italy and Britain. 'Yes, there were fascists among them. My father was a member of the fascist club. But it was more to do with their identity as Italians actually, it wasn't that they were politically-minded at all. But I think they did appreciate what Mussolini did for Italy, previous to him joining the heathen Hitler.' (Camy Rea, Middlesbrough).

But typically, too, the average Italian immigrant was an apolitical individualist with no fondness for officialdom; his priorities were his family, his job, his attachment to his old home community to which he hoped to return a prosperous man, and perhaps his religion, though this too was largely shaped by parochial memories of village patron saints and festivals. His great failing in the eyes of the fascist converts multiplying around him who mostly shared his same priorities was his lack of 'Italianness', *italianità*, no national feeling, no pride in Rome, Dante, and the Duce, no sense that Italy's sacred destiny mattered infinitely more than his own uncertain future. The animus and language of fascism ('Believe, Obey, Fight!') were of the war generation; and if he had not fought for his country, or thought the casualties of war not heroes but poor victims of grand illusions, then the 'hard-working and great-hearted' emigrant felt little urge to 'rally to the black pennants'. Consequently, although enthusiasts had started *fasci* in every major city in Britain by 1924, their ascendancy was a more gradual process and not more or less universal until around 1930 when the regime in Italy had long since silenced or tamed its most radical elements and bore the reassuring face of middle-class respectability and conformity. Fascism was no longer even presented as a political choice but a birthright: 'All Italians are fascist inasmuch as they are citizens of Italy', declared Prince Colonna, head of the London *fascio*, in 1927. That this happy state was not so all-inclusive is shown by the fact that for the regime and its loyal police 'good Italian' and 'good fascist' were interchangeable terms. All were potentially under *fascio* surveillance, even abroad. And for those with property in Italy, taxes to settle, money to transfer, a pension to claim, it paid to be good.

Politically motivated anti-fascism, as opposed to instinctive wariness of fanatics and windbags, was minimal among the Italians in Britain, mostly confined to the capital and debilitated by disputing rival ideologues with little concern for hard campaigning among their humblest compatriots. Brave attempts at launching anti-fascist broadsheets soon folded for lack of subscribers as much as fascist intimidation. *L'Italia nostra,* the embassy-backed official voice of Britain's *fasci*, dismissed all non-believers as delinquent anti-Italians, yet it is good to know that during all the conformist years a few stubborn individuals, stalked by Scotland Yard as well as Italian fascist agents and informers, still kept the lines of defiance open between London and Paris, the headquarters of European anti-fascism. One or two very prominent opponents of the regime also spent some of their exile years in London, but they lobbied at a high level and had no impact among the Italian settlers at large. The new creed of Mussolinian nationalism ('Mussolini Is Always Right') had a relatively easy ride among Italians in Britain, certainly compared to the early years of fascist proselytising in the United States and especially South America where anarchism and socialism enjoyed a long pedigree among a vocal minority of immigrants, or France and Switzerland where Italians made up a considerable portion of the workforce in industry and construction and were much more receptive to oppositional thinking than Britain's mostly small-time self-employed Italians, or lowly operatives in the world of catering.

In any case, when almost all one's knowledge of the public domain in Italy came from respectable believers in black shirts or black soutanes who all appeared to be saying the new faith stood for nothing more controversial than nation, hard work, and family values (of the good old patriarchal sort), what reason was there to be anti? These well-spoken proud-to-be-Italian folk stood up for your own kind among a population that looked down on foreigners and even proclaimed that nothing was more fascist than your daily struggle to better your lot in the world. Proof of the eventual conversion or acquiescence of the majority is that the twenty-five *fasci* sections and sub-sections in place by the mid-1930s provide a reliable map of the extent of all major and minor centres of Italian settlement in the British Isles: London, Bristol, Southampton, Birmingham, Manchester, Cardiff, Swansea, Burton-on-Trent, Sheffield, Bradford, Leeds, Liverpool, Hull, Middlesbrough, Newcastle-on-Tyne, Carlisle, Glasgow, Greenock, Edinburgh, Stirling, Dundee, Aberdeen, Dublin, Londonderry, Belfast.

By no means all were deeply involved. Within the territory covered by each *fascio* only a small number of men (few women) were full party members (*iscritti,* or *tesserati*), while from a quarter to half the remainder might be classified by the authorities as affiliates (*organizzati*), ranging from assiduous to occasional attenders who at the very least subscribed to the *fascio*'s social ideal of Italian brotherhood, while the rest simply got on with their lives, too busy or indifferent or alienated from their origins to be bothered with it. In most cases, including the North East, the *fascio* activists were from the more prosperous end of the community, self-made men who could readily associate their own personal success stories with Italy's 'resurgence'.

The back-lane barrow lads, the asphalters, the terrazzo workers, even if few showed up for meetings, no doubt found some consolation for their tough lives in the quasi-religious message that somewhere back home a great man cared about them.

By 1928 the regime had evolved a comprehensive ideology and policy with regard to the emigrant millions. As entry restrictions were tightened by the traditional receiving countries, including Britain and notably the United States with its barely disguised bias against Jews and Italians, fascism was forced to view mass emigration less as a necessary evil and more as a long story of national humiliation. It had to be controlled, it made foreigners suppose Italians were all ignorant peasants and that even under the Duce's infallible leadership the motherland could not provide for her sons: professionals and the highly skilled might be given new passports to leave, the rest should be draining marshes and building *autostrade* at home, or 'tilling uncultivated lands' not in Brazil and Argentina but in Italy's three desert colonies in Africa. On the other hand, those who could not be tempted back, and whose remissions home were so precious to the economy, could be turned into a ten million-strong army[4] of fervent patriots keen to present only the most positive image of the orderly and disciplined new Italy all over the world. All they needed was a more positive image of themselves. With one wave of his masculine arm the Duce transformed them all from common emigrants into respectable and self-respecting 'Italians abroad', *Italiani all'estero*.

In his ultra-nationalism Mussolini and his collaborators were harking back to a more or less discredited earlier era of Italian colonialism in the first decades after national unification. Then too the spin was that mass emigration was not mass defection but a mighty demographic process of peaceful world colonisation by a prolifically fertile and creative young 'proletarian' nation, and then too the great enemy of *italianità* was sneeringly labelled *snazionalizzazione*, the de-nationalising effect of cultural and linguistic assimilation in the host countries. To check and reverse the menace, the regime's reorganisation of the state and indoctrination of the masses back home was projected onto the consular corps abroad by 'fascistising' its personnel and priorities and ordering it to organise and educate all Italians abroad, in particular the young who were most in danger of being lost to Italy.

So all the *fasci italiani all'estero*, the more or less self-generated fascist sections abroad, became government-vetted foreign branches of the PNF with, in the case of Britain, prestigious headquarters in London under the presidency of the Italian ambassador, himself a 'first hour' fascist, answerable to a general secretariat of all *fasci all'estero* at the Ministry for Foreign Affairs in Rome. All children were expected to join appropriate local sections of the fascist youth movement and study the language of their parents. Welfare work, formerly left almost entirely to church missions and workers' self-help organisations, was fascistised by subjecting every emigrant occupational and cultural organisation to *fascio* supervision and scrutiny, while the Bonomelli Foundation, the worldwide Catholic organisation dedicated to emigrant welfare, was simply dissolved and its duties allotted to the consular authorities and women's sections of the various *fasci*. Though state-sponsored, provincial *fasci* such as that in Newcastle received no funding beyond being allowed to keep three-fifths of the income from PNF subscriptions, but in enthusiastic hands the need to be self-financing could stimulate greater activism.

The impression of one harmonious 'colony' solidly united in its devotion to Italy and the Duce was fostered everywhere in Britain by scheduling communal events to coincide with the main dates in the fascist national calendar: 6 January, *la befana fascista*, or fascist version of the traditional Epiphany present-giving to children; 21 April, *il natale di Roma e festa del lavoro italiano,* Italian Labour Day on the legendary anniversary of the founding of Rome; 15 August, *ferragosto,* feast of the Assumption and peak of the summer holiday season in Italy, but also regular fixture for the annual reunion of Italian fascists in Britain; 28 October, *la marcia su Roma,* anniversary of the 1922 'march on Rome', the birth-date of the new 'fascist era' (destined to supplant the Christian era, and expressed of course in Roman numerals); and 4 November, *la Vittoria,* the anniversary of Italian victory over Austria in the Great War, commemorating also the heroic dead. These last two crucial dates with history falling only a week apart were generally celebrated on the same day.

For events of this kind party members donned black shirts and reported to their local *fascio* assembly hall, *la sala del fascio,* with their little ones in tow dressed in the party youth uniforms for boys *(balilla)* and girls *(piccole italiane),* from which if not too bored or disillusioned they could graduate to teenage *avanguardisti* (male) or *giovani italiane* (female). Both sexes, taught separately to preserve decorum, were instructed in Italian and in Italian nationalism at regime-financed after-hours 'Italian schools'. Through the *fascio,* which of course controlled PNF membership, ambitious parents could compete on behalf of their children for much-contested places in the *colonie estive,* paramilitary youth summer camps in Italy entirely funded by the regime once the children were inside the country. Wealthier members of the community made conspicuous donations towards other travel costs. The children, up to 200 from all over the British Isles, would assemble outside PNF headquarters before parading through central London for an emotional send-off by tearful parents and fascist dignataries at Victoria station. The less fortunate could always attend one of the military-style 'Benito Mussolini' holiday camps run by the London *fascio* in Felixstowe and Maidstone, or by the Scottish *fasci* at Portencross on the Ayrshire coast. 'Dawn of life, hope of the Motherland,' crooned the Duce, 'and above all army of tomorrow.'

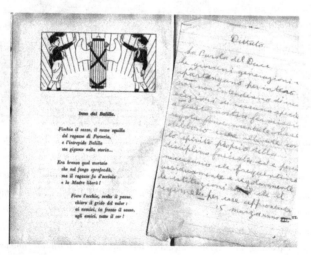

'The Duce Says': a sheet of dictation found in the pages of a primer used in the fascist regime's Italian schools in Britain. The chorus of the Balilla anthem translates: 'Proud his gaze, sure his tread/ One brave summons he sends:/ For the foe a stone in the head,/ All his heart for his friends.' The boy hero Balilla, a legendary figure in Genovese folk history, supposedly threw the first stone in a successful insurrection against Austrian troops occupying the city.

NEWCASTLE-ON-TYNE. — Gli alunni della Scuola Italiana ed i loro valorosi Insegnanti.

St Andrew's RC church hall, Newcastle: 'The Italian School pupils and their valiant teachers' (photo from L'Italia nostra, *April 1932). Supervised by Nestore and Rita Tognoli, the boys sit to one side and the girls to the other.*

La befana fascista *or Fascist Twelfth Night party, Newcastle, about 1932 (press cutting from a family album).*
The boys wear the standard balilla *outfit prescribed by the regime, a blackshirt version of the international Boy*
Scout uniform; the girls or piccole italiane *wear a black skirt and tie with white shirt and stockings. Each year up*
to ten young scholars from the three Italian schools in the region were selected to attend the immensely popular
summer camps in Italy paid for by the regime. A 'balilla' of the time recalled half a century later how special it felt
to be chosen: 'Through the Fasci Italiani all'Estero I was given a medal by the Italian school in Middlesbrough,
and a scholarship to go to a camp in Italy, at Cattolica on the Adriatic Sea. It was the summer of 1937 and we
were there for six weeks. We were fitted out and kitted out and drilled and trained in the use of rifles – the wooden
ones! On one occasion we were inspected by Count Ciano, Mussolini's foreign minister. It was the most wonderful
time I'd ever had. But it was a propaganda time, no question of the fact. We were called together and shown films
of priests and nuns being burned and of Italian soldiers sacrificing their lives. This was during the Spanish Civil
War, and we were told how terrible it was, and how the Italians had gone out to Spain to save them.'

Other national governments resented these unprecedented actions by branches of a foreign party, and protested accordingly – in the United States so strongly that Mussolini ordered the suppression of all *fasci* there in 1929. But although the Home Office did eventually fret a bit about the legitimacy of this Italian state posturing on British soil it never put any pressure on Rome, indeed obliged the regime by keeping tabs on resident Italian antifascists. As for our press, all this activity, when noticed, was observed with a mixture of curiosity and benevolence. Photographs of Italian blackshirt meetings, school parades, children's parties, departing holiday campers, were published without adverse comment. They simply reflected the happy and orderly society which everyone knew was Mussolini's new Italy. On Armistice Day in Newcastle, as in other cities, representatives of the North-East colony headed by the vice-consul and the secretary of the Newcastle *fascio*, routinely joined the civic parade to the cenotaph in Eldon Square to lay a wreath in memory of the Italian fallen.

Gaetano Salvemini, one of fascism's fiercest and most effective critics who spent nearly ten years in Britain as a political exile and travelled often to the United States to try to open the eyes of influential people over there, in the end had to acknowledge despairingly that the regime's propaganda machine was extraordinarily successful both in winning general approval abroad and in feeding millions of emigrants' yearning for improved status and self-esteem: 'They had felt themselves despised by everyone because they were Italians – and now they heard everyone say, even Americans, that Mussolini had turned Italy into a great country, that there were no unemployed, that everyone had a bathroom in his house, that trains ran on time, and that Italy was now respected and feared. Whoever contradicted all this, not only destroyed their ideal country, but insulted their personal dignity'.

'ANTIFASCIST, ABROAD, ENGLAND'

Italian political police file on Giuseppe Zari, resident in Newcastle. The state central archives in Rome from the fascist period contain thousands of files on suspect individuals, 382 of them Italians in Britain. In November 1926, anticipating embarrassing protests or even an assassination attempt during Mussolini's forthcoming visit to Britain, the Ministry of the Interior in Rome requested reports on all known resident 'subversives'. The Liverpool consul-general De Carolis wrote of Zari, a terrazzo specialist employed by Rowles Ltd of Newcastle and evidently a man of some means: 'He is naturalised British and fiercely anti-fascist, capable of materially and financially sponsoring any plot against the Head of Government. I have arranged for special surveillance of his words and actions in order to determine his movements.' Nothing else of consequence appears in the file. Consular staff depended on a network of not

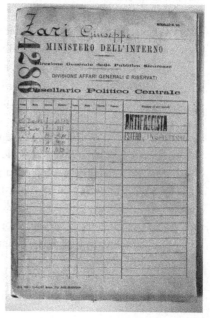

aleays reliable informers. After a tip-off that a café owner in a Durham pit village no longer attended the monthly fascio meetings because he was a covert mason and communist, vice-consul Tognoli paid a visit to the man and found the truth more prosaic: 'Following repeated communist demonstrations in the village and fearing his business would be totally ruined if his fascio membership were known, he and his brother have ceased attending.' Fears about an anti-fascist anarchist cell in the North East comprising 'about twenty' of the Newcastle asphalt and terrazzo workers 'from North Italy' (i.e. Friulans) also seem to have proved unfounded after closer investigation of the main personalities involved, including presumably Zari. Interestingly, another file contains political clearance of an individual provided by the chief constable of Durham police.

Italian fascist clubs in the North East

Although the largest regional spread of Italians outside London and the central belt of Scotland was in the North East – almost 3000 in 1935 according to Italian figures which always include children of Italians born here – the presiding authority remained the consul-general in Liverpool, with responsibility for a further 2000 nationals in the North West and Midlands, mainly concentrated in Manchester.[5] To answer their needs and those of British-Italian commercial interests in this large constituency, consular agents were maintained in other centres of migrant settlement and trade with Italy: Manchester, Bradford (including Leeds), Hull, and Newcastle. Each had its own *fascio*.

The Newcastle *fascio* was started as early as October 1923 under the auspices of the consular agent Renato De Carolis, an importer of Italian marble and a veteran of the recent war. On his promotion to vice-consul in Liverpool in 1924, the agent's post passed to Captain Francesco Valle, a ship's provisioner and importer of Italian food products who was also fascist party overseer, *fiduciario del fascio*, for the North East and Cumberland (another early *fascio* had been started by enthusiasts in Carlisle). Ever since the war the Newcastle chamber of commerce had pressed for Italian representation at vice-consular level, as had been the case until 1899, but only in September 1928, as part of the reorganisation of policy toward the worldwide emigrant population, did Rome give the go-ahead.

The prestigious appointment went not to Valle but to Nestore Tognoli, a language teacher and commercial translator who was then secretary of the Newcastle *fascio*. Tognoli had proved his credentials by leading an anti-Valle faction in the *fascio* which accused the *fiduciario* of obstructing Rome's orders to set up a permanent clubroom (*sede del fascio*) and a language school for the children of immigrant families. As well as losing his consular job, Valle was expelled from the party, while Tognoli's post of *fascio* secretary went to Federigo Moscardini, the Stanley temperance bar proprietor from Sommocolonia whom we met in chapter 5. (Giuseppe Castellina was secretary from 1930, Marco Casella from 1932, and Claudio Bava from 1934 until the war).

Tognoli, a northern Italian who is said to have needed an interpreter in his dealings with his many southern compatriots, was an able and conscientious organiser who grew to be a popular figure among the North East's Italians, trusted for his energy and commitment to their welfare. In Saville House, Saville Row, a large city centre building which already housed the Italian consular office and Gouin Language School where he taught, Tognoli opened a tricolour-bedecked *sede del fascio* and a small reading-room, and also revived Montaldi's pre-war classes for Italian children.[6] Liverpool covered teaching costs for these Saturday classes and supplied the recommended elementary school textbooks designed to instil military valour in boys and domestic virtues in girls. All pupils wore the prescribed youth uniforms. The boys were taught by Tognoli himself, while his no less energetic wife Rita took the *piccole italiane*. In June 1929, a small theatre was opened with much fanfare in Saville House, and here the children would stage end-of-term recitals of patriotic poems and prayers and songs, or perform improving playlets contrived by Rita who regularly received a bouquet for her hard work which also included devising and sewing the costumes. In 1932 the little school of forty to fifty pupils moved to new premises at St Andrew's RC church, the traditional place of worship for the city's Italians. Signora Tognoli also headed a *fascio femminile*, or women's committee, which organised the Twelfth Night *befana fascista* party and prizes for young stars of the school, as well as charity work among needy immigrant families, of which there were not a few in those years of general economic hardship. Never had local Italians experienced anything like this scale of official involvement and concern for their lives.

Since Cumberland and Westmoreland were also within his remit, the new vice-consul kept an eye on the struggling Carlisle *fascio*, and also on developments in Middlesbrough where a *fascio* had been set up in March 1928 as part of the regime's overhaul of its international network. The launch in the Hotel Excelsior was attended by the Liverpool consul-general, its instigator, and fifty local Italian 'fascists'. But the Middlesbrough *fascio* was never to possess the sort of resources enjoyed by its wealthier cousin in Newcastle. Members attended monthly meetings in a room above Lena Martino's cafe in Newport Road, opposite the Princess Alice pub, and for grand occasions booked space elsewhere including the Town Hall. Umberto Panico, proprietor of a popular ice-cream parlour in Hill Street, remained secretary of the Middlesbrough *fascio* right up until the war. The Middlesbrough *scuola italiana*, with up to thirty pupils, convened at the Mill Hill St Mary's junior school, but in the later thirties following some sort of 'altercation', possibly political, decamped to a room above a grocer's shop near the Infirmary. Alberto Scappaticci, the college-educated son of the unlettered Francesco Scappaticci who had once dominated the pre-war Teesside ice cream world, took the boys. Signora Tognoli commuted weekly from Newcastle to teach the girls. Sunderland, despite grumbles, never got its own *fascio*. Those interested attended meetings and events in nearby Newcastle, or from 1932 went through to Durham where the vice-consul had set up a small school and meeting-room above Dimambro's shop on Claypath. Here the teacher for the Wednesday evening classes was again Rita Tognoli, whom one former pupil, Tony Sacco, who later fought with the Durhams in North Africa and Italy, remembered as 'a real fire-cracker who wouldn't stand any nonsense, so we used to really look up to her'.

These subsidised classes offering children basic after-hours tuition in Italian were viewed by the authorities as a crucial medium for the education of the entire immigrant community, since apart from hoping to turn out good little fascists able to chant a few phrases and songs in standard Italian, which for most was not their first language, their learning activities and mini-parades were a perfect vehicle to impress and involve the parents whose own level of education and sentiments of *italianità* might scarcely come up to those of their anglicised children. Some mums and dads had not seen Italy since they themselves were kids. 'The work of the schools,' the Liverpool consul-general reported to the Foreign Ministry at the end of 1928, 'and the evident benefits they bring to the new generation are rousing a vague awareness in the adults of their duties toward their own country'. Selling nationalism always had to contend with the inescapable fact that as far as his own country went every emigrant had turned his back and voted with his feet.

All the same, a combination of any exile's idealisation of home, up-beat speeches at social gatherings and genuine intervention on their behalf won general acceptance, if not necessarily deep politicisation. As Louis Ciaraldi, an observant little boy at the time, pithily put it fifty years later: 'There were meetings every month to hear a couple of blokes talking about how good Mussolini was doing for Italy and all that carry-on. A lot couldn't read or write. They'd been here thirty or forty years, and they'd say, "He must be doing good, because it was terrible when I was there!"'

The at best rudimentary education of the mass of migrants no doubt made most fairly easy converts to the basic chauvinist myths of fascism (and unassimilated nationals abroad are normally much more patriotically inclined than their equivalents back home) but equally their political naivety was the despair of the bureaucrats who hoped to make effective operatives of at least some of them. Back in 1925, Renato De Carolis, who knew our region very well, declared he was unable to recommend a single local replacement for the unsatisfactory Captain Valle as Newcastle consular agent: 'to the best of my knowledge there does not exist in that city even one of our compatriots whose financial, social and cultural circumstances would enable him to represent Italy and the royal government with dignity and efficiency.' Again in 1936, when vice-consul Tognoli unexpectedly threatened to step down, the new Liverpool consul-general Count Ottavio Gloria found 'in Newcastle and neighbouring localities no co-nationals or foreigners who can be entrusted with the job of managing our consular office.' Even as late as 1940, the following unwittingly poignant report by the count's successor shows once more how for the bulk of poorly educated Italians if not their cultured minders 'fascism' was little more than another word for unquestioning patriotism.

'KEEN AND (ALAS!) ILLITERATE'

The criteria which prompted the organisation of the Fasci in this consular district were laudable at the time they were set up... Nonetheless, in the light of subsequent experience and the level of results it would be fair to say that from the outset too many Fasci were created, particularly considering it was plainly not enough to have plenty of keen and (alas!) illiterate Italians, but for every Fascio to function autonomously those selected as secretaries had to possess not just enthusiasm and goodwill but the ability to interpret soundly and fully implement the Secretary General's instructions, while also maintaining and ensuring an active and tangible correspondence with the Secretariat. Thus it happened that once the Carlisle and Middlesbrough Fasci were made independent entities the persons appointed believed (note that both localities are several hundred kilometres from Liverpool) they were wholly fulfilling their duties by maintaining the enthusiastic spirit they always demonstrated whenever Consul-General Count Gloria visited them, and by carrying out admirable work of brotherhood and solidarity among the fascists, while at the same time evincing no interest in anything resembling organisation. Living in isolation and goaded into this state of personal enthusiasm by a hostile environment, in thrall as it were to their very enthusiasm, in good faith they considered any sort of stable and planned organisation superfluous, not least because their rudimentary education was not up to deciphering the Secretary General's circulars which to their eyes frequently appeared nothing short of an enigma. Hundreds of kilometres from centres with larger nuclei of Italians, and more able and capable Italians, hard at work all week, it was often impossible for them to find anyone to turn to for enlightenment and advice, thus in the end they fell into the habit of simply receiving the Secretariat's letters and not answering them. In sum, when the Secretariat sent out a letter some months ago reproaching several of them for their inactivity I had to adopt the most humane approach and the greatest tact in transmitting the reprimand, in particular with two whom I ran into in November at a meeting in Manchester attended by many Italians from the region. Even so, these two people did not even understand what it was they were being reproached with; they were as hurt as if they had been accused of harbouring anti-patriotic sentiments. From the way in which they interpreted the Secretariat's letters I am now convinced that a not unreasonable measure to propose is that both these Fasci be closed down and made branches of the Fascio in Newcastle under the suspervision of an overseer.'

(A. Rotini, Liverpool consul-general, 22 January 1940, to the Foreign Ministry in Rome)

Another photograph of one of the annual November banquets, County Hotel, Newcastle. The walls are decorated with Italian flags, the banner of the Newcastle fascio (behind the tallest of the standing dignitaries), and portraits of Italy's king and queen flanking that of the Duce.

The most important social event in the Italian North East calendar, attended by immigrants from all over the region including representatives of the Carlisle and Middlesbrough *fasci*, was the annual celebration of the march on Rome and victory in the Great War. Always held in Newcastle in the same week as Remembrance Day, the great day opened in St Mary's cathedral with a morning mass for the fallen with the whole congregation gathered behind the national flag and local *fasci* standards. Those who could afford the five-shilling ticket then repaired to the County Hotel for a long lunch to the strains of classic Italian numbers performed by Colombo Riani's all-Italian band in a dining hall decorated with red, white and green national flags and flowers, and portraits of the royal couple and the Duce. The entire event of course was masterminded by vice-consul Tognoli and his Signora who together with local ice cream kings Marcantonio, Moscardini, Bertorelli, and Mancini, regularly donated big prizes for the raffle in aid of needy Italian families. 150 attended the 1931 banquet when the guest of honour was Liverpool consul-general Giuseppe Biondelli (promoted to London in 1936). He warmly congratulated the gathering on their customary wondrous show of communal solidarity before delivering a rousing speech on 'the remarkable progress Italy has made under the Fascist Regime, showing how Italy is now a world leader, and how much can be learned from Her, even by richer and more powerful older nations' (*L'Italia nostra*). Singing the *balilla* anthem, the Italian school's uniformed boys and girls filed past the regime's illustrious representatives and then entertained the company to patriotic songs and sketches. After more food and dancing, festivities concluded at eleven o'clock with all up on their feet singing *Giovinezza* and *Fratelli d'Italia* followed by hurrahs for the king, the Duce, and Italy.

There will be readers who hearing of these things today are appalled at such wholehearted enthusiasm for fascism. Fascism in its too many guises is a pernicious and contagious creed whose dismal history shows to what extremes of inhumanity blind nationalism and hostility to its presumed enemies can lead. But in the *Italian emigrant* form I am documenting here, intellectually and geographically remote from the unquestionably dangerous and manipulative opinion-makers in Rome and the Italian embassy in London, fascism was really nothing more threatening than a fellowship of credulous and isolated expatriates trying to create a little bit of heartening space for themselves (see Biondelli's words above) within a country that in the name of enlightened imperialism ruled a quarter of the globe. For most of these people 'fascism' meant little more than 'Italian', their team, and all the better if the English had actually heard of it. This, I am sure, is the sense in which to interpret the seemingly bizarre news that an Italian wedding in Middlesbrough in 1930, complete with a black-shirted guard of honour, was proudly billed by its organisers as 'the North East's first fascist wedding', or that the Blackshirts was a football team in the upper Wear valley managed by a syndicate of soccer-mad local Italian ice-cream men. If such naivety or hootspah is still considered inexcusable, then it need only be remembered that in one way or another almost every Italian in Britain, guilty or innocent, suffered for it when war came.

Toward war

One perturbing factor conditioned every Italian's response to the rallying call of the *fasci*: all immigrants were keenly sensitized to anti-Italian feeling in the larger society within which they

Meeting of the Newcastle 'Fascio', County Hotel, Newcastle, in the mid 1930s. Centre, behind the table under a framed portrait of the Duce and the banner of the Newcastle fascio, stands the guest of honour, the Italian consul-general for Great Britain, Giuseppe Biondelli, flanked by Newcastle vice-consul Nestore Tognoli and his wife Rita. 'It was in the paper about the consul having meetings. The police tried to discourage things, and a lot dropped out. They'd come to the house and quiz you, in a roundabout way, because you were an alien.' (Louis Ciaraldi, referring to the increasing tensions for Italians in the later 1930s)

were here to make a living. In the very first years of the new regime two events in particular shook the general impression abroad that now fascism enjoyed the responsibility of power it rejected its brute origins. British public opinion was deeply hostile when in 1923 in retaliation for a minor incident Mussolini ordered the bombardment and occupation of the Greek island of Corfu, the first act of war in Europe since 1918. Next year the regime nearly collapsed under the pressure of worldwide outrage at the assassination of its most persuasive parliamentary opponent, the socialist leader Giacomo Matteotti. An antifascist rally filled Trafalgar Square, and for once a British government (Labour, briefly in power that year) was openly critical. Immigrant support drained away. On the other hand, by 1926, the year of the General Strike, membership was picking up again with the Tories back in command and right-wing politicians and media once more lauding the 'strong man' in Italy who had knocked the workers into line by outlawing socialism and communism, banning strikes, and bringing trade unions under state control.

By the early Thirties fascist rule excited little opposition in either Italy or abroad, and this was reflected in the overall immigrant support for the *fasci*. A worrisome cautionary lesson though was the scale of popular hostility to Sir Oswald Mosley's British Union of Fascists (BUF), with opposition particularly well-organised and effective in the North East after Hitler's accession to power in 1933. Back in 1927, while still a Labour MP, Mosley had mocked home-grown National Fascist adherents as 'black-shirted buffoons making a cheap imitation of ice-cream sellers', but a visit to Rome in 1932 left him dazzled by the Duce and the country's apparent ability to ride the world economic recession through a policy of wage cuts, state takeovers of failing firms, and enormous investment in public works. To Mosley and others, Britain in the midst of the Depression seemed ripe for similar treatment, but his fatal fascination with Mussolini, and soon Hitler even more, was probably a greater deterrent to support than the movement's growing reputation for violence. It scarcely even looked British. The BUF paraded in black shirts, adopted the *fasces* and the Roman salute, and belted out 'Onward Blackshirts' to the tune of *Giovinezza*.

Though naturally sympathetic, Italian fascists did not turn out alongside Mosley's men, not even in 1934 at the time of the BUF's maximum popularity when Lord Rothermere notoriously used the pages of his *Daily Mail* to shout 'Hurrah For The Blackshirts!' There were discrete contacts at the highest level, in fact the Italian embassy was secretly paying a lavish £5,000 monthly to the BUF as well as subsidising various other British enthusiasts for the Italian regime, but extreme care was taken not to involve the organised immigrants in such a patently controversial area of domestic politics. More than foreign mini-Mussolinis, the Duce needed continuing high-level political support abroad for his own regime, particularly now that his foreign policy was poised to take a much more audacious turn. Fascism was not for export, he famously said, for how could *italianità*, its core belief, be shared by anyone not of the unique Italian race? His first two 'commandments' for the conduct of Italians abroad instructed them to respect the laws of the host country and have nothing to do with its politics. This stopped them tarnishing the good name of Italy, protected them from fascism's many foreign opponents, and preserved them for loyal service to their own country.

A fundamental test of that loyalty came in mid-1935 when it became apparent that Italian troops were massing in Italian Eritrea in order to annex neighbouring Abyssinia (Ethiopia), the last large uncolonised country in Africa, and with a long and honourable history of resistance to Italian imperialism. British public opinion rose massively for the underdog against the 'bully'. Anti-Italian feeling ran so high that several Italian businesses in London were attacked after some newspapers and politicians called for armed intervention over this flagrant flouting of League of Nations principles by one of its signatories. Friendship with Italy had been Britain's undeviating policy ever since the Risorgimento, and with another nationalist dictator flexing his muscles in Germany appeasing Mussolini now seemed even more urgent to Britain and France, Italy's old wartime partners. But democratic governments also have public opinion to appease, so a few more battleships were sent to the Mediterranean, and once the invasion of Abyssinia got going Britain backed League of Nations sanctions against the aggressor. It was largely bluff. Britain made sure sanctions did not apply to oil and kept the Suez Canal open to Italian supply ships, and very soon it emerged that for the sake of a quick return to peaceful relations France and Britain were happy to cut a scandalous deal which would have handed Italy two-thirds of Abyssinia without a fight. Mussolini of course wanted the lot, and besides was well served by the British-led boycott which conveniently bolstered Italian jingoism, an aggrieved sense of victimisation by nations with bigger empires. In May 1936, having completed his 'civilising mission' with the aid of aerial bombardment and mustard gas against spear-wielding tribesmen, Mussolini stepped out onto the famous balcony of Palazzo Venezia in Rome to announce to delirious crowds the founding of a new Roman empire.

The Duce's defiance of world opinion had made the regime more popular than ever, just when national support had been showing ominous signs of slippage. During the seven-month contest Italy's historic ally and mentor became 'perfidious Albion'. Banners and lapel badges proclaiming 'God damn the English' (*Dio stramaledica gli inglesi*) were prominent at official Pro-Patria appeals for cash and gold toward the war effort. A quarter of a million women, including the queen, gave up their wedding rings in exchange for cheap iron ones.

Primed by years of assertive patriotic rhetoric, the 'colony' in Britain also rose to the occasion. *L'Italia nostra* mounted a counter-boycott ('Patronise Italian tea-rooms', 'One glass of Italian wine is worth ten of beer'), and with embassy money rushed out 20,000 copies of a new weekly English-language bulletin to promote the Italian version of the truth about the war against Christian Abyssinia. In the nationwide Pro-Patria appeal organised through the *fasci* the Newcastle *fascio* was the first to call for cash donations to the Italian Red Cross, Tognoli's favourite charity, in solidarity with the Duce's 'sacred colonising mission'. The North East's final cash total, plus kilos of gold and silver and other valuables, was over double the combined contributions of the Liverpool and Manchester *fasci*, proof not only of the level of local patriotic fervour but the substantial prosperity enjoyed by many of the region's Italians in the Ice Age.

Vice-consul Tognoli must have derived enormous personal satisfaction from this incontrovertible demonstration of how successfully he had promoted fascist nationalism among the North East's Italians. He and other men at the top pitched in with fivers and tenners, and numerous humbler folk including some who had never had much to do with the *fascio* gave a hard-earned shilling, or even five bob. At the great patriotic November 1935 banquet (now reduced to basic military rations in solidarity with Italy's fighting men) an appeal for donations in gold and silver spurred 'a truly moving rivalry' led by Rita Tognoli in which 'various ladies stripped off wedding rings, necklaces and other precious objects.' Men denuded themselves too: cufflinks, gold watches, tiepins, cigarette cases and lighters, gold buttons, twenty dollar pieces, even war medals. *L'Italia nostra*'s weekly listings of names and donations no matter how small from all over the country kept up the momentum and peer pressure here. Eight male wedding rings eventually joined the wives' nineteen. At the final cash count in February 1936, the region's front runners by several lengths were Benedetto Notarianni (Sunderland) with £30 – more than a half-year's wages for a shop-girl – and Aleardo Rossi (Stockton) with £29, though the moral winner was surely Alfredo Gallone (Ashington) who donated ten pounds plus his war pension. The UK grand total – 'our retort to the sanctions' (*L'Italia nostra*) – was not far short of £2 million by today's reckoning.

But this was only the official, triumphalist face of things. Underneath lay another reality. In the contest between poor 'proletarian' Italy and mighty 'plutocratic' Britain most of the community 'felt Italian', yet on the personal and practical level few had any deep quarrel with the English. Everyone had lived here peaceably for years, a number had married locally, and all had livelihoods to consider, not to mention the future of grown sons who if born in England would be liable for call-up if ever war came. The North East's response in cash and gold had been truly magnificent, well worth a telegram to Mussolini ('These Italian workers are all up on their feet awaiting their Duce's orders for the glory of Italy'), but the Liverpool consul-general who composed the telegram also privately reported 'strong currents of *snazionalizzazione*' throughout the region. In another despatch to Rome he blamed 'the violent campaign against our country in recent months, artfully spread rumours about the internal and external situation of Italy, and the intensification of the most insubstantial tales about the consequences for our co-nationals here of an eventual state of war between Italy and England.'[7]

Yet this was the eventuality toward which everything was inexorably moving. The most ominous consequence of the clash over Abyssinia was Mussolini's rapprochement with Hitler, his sudden talk of a 'Rome-Berlin axis' when just two years earlier he had stood up to the Führer's designs on Austria with threats of armed intervention. The clash with Britain and France had driven the country to depend increasingly on German investment and German coal, and within only months of the Abyssinian annexation the two dictators were intervening together on Franco's side in the Spanish Civil War. Again Britain shirked conflict, even when Italian planes sank British ships in Spanish ports. In September 1938, during the crisis over the fate of Czechoslovakia, Mussolini claimed his sway with Hitler had preserved Europe from a second world war, and he continued to pose as indispensable arbitrator and man of peace, despite scooping up Albania after watching Britain and France again do nothing when Hitler finally took Czechoslovakia in March 1939. By then the Duce had introduced the goose step and anti-Semitic laws on Nazi lines, and in May he was to commit his country to a full military alliance with Germany, although the immense costs of colonising Abyssinia and assisting Franco had left Italy in no condition to contemplate a far more demanding conflict. When war came in September, Italy prudently remained 'non-belligerent', Mussolini's euphemism for the more craven-sounding 'neutral'. Most of the population, as in 1914, and even his High Command, were greatly relieved.

The *fasci*'s long holiday in Britain was over. Special Branch had finally begun to take an interest in their activities during the Abyssinian conflict, and as Italy and Germany drew closer together there was sudden anxiety about spies and sabotage. Churchill, the leading anti-appeaser, called on the Chamberlain government to ban both the *fasci* and their Nazi imitations, the Landesgruppen or Auslands Organisation, but despite repeated heart-searching in cabinet no action was ever taken for fear of worsening relations with both organisations' masters. All the same, the Public Order Act (1936) banning paramilitary uniforms, a measure designed to reduce BUF clashes with anti-fascist protesters, also had the side effect of driving the *fasci all'estero* off the streets. Tognoli's dwindling Newcastle and Durham pupils now changed into their fascist youth outfits on school premises.

Snazionalizzazione was right out in the open now. Distressed at the change of mood and fearing where it was leading, some families took the precautionary disguise of Englishing their surnames, and I have been told of an Italian husband who adopted his English wife's surname, and a son, once a stalwart of the Middlesbrough *fascio,* who assumed his English mother's maiden name. Applications for British citizenship soared. The general anxiety about imminent war affected business too. While the going was still good, some families sold up and decamped to the old country along with their carefully accumulated savings. In these strange times repatriation could seem a patriotic action. The regime was pressuring emigrants to return and boost the economy, and some funding was available to aid the move.

Things were cracking at the highest level too. In July 1939, after Hitler and Mussolini concluded their 'Pact of Steel', the Italian ambassador Dino Grande, a hero of early fascism known for his pro-British sympathies, was summarily replaced. When Britain finally declared war against Germany over the Nazi invasion of Poland, the Liverpool vice-consul Ugo Antona Traversi immediately resigned declaring 'in the case of conflict between our country and England I would be resolutely for the other side.' His resignation letter accused consul-general Rotini and the Liverpool *fascio* secretary of expressing pro-Nazi views when Italy's official policy was non-belligerence. But what real hope was there for belligerence, he could have asked, if by his boss's own admission even the 'very best' Italians who rashly chose to marry English women were no match for their wives?

THE PERILS OF INTERMARRIAGE

Dazzled, regrettably, by the prestige of the British race, many of our male co-nationals (especially Italians from the south) have married British citizens from the poorest backgrounds who are nonetheless full of ignorance and bloated with pride, and whose origins preclude any intelligent understanding not just of Fascism but even of Italy's enduring achievements in the arts and the humanities, or simply the sheer grace and charm of life.

In the first days of September [after Britain declared war on Germany] I saw with my own eyes the tragic plight of these compatriots who being sincerely attached to the Motherland and its institutions were more than ever set on repatriation yet had to endure exceptionally painful family dramas, since in almost all cases their English wives were in their turn more reluctant than ever to abandon England and more determined than ever to keep their children in England. Sadly, not only have these husbands failed to imbue their homes with an Italian and fascist spirit and impart a good Italian upbringing to their offspring, but more often than not their British wives know nothing about their husbands' country of origin and refuse to speak even just a few words of our language. The family's homogeneity and unity is thereby compromised and shattered, and the husbands, Italian citizens and fascists, suffer this profound fracture in silence.

Are they at fault? Even those who in themselves are the very best Italians surely have one failing in common: that of not having brought into the family, both before and during the marriage, a racial pride as strong and exacerbated as that of their English wives.

(Consul-general A. Rotini, 22 January 1940, reporting to the Foreign Ministry in Rome.)

It must have been painfully hard for the majority of Italians who opted to stay on in Britain to be forced to choose between their adoptive country and their native land. Many clung to a wild hope it would never get as bad as that. If Mussolini really wanted war, they argued, he would have been in at the beginning. And just as well he was mates with Hitler, it forced Britain to woo him all the harder. Even after six months and more the war still looked like stalemate, not too many were dying, and despite the risk of mines Italian merchantmen were still fetching coals from Newcastle. Somehow it would all soon be over. 'So why fret, Mario, our lot are non-belligerent, right?' 'Aye, brilliant policy, never gets it wrong, does he?' 'And pope's working behind the scenes, I doubt.' 'Remember old Tognoli at the last March on Rome do?' 'That ancient gramophone.' 'No, listen: "Our duty is to remain completely calm in the face of the present international situation and have absolute faith in our Great Leader who is working tirelessly for the power and greatness of our beloved country."'

'Where War was Forgotten': Christmas party at the Italian School, Newcastle, December 1939.

P. N. F.

Fasci Italiani All'Estero,

Fascio di Newcastle-on-Tyne.

"Nazario Sauro."

OGGETTO RITRATTO DI MUSSOLINI

17-Gennaio 1940 XVIII·

N. 24

On.Ispettorato per i Fasci
della Gran Bretagna,
LONDRA
4, Charing Cross Road,

In relazione al foglio surriferito ho
il pregio, qui unito di trasmettere a codesto On.Ispetto-
rato Postal Order di Sh.3/6 a pagamento cartello portante
in italiano ed in inglese, il RITRATTO DI MUSSOLINI.

Tengo ad assicurarVi che tale cartello
si trova già appeso sotto la fotografia del Duce nella sala del Fascio. Gradirò un cenno di ricevuta.

Distinti saluti.fascisti.

Claudio Bava

Segretario.

17 January 1940 (Year XVIII of the Fascist Era): barely five months before Mussolini's declaration of war on Britain and France, the secretary of the Newcastle fascio writes enclosing a 3s 6p postal order in payment for the official nameplate, in both Italian and English, which now reposes beneath the Duce's portrait in the assembly hall, la sala del fascio. Claudio Bava, a waiter by profession, was to be a victim of the torpedoing of the Arandora Star. The Newcastle fascio had been named after the nationalist hero Nazario Sauro at a well-attended ceremony in Saville House in 1932. (Archivio storico diplomatico, Rome).

The tommy-gun is greased, the sawn-off shotgun is loaded.

There is a stinking wind from the Mediterranean which bodes no good.

Yet we still tolerate Mussolini's henchmen in this country!

The government of Italy has thousands of loyal followers here.

Italians by birth. Fascists by breeding.

And I'm presenting this memo in the hope that this fact isn't being overlooked when the various 'Fifth Columns' are probed.

London alone shelters more than eleven thousand of them.

The London Italian is an indigestible unit of population.

He settles here more or less temporarily, working until he has enough money to buy himself a little land in Calabria, or Campagnia, or Tuscany.

His first object is to start a business; frequently a cafe.

He often avoids employing British labour. It is much cheaper to bring in a few relations from the old home town.

Individually, these people are usually inoffensive, decent and likeable.

BUT...

Mussolini keeps in touch with them constantly. He has always sent out agents. And the agents or other zealous Italians, formed Fascist clubs.

So now, every Italian colony in Great Britain and America is a seething cauldron of smoking Italian politics. Black Fascism. Hot as hell.

Even the peaceful, law-abiding proprietor of the back-street coffee-shop bounces into a fine patriotic frenzy at the sound of Mussolini's name.

The youths learned the principles of fascism – British nationals, yet keen and enthusiastic Fascists.

Many of these lads are now soldiers, wearing the khaki of Britain.

Wearing it gallantly no doubt. In most cases... But in other cases? What a source of potential danger!

They are, let us say, loyal to Italy, just as we in Italy should remain loyal to Britain.

We ought to smoke out our Fascist wasp-nests. At least we ought to watch them.

Mussolini would never for a moment tolerate twenty thousand such nests of divided loyalty, or worse.

But we always were the mugs of the world... **AND WE ARE ALWAYS SORRY AFTERWARDS.**

(John Boswell, *Daily Mirror*, 27 April 1940)

10 June 1940

6 p.m. on 10 June 1940, a Monday, was the fateful hour long dreaded by Italians resident in Britain. From the famous balcony, facing a vast crowd packed beneath the colossal marble monument commemorating the unification of the country he was about to lead to disaster, Mussolini announced that Italy was at war with France and Britain. Twenty thousand Italians in Britain instantly became enemy aliens.

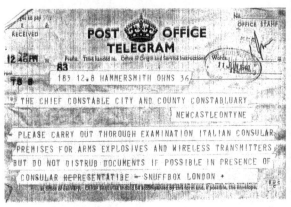

'Operation Snuffbox': Telegram received by the Newcastle constabulary, 11 June 1940. (Tyne and Wear Archives)

Flying Squad detachments throughout the country at once began 'combing out' the males. Even as the police moved to detain them, crowds converged on Italian-owned premises to vent their feelings. There were acts of anti-Italian violence all over the country, but the worst excesses of the night occurred in Swansea, Cardiff, Liverpool, Glasgow, Edinburgh, and the North East, all areas afflicted with economic depression and high unemployment.

Next day the Newcastle *Journal and North Mail* reported several shop windows smashed in the city, but only detailed an 'anti-Italian demonstration' outside Peter's snack bar[8] opposite the Central Station which had bizarrely evolved into a 'spy scare' assault on a press photographer who was snapping pictures of the event. The same paper also rather laconically reported 'a demonstration by hundreds of people outside the homes of several Italian families in Sunderland. There were catcalls and shouting, but eventually the crowds dispersed without further incident.' The feelings of those trapped inside their homes can easily be imagined. Although it was everywhere a fearful night for all Italians, many businesses and homes escaped attack, for reasons suggested in some of the personal reminiscences given at the end of this chapter. Some smaller centres (the local press specifically mentioned Stockton, Thornaby, and Tynemouth) experienced no anti-Italian disturbances at all. In the pit villages the cafés and temperance bars which remained unmolested tended to be those which had put something back into the community to which they owed their livelihood.

The most frightening place to be that night was Middlesbrough. According to the town's chief constable, 'the spark to mounting feelings which otherwise would not have led to rowdyism' was 25-year-old Antonietta Panico's defiant shout of 'Heil Hitler!' – 'or something like it' – at a crowd gathering outside her home in Borough Road as the men of her family were being taken into custody. Since her father Umberto had served for over ten years as secretary of the Middlesbrough *fascio* and was surely well known for his views, the implication that all would have passed off peacefully but for his daughter's rash intervention is by no means assured. In any case despite the police presence the crowd proceeded to ransack the place, then split up to menace every Italian business in town. Over the next few hours six well-known ice cream parlours in or near the city centre and Greco's wafer and biscuit factory in Suffied Street were wrecked and pillaged. Women and children, mostly with their men already in custody, cowered behind shattered upstairs windows while their shops were trashed beneath them. Just one man was arrested for affray. In the early hours of the morning, long after the damage was done, a further fifteen men and women were picked up for looting from the wreckage. Apart from helping themselves to coveted food supplies such as coffee, sugar, sacks of flour and tins of biscuits, they were variously nabbed carting off chairs, tables, a bureau, a bedstead, even an accordion. Italians who were young at the time remember other kids coming to school next morning with pocketfuls of goodies.

Many residents were shocked at the vicious scale of the 'rowdyism'. The Middlesbrough-based *North Eastern Daily Gazette* of 12 June appealed to readers to comprehend the Italians' predicament and called for exemplary action against the perpetrators: 'A certain section of the community of Middlesbrough have disgraced themselves and their town by their unthinking destruction of Italian-owned shops and establishments. Many of these people are naturalised British subjects of friendly disposition to our cause and totally devoid of sympathy for the elements responsible for the entry into the war of their native land. The lot of these Italian people is hard, for they are with us, some of their colony already having laid down their lives fighting with our own soldiers against the despotism of the dictators. There is no quarrel between the Italian and British peoples and those responsible for this mob violence should be punished.'

Except for two 18-years-olds without previous convictions who were given probation, all the accused including five women were sentenced from one to three months' hard labour. 'Most of the people charged with larceny stated that they found the articles concerned in the street, and some said that they took them home to look after them' (*Daily Gazette*). Weeks later, another seven men were convicted for stealing the safe from Greco's premises.

No local paper mentioned that all over the North East there were also many heroes that long midsummer night, ordinary people prepared to stand up to the mob. Sons and daughters of Italians inevitably recall the terrors, but very often also how English friends and neighbours

Fedele Costantino's ice cream parlour and home in Newport Road, Middlesbrough, under police protection the morning after the riots of 10 June 1940 (North Eastern Daily Gazette). But for Edinburgh, where vicious rioting and looting resumed next night, the police had the situation under control everywhere in the country by morning.

rallied to protect them and their families. These testimonies of spontaneous support make heartening reading. They show, even at such a high moment of official and public hysteria, how far from the truth is the claim that Italians in Britain were universally felt to be an enemy within, that 'indigestible unit of population' both feared and oddly relished in the *Daily Mirror* article which was only one of the fiercest of many press disparagements in the run-up to the 10th of June.

'I REMEMBER THAT NIGHT'

Middlesbrough: *The Italians were well respected in Middlesbrough, and when they had the trouble in 1940 with the hooligans raiding premises, those were not the typical English people. They were just the same horrible creatures who are causing trouble at football matches. My mother and my sister were on their own, and there was a doctor who lived round the corner who arrived to help with a community of men. There must have been twenty men from families round about who came and stood on my father's doorstep to stop them.* (Camy Rea)

Middlesbrough: *I was there when these gangs were roaming round. They smashed nearly everything they possibly could. We saw them smash a small lock-up shop near St John's church, then they were coming on to my grandmother's place in Russell Street, so we knew what was going to happen. Quite a few of us rallied round, the cousins who were dockers from down the market and some others, and we just stood there, and they didn't do anything to that particular shop. Borzamato's on Cannon Street they also didn't touch, because Borzamato and the lads were strong, they weren't to be trifled with, and it was known one of them had finished up in the Black Watch. But another shop on Cannon Street was knocked about. And Lucantoni on Newport Road, they smashed the front in and pillaged the shop, looted it all. The same with Martino's and Costantino's, and another on Union Street.* (Francis Hynes, of the Scappaticci family)

Newcastle: *Three of our places were smashed up. War was declared and I was in the Shields Road shop. I think that was about six. And then about ten – I had sent home the other girls – I said to the manageress, 'You can go, I'll close up.' And she went out and she came back and she said, 'Miss Toney, I'll stay with you.' I said, 'Why?' She said, 'I'll lock up the front, you go out the back.' 'Why?' I said. 'Well, have you seen what's going on outside?' So I went to the door and I looked out and the traffic was stopped, the roads were blocked with people, there must have been hundreds of them waiting for me to go out. I was really shattered, I just didn't know what was happening. So I said to her, 'You'd better go, in case there's trouble.' She didn't want to, but eventually I made her go. And then I locked up and I walked out, and they sort of made way for me. Then someone threw a brick at me. Fortunately I felt it grazing the back of my head, and – by this time I was on next door's shop – it went through that window. It just missed me by a fraction of a thing.* (Mary Marcantonio)

Newcastle. *These two big men came to the door after Italy came into the war and asked for my mother. I didn't know what they were. She was away in town, gone shopping. So he says, 'Well when she comes in will you tell her to come up to the Pilgrim Street police station.' So when my mother got back I said,*

'You've got to go the Pilgrim Street police station.' She says, 'What for?' 'I don't know what for, two men came here.' So she says: 'Go for Mrs Monroe.' Mrs Monroe was a very good woman, if you had a baby she was there, if someone died she was there. I went for her, and she came and she said, 'What did they say?' ' Nothing, just go to the Pilgrim Street police station.' 'Well, I'm going with you!' So she went too, and they said something about my mother could be interned. 'Interned!' – Mrs Monroe says –' What do you mean, she's never been out of Newcastle, we'll not let her go, there's no way you're taking her. If you take her you take all Trafalgar Street!' (Tillie Rennie, née Giordano)

Sunderland: *I remember there was the Someo family in Drury Lane, down the East End. They must have had five hundred bricks going through those windows, upstairs and down. Bricks and half-bricks. It wasn't the neighbours went for them, it was the surrounding streets. It was the neighbours actually saved them, chased the others away. The old man was about seventy-five, the wife was about seventy-five, and the daughter forty-odd. The only place they could go was the bathroom under the stairs, just a bath and a toilet and a small window, and they had the sense to run in there. They were in there about half an hour before the other people in the street said, "Ah, don't do that, man", "Eh, stop it, neighbour", "Get yerselves away..." Because it only takes a couple, doesn't it?'* (Louis Ciaraldi)

Bedlington. *When the news was heard in Bedlington a large band of local people began to gather outside the business premises in Bedlington Station and started to break the windows. They kept shouting for my father to come outside, intimating that they were going to "string him up". Several people did not particularly like my father. It undoubtedly stemmed from xenophobia but it was also probably due to jealousy of his success in business. Added to this, Father was a staunch patriot and very proud of his Italian nationality. Although he was not a paid up member of the Fascist party he had always been a fervent admirer of Mussolini. I remember that a large photograph of Il Duce took pride of place on the wall above the fireplace in the flat above the shop. This may possibly have been one of the main reasons for his unpopularity. Whether this unruly mob would have really killed my father is a matter of speculation for the police soon arrived to restore order. They immediately arrested my father and took him away to intern him as an enemy alien. My brother John, who was only fifteen, was absolutely terrified. The police advised him that, although he was a British subject, it would be wiser if he did not remain all on his own in the flat above the shop. John went to stay with the Bacci family across the road. Mr Bacci had been arrested along with Father, but Mrs Bacci and her daughter Nita had temporarily been allowed to remain in their house.* (Bernard Moscardini, in his memoir *La vacanza*)

North Ormsby: *Oh I remember that night. Just seeing them come and take your dad, it was awful. The police pulled the house to bits looking for papers and things. Yet my dad was well-liked, they all knew him. They said, 'Oh we're sorry, oh we're sorry,' even when they were taking him out. Mind, we had no trouble like there was in Middlesbrough, no trouble at all. We had good neighbours, we had none of that. They stayed up and looked after us, in fact stood round that shop all night to make sure nobody tried anything.* (May Crolla, daughter of Domenico Rea who was lost on the *Arandora Star*)

Berwick-on-Tweed: *That was frightening actually. There was a crowd outside, I don't know how many, when you're a kid a crowd seems huge. Suddenly a brick came through the window. I can't remember seeing any police. But when we closed there was one English fellow, in civvies at the time but* *he was in the RAF and home on leave, and he stayed in with us. He chose to remain with my dad and try to comfort my mother. Next day no one would come in the shop. But the manager from the theatre next door, who was English too, he stood at the door and said, 'Come on in and have a coffee, come on in and have a coffee!' So you always got the nice ones as well that understood it's not your fault. That morning of course I was frightened to go to school. But my father says, 'No, you're still going, show them you'll still go.' I didn't get any trouble at school, in fact the teacher even says, 'Do you want someone to walk you home?' And I says, 'Oh no, I'll go myself.' Brave lad! But you did get the awkward ones as well, because I did get hit at the door of the shop once. We were closed and I'd come back and I rang the bell. I was just standing there and something hit me, and I can't remember anything else, just started seeing stars. I don't know who it was. I was thirteen.* (Alfie Forte)

BOOKS AND SOURCES

Fascism in Italy and Britain. The attempted mass 'fascistisation' of the population in Italy is the key to understanding the regime's policy toward Italians abroad: E.R. Tannenbaum, *Fascism in Italy. Society and Culture, 1922-1945* (1973), T. Koon, *Believe, Obey, Fight: Political Socialization of Youth in Fascist Italy, 1922-1943* (1985). On British fascism: M. Pugh, *Hurrah for the Blackshirts! Fascists and Fascism Between the Wars* (2006), and S. Dorrill, *Blackshirt: Sir Oswald Mosley and British Fascism* (2006). Nigel Todd's *In Excited Times: The People against the Blackshirts* (1995) documents the resistance to Mosleyite fascism in the North East but also the appeal of Italian and German fascism to some prominent business figures and some senior members of the region's political class (both right and left). For the establishment's generally positive assessment of Italian fascism, see A. Hamilton, *The Appeal of Fascism* (1971); P.G. Edwards, 'The Foreign Office and Fascism 1924-1929' and A.J.B. Bosworth 'The British Press, the Conservatives, and Mussolini', both in *Journal of Contemporary History*, 5, 1970.

The fascist organisation of Italians in Britain. My sources for information about the *fasci* in Britain were the *Guida generale degli italiani in Gran Bretagna* (London 1936 and 1939), and the London-published Italian fascist weekly *L'eco d'Italia* (July 1922 – June 1928) and its successor *L'Italia nostra* (September 1928 – June 1940). For the evolution of fascist policy toward 'Italians Abroad': Z. Ciuffoletti and M. Degl'Innocenti, *L'emigrazione nella storia italiana 1865-1975*, vol 2 (1978); E. Gentile, 'La politica estera del partito fascista: ideologia e organizzazione dei Fasci Italiani all'Estero, 1920-1930', and R. Suzzi Valli, 'Il fascio italiano a Londra', both in *Storia contemporanea*, 26/6 (1995). L. Sponza, *Divided Loyalties: Italians in Britain during the Second World War* (2000) opens with the inter-war years. A. Bernabei, *Esuli ed emigrati italiani nel regno Unito, 1920-1940* (1997) is an impressive study of a few dedicated Italian antifascists in London, with much on Italian fascist activity in Britain and its official toleration for the sake of good Anglo-Italian relations.

Italian fascist clubs in the North East. The social activities of the various provincial *fasci* were regularly reported in *L'Italia nostra*. Correspondence generated by the office of the

Italian consul-general in Liverpool, which had responsibility for the North East, is in the Archivio Storico Diplomatico at the Foreign Ministry, Rome (*Rapporti dei consolati e agenzie consolari*). The *Casellario politico centrale*, the archive of secret police files on antifascists, is held in the Archivio Centrale dello Stato, Rome.

Toward war. D. Waley, *British Public Opinion and the Abyssinian War* (1975). D.Mack Smith, *Mussolini's Roman Empire* (1976).

10 June 1940. L. Sponza, 'The Anti-Italian Riots, June 1940', in P.Panayi, *Racial Violence in the Nineteenth and Twentieth Centuries* (1996), reworked in Sponza's *Divided Loyalties*. Apart from the Middlesbrough *North Eastern Daily Gazette*, which published an editorial and readers' letters, no other local papers followed up their own cursory reports of the night's disturbances.

Agostino ('Gus') Giordano, one of the stars of the Newcastle Italian school, in balilla uniform. Gus fought with the Eighth Army against the Italians and Germans, and died aged 22 in 1944 after being invalided home from North Africa.

Angelina Rea, Jarrow

Giuseppe Angelo and Flora Risi, Newcastle.

*Maria and Alberto Scappaticci,
Middlesbrough.*

Angela Valente, Sunderland.

Elizabeth and Antonio Ranaldi, Shildon.
(See illustration page 119)

Matilda and Agostino Giordano, Newcastle.
(See pages 98 and 198)

Mary and Joe Biesi, Middlesbrough.

Lorenza Paolozzi (seated) with her sister
Angelina Sebastianelli, Newcastle. Lorenza's
third son was the North of England lightweight
boxing champion, Alfie Paolozzi.

Forte wedding, Washington (See illustration page 117)

Chrisanella and Giuseppe Valente (standing) with their eight children, Sunderland. (See page 105)

Osea and Addolorata Briganti, Newcastle

Santi Rea (centre) and sons, Middlesbrough. Second from left is Domenico, lost on the Arandora Star.(See page 149)

Rosalinda Reale and her first five children, with (back row) nieces brought from Italy to mind them, Newcastle. (See illustration page 122)

Marianna Arrighi, with Rosa and Pietro, Seaton Deleval. (See page 234)

Basilio and Anita Pieroni, Blackhall.

Anita, now Maggiore, with sons Ivo and Basil, Ryton.

The Martino sisters, Middlesbrough.

The Fionda sisters, Newcastle.

The Pacitto sisters, Middlesbrough.

Elisabetta Pompa, Sunderland.

Raffaele Ranaldi, ice cream vendor and amateur weight lifter, Middlesbrough.

(Right) Giovanni Forte, café proprietor, Washington.

Nicola Fionda, ice cream dealer, Hebburn.

Domenico Dragone, café proprietor, Felling.

Angelo Rea, Middlesbrough, at the Italian front, World War I.

Tony and Assunta Quadrini, Newcastle, 1940.

7

AT WAR

France was broken and Britain in retreat when Mussolini finally threw Italy into the fray alongside Germany, calculating a short victorious war. He could hardly wish otherwise. His previous aggressions, the seizures of Abyssinia and Albania and the long intervention on Franco's side in Spain, drained the economy, alienated his former allies, and left the country perilously reliant on Germany for raw materials and fuel. Negotiating the fateful 'Pact of Steel' with Germany in May 1939 his envoy had had to plead for time: Italy would need four more years before contemplating a major war. So the 'Axis' alliance was unequal

Two couples, four friends: Tommy Mitton (left) from West Cornforth met Pina when he was with the British Army in Rome; Pasquale Cubello, from Catanzaro, met Mary when he was a POW at Coxhoe Hall camp.

from the start. The Duce liked to flatter himself that the Führer was his enthusiastic junior pupil but feared this Teutonic monster on the move which seemed to be encircling Italy by swallowing up first Austria and now France. In the end his dream of dominating the Mediterranean and building a new Roman Empire hastened the collapse of Hitler's even more boundless ambitions by overstretching Nazi forces to bail out beleaguered Italian armies in Greece and the Balkans, then in North Africa, and finally to make a prolonged and desperate stand against the invading Allies in Italy itself.

In the face of the immeasurable suffering of whole populations over the six years of world war, the trials of the relatively small number of Italian 'enemy aliens' settled in Britain might seem of little consequence. But personal misery is not cancelled out by greater miseries, and it should never be forgotten that Italians here suffered more than their due measure of violent death.

Comb-out

It was the misfortune of the approximately 20,000[1] Italian civilians in Britain that the timing of their country's long-delayed entry into the war coincided with a sudden hardening of policy toward the far larger population of German and Austrian 'enemy aliens' here, almost all of whom had been left at liberty for the first eight months of war.

The indiscriminate imprisonment of enemy nationals in World War I had later been acknowledged a gross injustice, so this time, precisely in order to eliminate any need for mass internment, special tribunals had rapidly – often too rapidly – processed the over 70,000 holders of German and Austrian passports, dividing them into categories A, B and C, according to their supposed risk to security. That nearly all were graded C as 'friendly enemy aliens' is hardly surprising given that 75 per cent were also classed as 'refugees from Nazi oppression'. Only the few hundred graded A, or 'dangerous', were immediately detained. Category B covered 'doubtful' cases, in practice when tribunals failed to agree on granting an exonerating C.

In April 1940, however, as the war situation abruptly worsened with the swift fall of Denmark and Norway to Germany, panic about a supposed huge 'fifth column' of Nazi sympathisers and saboteurs not only in those two countries but deep inside Britain gripped not just the popular press but very soon the security service and combined chiefs of staff, and, when Churchill replaced Neville Chamberlain as prime minister, the war cabinet itself. On May 12, two days after Churchill took office and as German armies were overrunning Belgium and Holland, the order went out to arrest, regardless of category, all German and Austrian males in coastal areas where invasion seemed imminent, right from Hampshire to Inverness. Over the next weeks countless more opponents of Hitler were swept into the net as the cull escalated to all men and women in category B wherever they lived, and finally, after Dunkirk and the fall of Paris, even to all males in non-suspect category C, some of whom had already experienced Nazi concentration camps. By the end of May even the 164,000 'non-enemy aliens' in Britain, which still included Italians, were living under a 10.30 pm to 6 am curfew and banned from owning cars and even bicycles.

Given this background of mass internment and suspicion of all foreigners, and then the universal outrage which greeted Mussolini's opportunistic 'stab in the back' on 10 June, it is evident no exception was going to be made for Italians.

'Collar the lot', famously, was Churchill's blunt order. Fortunately 'the lot' was still understood to mean only those covered by secret instructions issued to all police constabularies six weeks earlier in anticipation of an Italian declaration of war: all Italian males between 16 and 70 (later reduced to 65) who had been resident here for less than twenty years, plus 1,500 named 'desperate characters' including some 400 'duals', that is British-born men (and a few women) of Italian blood whom MI5 wanted held under the notorious Defence Regulation 18b whereby any British citizen considered a security risk could be held indefinitely without trial. In the general haste and confusion, however, many who did not remotely qualify were still picked up: men who had lived and worked here for thirty and even forty years, long naturalised British, and even some who were infirm or underage. Only the huge numbers already detained and the absence of 'facilities' for thousands more spared non-suspect women, whether German, Austrian or Italian, from the same immediate fate. But they were marked out for similar treatment just as soon as sufficient men could be cleared out of the country to make room for them. Meantime, 'enemy alien' women employed in so-called work of national importance were suspended. Emma Petrucco, an auxiliary nurse at Newcastle General Hospital, was told her services were no longer required.

Aside from several hundred Italian merchant seamen serving on British ships or taken off Italian vessels seized as prizes of war in British waters, around 4,500 Italian civilians, that is over a quarter of the entire adult Italian population, were arrested within the first three weeks of war with Italy, almost all during the turbulent night of 10th June or early next morning. In the provinces, given the relatively small number of these mostly innocuous shopkeepers often with good friends in the police and certainly in the local community, the comb-out was swift and thorough. Less so in the vastnesses of London where some well-off fascists with friends in high places and other suspect characters slipped through the net, if they had not already fled to Italy.

I have only heard of one attempt to avoid capture in the North East. Though many homes were unceremoniously ransacked by CID and police searching for weapons and other 'evidence of plans for assisting the enemy' (cameras, radios, atlases, letters in Italian, busts of Mussolini stuffed under the bed), most men went quietly. One undoubted reason for this is that it was police practice to insist they would only be very briefly detained and need only pack the bare minimum. In some cases men were assured they were simply being taken into custody to protect them from the wrath of the public, though this hardly explained why women and children should be left to their fate. For some that public was right outside the door: 'After he was taken,' reports Domenico Greco's granddaughter in Middlesbrough, 'the family hid under the stairs terrified while a mob outside tried to get to them'.

Since no police lists have been found it is impossible to say just how many Italians were taken in the North East. Local papers spoke of 'several' in Sunderland, 'about a dozen in Newcastle', 'about half a dozen in Whitley bay', 15 in South Shields, 28 in Middlesbrough, 'several' in Redcar. In Tynemouth, apart from three residents, 57 crew members were taken off two Italian ships and held under armed guard in the Albion Assembly Rooms to be driven away next day in double-decker buses under military escort. These scattered reports would suggest at most eighty or ninety civilians, but when the full regional spread of Italians is taken into account (see Appendix) it seems more probable that at least 200 vanished into custody.

The prisoners were mostly held in local jails for the first few days, then in intermediate holding points, before joining almost all the country's interned Italians at Warth Mills 'camp' near Bury in Lancashire. This was in fact a huge derelict cotton factory sealed off by barbed wire where conditions were atrocious. On arrival all were stripped and searched by armed guards and made to surrender money and valuables, some of it never to be seen again. Sanitation was almost non-existent, food inadequate, and the captives slept side by side among rats and machinery on the filthy floor. Worst of all, they were allowed no contact with the outside world. And there they remained, day after day, with no idea what fate awaited them.

'WHAT YOU DONE WITH ME DAD?'

Luigi 'Big Louis' Ciaraldi (second from right, seated) at a family gathering for the wedding of his daughter Maria (centre), Sunderland 1947. Louis Jnr is second left in the back row.

It was a Wednesday. I'd been to school, so it was about ten past twelve, my dinner was on the table and me mam was out down the street at the shops. Ten past twelve comes a big rap on the door. 'Yes?' I saw a car outside and two plain clothes CID blokes, and I says, 'Come in.' 'Dad – Sunderland police CID!' He couldn't understand the language a lot. 'Mr Ciaraldi?' 'Yes.' He'd just washed his feet, because he had hard skin, I'd put some soda in the water. 'Dad, I'll throw the water away and dry your feet and put your socks on.' Because he couldn't stoop down, see. 'There's no socks here,' I says to them, 'but me mam's only down the road – can you wait?' The policeman says, 'Dry his feet.' I says, 'There's no socks here.' 'Dry his feet, son, just put his boots on.' Because me dad couldn't wear shoes. 'What about his socks?' 'Just put his boots on, we'll take him down in the car, and we'll fetch him back in ten minutes.' Me mam came back, and I says, 'They've taken him down the police station.' She knew about Italy. 'It's just something to do with Italy declaring war,' I says, 'they've took him down the police station.' She says, 'He's got no socks.' I says, 'I could have put those on, but they says, No, we'll bring him back.' Twelve-thirty, one o'clock, he still wasn't back. Only me and my mother, my two sisters were at work. One-thirty. Two o'clock. Still not home. She says, 'We better go down and get your sister, go down in tram car.' Me mother couldn't speak all that good English.

We goes to the shop she worked at, Fella's in Silksworth Row (they didn't take him, he was still at home), and me mam says, 'Here, you'd better come down to the police station, they took your dad away at twelve-thirty and now it's half-two, they said they'd ask him a few questions and bring him back.' 'What you done with me dad?' my sister asks them, 'he's got no socks on, just his boots, just his coat, his jacket. Where is he?' 'We couldn't tell you, we don't know, he's been taken away at one o'clock.' 'You've brought him down here, you were supposed to bring him back!'

My brother was stationed at Melrose, so my sister sent him a telegram: "Dad taken away by police, don't know where, ask CO if he'll give you leave." He shows it to the commander, the CO, who says to him, 'You can go straightaway, son.' So they give him compassionate and he was in our house by 6 pm. 'What's happening?' 'They've took me dad away but we don't know where.' Down to the police station again, about seven o'clock. 'What you done with me dad?' 'I'm sorry, we don't know where he is.' 'Look,

I'll have to know where he is, I've got special leave.' So the officer in charge: *'We'll have to tell him, because he's a soldier. They've taken him to Newcastle, to Fenham Barracks, that's where he is.'* Mother had me dad's kit packed, his underclothes, socks, all sorts: *'He's got nothing with him – here, can you take this?'* *'We can't accept anything, you'll have to take it back home.'* *'I want to see the inspector, I'm in the King's Own Scottish Borderers.'* *'We can't take nothing, that's our orders.'* They were in a panic, Dunkirk, France falling. *'I'm not going back to my unit, mind.'* *'It's up to you,'* he says, *'you'll only get arrested, you've got 24 hours, after 24 hours the military police will be seeking you out.'* So my mother says to him, *'You better go back, don't go on the run, they might... God knows what will happen. If you stay home they'll come for you.'* She was worried, we didn't want the military police after him.

Well, we never heard nothing until 19 July, I think it was. A letter from the Isle of Man. But it was a government letter, only one page, a blue government letter, not like an ordinary letter, perforated on the edges, sealed in the machine, you had to take it apart bit by bit: "Keeping all right, hope to see you." And a paper stuck on top: "CENSORED." But at least we knew where he was.

It was in Leeds a year later, 1941, about 20 September, and I was in the house about 25 past five. There was a little corner shop, Coopers, where you could get a few things. I gets me bag, comes down the corner to the main road, turns the corner, and passing by the shop here's a tap on a car window. A big finger: rat-tat-tat, like that. It was me dad in a taxi! He didn't know where we lived, did you know that? Never received our letter. But he knew we lived in Leeds, he'd been to Leeds about twenty years before, knew there's loads of Italians, someone's bound to know where our family lives. *'Get in the car,'* he says. Instead I flew up the street and the taxi followed and I said to myself, I'll beat you to the top! – it was all cobble stones and a car can't go on cobble stones. *'Mam, here's me dad!'* She thought I was joking. *'Oh Mam, he's here in a taxi.'*

(Louis Ciaraldi remembering back, in 1990. In 1898, his father ran away from Cervaro to work for Paolo Margiotta in Sunderland, where later he set up his own street vending business. By June 1940, aged 62, he was suffering badly from diabetes. See pages 135 and 228)

Disaster at sea: the Arandora Star

Today it seems extraordinary that the government's original intention in the case of war with Italy was to arrange a mutual exchange of resident enemy aliens, with Italy repatriating its 2,000 or so British subjects and Britain shipping ten times that number back to Italy, that is every Italian-born man, woman and child in the British Isles. By 10 June, however, given the invasion panic wholesale expulsion was clearly unfeasible, so in the end the only ship to leave for Italy carried a few hundred privileged evacuees, Italian diplomatic personnel and their families with other prominent figures recommended by the Italian ambassador. It was thus that Rita and Nestore Tognoli escaped the fate of their compatriots in the North East whom they had sought to enthuse with the now incriminating doctrines of Italian nationalism and fascism.

'The world's most delightful cruising liner' – the Blue Star Line's SS Arandora Star.

With wild fears of German troops parachuting into POW and internment camps in Britain to raise rebellion, transportation overseas still seemed the best option for disposing of suspect foreigners. Canada and Australia were persuaded to take the first shiploads, plus the still relatively few German merchant seamen and prisoners of war in Britain. Three passenger liners and two troop ships were commandeered for the purpose. The first liner, the *Duchess of York*, left Liverpool for Canada on 20 June crammed with 2,600 German and Austrian civilians and POWs. Ten days later, more than a thousand Italians were herded from Warth Mills camp to Liverpool for inclusion in the next two sailings, the *Arandora Star* and the *Ettrick*. Since no steps had been taken to sift the Italians into the three standard security categories, and not even half MI5's fearsome number of 1,500 'desperate characters' could be identified from the lists supplied, the authorities simply made up the Italian quota for deportation by adding the first unfortunates available. At least in the case of the *Ettrick* an attempt was made to choose single rather than married men – all were told to line up according to marital status – but in the general confusion several swapped places so that close relatives could stay together. State papers which even after more than seventy years have still to be released may one day explain how it was that certain well-known Italian fascists escaped the round-up, while among the many staunch friends of Britain expressly listed as dangerous and due for deportation were even Italian Jews who had fled Italy's harsh anti-Semitic laws, prominent Italian anti-fascists well known to MI5, and hundreds of German and Austrian Jews and anti-Nazis.

The *Arandora Star*, touted in peacetime as 'the perfect ship for the perfect holiday' and now a grey-painted prison ship bound for Newfoundland with over three times its usual complement of passengers, was torpedoed in the Atlantic some 75 miles north-west of Ireland in the early morning of 2nd July. Struck amidships, she sank within half an hour with terrible loss of life: 446 Italian civilians, 175 German civilian internees and POWs, 58 officers and crew including her captain, and 94 military guard.[2] Half her human cargo, and nearly two-thirds of her Italians. Mercifully the sea was relatively calm, and within only hours the *St. Laurent*, a Canadian destroyer, was pulling survivors aboard. Many more lives would have been spared if standard precautions had been observed. The ship was grossly overcrowded, with most Italians packed into the lowest deck. Life vests had been issued but there had been no boat drill for fear of spreading alarm if it should emerge there were too few lifeboats. Barbed wire enclosures on deck impeded movement. She had no Royal Navy escort to protect her and nothing but a swastika pennant flown below the Red Ensign to indicate her mission and deter predators in waters well known to be infested with enemy submarines. So Germans and their closest ally's nationals were sunk by U-boat 47 which had already accounted for eight British merchant ships and on an earlier mission had sunk the *Ark Royal*.

The bare statistics of the Italian 'desperate characters' drowned in the cold Atlantic make pathetic reading. They included 67 'waiters', 56 'café/refreshment house owners', 51 'confectioners', 40 'shop assistants/barmen', 30 'restaurant proprietors/managers', and 24 'chefs/cooks'. Their average age was 47 and nearly ten per cent were over 60. Even if able to swim the survival chances of such people were minimal.

In age and trade most of the fourteen victims from the North East were no different. But for 53-year-old Claudio Bava, a Gateshead waiter and secretary of the Newcastle *fascio* since 1934, hence a doubly desperate character, all were working on Teesside when rounded up. The youngest by far, Luigi Bertoia, still only nineteen, was one of a Newcastle-based terrazzo team picked up in Middlesbrough on 10 June which also included another victim, 50-year-old Leandro Beltrami. The remaining eleven men, with an average age of 51, were all senior members of well-known Teesside ice cream families who came from neighbouring communities in Ciociaria and had been settled here for decades. The two eldest, Camillo Rea, 61, and Giuseppe Tortolano, 59, had lived in Middlesbrough for over forty years. The long-serving secretary of the Middlesbrough *fascio*, Umberto Panico (see page 196), another ice cream dealer, would almost certainly have shared their fate had he not been hospitalised after suffering a heart attack within hours of being taken into custody. The level of danger he or any of his colleagues posed to national security can be judged by the sceptical assessment of the Middlesbrough *fascio* made barely six months earlier by the Italian consul-general in Liverpool, quoted on pages 186 -7. Of no account to the authorities was the fact that six of the victims had sons serving in the forces and four had English wives. The deaths of just the eleven Teesside men left fifty-four children fatherless. (Despite their shared surnames Camillo and Domenico Rea, and Domenico and Tullio Greco, were not closely related.)

CLAUDIO BAVA, waiter, Gateshead, born Montechiaro d'Asti 1887
LEANDRO BELTRAMI, terrazzo worker, Newcastle, born Massemino1890
LUIGI BERTOIA, terrazzo worker, Newcastle, born Montereale 1921
ALESSANDRO BORSUMATO, ice cream dealer, Middlesbrough, born Cassino, 1896
DOMENICO GRECO, ice cream dealer, Middlesbrough, born Santopadre, 1885
TULLIO GRECO, wafer and cornet manufacturer, Middlesbrough, born Arpino, 1897
AMEDEO LUCANTONI, ice cream parlour owner, Middlesbrough, born Rome 1897
ANTONIO NARDONE, ice cream dealer, Middlesbrough, born Cassino 1892
DOMENICO PONTONE, café proprietor, Seaton Carew, born Cassino 1885
ANTONIO RANALDI, ice cream dealer, Middlesbrough, born Arpino 1884
CAMILLO REA, café owner and ice cream dealer, Middlesbrough, born Arpino 1878
DOMENICO REA, café proprietor, North Ormsby, born Arpino 1900
ANTONIO TODISCO, ice cream parlour proprietor, Redcar, born Vallerotonda 1893
GIUSEPPE TORTOLANO, ice cream dealer, Middlesbrough, born Cassino 1880

For the three long weeks since 10 June all information about the whereabouts of the Italian internees had been suppressed, so when news of the sinking broke in the papers frantic relatives had no way of surmising who might have been on board. Almost every Italian family in Britain was terrified of receiving bad news of relatives or friends. The government stuck to the line that all were Fascists and Nazis the country was well rid of, and did nothing to refute a baseless report of the exemplary composure of the British guards and crew in contrast to unseemly panic-stricken fighting between brutal Germans and craven Italians, no doubt put about to justify the high death toll among the latter. No expression of apology, let alone regret, was ever uttered. The cobbled lists of those 'missing, presumed drowned' were made available only to the War Office and the Brazilian consular authorities (who were handling British diplomatic relations with Italy and Germany) in London and

Glasgow, which made families in the North East feel even more lost and isolated. The chilling Home Office letter to Adelina Borsumato, reproduced on page 218, arrived seven weeks after her husband's loss.

As for the almost 300 Italians rescued from death by the *St Laurent,* the luckiest were the 64 admitted to hospital for urgent treatment, since within barely a week of their ordeal all 202 shaken Italian survivors judged fit enough to leave, including three from the North East[3], were forced to suffer the trauma of being shipped out of Liverpool once again. They had not been permitted to contact relatives and most had lost all their possessions. During the two-month voyage to Australia on the troop carrier *Dunera,* besides enduring horrendous living conditions and narrowly escaping another torpedo attack in the Bay of Biscay, they and the 2,500 'enemy aliens' of other nationalities had to put up with constant brutal abuse from guards and even senior officers. The day after the *Arandora Star* went down, other men from our region were deported to Canada on the troop carrier *Ettrick* along with another 400 Italian civilians. Caged below decks behind barbed wire, they too were subjected to organised theft and bullying. The only veteran of the *Ettrick* I have met, Natalino Valente of Durham, never wished to speak of it.

Even wartime secrecy and dissembling could not stop some of the truth of these horrors from entering the public domain. Within days of the loss of the *Arandora Star* prominent figures in both houses of parliament were denouncing the bungling inhumanity of the government's entire internment policy. The official enquiry they demanded was a whitewash when finally delivered (it was never published in full), yet in the face of mounting public indignation, particularly at the revelation that so many on the *Arandora Star* held anything but Fascist or Nazi convictions, even Churchill was won over to a softer approach. There were to be no more deportations or 'category C' arrests, and new machinery for the review and release of harmless internees was finally put in place.

In time the plight of the hundreds of Italian deportees languishing in camps in Canada and Australia was also addressed. Among those whose internment order was finally rescinded was Colombo Riani, one of the most popular figures in the entire North-East Italian community. His fate was particularly cruel. In August 1942, after surviving the sinking of the *Arandora Star* and narrowly escaping a similar attack on the *Dunera,* he perished when the ship bringing him home from Australia was torpedoed. True, as band leader at the consul's annual banquets in Newcastle he had made no secret of his Italian patriotism, and with Antonio Volpi (see page 300) had co-written a new setting to a song extolling Italian fascist youth abroad, yet Colombo also happened to be happily integrated in British society, not only as the proprietor of the liveliest café in Houghton-le-Spring but as leading trombonist in the Darlington Hippodrome orchestra.

Police cells beneath Middlesbrough town hall once held some of the men remembered on this Arandora Star memorial plaque unveiled at the town hall on 2 July 2009. Standing beside the plaque that same day are Alessandro Borsumato's daughter Marlene and his sons Michael (left) and Andrew (right), with Anthony and Catharine representing the next generation. On this memorable occasion, attended by some seventy close relatives of the Teesside men lost at sea, the mayor, Ray Mallon, offered a profound apology on behalf of the people of Middlesbrough for the treatment of Italian civilians in their community during the war. The memorial is part of a wider British-Italian effort to ensure that one of the darkest episodes in the worldwide history of Italian immigration is not forgotten. The earliest Arandora Star memorials are the 1960 bronze relief on the facade of St Peter's Italian church in London and a mosaic in the former Casa d'Italia in Glasgow (no longer accessible). In 2005 a plaque was erected on the small Scottish island of Colonsay where the bodies of several victims were washed ashore. In 2008 a plaque was unveiled in Liverpool, the port of embarkation. On 2 July 2010, the 70th anniversary, a plaque was unveiled in St David's cathedral, Cardiff, to honour the 53 victims from Wales, and on the same day a memorial garden beside St Andrew's cathedral, Glasgow, was opened by Mario Conti, archbishop of Glasgow, to commemorate the 80 Italians from Scotland who lost their lives. In 2012 a new memorial naming 241 London Italian victims was unveiled at St. Peter's Italian church. In Italy, a chapel in the small Apennine town of Bardi dedicated to the memory of 48 townsmen who went down with the ship has become something of a universal memorial to all who died. There are five other memorials in Italian localities, including Picinisco which lost 17 men. In 1990, the fiftieth anniversary, the 21 survivors still living were awarded one of the highest honours of the Italian republic. 93-year-old Rando Bertoia of Glasgow, who like his less fortunate cousin Luigi Bertoia of Newcastle was 19 at the time, is the last remaining survivor.

Antonella and Antonio Nardone soon after their arrival in Middlesbrough from Cassino. The couple, who later opened an ice cream parlour in Newport Road, had lived in this country 35 years and raised ten children before their shop was wrecked and Antonio was arrested and deported. Antonella did not give up hope until a clipping from an Irish newspaper was mailed to her in August reporting the recovery of a body near Black Rock, County Cork, identified as Antonio Nardone from the Newport Working Men's Club membership card found in a pocket.

Adelina and Alessandro Borsumato, on their wedding day, Middlesborough, 29 October 1924. The couple ran a small ice cream business in Princes Road.

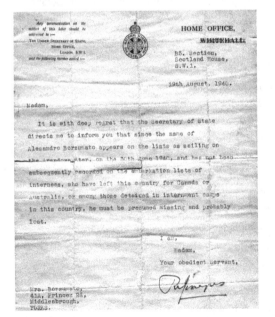

(Left) Home Office letter to Mrs Adelina Borsumato. 'My dad was taken without warning in the night,' recalls her daughter Marlene, 'and I have this memory of my brothers and me kneeling in a circle on the floor crying with my mother and praying. Life was terrible after that. Italians with businesses in the town had their windows put in and we wouldn't have survived without family help.'

218

Domenica and Amedeo Lucantoni with the first of their six children, Middlesbrough about 1930. Amedeo, who was lost because he went back below to search for his close friend Camillo Rea, first worked for Rea and Scappaticci in Middlesbrough before World War I. After enlisting he returned to open an ice cream parlour on Cannon Street, and finally in Newport Road. His son Romano recounts that his father and his brother Guido, still a schoolboy, were both arrested on the night of 10th June 'leaving my mother alone with a three-year-old daughter to face the angry crowd who smashed up the family business and looted the stock. My uncle Frank, wearing his army uniform, was able to placate the crowd to a certain degree by pointing out that he was a soldier, not long back from Dunkirk.'

Internment

A new line in concentration camps awaited 'aliens of enemy nationality' not fated to end up at the bottom of the sea or in a remote British dominion. As in World War I, the War Office selected the self-governing Isle of Man, suitably isolated in the midst of the Irish Sea, as a substitute for full-scale deportation. This time, instead of disfiguring the holiday island with vast compounds of grim huts, entire terraces of hotels and boarding houses were summarily requisitioned and emptied during the May 1940 flap. For the islanders it was no honour but not bad for business: the war had killed off tourism and the ousted householders and hoteliers were reasonably compensated, while the precipitous arrival of thousands of involuntary visitors and their minders provided new jobs and a good market for local farmers and other suppliers, and soon even a foreign labour force on the cheap at a time when surplus fit men were hard to come by. By August 1940, the moment of maximum density, 14,000 people were held in nine of these rambling detention centres dotted about the island. Six were in Douglas, the capital.

Metropole Camp, Douglas, Isle of Man. The only outdoor space for up to one thousand men confined in these buildings was the ten-yard strip of roadway visible here beyond the double wall of barbed wire. In August 1941, when there were still 600 prisoners, the camp leader Landini urged the camp commander to do something to alleviate the claustrophobic conditions, describing 'passers-by looking on the barbed wire enclosure and its inmates as a sort of cheap attraction and pastime, especially on a Sunday afternoon,' and conversely, 'the unpleasantness of internees standing by the barbed wire looking on with envious or critical eyes on the people outside, either walking happily on the promenade a few yards away, or bathing on the beach, on courting couples or at nightfall on those not-so-few who have had one too many.' The camp remained unchanged until the end of the war. (Photo: Getty images)

Palace, Metropole, Granville, all located on the Douglas seafront promenade, were the three 'camps' assigned to Italian males. Each took its improbable name from the largest peacetime hotel it incorporated and provisionally demeaned with hordes of long-stay guests and an awful lot of barbed wire. A small number of Italian female internees joined 4,000 other 'enemy alien' women and children held in two requisitioned villages on the south coast of the island, most of them refugees from Nazi Germany and Austria.

Even with three or four men crammed into a small B&B bedroom conditions were a vast improvement on Warth Mills. As things settled down the authorities went out of their way to accommodate relatives and friends together, and inmates could even ask for transfer between camps. A common reason for applying arose from the authorities' difficulties in handling tensions between political incompatibles, fascist and anti-fascist, pro-British and anti-British.

Those deemed to have 'fascist or doubtful sympathies' were held in Palace and Metropole, with a combined capacity for up to 3,000. Granville, with space for just 750, was opened in November 1940 to segregate those considered 'pro-Ally or at least non-fascist'. These tended to be older men who were more tolerant, or suitably humble, toward the country which they felt until now had given them so much. Beside civilian internees Metropole also held merchant seamen, classed as POW's and all taken to be 'rabid fascists'. Such broad distinctions were no guarantee of harmony. In June 1941, on the first anniversary of Italy's declaration of war, there were wild celebrations by pro-fascists in Palace and a convenient 'traitor' was savagely beaten up. The perpetrators received six months hard labour.

Boredom and aimlessness were alleviated to some extent by giving inmates responsibility for most aspects of their daily lives, leaving their guards to do little more than man the wire, enforce discipline (Metropole had six detention cells), and supervise roll-calls, morning physical exercise, the drawing of rations, and the comings and goings of visitors. The cleaning, the cooking, the camp post-offices, the camp libraries, sports and education and entertainment, the camp bands, even the sick bays, were manned and run by the internees. The Young Men's Christian Association (YMCA) did what it could to help with the provision of classes and procurement of books, footballs, and musical instruments. Apart from the food (the Italians craved less meat and potatoes, more pasta and bread and fish), the biggest grievance was the mail. Correspondence was channelled through a censorship unit in Liverpool which in the early weeks of mass internment was overwhelmed by thousands of desperate communications between detainees and the families which had so suddenly lost touch with them. In that period of greatest bewilderment and anguish very few letters or parcels reached their destination. Months later, post could still be held up twenty days. Prisoners were permitted to write two letters a week on specially prepared paper.

As things eased up, the authorities organised country walks and bathing parties to relieve the tedium, and much later even weekly visits to the cinema, all under military escort of course. There were board games and card games, boxing and *bocce*, and lots of football, even an inter-camp football league. The priests who had been rounded up engaged in conflict resolution as well as the curing of souls, some in acute distress, and conducted well-attended Sunday mass (rare for Italian males in normal circumstances) in hotel reception rooms set aside for worship and lovingly decorated by inmates with artistic talent. The most fervently political detainees kept alive the spirit of *italianità* by enforcing the fascist salute, scheming against presumed enemies, and elaborating fantastic alternative readings of the ever grimmer news from the front. Mostly younger men, their ethos of Italian solidarity in the face of incarceration by the supercilious British made them the natural leaders in the two camps where they predominated. Records show that their British overlords, while keeping them down, in fact respected their bloody-minded chauvinism.

But as Claudio Gallone's reminiscences given at the end of this section make plain, most inmates worked hardest at killing time and making the best of it. They missed their families, yet this weird freedom from responsibility in the midst of a war, the feeling of all being in it together as Italians, the comradeship, none would ever again experience anything like it. Tailors, shoemakers, and hairdressers had plenty of customers, as did craftsmen whose ingenious trinkets and gadgets made from recycled materials mysteriously found their way onto the local market as well. Master chefs from the grandest restaurants in Soho turned basic rations into something palatable, bootleggers turned almost anything into alcohol.

As early as August 1940 the authorities began operating a voluntary scheme for 'alien labour on farms', and as time went on more and more opted to get out of camp and earn a shilling a day (of which just four pence was theirs to keep) by helping out local farmers and market gardeners. At first no visitors were allowed but after two months the military authorities relented and a permit system was set up for closely monitored visits in the presence of an Army Intelligence officer. The trick was to get precious rationed food and clothing and black market cigarettes past him and the boys on the gate. Prisoners were allowed newspapers and could listen to the radio, even enemy Radio Roma (so their reactions could be monitored). Married couples were interned separately but permitted to meet up just once a month, under guard in a Port Erin café. There were no bombing raids by enemy aircraft. Not too many suicides. Rumour soon had it these enemies of Britain were having the time of their lives. Ministers had to reassure parliament that no person detained under the Royal Prerogative enjoyed better rations or more cigarettes (forty a week) than the rest of the population.

At least fifty men of all nationalities had brief tastes of freedom. To an Italian from Palace goes the honour of being first to cut through the wire. Another was apprehended in bed with his wife after a tip-off from the hotel where she was staying right next to his camp. He protested the English had 'no sympathy or understanding of these matters'.

It is not known exactly how many Italian women were interned, only that twenty still remained behind barbed wire in October 1943. Wives with families left more or less destitute on the outside pleaded in vain to be allowed to join their husbands. After more than a year of separate captivity, and when already over half the Italian internees had been released, all interned spouses were finally permitted to be united in a 'married camp' at Port St Mary along with their children. At least two families from our region benefitted in this way. Diomira Gallone with her two teenage sons was joined by her husband Ginesio, a founder member of the Newcastle *fascio*. The whole family had been picked up in Durham where they ran the popular 'Vaudeville' ice cream parlour in North Road. Maria Rossi, from the well-known Stockton ice cream family, also finally moved under one roof with her son, two daughters, and her husband Aleardo who had been one of the North East's most lavish benefactors of the Pro-Patria fund. Since both families were still on the island in October 1943, two and a half years after arrest, the authorities no doubt considered them exceptionally solid in their fascist convictions. Still, seeing that all this time the Rossi's other daughter, Olimpia, had been allowed to keep the family business going in Stockton one does wonder what actual *danger* they posed.

This was the big question exercising the illustrious panel of minds on the 'Loraine tribunal' which met more or less continuously in Douglas from October 1940 to assess the 'friendliness' of Italians who applied for release. Beside the sick and elderly, and boys under eighteen, priority was given to the 'duals', being after all British citizens. The tribunal was named after its chairman, Sir Percy Loraine, who as British ambassador in Rome had come to know the Italians, and their Duce, pretty well. Though sensitive to the plight of most of Britain's Italians, his instinct and judgment were constantly hampered by MI5's insistence on presumption of guilt for former *fascio* members since all on joining had had to swear allegiance to Mussolini. Most internees had had something to do with the *fascio* or its youth wing without being actual party members, and for them it was easier to argue that pride in their Italian blood and feeling pro-British in the present conflict were not incompatible. This, at the very least, was what had to be claimed if they were ever to be released as that curious hybrid, a 'friendly enemy alien'.

Italian internees at Palace camp, Isle of Man. Second from left in second row: Giovanni Di Mascio (Spennymoor). Back row, third from left: Amerigo Notarianni (Houghton-le-Spring), and extreme right: Cesare Niro (Stanley).

Group photo of another 'house' on the steps of the Palace Hotel. Back row, second right, in cap; Domenico D'Americo of Hartlepool (see page 231)

Even so, being neither political enemies of the regime nor refugees from oppression, simply what Mussolini called 'Italians abroad,' it must have been very hard to come across as desiring one's own country's defeat, whatever its reasons for going to war. On the other hand the tribunal knew that most people's deepest loyalty was to their families and the accident of being Italian did not make them potential spies or saboteurs.

Although all who were released had to sign a declaration of allegiance to this country and willingness to assist the war effort, the authorities could only persuade a few hundred males to don uniform and join the Auxiliary Military Pioneer Corps for non-combative duty. The majority were therefore enrolled in Alien Labour Battalions to assist the war effort by doing such things as road building or bomb damage clearance, labouring on a farm or in forestry, or working down the pit, as Diamante Jaconelli of Houghton-le-Spring opted to do in order to be near his family again. Older men were allowed to do 'work of national importance' locally, as say postmen or air raid wardens, although later on the Ministry of Labour conceded they could be placed in 'British restaurants and canteens, the type of work to which many of these Italians are accustomed'. Anyone not securing approved work risked re-internment.

Since every applicant was personally cross-examined the tribunal was not a speedy process, and a full year passed before about half the Italians had had their liberty restored. At this point, in late 1941, Granville and Palace were closed down and the remaining prisoners were merged with Onchan and Mooragh international camps, both outside Douglas. Over the next year and a half, 500 more Italian civilians were gradually released, leaving a core of some fifteen hundred 'fascists' (divided into 'extremists' and 'moderates') still interned when everything was changed by Italy's unconditional surrender to the Allies in September 1943.

The camps' extremists had already been shocked by the fall of Mussolini in July, removed by his own most senior party officials, and followed up by a royal decree disbanding the Fascist party. When after taking Sicily the Allies invaded the mainland meeting massive German resistance the new Italian government suddenly exhorted compatriots everywhere to join in the struggle to liberate the country from German occupation. The turn-around occurred at a terrible juncture and at terrible cost: Italian troops suddenly found themselves helpless and despised prisoners of the Germans not only in Italy but in occupied Russia and Greece. In a further dramatic turn of events the ageing Mussolini was rescued from captivity by German paratroopers and resurrected in Nazi-occupied central and northern Italy as nominal head of state.

At once, like Italy itself, the remaining Isle of Man camps were split between those who supported the king and his new anti-fascist government, and diehards who remained true to their Duce. The first category, numbering some 1,000 and including some of the merchant seamen, were let out over the next few months, leaving about 500 seamen and 500 of the original Italian civilian internees to sit out the rest of the war. The defiance of these mostly second generation British-Italians could be likened to that of disaffected young Muslim Britons today. Most were born in this country and English was their first language, yet they had grown up with 'Ay-Tie' slurs in the schoolyard and had endured seeing their parents patiently put up with racist innuendo for the sake of the family's security and advancement. At the same time the social and above all ideological activities of the *fascio* had armed them with an epic alternative account of their own worth and heritage, and to this they clung for inspiration and consolation after the humiliations of June 1940 seemed to be the most brutal confirmation of rejection by the only society they really knew. Outside captivity, most would have soon accepted the new reality, but being all locked up together gave them the grim satisfaction of having something to fight.

Bitterness and alienation were not confined only to the young and unattached still interned. Perhaps the most telling evidence for this is the very resilient rumour or suspicion – I have heard it aired decades later by some of the old folk – that the *Arandora Star* was deliberately sent off to certain doom, even purposely sunk by a British submarine. To understand such feelings it is worth recalling that during the invasion panic of May-June 1940 German, German-Jewish and Italian civilians were rounded up not only in threatened Britain but wherever else the British held sway, in Africa, Australia, India, Canada, all of them at that stage remote from the theatre of war. By contrast, when the United States came into the war its far larger communities of German and Italian nationals remained virtually untouched. Only 1,228 Germans and 228 Italians were considered sufficient security risk to intern, and all were released in under a year. America's Japanese on the other hand received very different treatment, with the entirety of 120,000 men, women and children being held in remote camps in horrendously substandard conditions for the duration. In 1988 the US government paid out compensation to all surviving Japanese internees, publicly acknowledging their captivity had been an act of racial discrimination. To many Italians in Britain, especially during the first harrowing months of their collective ordeal, something very similar seemed an unstated additional explanation for their treatment.

If there is a lesson to be drawn for present times, it must lie in the view expressed to the press after the Middlesbrough plaque unveiling ceremony by Peter Rovardi whose grandfather Liberato Greco was on the *Arandora Star* along with his two brothers, one of whom perished: 'The memories are painful, but it makes you understand the problems modern immigrants have in this country, and the discrimination they face.'

'IT WAS A UNIVERSITY EDUCATION TO ME'

I was interned when I was nineteen, and there were men in there sixty-odd years old. I have to say I enjoyed it, the experience, the company.

In our house there were about twenty-eight of us, mostly all young lads. My dad was there as well, and my uncle Alf who had the 'Venetian' in Whitley Bay. They were the heads, we were the grafters. Me and my friend Alfie Russo from Amalfi were in the kitchen. There was no dressing up, we just had to make the best of what we had. We used to make a ravioli without meat and without tomatoes. We bred rabbits to augment the rations. We made grappa from the kitchen peelings, so everyone got a drop in their coffee.

As people were getting released they used to shut a house down. So a little chap from number 40 comes down to our house, 32, to see if we'd let him come in with us. Mr Piccolo they called him, a proper little gentleman. 'Why aye,' all the lads said, 'let old Mr Piccolo come'. Well, it ended up he was head of the LMS restaurants before the war – and remember, we two were the cooks!

'Oh,' Mr Piccolo used to say, 'I marvel at the way you lads do it.'

And he used to say, round the fire on a winter's night telling a tale, how he started off in Negrasco's in Nice, polishing silver. And he showed us photographs of him and the king, King George VI back when he was Duke of York in Kruger Park with the lions and that, just the king and Mr Piccolo and the bloody car! Oh you learned a lot in there, it was a university education to me. Mr Piccolo had been sent to South Africa to organise the South African Exhibition, catering, sometime about 1932.

I was brought up with Italian parents, but my grandmother was the talker. She wouldn't speak English and that's how I picked it up at first. Then being in the camp where there were all types you got a bit of everything. There were Sicilians, there were Friulans, there were Piemontese, Toscans, Barghigians. When I went back to Valvori after the war they found I could sing songs even they didn't know, songs that I learned in the camp. I could play all the card games. I was more Italian than them!

Mind, we done some queer things. One day Joe Maccari comes in with a

Pia and Claudio Gallone, Redcar, 1989. Born in Valvori in 1921, Claudio was helping out in the family café in Wingate at the time of his arrest in June 1940. During four years of internment he experienced Palace, Metropole and Onchan camps. After the war he ran an ice cream shop on Redcar promenade, and finally his own wafer and cornet factory. Claudio died in 1994.

lump of tubing, I don't know where he'd get it, I mean we were fenced in – Joe Maccari from Casalattico, a cousin of Carlo Forte, Charles Forte who was in there a few months too. And Joe says to my dad, 'Make us a catapult of this.' My dad was handy, he made him a catapult. Right opposite the houses the seagulls in the evening and pigeons seemed to come there a lot. Bang! Three pigeons and a seagull! So me and Alfie take them in the kitchen. And old Parolli from Sant'Elia, Michele Parolli: 'I'll eat the pigeon', he says, 'but I don't want no seagull.' 'Fair enough, you eat what you want, we'll eat what we want'. So they all get a bit apiece. 'Hm', says Michele looking at his plate, 'what the hell's this? This is dark, and that's light'. I says, 'That's the dark pigeon, and that's the white', and he ate it all. 'That was lovely', he says. So I says, 'Oh Michele, era buono il seagullo? You liked the seagull?' He says to me, 'What was the seagull?' 'The white one!' And he turned round and he says, 'Well, if I'd known before you might have turned us off it. But I enjoyed it.'

No, I never tried to get out, to tell the truth. First of all, I would've had to join the Army. So I thought I'm better off here than in the Army. Didn't know what'd happen, did I?

There was a doctor there, a major in the First World War. He said to me, 'You know they question you, son – so do you want a bit of advice?' I says, 'I don't mind, doctor.' He liked the title. 'When you go in front of them,' he says, 'don't start expressing yourself or anything. When they ask you a question say just yes or no, then they can't say you've said anything funny.' And how true that was. No use telling them anything, they could always turn the bugger round.

You must remember this, Hugh, it was taken for granted: Mussolini was in charge. They were fascists so everybody was a fascist. You know what I mean? Propaganda. If you were listening to the same thing for a whole week you could turn round and go and shoot the Queen, couldn't you? Brainwashing.

But there were also men of seventy in there. One old man, Castagnaro we used to call him because he was a chestnut roaster – poor old fellow, what the hell was he picked up for? You get my point?

And there's another old man I'll always remember. A Friulan from Fanna, up there. A terrazziere he was, in fact he had that cement on his lung and that's what he died of, poor old bugger, silicosis sort of thing. He was in next-door to us, house 31, and we were all young lads and he used to come in a lot, old Osvaldo, and we used to give him a cigarette now and again. You used to see him in the camp picking up the dog ends, if he could find any. He had some relations in America, and he used to get a parcel about once a month, two or three packets of Chesterfields and a bit of shag, that American baccy, like scent. And as soon as he got his parcel he used to come straight in our house: 'Mi fai una per me e una per te.' One for me and one for you. He'd go round all us lads that used to look after him, and of course they wouldn't last him a day. And then he was picking them up again.

Now in house 30 there were about fifty priests that had all been interned with us, and poor old Osvaldo, he never used to go to church much. 'Three times a year I go to mass: Easter, Annunciation, and Christmas. Those are my days, and I don't need them telling me to go. Those three days I always go.' So one day he comes down with his enamel mug, gets himself some hot water to shave. Dinner-time comes: no Osvaldo. We went up. Dead! That's how it goes. The military came, the commandant, the medical officer and all that – and of course, away Osvaldo. Well, Alfie still owed him five shillings. ' Eh hell, I never give Osvaldo his five shilling back, and now he's dead!' I said, 'Well then, give it to a priest there and tell him to say a mass for him.' So Alfie gave him his five shillings and got a mass said at the funeral, and the lads all put a couple of coppers together and we bought him a wreath. Then they took Osvaldo away and buried him.

About a month after there was a Sivori died. Big people in Shrewsbury, lot of money the Sivori, the whole camp was in mourning for a week. All went to mass, High Mass, about ten priests at the altar, and the military walked us to the cemetery. Well, you know the lads they were all against the priests after that, because they'd said that Osvaldo was a peccatore pubblico, a public sinner because he didn't go to mass. It was bad really. Poor old bugger. You get it in the mines today. It came from the cement dust, polishing the terrazzo.

(Claudio Gallone)

How families coped

Distress was not confined to those behind barbed wire. A wife suddenly left responsible for day-to-day survival might have to manage not only without the family's main breadwinner but without the support of sons and daughters in the forces, or other close family members who chanced to be trapped in Italy. Her teenage lad guilty of being born in Italy and

Wartime in Jarrow: Risi's corner shop boarded up for protection 'because the windows were put in that often'.

now perhaps indispensable to her in the shop would become an enemy of the state on his sixteenth birthday and be removed to prison. Personal calamity prompted plenty of sympathy and offers of help from those who knew them well, but the drastic police action and then all the subsequent petty official harassment fed the general suspicion and prejudice. Bricks through windows were not limited to 10 June, Italian premises continued to be targets for random attack throughout the war. Suppliers hesitated to do business with 'the enemy', old customers made a point of staying away, and there might be no place in the communal air raid shelter for Italians. The old rule of only using English in the shop was observed more strictly than ever. Any connection with the host country was emphasised. The Seghini family in Blyth kept pictures of their two sons in British Army uniform in the shop window all through the war.

Few received compensation for premises and homes wrecked on the night of 10 June. Sudden removal of the menfolk had wrecked family equilibrium too, and wives and mothers left behind were not always in a state to lodge an appropriate claim with the police authority within the statuary 14 days, even if informed of the correct procedure. Where the Riot Act had not been read out by a magistrate the local authority could even repudiate responsibility. In Middlesbrough, the worst hit town in the North East, the council refused to grant the 42-day extension for submission of claims allowed by law in exceptional circumstances, arguing that all British landlords leasing property to Italians had made their claims in good time. As for the irreplaceable human loss on the *Arandora Star,* enemy aliens had no right to compensation.

Mob action, internment, and loss at sea were not the last of the Italians' sufferings. Following 10 June, under Defence Regulations non-interned Italian nationals living in so-called 'aliens protected areas', that is within a 20-mile coastal belt, were served three days' notice to quit. Age and infirmity were of no account. 65-year-old Carmine ('Jack') Rossi, who had been spared internment on grounds of ill health, still had to get out of Consett where he had run the town's favourite ice cream parlour since 1911. On the day he left his son Tony went into the Army. In the general emergency the Italians had to pull together as never before. Most of the expelled and their children were taken in by relatives or friends further inland. The Fiori family in Hexham took in not only their Brunini cousins from Murton but also girls from the Riani and Donnini families of Houghton-le-Spring and Easington.

Teresa Ciaraldi (now Atkinson) was five at the time: 'I had two sisters, one born in Italy, one born in England, so suddenly one sister was a friend and one was an enemy alien.' As we saw earlier, her ailing 62-year-old father Luigi, with three sons already in the Army, had been interned almost immediately. With her four remaining children, Teresa's mother Rosa left for Leeds in the company of other Sunderland Italian families, taking whatever they could manage to carry. In Leeds a widow called Margiotta from their same home village of Cervaro, herself with three children and a 19-year-old son who had been interned, somehow accommodated them all in her two-bedroom house along with Teresa's godmother Pasqualina Prenelle and her daughter, also refugees from Sunderland. Next day, says Teresa, her mother went straight out to rent a tub and barrow so she could start making and selling ice cream. There was a close Italian community in Leeds and the family managed to make a bit of a life there. When they returned to Sunderland in 1947 their home had been vandalised, stripped bare.

Most displaced Italians were back home by latest mid-1941 but still remained subject to restrictions 6a and 9a on enemy aliens 'at large': the nighttime curfew, the ban on using bicycles and motor vehicles (driving licences had to be handed in), and the need for police permission to travel outside their immediate locality. By this time local constabularies in liaison with the security services had been tasked with recommending individuals for exemption, being specially cautioned not to be lenient on 'Italians with long residence whose sympathies and attitude still remain Italian.' In March 1941, F.J.Crawley, chief constable for North Tyneside, cleared 77 Italian subjects within his jurisdiction, among them 18 British-born wives and 31 elderly or middle-aged men long resident here. Ten had sons serving in the forces. Possibly there was nothing exceptional about this, but that Crawley was a man of independent views is evident from the fact that eight of his recommended women had husbands still interned (one was the drowned boy Luigi Bertoia's mother Emilia, with two younger sons to care for). Crawley's assessment of Giacomo Tassi, 62, then on temporary release to be with his gravely ill wife, explicitly rejected all kneejerk 'desperate character' assumptions: 'Tassi was specially listed for internment by MI5 owing to him being one of the leading members of the Fascio in this area. He is well known to me over a period of years and I have no reason to think he was in any way hostile to this country.'

The twin blows of internment and forced removal from the protected areas affected almost everyone's livelihoods, some irreparably. Some businesses went to the wall, others were consigned to the Custodian of Enemy Property to be returned after the war. The same agency was charged with attempting to collect all business debts owed to internees, most of whom had had no time to make any provision for transfer or sale of their undertakings. Interned men with no family members of British nationality to take their place handed over the keys to others to run the shop, and not in every case did they get them back on their return.

The Italians had always prided themselves on managing on their own, but inevitably there were now some in the position of Filomena Pacitti who with three young children on her hands in Newcastle and no income after her husband was interned had to apply for public assistance (18s 6d a week). Coming from a culture where wives were expected to labour in the fields as well as raise a family, the shop-keeping women had worked as hard as their men and often harder, but until this point most had played a background role in business and consequently often had very little English. Now they had to learn to face the outside world of salesmen and the taxman, not to mention the overweening but indispensable black market fixer. The experience turned out to be the making of some very effective female entrepreneurs in our region in the post-war years.

In Middlesbrough, after the loss of their men on the *Arandora Star* and the trashing of their hard-won shops, neither Amelia Greco nor Antonella Nardone had the means or will to start again. In Redcar the Todisco ice cream parlour and café on the High Street had come through unharmed, and with support from the local Catholic community Gilda Todisco somehow managed to pick herself up after her husband's loss at sea was finally confirmed. The premises remained shuttered for a while, but there was the rent to pay and three children to feed.

In North Ormsby, Domenico Rea's widow Carolina was left with four young daughters as well as the shop to run. 'It was a real bad time, it hit her very hard,' recalled Dominica ('May') who was then thirteen. 'She always thought he'd come back, every morning we used to go to church to pray for him. She used to faint, and we learned to all go round after her with the smelling salts. But when people heard my dad was missing they started coming to the house with all the money they'd borrowed, money she knew nothing about. Because he was that sort of man, anyone with a sob story he'd give them money. She worked hard, she kept us going, we were only kids.'

English women married to Italians, and deprived therefore even of the dual status of their own sons and daughters born in England, were subject to the same restrictions hampering all

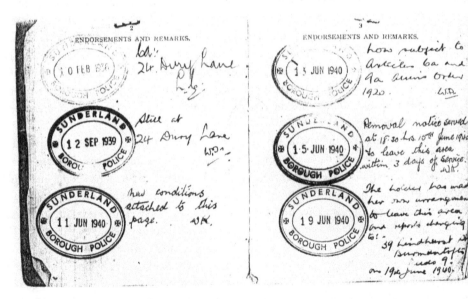

Pasqualina Prenelle's Aliens Certificate of Registration showing the police order (in red ink) to leave Sunderland within three days, dated 15 June 1940. Pasqualina, who had lived in the city since the age of four when brought here by her parents, had recently lost her husband Antonio Prenelle, an ice cream dealer who had served in both the British and Italian armies in World War I. With her daughter Charlotte she found refuge with the Italian community in Leeds until her restriction order was lifted in July 1941.

Gilda Todisco, whose husband Antonio was lost in the Arandora Star disaster, with children Rita, Tony and Patricia. Gilda and Antonio, both from Vallerotonda, had worked together for other Italians in Glasgow and Weston-super-Mare before opening an ice cream parlour in Redcar in 1932. 'My mother was a quiet lady,' Rita recalls. 'We'd lost our father, people just felt sorry for us. Even with the name up over the shop nobody insulted us.'

Domenico D'Americo (Amerigo) reunited with his family after release from internment, Hartlepool, 1942. His daughter Ann Marley writes: 'My dad didn't talk about his internment too much, but he told my mam and my older sister that when they were being transported before sailing to the Isle of Man they were chained up to walk through the streets and people were spitting at them. During the time he was interned quite a few neighbours shunned the Italian families; they would walk on the other side of the street rather than walk near them. He was a very quiet, polite and unassuming person and the most loving and caring Dad anyone could wish for.'

'aliens'. In the hope of improving their own and their husbands' lot many applied for naturalisation only to be informed no applications would be considered until after the war. However, from the summer of 1941, as a more humane appreciation of the position of Italians in Britain began to take hold in the Home Office a large number of wives were given back their British citizenship. Blocked naturalisation applications made just before the outbreak of war by Italian males with long residence in the UK also began to be reassessed.

Not all Italian businesses were adversely affected by the war. In the end a number did very well. After June 1940 some local Food Control Committees, including Newcastle, punitively sought to disrupt Italian ice cream dealers' businesses by refusing to approve the transfer of licences from internees to their nominated successors on the grounds that the Ministry of Food had declared ice cream 'non-essential'. The truth is ice cream was selling even better than in peacetime, a favourable situation which continued for two more full seasons until September 1942 when it was suddenly banned outright as a waste of precious sugar and milk reserves. Even then, old hands still in business continued to benefit by the restrictions on sweets and above all from the sudden absence of competition from large national producers like Walls and Eldorado, now compelled to turn to 'essential food' production. Under the influence of American technology and fads most standard Italian ice cream in Britain had abandoned its pure milk and egg custard origins long before the war, and now that rationing made synthetic ingredients and flavourings unavoidable it took little ingenuity even after the ban to come up with new substitutes (popular imagination fixated on Vaseline and Brylcreem!) to keep satisfying the high demand. The Reas and the Risis of Newcastle remember how jellies and blancmanges sweetened with unrationed glucose and saccharin went like a bomb. In addition, those with suitable machinery stepped up production of wafers and biscuits, now happily listed as essential foods.

As for the many little confectioners and cafés in the colliery villages which had had such a hard time surviving in the pre-war decade of idle pit-wheels and out-of-work men nursing one cup of Oxo for hours, they too began to pick up good custom. Once more the needs of war had transformed the fortunes of coal, providing full employment locally and eventually almost doubling the pitmen's peacetime earnings.

Proof of returning confidence when almost everyone had been released from internment and Italy was on the 'right side' again was the revival of the Northern Division of the Ice Cream Alliance at the end of 1944 when production was suddenly permitted once more. Almost all the top posts in the divisional and branch committees went to the old families which had dominated North-East ices in the pre-war years: Bertorelli of Whitley Bay, Risi of Newcastle, Moscardini in Stanley, Coia in Spennymoor, Pompa and Maggiore in Sunderland, Bianco of Hartlepool, Greco and Rea in Middlesbrough. The newly elected chairman was Percy Brown of the Variety Wafer Biscuit Company of Chester-le-Street, an Englishman of course, but for long a great friend of the Italians.

Even so, any impression that Italians were doing well out of wartime conditions always risked aggravating the widespread resentment of all these 'Wops' in whose country after all the British were still fighting right up to April 1945. Mary Marcantonio preserved only bitter memories of the years when with her father interned, her brothers in the forces, and her mother in poor health, she and her younger sisters struggled to keep Mark Toney's last shop in Newcastle running. 'I lost every friend I had. No one would speak to me. Shops that I used to deal with wouldn't serve me. If I got a bus to go home people used to recognise me and start creating. I used to have to get off and walk home. On one occasion there were small incendiary bombs dropped near our home and after it was over everyone was running to see if they could help. I was running too, and my mother with me. Then I heard someone say, "Huh, they should have dropped it on that bloody house along there, the Mark Toney's house." And I said to my mother, "Come on, come home, we came here to try and help." And we just walked away. This was the attitude. So it was a very, very bitter feeling, and it lasted a lot of years.'

Mary's father had been a keen member of the Newcastle *fascio*. That was no sin until 1940, but for it he was interned and only released two months after Italy's capitulation in 1943 when he was already sixty. His case was little different to that of Giacomo Tassi, another fervent supporter of the *fascio* but from whom we saw chief-constable Crawley believed there was nothing to fear. Antonio Marcantonio had known Newcastle as a teenager before the turn of the century and more than thirty years before his arrest as an enemy alien had returned to make a life and career here which was broken only to fight against Britain and Italy's mutual enemies in the Great War. Six of his seven children were born on Tyneside, and during the three and a half years he spent detained at His Majesty's pleasure his two sons and a son-in-law were in the forces. Tassi, too, had two sons in uniform at the time, and all his eight children were born and educated in this country. In the case of Michele Prenelle of Sunderland, six sons in uniform were not enough to prevent his internment. Such were just some of the painful paradoxes Italians in Britain had to face in this war.

(Left) Luigi Bertoia, lost on the Arandora Star, 2 July 1940, aged 19. (Right) Dennis Donnini VC, died in action, Western Front, 18 January 1945, aged 19.

The paradoxes of war

'I was in the DLI along with Tony Sacco of Langley Moor and Manzuotto, the terrazzo worker from Gateshead. When I was wounded and transferred to hospital in Pompei the stretcher bearer was a Bianco from Hartlepool. Then in Naples I bumped into Jock Tricchi from Ryton...'
(Pte Ivo Maggiore DLI, born in Sunderland, whose father and brother, being Italian-born, were both interned as enemy aliens.)

Young men of military age born in Britain who refused to be conscripted because they considered themselves Italian were interned along with other dual nationals held under Defence Regulation 18b. Their case is clear enough. Other second generation men who declared they could not fight for Britain against Italy but were prepared to help the war effort in other ways were routinely placed in the non-combatant 'aliens' unit of the Pioneer Corps. It therefore seems to have been tacitly acknowledged they had some right to be recognised as conscientious objectors, and indeed the Home Office also advised exemption for women of Italian extraction who professed scruples about munitions work. Far more numerous, however, were the many British-born sons of Italians who volunteered for the forces or had been called up without demur, but then protested by every means they could in June 1940 when they learned how the nation they served was treating their Italian-born fathers and uncles and brothers. The Home Office and local MPs were deluged with pleas for justice from concerned families and their servicemen sons, many of whom at first refused to co-operate in the hope their protest might move the authorities to release family members from captivity. For refusing to wear uniform while his father was interned and allegedly 'deserting with intent to avoid foreign service' Geraldo Marcantonio of Newcastle was sentenced to eighteen months in jail by an Aldershot court martial. All British Italians in the army experienced anti-Italian feeling at times, and there is some evidence it received more or less official endorsement in the RAF and Royal Navy where applications were routinely turned down on the grounds of Italian parentage. On the recruiting officer's advice Alfredo Amerigo of Hartlepool used his mother's name when signing up. As Alfred Crosby he fought in both the North African and Italian campaigns.

Emotions had a terrible poignancy in the case of those who lost family on the *Arandora Star*. Andrew Ranaldi of Middlesbrough was serving in the artillery in the south of England when his English mother wrote telling him his father was one of the victims. 'I only wanted a couple of days,' he remembers, 'but they wouldn't give it to me – I was raging.' Despite the extreme circumstances he was refused compassionate leave, and as an extra precaution was compelled for a second time to sign the oath of allegiance to the King. When Joe Greco's call-up papers came his father Liberato, who had survived the tragedy though his brother had been lost, was still interned on the Isle of Man. 'Until they released my father I didn't think it was right to go. And when they did I went.' Three days after reporting for duty at Brancepeth Castle he heard his father had been reinterned. 'So what did I do? Got on my motorbike and came home. I did the glasshouse...'

Other Italian families in the North East were split simply because members happened to be in the wrong place at the wrong time. Dina Moscardini from Bedlington, who had returned to Italy with her youngest son Bernardo in mid-1940 to have her third child in the peace of a country not at war, was stranded in Sommocolonia for the next six years which included terrifying months in the thick of the fighting when the village was right in the front line.[4] When Benedetto Notarianni returned to Sunderland with his eldest daughter after holidaying in their house in Valvori he had no idea he was leaving the rest of the family trapped in Italy for the duration. Serafino Reale of Newcastle, staying with cousins in Arpino in June 1940, hid out in the forest for fear of internment on account of his British passport. Instead, owing to his Italian parentage, he was conscripted into the Italian army but then for health reasons soon discharged.

Pietro Arrighi, another British-born son of military age, was also caught on holiday in Italy in June 1940, and with unpleasant consequences for his family in Seaton Deleval, Northumberland. He too was conscripted, an accident of fate which made him a traitor in the eyes of local people who boycotted the family café throughout the war, assuming he had deliberately gone off to fight for Mussolini. With their father interned and their mother compelled by the 'protected area' restriction to seek refuge with Italian friends in Carlisle, Pietro's sister Rosa was left entirely on her own to cope with the café. 'She suffered quite badly,' her daughter Milvia says about those hard years, 'in fact people she grew up with ostracised her and the family completely. My grandmother couldn't understand that. In fact she died before the end of the war, and mainly they say of a broken heart because she couldn't accept how the village had turned against her.'

In East Africa, in North Africa, in Sicily, British Italians fought Italians. A particularly grim irony was that during the subsequent long campaign in peninsular Italy the bitterly contested front line ran through the very zones which had been the main sources of emigration to Britain, at Cassino in the winter 1943-44, and in the Tuscan-Emilian Apennines in the winter 1944-45. In both these territories the civilian population experienced appalling suffering: bombardment, rape, theft, eviction, hunger, and German slaughter of civilians in reprisal for assisting partisans or helping escaped Allied prisoners of war. The first time Tony Sacco from Langley Moor had set foot in Italy since the age of nine was with the Durham Light Infantry at the battle of Salerno. The night before, during the long crossing from Bizerta, his captain asked him where his family were from and he answered it was a little place called Cassino. 'He'd never heard of it. But after that he would say to me: Cassino, we're certainly hearing plenty about it now!'

When Italy switched sides in September 1943 thousands of British prisoners of war who had been captured in North Africa hid out in the Apennine mountain range after being set free behind German lines by their Italian guards. If any before had doubted the humanity and courage of ordinary Italians they discovered it then, when countless numbers risked their lives to protect them. Generally unfailing in their support were the returned emigrants from America and Britain.

One former British fugitive who spoke with the warmest admiration of the peasant people he chanced to fall in with was Alfie Longstaff from Middlestone Moor, near Spennymoor. 'The Italian working class,' he would repeat with deep affection and gratitude, 'oh dear me, they'd give you their last – and the backbone of Italy is the women!' With his friend Johnny from Banff he had hidden out for weeks in the rugged mountains above Cassino before falling desperately ill and becoming entirely dependent on the care of Maria Ciccarelli who nursed him back to health in her home in the village of Campoli Apennina, near Arpino. The area was thick with Germans on the look-out for escaped POWs and deserters from the Italian army and even their own forces, and the penalty for assisting them was death. Yet seven English, eleven Italian deserters, and one Austrian managed to live among the villagers without ever being discovered or betrayed. With some of these fellow fugitives, when he was fit again, 'Alfredo' formed a partisan band which carried out a number of operations against German fuel depots and ammunition dumps over on the Adriatic side of the mountains, losing three men in the process. Maria's children were a boy of fifteen, and Elena, still a little girl. Today if you care to buy something from one of the family's fleet of ice cream vans in and around Newcastle you will be doing a little bit to sustain the firm which Alfie's rescuer's daughter, Elena Ciccarelli, founded some twenty years after the war with her late husband Donato Gregorio, an immigrant steelworker.

Alfredo's experiences in Ciociaria tellingly point up many of the contradictions and coincidences, not all unhappy, that characterised the war years from both a British and Italian standpoint.

'WITHOUT THAT FAMILY I WOULDN'T BE HERE TODAY'

One day Johnny and I left Maria's to see if we could collect some dandelion leaves and snails along the road. We were in this field when some horsemen came by, about twenty Jerries on horseback. The wood was too far away from us, so I says, 'Don't look up, Johnny, keep picking up the food on the bottom even if it's only grass' – and at that same moment one of the horsemen fell off. So then the game was on. They crowded round and we thought it was all up for us. But eventually they got him back on his horse and we two carried on, and when we got to the bottom of the road and turned right there was this house there, and we went and asked if there was any spare food. 'Who are you?' the man says. We told him point blank that one was English and one was Scotch: 'Oh, come on in!' So we had a glass of vino, quite a few glasses in fact, and he says – he could speak a bit of broken English, he'd been in America – 'What part of England do you come from then?' 'Oh,' I says, 'I'm from the north like: il nord.' And he says, 'Bishop Auckland?' 'What?! What do you know about Bishop Auckland?' He says, 'I'm the godfather of one of the Gabrieles!'

Well, we bid him good day, and went on a bit farther, and as we got out toward the bottom of the place, onto the Arpino road, there were about five big houses where we were told there were Germans. But all the same I says, 'You cover me off, Johnny,' and I went and knocked on this door. A young lad came out, about eighteen, nineteen, and I asked him for something to eat: 'Poco mangiare?' 'Nient', he says, 'Voi tedeschi?' But he spoke with a Geordie accent, Newcastle. So I says, 'Eh, do you come from Newcastle?' Oh dear me, his eyes went wide and you should have seen the sweat coming on, he'd thought I was German. 'Don't be frightened', I says. 'I'm English, and you see that lad up there that's watching you, he's Scotch'. 'What do you want?' he says. 'A bit of food.' 'When are you going back?' 'When they'll let us. We've already had one try and it's very difficult, but we'll try again'. 'Well, will you take a letter through for us,' he says, 'a letter to me mam?' I says, 'We're going to try and go again in November. If you've got this letter now I can memorise everything, that will be the best plan. You keep the letter, I'll memorise it. And I'll memorise where your mam lives in Newcastle'. And he says, 'They don't know that I'm married. What happened was I came out here for an ear operation and the war was declared, I'm detained and they've never heard from us since.'

So when I did get through the lines, and back home eventually, I went up to Rea's, the two sisters living near the Scotswood Road, going up towards Benwell. Eh, they couldn't believe it! After that we used to go up regular to see them, the wife and I and the daughter, because they always asked us up. And then one day they made us a coffee as usual – and who was it brought the bairn some milk? Elena! Dear me, I recognised her, and I'd only seen her when she was a bairn at Campoli when I used to pick her up, chuck her about, and she used to think it was great. I looked at her and I says, 'Elena!' And you know, without that family I wouldn't be here today.

(Alfie ('Alfredo') Longstaff, Middlestone Moor, 1990. The Scotswood Road sisters were Vera and Angela ('Florrie'), daughters of Angelo Rea, from Arpino, one of the earliest settlers on Teesside along with his brother Santi.)

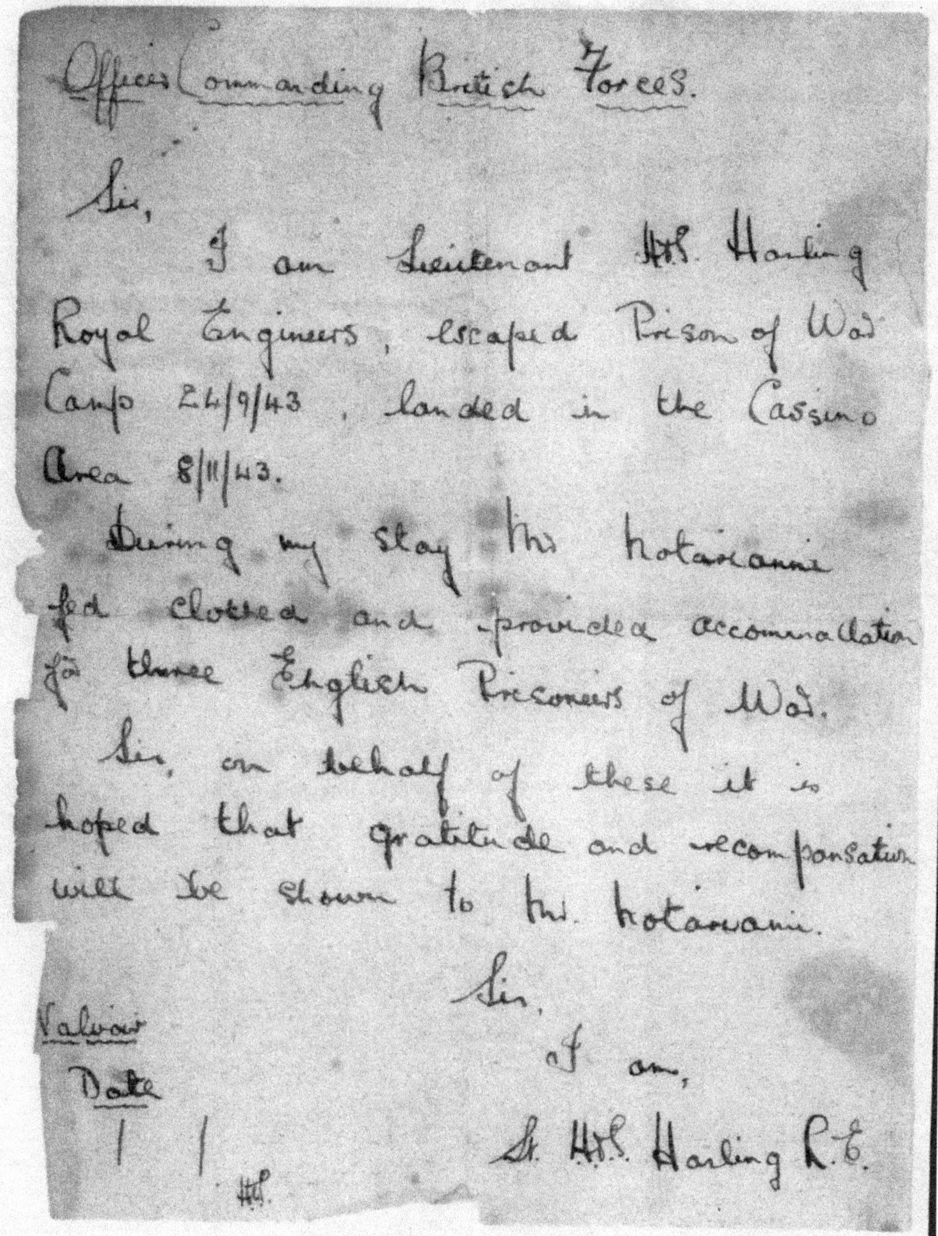

Officer Commanding British Forces.

Sir,

I am Lieutenant H.S. Harling Royal Engineers, escaped Prison of War Camp 24/9/43, landed in the Cassino Area 8/11/43.

During my stay Mr Notarianni fed clothed and provided accommodation for three English Prisoners of War.

Sir, on behalf of these it is hoped that gratitude and recompensation will be shown to Mr. Notarianni.

Sir,

I am,

Lt. H.S. Harling R.E.

Valvori
Date
/ /

In winter 1943, shortly before the SS requisitioned their home, members of the Notarianni family of Sunderland stranded in Italy had risked their lives to shelter three Allied POWs on the run. This is the chit they left. The Notarianni house in Valvori, the Marcantonio house in Picinisco, the Reale house in Arpino, and the Moscardini house in Sommocolonia, were all commandeered by the Germans for their size and the vantage point they offered when these high hill villages found themselves in the front line.

Christmas message from Luigi Citrone to his parents in Chester-le-Street, sent from the Italian front, December 1944, with English summary in his own hand added for the censor. His parents had been interned in 1940.

But the most extreme wartime paradox, or the supreme twist of fate which possibly reconciles them all, is the unparalleled case of Dennis Donnini, the Easington-born son of a pitman's daughter from Sacriston and an Italian ice cream dealer from Castelnuovo near Barga, who in giving his life for this country became the war's youngest winner of the VC. His father Alfredo Donnini had been settled in England for over forty years and therefore was not interned in June 1940, yet even so as an enemy alien he had still to quit the 'protected area' where he and Catherine had run an ice cream parlour and billiard saloon since 1912 following a first venture in Ferryhill. Along with 'Denny', then only fourteen, they were taken in by Barghigiani relatives in Crook in the upper Wear valley.

The posthumous investiture presented the Palace with a baffling quandary: the hero's next of kin was not a British subject. Finally somehow ancient protocol was overruled, some say with the tactful intervention of Easington's Catholic priest, and on the appointed day the possessor of alien's identity card no. 60058 and his eldest daughter were ushered into the royal presence. Under the headline 'Mr Donnini Goes to the Palace' Reginald Butler's article in the local paper strove to capture all the incongruity and solemn pathos of the event.

MR DONNINI GOES TO THE PALACE

At 10.16 a.m. precisely, as Mr Donnini and his daughter Silvia passed between the Palace gates, a precedent was created.

It was the first time since the London home of the Royal family was built in 1703 that an alien, officially an enemy, had crossed the threshold of the building which symbolises the British Empire. As they passed between the drawn-up lines of 6ft. stiff-backed Grenadier and Welsh guardsmen in the Palace forecourt, three lorries full of Italian non-co-operator prisoners-of-war drove past the front of the Palace.

Inside the Palace the grey-haired Italian, his black hat crushed in his right hand, was almost overcome by the majesty of it all. Beads of perspiration appeared on his white brow as the marshal called his name, told him that he would be No. 3 on the list of recipients.

Silvia stood closely by his side, slipped her hand in his when the King, wearing the uniform of a marshal of the RAF, came on to the dais. Mr Donnini bent his head, murmured in broken English: 'My Dennis... If only he was here.'

A court official called out: 'Mr Alfredo Donnini.' With his daughter at his side, the one-time ice cream vendor – who came to Britain when he was 17, started working making ice cream for 6s. 3d. a week and his keep, and always forgot to apply for naturalisation papers – walked slowly towards the King, holding Silvia's left hand.

The King looked at the old Italian as the citation was being read, realised from his white face and perspiring brow that he was ill at ease. When the citation ended the King held out his hand, smiled, and as Mr Donnini extended his right hand he knew his first peace of mind since he set out from his Easington home on Monday morning.

The King asked about young Dennis, shook his head as Mr Donnini told him that he was the baby of the family and had been killed in action only seven months after he had joined the Army.

The King surprised his visitor by telling him that he knew of the service which the Donnini family had given to Britain during the war. Two sons had given their lives, a third was a prisoner for five years, and the two younger daughters were serving in the ATS.

Mr Donnini straightened his back. He looked at the King, said: 'Thank you, sir'.
The King smiled.

As soon as news of the award broke, the Northern Division of the Ice Cream Alliance resolved to launch an appeal for a fund to commemorate Dennis Donnini by endowing a bed in Durham County Hospital. The call for donations was taken up enthusiastically by the *Ice Cream Industry* journal which lost no time in proclaiming Dennis 'the hero of the trade'. The ambitious target of £1,000 was reached within eighteen months. Donations poured in from ice cream people and sympathisers from all over the country, by no means all of Italian descent though by far the greatest number of subscribers were the North East's Italians, some of them donating several times over. Inevitably, many were the same who only ten years previously had contributed to the Duce's fund for gold at the time of the Abyssinian War.

One is left with the poignant impression that after the intervening decade of confused emotions and accusations and prejudice the fact that 'the bravest of the brave' happened to be the son of an Italian father and an English mother was felt both to vindicate the gallantry and honour of Italians and to represent an exemplary sacrifice which could go a long way toward healing the painful wounds amassed in the long years in which their own loyalty to their adopted country had been so drastically called into question.

'Italian Father Gets His Boy's VC' (Newcastle Journal). Flanked by his daughters Corinna and Silvia (right), both in ATS uniform, Alfredo Donnini displays his son's VC to the press outside Buckingham Palace on 17 July 1945. All three sons served in the British Army: Alfie was captured at Dunkirk and endured five years as a prisoner of war in Germany, Louis died of his wounds, and Dennis, the youngest, was killed in the action which gained him the Victoria Cross. Aged just 19 and only 5ft. 4in. tall, Dennis Donnini was not only the youngest but the smallest serviceman to win the VC in World War II. Remembered by his family and friends as 'a bit of a scrapper' and 'always smiling', he left home promising his mother he would win the VC. His memory is honoured in Donnini House, a block of 24 flats for the elderly in Easington Colliery, Donnini Place in Durham City, and Donnini Court in Ayr, the home base of his chosen regiment, the Royal Scots Fusiliers.

THE COMMENDATION

THE KING has been graciously pleased to approve the posthumous award of the VICTORIA CROSS to –

No.14768011 Fusilier DENNIS DONNINI, The Royal Scots Fusiliers,
(Easington Colliery, County Durham)
Gazetted 19th March, 1945

In North-West Europe on 18th January, 1945, a battalion of the Royal Scots Fusiliers supported by tanks led the assault on the German position between the rivers Roer and Maas. This was a broad belt of minefields and wire on the other side of a stream. As a result of a thaw, the armour was unable to cross the stream, and the infantry had to continue the assault without the support of the tanks. Fusilier Donnini's platoon was ordered to attack a small village. As they left their trenches the platoon came under concentrated machine-gun and rifle fire from the houses, and Fusilier Donnini was hit by a bullet in the head. After a few minutes he recovered consciousness, charged down thirty yards of open road, and threw a grenade in the nearest window. The enemy fled through the gardens of four houses, closely pursued by Fusilier Donnini and the survivors of his platoon. Under heavy fire at seventy yards range, Fusilier Donnini and two companions crossed an open space and reached the cover of a wooden barn, thirty yards from the enemy trenches. Fusilier Donnini, still bleeding profusely from his wounds, went into the open under intense close-range fire and carried one of his companions, who had been wounded, into the barn. Taking a Bren gun he again went into the open, firing as he went. He was wounded a second time, but recovered, and went on firing until a third bullet hit a grenade which he was carrying and killed him. The superb gallantry and self-sacrifice of Fusilier Donnini drew enemy fire away from his companions onto himself. As a result of this, the platoon were able to capture the position, accounting for thirty Germans and two machine guns. Throughout this action, fought from beginning to end at point-blank range, the dash, determination, and magnificent courage of Fusilier Donnini enabled his comrades to overcome an enemy more than twice their own number.

Italian prisoners of war in the North East

Until the country itself became a battlefield, the bleakest proof of the catastrophic collapse of Fascist Italy's dreams of Roman conquest was the vast number of Italian prisoners of war held by the Allies – about three quarters of a million by the end of 1943. The 400,000 who surrendered to British forces in North Africa and in Italy's East African dominions were dispersed throughout Britain's own African colonies and protectorates, or to neutralise them further were

Italian POWs at Darras Hall camp, 1944. (Photo: Tatoli).

transferred as far as India and Ceylon, Australia and New Zealand, Canada and the West Indies. Ahead of them all lay years of captivity. Despite abundant instances of individual courage in the field, no great collective military feats had come from this huge but ill-equipped and poorly led conscript force waging an incompetently planned war for a cause which few of its foot soldiers understood.

Britain from June 1940 was a nation under siege. Cut off from German-occupied Europe and prey to heavy losses on its transatlantic supply routes, the country's survival depended not only on its military response but on boosting food productivity to achieve near self-sufficiency. Even with an 80,000 strong Women's Land Army raised to compensate for the manpower shortage on farms it was inevitable the captured Italians would come to be viewed as a vast reservoir of cheap labour, just as had happened with German POWs in the First World War. Legal scruples about the rights of prisoners of war under the Geneva Convention were routinely flouted, in particular the obligation to keep enemy prisoners out of danger. Over five times as many Italians died on torpedoed vessels bringing them to work in Britain as perished on the *Arandora Star,* and now with no outcry at all, but when your own troops are dying in large numbers and your cities are under nightly bombardment fatal accidents to enemy personnel break no hearts.

The first batch of 1,500 POWs arrived from North Africa in July 1941 and were immediately put to work erecting barbed wire encircled camps of prefabricated huts for the massive intakes to follow: 40,000 over the next twelve months, peaking at over 155,000 by the end of 1944, when even this number was eclipsed by the arrival of some 400,000 German POWs in the very last stages of the war.

First reports found the rapidly growing army of handpicked men were willing workers, 'disciplined and cooperative', glad to be freed to work out in the open during the day, and all the more welcome for being fit young men mostly from a farming background who cost their hirers a lot less than local labour: 38 shillings a week, of which the prisoner himself received at most five in the form of token money he could only use in his camp canteen, plus 35 cigarettes, the rest going straight to the Treasury.

Since their work placements were scattered over large tracts of countryside a system quickly evolved of erecting a large parent camp at the centre of a particular area of need with dependent detachments of 70 to 100 men with 'good conduct' records billeted in outlying hostels supervised by British Army NCOs. Very similar arrangements and work allocations were experienced by their British counterparts in POW camps in Italy. Unless engaged on large schemes like land reclamation or road building, all were trucked or marched (and later to the outrage of many civilians even permitted to bike) to individual farms for day work. Though locked up in their camps and hostels every night, they were seldom under surveillance at work. Some of course absconded, but were easily spotted in their standard British battledress jackets dyed chocolate brown with a yellow patch on the back, and further patches on the front of the right trouser leg and the back of the left. A fortunate few (still only 800 at the end of 1942) were directly billeted on the more remote farms. For them, at least, it was impossible to adhere to the rules against 'fraternisation' enforced by both the military and local police, often responding to tip-offs from nosy locals. Outside the workplace the Italians were permitted no contacts with the public, the sole exception being Sunday church attendance under guard where a hostel had no chaplain available. This, fortunately, led to the Catholic Church becoming the only charitable institution apart from the YMCA to take any interest in their plight. Hostility was the norm, and particularly virulent or petty in the press even long after Italy had ceased to be an enemy power.

Most camps in the North-East were set up during 1942-3 and built by local contractors with large detachments of POWs working alongside them. The main camps, with a capacity for at least 700 prisoners and at times many more, were at Darras Hall near Ponteland, at Fir Tree near Crook in Weardale, at Wooler in Northumberland, and later at Featherstone Park, also in Northumberland, which served first as a training camp for American forces preparing for the D-Day landings, then as an Italian POW camp, and finally as a re-education centre for Nazi officers. Aside from Italian medical and dental officers and chaplains who served the needs of all ranks, the POW labour camp system had no use for officers since the Geneva Convention exempted them from work. Officers were held separately in Walworth Castle, and naval personnel in Windlestone Hall, otherwise all other camps for Italians in the North-East were for army non-commissioned officers and other ranks, and the Italian camp leader was therefore typically a sergeant-major. As can be seen from the list overleaf, large country houses were routinely requisitioned for smaller camps and hostels, within the house itself or in the grounds. Each camp was self-regulating, with British administrative and security personnel billeted apart in an adjacent compound. International Red Cross inspections concurred that despite the nation's extreme shortages the prisoners were adequately fed and clothed and housed, and well treated. The happiest camps were those where the three chief authority figures, the English commandant, the English interpreter officer, and the Italian camp leader, worked harmoniously in the interests of all concerned. In the winter months when there was less work in the fields the POWs were diverted to projects like ditching and road building, or snow and bomb damage clearance. Bedburn hostel POWs built an open air swimming pool for the village. From September 1944 most of the Italian 'co-operators' were transferred to low-security smaller camps and hostels in order to make room for the huge influx of still untamed German POW workers. The camps listed with numbers in the 600s were expressly created to take these dislodged Italians in the last months of the war.

n. 4 Windlestone Hall camp, Rushyford, near Durham, later a sub camp for 93.

n. 18 Featherstone Park camp, Haltwhistle, Northumbria.

n. 36 Walworth Castle camp, near Darlington.

n. 69 Darras Hall camp, Ponteland, with hostels at Catton, Colwell, Gosforth, Longhorsley, Prestwick, Raylees (near Elsdon), Wylam.

n. 93 Harperley camp, Crook, with hostels at Bedburn, Bishop Auckland, Consett, Hamsterley Hall, High Spen, Lanchester, Langton Grange, Mount Oswald (Durham), Usworth, Windlestone Hall,

n. 105 Wooler camp, Brewery Road, Wooler, with hostels at Druridge Bay, Embleton, Seaton Deleval, Whittingham.

n. 133 Hetton House camp, Chatton, near Wooler.

n. 139 Wolviston Hall camp, Billingham, with an associated Italian Labour Battalion at Coxhoe Hall (camp 139b), and hostels at Bewley, Bishop Middleham, Cowpen, Hart, Kirkleatham, and Rift House (West Hartlepool)

n. 291 Kitty Brewster Farm camp, Blyth

n. 605 Urpeth Lodge camp, Birtley

n. 605 West Boldon camp, Down Hill Quarry, Sunderland

n. 667 Byrness camp, Redesdale, near Otterburn

n. 699 Gosforth camp (Tyne 'J' camp), Newcastle, a subsidiary of camp 69.

According to local informants, Italian POWs were also present in small numbers at Barnard Castle, Cox Green (Sunderland), Dudley, and the Hermitage in Chester-le-Street. Local RAF stations also used Italian POWs to perform menial tasks.

Fifty huts of the former POW camp 93 still remain on this hillside near Harperley in Weardale, a melancholy reminder of the years in which Italian and German prisoners of war were set to work within our rural communities. Despite gaining scheduled monument status in 2002 most of the 18-acre site remains derelict after lack of funding scuppered a project to turn it into a 'themed' World War II museum along the lines of Eden Camp near Malton in North Yorkshire. Until the arrival of German POWs in late 1944 the camp routinely housed up to 1,000 Italian POWs. Alongside administrative buildings and billets for the guards and a detention block, there were vegetable gardens, a football pitch, recreation rooms, a library, a church hut, and a theatre hut equipped with tiered seats built by the prisoners. Other huts were set aside for dental and medical care, while graver cases were handled in a special POW unit in Bishop Auckland Hospital. An article in Il Corriere del Sabato for 18 March 1944 by a resident POW reported that 'in Camp 93, too, something is being done to relieve the boredom of these last days of prison life' (wishful thinking, alas!), instancing the arrival of a 'good projector' for the camp cinema and 'tender memories of the past' evoked by the camp band's musical evenings under the 'talented maestro Sorrentino'. The camp school was well attended by those 'keen to make the most of their scant spare time', while 'Fulmine' and 'Lampo' football teams were training hard for the inaugural match on the nearly completed sports field, and a forthcoming boxing match was generating great excitement among rival fans. All these initiatives were attributed to the able efforts of the camp leader Sgt-Maj. Pasquale Galluzzo working in collaboration with the camp commandant and the English captain who was also camp interpreter.

Sunday afternoon concert party in the theatre hut at Coxhoe camp. Note the prisoners' paintings on the walls. On the right, standing, is the camp commandant; on the left is the band's singer, Maurizio. The clarinet player to the right is Donato De Grecis, a cabinet maker in peacetime who was to marry local girl Katie. The couple settled in Coxhoe where they raised seven daughters. (Photo: De Grecis)

Derelict hut at Harperley camp today.

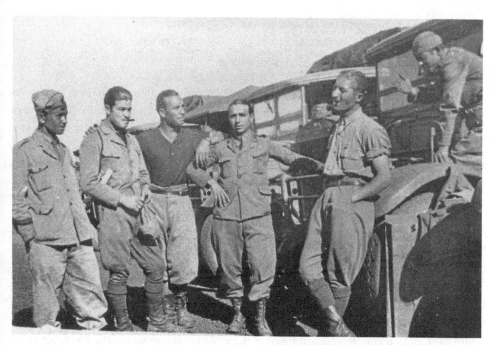

Pte Donato De Grecis (second left) before capture, with comrades-in-arms in North Africa.

As in the Isle of Man internment camps, the YMCA took upon itself the immense humanitarian task of attending to the prisoners' recreational and educational needs, boldly declaring its purpose was nothing less than to help 'every man in camp gain the victory over the great enemies of all prisoners – monotony, futility, discouragement'. Accordingly its hard-pressed staff bought or scrounged radios and gramophones, books and play texts, footballs and musical instruments, and most notably trained educated POW volunteers to set up and run camp schools offering basic classes for their numerous less literate fellow prisoners. Extremely popular were the three small voluntary groups of professional civilian singers and musicians the organisation sponsored to tour the camps.

Most POWs were understandably sceptical of all news of Italy they received from British papers and BBC radio bulletins, for the very few who knew English, and from *Il Corriere del Sabato* ('The Saturday Courier') for the majority. This Italian-language weekly paper produced by the Political Intelligence Department of the Foreign Office was unabashedly aimed at re-educating these enemy subjects who were mostly too young to have known any political system but fascism. Even so, it remains a useful source of insights from the prisoners' own perspective since eventually it admitted vetted contributions from the POWs themselves. A crucial service was the inter-camp message page, the most poignant column being the numerous standardised one-line items printed in the *Sezione ricerche* in which prisoners, presumably after fruitless inquiries through the International Red Cross and the Vatican, sought news of close relatives who had also been under arms, adding (in brackets) the theatre of war and last date they had been heard of. For instance, on 13 January 1945 we find:

Sold. DOTTO Vittorio (C.93): fratello Aldo (Tunisi, maggio '43).

Cpl. M. FINOTTO Alberico (C.93): fratello Giacomo (Agedabia '41)

Sold. CONGEDO Santo (C.93): cognato FUSO Antonio (Bardia '41)

The first two of these three prisoners at Harperley camp (C.93) were hoping for news of lost brothers, the third of a brother-in-law. Note that two had vanished into the unknown almost four years before. These stark appeals are just one indication of how isolated these men felt, and what black thoughts they could be prey to at a time when even a long-awaited letter from war-ravaged Italy might only compound their misery. 'My wife wrote from Naples a while ago,' a POW writes the following week, 'saying our home was hit in the bombing. She had been starving for months, and she begged me if I can to bring back clothing because the Germans stole everything before retreating'. Mail from home took months to arrive, if it got through at all, and of course none came out of German-occupied northern Italy. Delivery of the prisoners' own censored letters was equally unpredictable.

Most *Corriere del Sabato* POW reports of camp activities are relentlessly upbeat. For instance, along with graphic accounts of key matches in a 7 a side football league competing for 'the cup' (a hoard of cigarettes) donated by camp leader Sgt-Maj. Parolini, four reports over the winter '43-44 from Wooler camp give a picture of intense communal involvement in *bocce*, volley-ball, table-tennis, frenetic card games, and a big boxing event coached and supervised by Sgt. Orofino with musical interludes provided by the camp band under maestro Baratta. Extravagant praise is heaped on the individually named scene painters, writers, producers, singers and actors (starring also in female roles) involved in the hilarious or not-a-dry-eye-in-the-house shows at the Teatro Aurora ['Dawn'], 'so aptly named by *capo campo* Sgt-maj. Parolini, its inspiration and impresario, because just as dawn heralds day so with our theatre life has returned once more, life with all its hopes of a bright tomorrow'.

The bright tomorrow so yearned for by these cooped-up young men, or living dead, who had not seen their families for years and who could work hard for the British but not befriend them, was a product of the immense hopes aroused by the armistice of September 1943. Within only a few weeks the whole of Sicily and much of southern Italy had been liberated, the king and his new government had rejected fascism and been rewarded by the Allies with 'co-belligerent' status. How much longer then before those from the liberated territories could go home, and even take up arms again to rid the rest of Italy of the common enemy, the Germans? Above all, when would there be a change in their POW status and conditions now that their country was a friendly power? Unknown to them, the Americans were already releasing prisoners in North Africa and enlisting ex-POWs from camps in the US.

The British had no intention of relinquishing 75,000 captive workers who were on the whole smoothly and efficiently supplementing the acute manpower shortage, nor the tens of thousands more Italians already earmarked for importation from even as far away as India. With Italy now our 'co-belligerent' we could have it both ways: the Italians would remain prisoners of war so we could still control them, but seeing the Geneva Convention applied to prisoners of war but obviously not to co-belligerents there was now nothing to stop them doing additional vital work for the war effort in formerly proscribed fields such as factory work, transport, dock labour, food distribution, and so on.

On Sunday 30 April 1944, after seven long months of waiting had crushed almost all expectations of some improvement and at least a start to the repatriation process, all the Italians were paraded in their camps and offered not a change in their POW status but a stark political choice: with us or against us, with your king and his government who now support us, or with Musssolini and the Germans, 'royalists' or 'fascists', 'co-operators' or 'non-co-operators'. Non-co-operators will live as before behind barbed wire and work for us at the standard five shillings a week. If however you volunteer to co-operate in our war effort you will receive an extra two shillings a week and live without barbed wire, though the perimeter fence will remain; you will be organised into Italian Labour Battalions in the camps and Italian Working Companies in the hostels run by Italian officers (a genuine but not wholly welcome innovation) and NCOs, though of course still under British command and supervision; and no longer will you wear brown uniforms with those humiliating patches but green uniforms with 'ITALY'[5] emblazoned on a shoulder flash in which during what time you have off you will be able to walk freely out of camp, though no more than two miles and without talking to civilians, and without entering centres of population or using public transport, or visiting any shop or pub or private home. It was a bit like Mussolini declaring all emigrants 'Italians Abroad': though dressed up differently co-operators were still POWs and Apartheid continued.

The authorities assumed nine out of ten would fall for the deal, instead they got just sixty per cent. The manoeuvre in fact precipitated a bitter rift, split the hard-achieved harmony in the camps by turning Italian against Italian, just as was happening in Italy itself, and exacerbated anti-British feeling not only among the small percentage of convinced fascists (whom the British estimated at no more than 15%). 'Non-co-operators' denounced their opposite numbers as collaborators, deserters, traitors who had sold out to the British, and as the strength of feeling mounted on both sides the two factions had to be kept apart for more than purely administrative reasons. Most who opted for non-co-operation did so from personal rather than political choice, for after years of confinement together it felt important to stick with your friends and the routine you knew. There was also concern that co-operation could lead to reprisals against family members in Italy now that Mussolini was reinstated as head of government alongside his Nazi ally who ruthlessly ruled the northern half of the peninsula. A contributor to *Il Corriere del Sabato* bluntly summed up what he believed to be most non-co-operators' feelings by referring instead to their captors: 'I am not a fascist. I chose not to co-operate for two reasons: first, because I don't want to give the English the satisfaction, and second, because the English don't show the least liking for us.'

The take-up rate did not notably improve even four months later when the need for more co-operators wrung significant new concessions from the authorities: access to shops and cinemas (but not pubs or other places of entertainment), visits to private homes (if invited), friendly (but on no account sexual) relations with civilians. 'Consorting' with a Briton remained a crime carrying a maximum penalty of two years imprisonment with hard labour, and it was rigorously applied in most cases which came to court. That was as far as the Fraternisation Regulation could go, and even so it unleashed a storm of scaremongering in the press.

The non-co-operators, still 30% of the POW population right up to the war's end, remained in their separate camps behind barbed wire, proud in their sense of honourable martyrdom. The co-operators meantime were made to feel more than ever like enemy aliens. Even after the two countries had been allies for over a year they were still forbidden to use public transport or to set foot in pubs, restaurants, cafés, and dance halls, and were often turned away from cinemas despite the new dispensation. Ion Megary, a YMCA organiser who wrote very affectingly of his work among the Italians whom he found to be 'generous and warm-hearted' and with 'a genius for personal relations', memorably summed up the co-operators' plight: 'Moving among free men but themselves subject to restrictions which were incompatible with freedom, they suffered more humiliation than they had ever suffered in the camps. Unloved, and unlovely, many of them, in their shoddy clothes they hung about the streets of every village in England with nothing to do, resented by the population and spied on by the police.'

It can be no surprise therefore that these half-free lonely men unable to speak much English gravitated towards any local Italian café they could find. In our region, as some of the accompanying photographs show, the warmth and kindness with which they were received resulted in several marriages between Italian POWs and British Italians. Equally, despite every unnatural obstacle to 'fraternisation', again and again love found a way even between the alienated POWs and the wary Brits.

'POSSEEBLE ONE KISS?'

I was standing at the fairground just looking, listening to the music and watching the rides go round, and these prisoners of war were coming up and speaking to me and I was just turning away. So he must have been watching me, and watching them coming and speaking to me, and me turning away like that, so he thought he would try. He came and said something to me and I just said 'No' and turned away. He was trying to speak to me and there was all the noise of the shows and everything going on, so I said to him, 'Look, come here.' I took hold of his arm to take him outside, away from all the noise of the music to explain that my father wouldn't allow me. So I was doing my best to tell him how my father wouldn't

POW kitchen staff at Bishop Middleham hostel (Camp 139).
Pasquale Cubello, from Calabria, who volunteered to 'co-operate' while in a POW camp in South Africa, is second from left in the front row. On the reverse of this photograph which he left with Mary Smith on his repatriation in 1946 he wrote: 'I hope some day you will be my wife for all my life. I never shall forget our dear love. You have been so kind with me, same your family, they have take me like their son.'
The couple married on his return to England in June 1948.

agree to it, and after all the explanation he said to me, 'Posseeble one kiss?' After all that trouble and all the explanation I'd gone through, that's what he said: 'Posseeble one kiss'! Well, I thought, that's rich isn't it! So I said I'd see him another night, and that's how it started.

One particular night, perhaps it was a Saturday night, I was supposed to be going out with him, and I'd been ill all the week so I said to my father, 'What's it like outside?' 'Well,' he said, 'it's not too bad but you cannot go out tonight, you've been ill all week, you'd better stop in.' So what do I do, I thought, there he is waiting outside? And of course Father didn't know. So I said, 'Well, if I can't go out could a friend of mine come in?' 'A friend – what friend?' I said, 'Well, it's an Italian, from the camp.' So he said, 'You know I don't agree with that.' But then he said, 'All the same, let him come in and we'll see what he's like.' He was very reasonable, my father, you had to do what you were told, but he wouldn't dismiss things out of hand. Another father would have said, 'He is not coming in, that's the end of it,' and then you'd have had to do things underhand. When I went across and told Pasquale he was a bit nervous about coming in. He thought, 'What's going on here, will he start on me when I go in?' But never mind. My father told him, 'I don't agree with it, my daughter is just a young girl and there is no future in it'. So Pasquale said, 'Well, just a friend, just a friend', because he didn't have a great deal of English at the time. 'Just a friend, company.' So then my father knew and it was out in the open. After that Pasquale used to come to chapel and it was a lot easier.

Well, time went on, and it was getting near the time for him to be repatriated, and this particular Sunday morning after my father came from chapel I could see he'd been thinking about something because he stood – I can picture him now – he stood with his back to the fire, and he said to me, 'Do you love that young man?' I said, 'Yes, I do.' So he said, 'Well, I don't want you to go to Italy, I know what countries are like after a war, you don't know anything about the world. But if he is willing to come back here for you I'll help you all I can'. And he did.

(Mary Cubello, neé Smith, Coxhoe 1991)

During the last half-year of the war, the first five hundred of finally some five thousand British servicemen returned home with Italian wives. They too had had to overcome fierce anti-fraternisation regulations and often extreme efforts by the military authorities to deter their marriage plans. At least four of the many Italian 'war brides' who settled down in our region with their demobbed husbands – Anna Richardson, Ada Bonelli-Morgan, Maria Melone, Ines Fox – went on to teach their mother tongue to countless numbers of local enthusiasts of all things Italian.

It is often erroneously asserted that the repatriation of Italian POWs took place well before the end of the war (May 1945). The impression presumably arose from the fact that Britain had not been at war with Italy since September 1943 and, as explained earlier, from late 1944 most Italians were moved out of the major camps to make way for massive intakes of German POWs. Instead repatriation was another story of shabby treatment and calculated delay.

Even with the war over, Britain's workforce of 130,000 Italian POWs (some 10,000 sick or unsuitable were released earlier) was much too usefully engaged to be dispensed with at once. Countless farmers had grown dependent on their labour, and with the Women's Land Army disbanding and returning to civilian life they were desperately needed at the very least until the last harvests were in. For this reason the Ministry of Labour intervened forcefully to hold back the longed-for process of mass repatriation until Christmas 1945. It was not in fact completed until July 1946, almost three years after Italy had thrown in its lot with the Allies. The longest serving POWs, seized in the former Italian colonies of Abyssinia and Eritrea in 1940, had therefore spent six years in captivity. Embarkation proceeded by age, working downwards, with the non-co-operators held over till last. Each prisoner was allowed a maximum of two kit bags of personal effects, providing none were 'gifts or comforts from any private source'.

Francesco 'Frankie' Trapani met Giuseppina Di Palma, of the Bishop Auckland ice cream family, while a prisoner at the Coxhoe and Bishop Middleham hostels after a long spell at Harperley camp. He became a well known local figure, with ice cream stalls in Bishop Auckland market place and Witton Lido. Among the bridesmaids are Angelina and Rosalinda Quadrini, and the best man (right) is Gaetano Rea of the Middlesbrough ice cream company.

Oreste Gracco (right) was one of three POWs to each marry one of the Reale sisters of Newcastle. The friends met Enrica, Amelia, and Marietta while based at Gosforth hostel (Camp 699). Others seen here at the Reale stall at the Hoppings are (from left) Domenic Reale, Frankie Rea, and (in the stall) Serafino Reale and his wife Lauretta.

MARRIED TO THE CAFÉ

Sgt. Franco Bonadies, from Corato near Bari, met Rosa Arrighi at the family café in Seaton Deleval, Northumbria, when he was camp leader at the nearby 'co-operators' hostel. Their wedding was held in Rosa's parents' home town of Barga, after which the couple returned to run together the celebrated 'Crescent Café'.

A BRIDE WHO CROSSED THE DIVIDE

Joyce Wrangham met Silvio Spaventa, an Italian airforce radio operator, when she was working at the Royal Ordnance Factory at Birtley and he was a POW at the Urpeth Lodge hostel. When her family protested about the liaison the commandant obligingly had Silvio transferred to a camp in the south, but Joyce unhesitatingly followed. The couple married in Italy and returned to England after the birth of their first baby in 1948, after which Silvio worked at Park Drift pit, then for Bove's café in South Moor and Niro's in Stanley. In 1983 the couple retired to Silvio's home town of Bomba, near Pescara.

LOVE OUTLASTS WAR

Ken Douglas of Newcastle met Anna Sica while briefly stationed at Alvignano village near Caserta in 1943, and before leaving for the Cassino front promised he would marry her if he survived. They were only able to meet and marry eight years later after Anna volunteered for millwork in Rochdale under the post-war bulk recruitment scheme.

What awaited the repatriated POWs in Italy? Domenico Tatoli, a bricklayer from Corato in Puglia who had been contentedly working on a Northumbrian farm for the past 18 months, had no illusions about what would be his lot at home, or that of other labouring men. 'I thought to myself: The war was in Italy, so how am I going to find work? If I go back I'll starve. Better to stay where I am and see if I can make a good life here.' In the end 1,400 Italians engaged in farm work all over England were granted temporary leave to stay as 'civilian volunteers' on a renewable annual contract, and most crucially were permitted to bring over wives and children. Domenico had not seen his wife Francesca and their little son Nicola for seven long years. Only in 1951 were resident Italian ex-POWs given refugee status and thus leave to remain indefinitely in this country. The very last German POWs were not released until 1948. This experience of using thousands of foreign workers to fill gaps in the labour market was to have far-reaching repercussions for Italian immigration in post-war Britain.

Domenico Tatoli and Cosimo Manfredi (first and second left) with other Italian 'co-operators' at an Allendale farm in 1944. The two friends, both from Puglia and easily identified on the left of the photo on page 242, were among the very few POWs granted permission to settle in the North East at the end of the war. For almost 20 years they remained working for the families they had befriended while billeted with them. On leaving Bishopside Farm in Catton, Domenico tried sheep rearing for a time before opening Domenic's café in Saltwell Road, Gateshead. After leaving Round Meadows Farm, also in Catton, Cosimo and his wife Natalina settled in Stanley where they opened 'Manfredi's' well known fish and chip shop.

BOOKS AND SOURCES

Lucio Sponza's *Divided Loyalties: Italians in Britain during the Second World War* (2000) treats with great authority all the principal topics discussed in this chapter, providing a wealth of information from government and other sources. Terri Colpi, 'The Impact of the Second World War on the British Italian Community' in *Immigrants and Minorities* (Vol.11, 1992) is an extremely useful overview. The same issue contains other contributions which situate internment (in both world wars) within a much longer history of anti-alien feeling in modern Britain. The National Archives hold the essential source material on deportation and internment under Home Office files 213, 214 and 215, and Foreign Office file 916.

Comb-out. François Lafitte, *The Internment of Aliens* (1940, reissued in 1988 with a new introduction by the author) was a courageous denunciation of the excesses of the internment scheme written at the very time. Forty years later the release of (by no means all) the relevant official documents enabled Peter and Leni Gilman in *Collar the Lot! How Britain Interned and Expelled its Wartime Refugees* (1980) to uncover a lot more of the unedifying story of the top-level manoeuvrings behind the programmes of internment and deportation. See also D. Cesarani and T. Kushner, *The Internment of Aliens in Twentieth Century Britain* (1993).

Disaster at sea: the *Arandora Star*. The memorable chapters in *Collar the Lot!* on the tragedy and its aftermath have inspired others to draw on accounts by survivors and their families: Pietro Zorza, *Arandora Star: il dovere di ricordarli* (special supplement to the paper *Italiani in Scozia*, 1985); D. Hickey and G. Smith, *Star of Shame: the Secret Voyage of the Arandora Star* (1989). The latest, a fine bilingual tribute to all who suffered, is Maria Serena Balestracci, *Arandora Star: Dall'oblio alla memoria / From oblivion to memory* (Parma 2008), which also lists the names of all known victims, Italian, British, German and Austrian. I am most grateful to Alan Davis for sharing his detailed knowledge of the impact the tragedy had on Teesside families, much of it recorded in an illustrated booklet with brief biographies and memories by relatives which he produced for the Middlesbrough unveiling, published by Middlesbrough town council (2009). www.colonsay.org.uk has information about victims' remains washed up on the island of Colonsay and at other locations. Available on YouTube under 'Arandora Star' is Brenda and Michael McRitchie's very moving 2008 video tribute to the numerous victims who lie in small graveyards along the north-west coast of Ireland.

Internment. The experience of German and Austrian, mainly Jewish, internees is recorded in R. Stent, *A Bespattered Page? The Internment of His Majesty's 'Most Loyal Enemy Aliens'* (1980), and Miriam Kochan, *Britain's Internees in the Second World War* (1983). C. Chappel, *Island of Barbed Wire. Internment on the Isle of Man in World War Two* (1984), follows among other stories the adventures of Giovanni Maneta, engineer on an Italian collier scuttled after leaving Newcastle on 10 June (see *Newcastle Journal*, 17.6.1940). Memories of internment dominate three publications by Italians: Cabisto Cavalli, *Ricordi di un emigrato* (Edizione La Voce degli Italiani, 1973); Gaetano Rossi, *Memoirs of 1940: Impressions of Life in an Internment Camp* (Rome 1991); Joe Pieri, *Isle of the Displaced: An Italian-Scot's Memoir of Internment in the Second World War* (1997). Cavalli was camp leader at Onchan camp; Rossi was interned as a young priest and went on to serve the Italian community in Scotland for fifty years; Pieri was deported to Canada. Personal accounts by six Italian ex-internees are held in the Imperial War Museum's sound archive.

How families coped. Most information here is from oral sources. Chief-constable Crawley's March 1941 report to the Home Office is in Tyne and Wear Archives. Mary Marcantonio's recollections were recorded by Beamish Museum.

Paradoxes of war. Most information is from oral sources. The Donnini family scrapbook, now in the possession of Mauro Ferri, Dennis Donnini's brother-in-law, was the prime source for information and photographs. R. Absalom, *A Strange Alliance: Aspects of Escape and Survival in Italy 1943-45* (Florence, 1991) documents the spontaneous help offered to British escapees by 'tens of thousands of Italian civilians'.

Prisoners of war. Beside the weekly numbers of *Il Corriere del Sabato*, the best texts for understanding what life was like for Italian POWs in Britain were written by two individuals who were tirelessly committed to their welfare, came to know them well, and were deeply saddened by the general prejudice against them: *The YMCA and the Italian Prisoners of War* (1946) by Ion Megary, and *"Not only Music, Signora"* (1947) by the Italian-born English concert pianist and singer Winifred Percival. To such honourable company can now be added Lucio Sponza whose long section on the prisoners of war in his *Divided Loyalties* is a fine blend of scholarly detective work and generous humanity. The following brief accounts of North-East POW camps are almost exclusively concerned with the later phases of occupation by German prisoners: J.S. Arcumes & J.F. Helvet, *Prisoner of War Camps in County Durham 1944-48* (County Durham Books, 2002), with good photographs of Harperley camp when still in use, and John Turner, 'POW Camp 69, Darras Hall', in *Pont Island News* (Ponteland Local History Society, 2005).

Survivors of the Arandora Star being helped aboard the Canadian destroyer St. Laurent.
(Photo given to Anna Chiappa, Ottowa, by a former member of the crew when researching for a Canadian TV documentary about the ill-fated liner)

8

'THE NEW ITALIANS': POST-WAR IMMIGRATION AND THE PRESENT GENERATION

Dear Sir,
I am instructed to ask that before any Italian miners are brought into the country, there should be a vote of the members as to their willingness to work with such miners.
Yours respectfully,
Edward Cain, Secretary, Wheatley Hill Lodge
(to Executive Committee Durham Area NUM, 20ᵗʰ August, 1955)

Recovery from the material and psychological damage of the war was something that Italians in Britain had to work at in one way or another alongside everyone else here. But there was a difference. An Italian could be no less revolted by the satanic alliance between Fascism and Nazism, and have had family members fighting to destroy it, but could still empathise with the pain and humiliation of fellow countrymen caught up in military collapse and two years of foreign armies slogging it out on Italian soil. Yet what could he retort to those around him who represented that tragic reality as nothing but an ignominious farce? The stark gulf between the Duce's strutting bravado and the generally miserable record of his vast armies determined a view of Italians that set back the old balance of good relations between the two countries and peoples for years. It took a long while, in those austere times, for the poison to work its way out of the system. In the 1950s kids at school were still putting up with playground taunts and fights. For some the war was never over.

'People now just don't realise how hard it was to be Italian then', says Paul Risi explaining how, even with the family surname safely changed to Rice, his father insisted on the curtains being drawn at mealtimes so there could be no risk of outsiders sighting the household in the outlandish act of consuming 'worms' together. Another friend from the war generation, Italo Rigali, wryly says the Italians have the more recent and more dark-skinned arrivals to thank, the Jamaicans, the Indians, the Pakistanis, the Bangladeshis, for finally providing an alternative target for prejudice.

Defeated, demoralised, desperately impoverished, Italy had little to offer her least favoured sons and daughters after five years of devastating war. Over the next thirty years, 1946 – 1976, seven and a half million left temporarily or permanently for anywhere there was some hope of improving their material situation. From about 1955 movement abroad began to be accompanied by at least as massive internal migration from the south and islands to the rapidly developing industrial centres of northern Italy, in particular Milan and Turin. Overseas migration now took in not only traditional destinations like the USA and Argentina but relatively untried lands like Venezuela, Canada and Australia. The bulk of those leaving opted however for much nearer destinations, generally in the short term, although often enough a first temporary job turned out to prelude a lifetime's work abroad. Switzerland, Germany, France, and Belgium, in that order, were the major receiving countries. Britain's intake was only a fraction by comparison, yet even so the Italian presence here was to surge to well over 100,000 by the time of the 1971 census, four times greater than at any point under the old migration.[1] Often whole groups of young men from the same village organised to leave together. Here in the North East it is not unusual to encounter elderly Italian emigrants from that time who come from large families where every son and daughter of their own generation now lives abroad, sometimes dispersed right across the globe between Europe, the Americas, and Australia.

Bulk recruitment

The vigorous revival of Italian immigration after the war was in part due to reactivation of the natural processes of chain migration which had been temporarily thwarted by the British and Italian restrictions, and of course halted totally by the war. The Aliens Order remained in place to bar entrants without a work permit, however government policy favoured admitting more Italians to the undersubscribed catering sector, and in the North East this meant some revitalisation of the traditional migratory links with the arrival of work-hungry young people from war-worn Ciociaria and northern Tuscany to take advantage of their connections with the population of ageing pre-war settlers of similar family and regional origins. Nevertheless the unprecedented increase in Italian immigration was to a far greater extent due to wholesale state-backed recruitment of low-skilled foreign labour from continental Europe. The use, or abuse, of cut-price prisoner-of-war workers had made up for acute manpower shortages mainly in the agricultural sector, and now this lesson was applied to other sectors of the economy in the years of post-war reconstruction. Many thousands of so-called 'European Volunteer Workers' were procured, most of them victims of the deprivations and population upheavals of the recent war: Poles, Ukrainians, Germans, Austrians, as well as Italians. From 1951, however, faced with accusations of favouring foreign over British workers the government shifted the responsibility and expense of importing manpower onto individual firms and employers, subject always to approval from the Ministry of Labour, in effect operating what was a quotas system in all but name.

Italian workers receiving training at Jarrow mill, 1957 (Photo: Beamish Museum).

With several million unemployed in Italy, and expectations of bolstering the economy through emigrants' remittances, the new Christian Democrat government eagerly cooperated in the mass recruitment of Italian manpower by the more rapidly recovering industrial economies of northern Europe. In Britain, significant shortfalls of unskilled labour at this moment of more or less full employment were identified mainly in heavy industry and coal mining, in the textile mills, and in the service sector, particularly in domestic service and low-grade work in hospitals. British recruitment missions competed with other northern European employment agencies to scout for 'volunteers' all over the historically disadvantaged south of Italy including the islands of Sicily and Sardinia, areas of higher birth rate and much lower per capita income where emigration had for long been a first line of escape from chronic rural poverty and underemployment. Selection procedures and medical tests were carried out in collaboration with the Italian authorities who also paid the train fares for each northward-bound batch of recruits, often numbering hundreds at a time.

The standard government-approved 'bulk recruitment' contract emphasised that the foreign worker in this country enjoyed the same rights and remuneration as his British counterpart, but with one crippling proviso: for four years he could not change occupation. Thereafter he was a free man, though with his movements monitored through obligatory registration with the police. This contract so highly favourable to employers had to be renewed in each one of the four years, and if a worker did not like it he had to quit the country. Inevitably, many new arrivals were unable to accept or adapt to the often harsh working and living conditions in the allotted first occupation and abandoned the dream of boundless opportunities in a more prosperous land long before their four years of servitude were up. Under the pre-1951 'Official

Italian Scheme', for instance, some 17,000 Italians, mostly single women in their early twenties, were brought over to work in low-paid jobs in the textile and ceramics industries, or as cleaners, cooks, and servants in hospitals, schools and private houses. For the most part they lived painfully isolated lives in barrack-like dormitories or as lone domestic servants in grand houses. If homesickness did not drive them back, a common route out was through early marriage, not with local men but within other groups of forlorn 'aliens' on similar schemes, as in the well-studied case of Italian women and Polish and Ukrainian mill workers in Bradford.[2]

From 1951 the Italian intake became predominantly male since the main allocations were now in brick manufacture, mining and steel, disagreeable heavy manual work which was failing to attract sufficient numbers of unskilled young British men. Over the next ten years, to meet the huge demand for building material during the post-war housing boom, some 15,000 Italians were drafted into the brick industry, a phenomenon which in Bedford rapidly led to the creation of the largest Italian community anywhere in Britain since the heyday of London's Italian quarter in the late nineteenth century. The resultant transformation in Bedford's ethnic make-up so alarmed the Town Council that in 1959 it voted unanimously to outlaw further bulk recruitment by local employers. Similar circumstances significantly Italianized the populations of Peterborough and Nottingham.

As for the newly nationalised coal industry, despite repeated government efforts to meet escalating demand by increasing manpower nothing like the same numbers of foreign workers were absorbed. Their imposition was bitterly resented in the workplace and only tolerated by the powerful National Union of Mineworkers (NUM) wherever a branch gave prior consent, and even then only for as long as no local pitman was without a job. The first experiment in 1951-2 with 2,400 Italians, predominantly Sicilians, met with such massive resistance that the National Coal Board (NCB) halted all bulk recruitment from Italy within the year. In many a South Wales and Yorkshire colliery, where most were placed, and in at least two pits in county Durham, local miners had refused to work with them. Immediately after the war the northern divisions of the NUM had already successfully manoeuvred to limit a planned intake of Poles to just a few hundred, and now these fresh 'difficulties' over the acceptance of Italians assured their number in the whole of our region's vast coalfields was never more than a few score. This might even be a pity, for since practically every colliery village had its Italian café more of these unfortunates might at least have found a little home from home. I have not heard of even one who stayed.

In the mid-1950s, with the coal industry losing underground workers at the rate of 5,000 a year the NCB once again considered resorting to foreign labour, specifically Italians and Austrians, with numbers as high as 15,000 mooted. Again determined resistance in all the major coalfields forced the Board to abandon the idea almost immediately. Faced with open revolt at branch level, the able general secretary of the Durham Miners Association, Sam Watson, who had repeatedly and forcefully pleaded for take-up, made no bones about his exasperation: 'It is particularly those who prate most about the brotherhood of men who act contrariwise. "All men are brothers" sounds very hollow on the lips of those who add "except Italians in the Mining Industry".

Post-war recruitment into the steel industry, on the other hand, was to lead to two small permanent settlements of Italians in our region.

Middlesbrough and Jarrow steel workers

In the autumn of 1957, Dorman Long in Middlesbrough took on around 200 Italian workers, and the Consett Iron Company subsidiary in Jarrow another 60. They were not raw recruits straight from Italy but casualties of the long demise of the Welsh tin industry which since 1949 had relied for survival in good part on Polish and Italian labour – more than 2,000 in the case of the Italians. True, some of the new arrivals had spent barely a few months in this country, but all had shared the same hot and hazardous work at the furnaces of tin-plate factories in the Swansea area and a social life little better than that endured earlier by their compatriots as prisoners of war; indeed the grim hostel at Morriston, a former barracks where all were initially housed, had served as a POW camp only a few years before. Technology at the plants was no less primitive: day and night, in eight-hour shifts, teams of six men armed with tongs and shod in protective metal-soled clogs or thick rags wrapped round their shoes constantly heated and re-heated, rolled, cut, folded, pressed and re-rolled, steel bars into thin sheet for coating with tin. Basic weekly pay in 1954 after deductions

Angelo Rago, from Roccavivara near Campobasso, at the Upper Forest and Worcester tinplate works, Swansea 1955.

for food and accommodation in shared cubicles was £3.16s a week for rollermen and £4.10s for the few Italians who progressed to furnace-worker. Even so, it was better than most could hope to earn in Italy, and some even declare they managed to save as much as £6 or even £10 a month. A lucky few who 'knew the right person' also secured a bit of clandestine extra work at the weekend or after the daytime shift. Whether married or single, all had family to support back home. Foreign workers at this time were still permitted to bring over immediate dependants so long as they could support them, so some recently married men with strong ambitions to settle long-term had small households to maintain in Swansea. Their wives, particularly if children had had to be left behind to save costs, were often desperately lonely in a climate and milieu that seemed to them unrelentingly hostile. Without exception these were country people hardened to agricultural work from an early age but with no preparation for the rigorous conformity of industrial labour. Absenteeism and friction with non-Italian co-workers was high, and of each fresh intake as many as half might leave long before the completion of the four-year term.

On arrival in the North East, the Middlesbrough contingent was billeted with local landlords, several to a room, and next day went off for induction in their new jobs in steel. The Jarrow contingent was housed in a foreign workers' hostel in Hebburn, which itself was incentive enough for some to seek alternative accommodation in town. As in Swansea, those who chose to move out tended to find rooms with Italian families long established here. Both contingents, like the POW 'co-operators' before them, mostly congregated and socialised in Italian-owned cafés in town. The presence of other Italians with local know-how and good English proved indispensable in the men's acclimatisation and their dealings with officialdom. Wherever they ended up, all say that both jobs and pay were an improvement on 'Sa-wanz'.

But Jarrow mill was to close within a few months, in May 1958, and over the next one to five years the Italians in Middlesbrough working for Dorman Long at Lackenby or the Britannia works were all made redundant as their line of hand-work became automated. Efforts were made to place those who did not want to return to Italy with firms in other parts of the country already employing Italians – brickyards in Bedford, steelworks in Sheffield, market gardens in the South East – but in that era of still abundant work in our region the majority chose to remain here. The Italians on Tyneside mostly found jobs in the firebrick industry and the shipyards, or in construction, including such major projects as the Scotswood Bridge, the Tyne Tunnel, and the new Newcastle Brewery. Most of the Middlesbrough ex-steelworkers transferred to ICI Billingham, where they report wages and conditions were better than anything experienced before. A number retrained as bus conductors. As time went on, more and more of these men new to the region married local women, or appealed to the family network at home to secure a partner for life. Faced with the financial strain of saving for a first small house while also raising a family, their spouses took up low-paid work in local Italian businesses, in clothing factories, or as child-minders, cooks and cleaners.

Since before everyone's eyes was the example of earlier Italian immigrant families, by now well into the second or even third generation, apparently making good lives in ice cream or fish and chips or running thriving cafés, there was also a strong incentive to break out and join the ranks of the self-employed. A common route was to gain essential experience with some well-established 'original' Italian family then attempt to branch out on one's own as the owner-driver of an ice cream van, or somehow raise funds to lease a shop, not infrequently from Italian proprietors on the point of retirement. A few ventured into the still virtually uncharted territory of Italian restaurant-keeping. Two former steelworkers who were destined to make a significant impact in this line were Giuseppe Arceri in Middlesbrough and Mario De Giorgi in Newcastle (see next section).

Though it folded nine years ago, the Middlesbrough 'Italia' Anglo-Italian Association, founded by a group of ex-steelworkers and their wives in 1985, played an admirable role in providing focus and comradeship for the close community of families which through the addition of children and grandchildren had by then grown to several hundred. For twenty years, as well as looking out for the welfare of the sick and elderly, the association held fortnightly social evenings at St Patrick's church hall in Cannon Park and regularly organised larger communal *feste*.

Lately, the few survivors of the original Jarrow contingent of steelworkers have seized a chance for socialisation with other pensioner-age Tyneside Italians at the weekly lunchtime get-togethers of the Amici d'Italia association in Newcastle (see page 306).

The following pages give, in their own words, some impression of the experiences lived by these men and women and their feelings about the long road they have travelled.

'WHY DID WE COME TO THIS COUNTRY?'

Donato and Maria Pallotta from Pietragalla, near Potenza, as portrayed in the newly married couple's aliens registration books. Donato arrived in Swansea in January 1956, and after a year Maria joined him.

I'd never seen a factory before. Where I lived there were no factories, just countryside, countryside, countryside.

In England we had a job, that was all. A hard dangerous job. And there were other snags, like the language, and people who didn't like us very much. They used to take the Mickey about the war, call the Italians cowards. All them things you had to put up with. A lot couldn't stand it. Before the four years were over, the contract period, a lot of the single lads who had no family went home. It was easier for them, they would be the only losers and they didn't have to worry about money so much.

Why did we come to this country? You know what young people are – crazy! They like to go. There was a very nasty crisis in Sardinia after the war, though it started to improve just a couple of years after we came here. But in those times, the 1950s, there was no work, just a day here a day there. In fact after I married I had nothing at all. That's what made me decide to get away.

I never went to school because we lived out in the country, and if you're in the country there's always work to do. My father wanted to keep me on the farm. But at fifteen I started taking a few evening lessons with a teacher, because if you've no education you always have to be at someone else's beck and call.

I decided to leave Italy because I didn't get along with my father. He was never satisfied with anything I did on the farm. We had maybe five or six hectares of land. There was the wine harvest and then the wine to make. We had chestnuts, and we had to pick the chestnuts when the time came, and walnuts, pears, apples, and we had five or six cows and I had them to mind too, cleaning out and feeding. I came

264

to England to be independent. I signed the contract and left next day. There were about thirty from my village. Only five have stayed here, the others have all gone back now.

We were five children. All of us went abroad, barring my sister who married the village sexton. The others went to France or Belgium, and I came here. My plan was to earn something and send it home. Nobody forced me to, but there were no pensions then and I knew my father and mother had no money. With overtime and working weekends I managed to send £10 home every month to buy salt, sugar, a bit of pasta, some sulphur for the vines.

They wanted the Italians because nobody else would do the job. There were Polish people, Ukrainians, and hundreds and hundreds of Italians in Swansea. The hostel we lived in was horrible – what a place to live! We slept two to a room, like prison. The food was no good and you had nowhere to cook your own. When the works started to shut down, in 1957, some had no choice, they had to go back. Others went to London, and a lot transferred to the brickworks in Bedford, and we were transferred to Middlesbrough.

We Italians love work, and that's how it should be. But after five months in Swansea it all finished. My friend said there was work in Middlesbrough at Dorman Long, and some of them went there. I got a job at Jarrow steelworks. I looked it up on the map and thought, that's not far off. I tried to find lodgings in Newcastle, but in those days nobody would open their doors to Italians. It was after the war, see, not like it is today. Newcastle was really run down, I was surprised at the conditions. The culture here was against good food, but I ate it anyway. I lived on milk and cornflakes.

I followed my husband after two years, with our two children. It was lonely without the language. I used to cry, I wanted to go back home. But I think when you first come you feel a bit awful about going back home straight away. So I told everybody we were okay.

My husband came here to work. I was 22 when he applied to come – but not for all his life, mind. But when we went back to Italy after four years he couldn't find any work. So we came back here, then the children came and so we stayed on. We go to Italy every two or three years, but of course we can't stay because all the family's over here. I have four children and seven grandchildren – so you can see why I can't just go off to Italy and leave all this. It's too late. All the same, it's been a very tough life because we always wanted to go back to live in our own country with our family all round us. It's so sad. Nobody would believe what we've been through, nobody can imagine what we felt.

I wish nobody ever had to emigrate like us. I'm not complaining now, we're doing alright, but we suffered a lot. It was horrible. Do you know how we used to live when we first came to Middlesbrough? We found a box of a room somebody gave us to rent, and with just a single bed. I was still poorly, and when the doctor came he couldn't even open the door, he couldn't fit in the room. There was nobody to look after us, nobody.

You get used to it being a foreigner, you get thick-skinned. But it never quite goes away. You feel an intruder sometimes. You're frightened just in case somebody calls you a foreigner or something. You know, you take it to heart.

They're more open, they go out, they enjoy themselves more. We Italian women are more reserved, even too much. We like family, we like helping, cooking, seeing to the family's needs.

Getting married here I had to adapt to the customs here, more or less, because the women here have a different character, they're brought up differently to Italian women. Women like we met here, there was none like them in Italy then.

It's good in England, you get help in everything, but there's not the sun like in Italy, or water like in Italy. In Italy a glass of water seems like a liqueur when you drink it. And I'll tell you another thing. Eat a bit of salami in Italy and a bit of salami here in England, the same salami, and it just doesn't taste the same. Maybe it's something to do with the temperature, the air, but the taste goes. A fortnight and it goes off. But in Italy it can wait years and years and it still has that flavour.

I didn't get any education in Italy because my father wasn't able to send me to school. But I believe in education. I don't want my children to have the same life I've had. I try to see they have their heads right and the Good Lord grants them a better life. And I want them to learn three or four languages, because they must be able to understand wherever they go. What I saw when I came to England and I couldn't say a word and understood nothing – for me that was terrible, and I don't want my children having to live through what I had to.

When the children get older they don't want to go back to the village. What is there for them to do there? There's no entertainment. My village is in the mountains, a whole hour by car from the sea, or three hours by bus and the only one leaves at six in the morning. Like here too there's more money now, and quite a bit of development, but if you go back to the Fifties and Sixties who went on holiday then?

You should see our kids. They've got everything, they're much better off than us. When we came we had nothing, just ourselves.

I came to England to work but I'm still Italian. I've never signed a bit of paper to say I renounce Italy. Now my head says 'Stay', but when I don't want to stay any longer I'll get my suitcase and go back to Italy because nobody's going to stop me.

I still feel a foreigner here, even after nearly fifty years. When all is said and done maybe it would have been better if we'd never left Italy, stayed in our own homes, at the very least you always have something to eat and drink. I hope I'll go back one day. Better to finish my days there. At least there's the sun.

This country saved me from hell.

[Contributors in alphabetical order: Leonardo Angelicchio, Giuseppe Arceri, Giosuè Brancati, Domenico Di Paolo, Donato Gregorio, Mario De Giorgi, Donato and Maria Pallotta, Angelo Rago, Libera Tempestoso, Mario and Irene Vargiù.]

October 1955: after a year in Swansea, Giuseppe Arceri's wife Maria and sons Marinello and Rossano have come from Sardinia to join him. The couple went on to found a veritable dynasty of restaurateurs in our region. (See page 275).

Left: Luigi Lanna (right), from Artena near Rome, when a tinplate worker in Swansea; and right, with his brother Gianni and colleagues after their transfer to Middlesbrough in 1957. The brothers later opened the Bacchus restaurant in Northgate, Darlington, the town's earliest Italian restaurant.

Well-earned retirement: Vincenzo Riggio, president of the 'Italia' Anglo-Italian Association, and his wife Rosa at their Acklam home in 1992.

Angelo Rago, secretary of the 'Italia' association, in his greenhouse the same year. As well as making their own wine and spicey sausages, country-born Italians in our region fill their gardens and greenhouses with Mediterranean staples: peaches, grapes, figs, aubergines, peppers, courgettes, chicory, rocket, garlic, rosemary, basil.

The pasta and pizza boom

In this age of dial-a-pizza, when of an evening our region's town centres reek of garlic to an extent no street in Italy ever has, and *panini* and *lasagne* are about as local as stotties and pasties, it is hard to believe that 'eating Italian' is a relatively new phenomenon. Yet go back little more than forty-five years and the first pioneers of Italian cuisine in the North East will tell you this was terra incognita, a land of long dark nights and hardly less dark rainy days in which apart from a few greasy-spoons and the occasional 'Indian' or 'Chinese' there was nowhere to go for an affordable sit-down meal. The people, *good* people, they always stress, *brava gente, rozza ma accogliente*, rough but friendly – the good simple people of the North East had no idea at all what real pasta was. On desolate quests through smoggy streets ('when you could smell fish and chips a mile away') for the kind of diet they were used to at home these exile souls found the only spaghetti readily available came in

'Sharing their Pleasures', by Eugenio Zampighi, in the Shipley Art Gallery, Gateshead. (Tyne and Wear Archives and Museums). Today there are no more popular foods on the planet than pasta, pizza, and ice cream, each perfected in Italy. The first two, requiring little more than flour and water, had for long been staples of the poor but were not consumed by all Italians until fairly recent times. Pasta only became standard in polenta and rice-eating parts of northern Italy in the first half of the twentieth century, and until well after World War II pizza had no presence at all outside Naples where it originated three hundred years ago. Its spectacular rise to world's favourite fast food in just the past thirty years owes its modest beginnings to Neapolitan immigrants in the United States a century ago.

tins, olive oil was sold for medicinal purposes in tiny very costly bottles at Boots, and wine was a rare luxury served in the dining-rooms of grand hotels. The hostel-bound steelworkers were horrified to discover the only use our native cuisine had for pasta was baked in milk as 'macaroni cheese' or warmed up canned spaghetti dumped on toast.

And yet, as we have amply seen, Italians had been catering for north-easterners for a very long time. But despite the mountains of homemade pasta consumed in their private quarters behind or above the shop, the nearest thing to an Italian food speciality on offer to customers was ice cream, and then only vanilla-flavoured white, or at most its standard British variants, pink or brown. In 1880s Newcastle a very few north Italians ran pubs, coaching houses, and eating-houses as 'licensed victuallers', but these too catered for local expectations[3]. In grander places any 'continental' flavour to the cuisine apart from the odd helping of soggy macaroni was bound to be French even if limited solely to the language in which the day's menu was composed, another way of saying 'posh'.

Posh was most certainly Gustavo Barawitzka's 'Criterion' in Market Street, Newcastle. With the Station Hotel it was the grandest restaurant in town until sold by Gustavo's descendants in 1952 after fully six decades in business. 'The Barawitzkas did much to raise the standard of cooking in this industrial city,' proclaimed a piece in that year's *Chronicle* lamenting the 'internationally famous' restaurant's passing. Gustavo, despite his surname, was a native of Vicenza and received his early training in restaurant kitchens in other parts of continental Europe before beginning his Tyneside career as an 18-year-old waiter at the luxurious Station Hotel in 1875. Contrary to the rigid occupational division by nationality in high-class catering at that time – *dans la salle les italiens, dans la cuisine les français*: Italians in the dining-room, French in the kitchen – the young commis waiter eventually rose to become head chef at the Station. His long experience of both haute cuisine and the complex formalities expected at front of house in those far-off days of bow-ties and tails must have been crucial to the success of the establishment he ambitiously named after one of London's greatest restaurants. His own 'Cri', which opened in one small room of the large building it was eventually to fill, was famed for its elaborate mixed grill and special rum omelette, and for the glittering list of stars from Sarah Bernhardt to Vesta Tilley and George Robey who had dropped in to dine when playing at the nearby Theatre Royal. Like so many Italian restaurateurs to try their luck here in our own time Gustavo soon married locally. The conspicuous neo-classical Barowitzka mausoleum in a corner of St Andrew's cemetery in Jesmond is the family's memorial to an astute young immigrant's achievement.

For long after the last war dining out remained an extravagance for the well-heeled few. The 'refreshment rooms' in our region, even when Italian-owned, were nothing more than sit-down cafés offering basic hot meals like soup and pies along with sandwiches and cakes, no different from their English counterparts except for the homemade ice cream. From the mid-1930s 'express coffee' had been on offer at the classier Italian premises in the region, expressed from lovingly polished Arduino and La Paloma copper boilers (some of which I remember still around in the 1960s), but tea and milk-based drinks and Bovril or Oxo remained

Modernity with an Italian flavour: the Bis Bar, Sunderland, about 1960.

far more popular beverages. The Espresso Bar craze which coincided with the adoption by Italian café proprietors of Achille Gaggia's much more streamlined coffee-maker was a youth-driven phenomenon of 1950s London and only reached the north in much diluted form toward the end of the decade, just as the universal modernisation fever was prompting local town planners to level our city centres in the name of progress. As Victorian terraces crumpled under the bulldozers the heavy but homely old furnishings of carved panelling and marble-topped tables in the Italian parlours and cafés were stripped out in favour of the chrome and Formica and ceramic surfaces thought more appropriate to jet-age times.

Notarianni's postwar expansion included the popular 'Bis Bar' in Park Lane, Sunderland, opened by the family's eldest son Gino. Here his wife Maria, who had learned to cook in her native city of Rome, began adding some simple Italian dishes to the menu in the late 1950s when the first package holidays on the Adriatic and Elizabeth David's ground-breaking *Italian Cooking* were beginning to spread the notion that our Mrs Beeton might not have had the last word to say on Italian cuisine ('Italians, with the exception of Macaroni, have no specially characteristic article of food', *Household Management,* 1861). Some longer established Italian-owned cafés also tried similar cautious experiments, and older members of Newcastle's Italian fraternity still treasure the memory of a Florentine chef named Sabatini who introduced authentic Italian dishes at the County Hotel.

However, the honour of first true Italian restaurant in the North East goes to a venture started with financial backing from local businessmen in 1963 in Low Fell, Gateshead, by three hotel-school trained young immigrants: Dante Calzini, Pasqualino Fulgenzi, and Mario Neri. By judiciously offering English dishes alongside Italian specialities the 'Dante' gradually won over even its most sceptical clientele from prawn cocktail and steak and chips to *penne all'amatriciana* and *pollo valdostana,* and, no less importantly, from quaffing 'broon' to sipping wine. But mass conversion to pasta and pizza was still a long way off. Even ten years later there were no more than six Italian restaurants on all of Tyneside. In that year, 1972, Benito Gianfreda opened La Capannella in Shakespeare Street, Newcastle, the North East's first pizzeria, and still felt safest offering both Italian and English fare. Around most of the country the slow spread of delicatessens was by now beginning to make essential Mediterranean ingredients more generally available, but Italians up here, both householders and restaurateurs, still had to rely on van visits from suppliers such as Glasgow's Fazzi Bros, Edinburgh's Valvona and Crolla, or Giordano's of London, and eventually two local pioneers of Italian provisioning: Antonio Rea with his 'Italcibo' in Middlesbrough, and Alessandro Rossi, also of Middlesbrough, whose van delivery business was taken over in 1972 by Mario De Giorgi, an enterprising veteran of tinplate days in Swansea who before long was to go on to greater fame as the innovatory *padrone* of Don Vito's, one of Newcastle's most popular all-Italian restaurants. Only in the early 1980s did the city gain anything like an authentic Italian *alimentari,* in the shape of Bruno Tavasso's little shop in Newlands Road, Jesmond, serving mostly the Italian restaurant trade. In 1987 Mary and Nicky Sparacio transformed it into one of the most richly stocked Italian delicatessens in all England.

Once local suspicions have been overcome, Italian restaurants start reproducing fairly rapidly by a mixture of fission and fusion: new restaurants are born out of the old when a long-time partner or some scrupulously trained staff member sets up with a new mate or starts his own baby. The tentative beginnings of the North East's now very extensive Italian restaurant network will serve to illustrate the pattern. In 1965, Mario and Pasqualino, long since Pascal to his English

Tyneside's first pasta pioneers: Dante Calzini, Pasqualino Fulgenzi, Mario Neri, (from left to right) photographed in Newcastle, 2011.

Mary and Nicky Sparacio at their 'Tavasso' Italian delicatessen, Newcastle 1990. (Photo: NCJ Media Ltd)

customers, parted from Dante in Gateshead and crossed the river to open their own 'Roma' in Collingwood Street, Newcastle, a very happy partnership which lasted for years until Mario broke away to open the Pinocchio, Sunderland's first Italian restaurant, and soon also his equally successful 'Mario''s in Newcastle's Westgate Road. In 1968, meantime, the 'Dante' had acquired new owners and a new title, the 'Italia', when its namesake also departed for Newcastle to take over Gino Visocchi's short-lived 'Latina' together with a Sicilian colleague, Santo 'Alex' Cuscani. This second 'Dante', in a prime location in Market Street (at the same address as Barowitzka's former Criterion) then fused into Cuscani's own 'Godfather' (the movie had just come out) when Dante embarked on a third partnership to open Dante & Piero's pizzeria and disco in Grainger Street, one of the city's most popular dives until its demise some fifteen years ago.

Nowadays most Italian-owned restaurants in the region are run by men who started out as waiters or assistant cooks with very little training and learned on the hoof, but these three close friends who pioneered what must now be by far the most popular way of dining out in our region were products of rigorously disciplined apprenticeships in Italy and Switzerland. When as young single men they decided to try England they were actually following a long established career path to restaurant or hotel manager, or head chef. As far back as the mid-nineteenth century numerous Italians, mainly from northern Italy like Barawitzka, had sought lowly posts in London's top hotels and restaurants in order to hone their professional skills and work at their English before returning home to better positions in their country's ever-growing tourist industry. Others stayed on in the hope of rising through the ranks while patiently perfecting an extreme self-effacing courtesy which was not always appropriately reciprocated. Some of these men founded and staffed Soho's first upmarket Italian restaurants which were as formal and stuffy as their English models, offering apart from a few bland pasta dishes a very similar Anglo-French cuisine masquerading under Italianified titles. Out in the provinces, though, where mostly hotels catered for those who could afford to eat out in some style, Italian entrepreneurship stuck to the well-tried formula of the friendly neighbourhood café-cum-ice cream parlour.

In the restive extended family of Italian eateries longevity is rare. Even the venerable Italia, if we discount its earlier Dantesque incarnation, before expiring in 2013 had only just surpassed the record of the Roma which with 'Newcastle's Oldest Italian Restaurant' blazoned across its Colosseum-inspired frontage finally closed its doors on New Year's Eve 2008 after 44 years in which Pasqualino Fulgenzi who claims never to have missed a day doubled as its expert head chef and genial *padrone*.

'WE KNEW IT WOULD CATCH ON'

My mother died when I was twelve and my father couldn't do anything with me. He wanted me to stay put in the village, be a tailor like my brother, but I wanted to see the world. My brother thought I was crazy. I tried L'Aquila, then Pescara, then Rome. Rome wasn't easy, not for a lad my age. We used to hang about Piazza del Pantheon, the square in front of the Pantheon, where there were always people in white jackets with black trousers and money pouches hoping for someone to come along and say, 'Want some work today?' La piazza della fame, we called it, Hunger Square.

We were there one time, a bunch of us, and this lad said he'd heard about hotel school and where we needed to apply. The others had only done three years of elementary school, and I'd done five, plus night school – a genius! We got our interviews, but the lady said there was nothing doing. Meantime luckily I was starting to get work in various places, some really famous, like Tre Scalini in Piazza Navona. Well, suddenly one day the call came – six months at hotel school in Bolzano, all paid for by the government: kitchen work, dining-room service, book-keeping, languages, and on top of that six months hotel experience in Switzerland. Unfortunately that turned out to be a little hotel deep in the countryside, and after three months I said to myself, What am I doing here, I'm a waiter not a farmer! So I got on to Mario in Zurich, a friend from hotel school, and he got me into the top hotel. There I learned a lot, in fact it's what really got me going. We'd done French and German at hotel school, but Swiss German is totally unintelligible. So I took a train to Munich and got a job in the Regina Palace Hotel. After eight months the season finished, so I said to this other friend of mine: Where next? How about Hamburg? All I had was a suitcase, I was only young. We got the train, only instead of Hamburg we ended up in Hannover working in a beautiful restaurant by the lake.

Pasqualino Fulgenzi, from the village of Calascio near L'Aquila, outside his Ristorante Roma, Newcastle, 1986.
(Photo: NCJ Media Ltd).

All this time Mario had stayed in Zurich, so when the Hannover job finished I went back to Zurich. Four of us shared the one room, and on top of that I had to get up early so the landlady didn't know there was one extra. Dante was with us too, we'd all done hotel school together and we all looked out for each other. I got taken on at the Savoy, and then went back to Germany for a bit, then back to another French restaurant in Zurich.

If you want to get on you need languages, everyone in our line of work speaks two or three. So Dante says, Let's go to England. An agency fixed me up with a hotel in Bath, the Royal, where the head waiter spoke French so somehow I survived. I did two seasons there, then this lad Antonio said, Let's try a ship! So we went to the P & O office in London and they put us on the SS Arcadia bound for Adelaide. Fourteen months we did with not a single day off, but we certainly got about: Australia, New Zealand, San Francisco, Honolulu, Tasmania.

There was an Englishman on board, Jim Wright from Chester-le-Street, a really nice guy, who was just washing dishes though he'd been a shoe shop manager in Birmingham. So after we got fed up with the ship that's how we came to Newcastle. My first job was at Michael's Club, the only club which stayed open till 2 in the morning. Next was the Downbeat, where 'The Animals' were created. When I first got here Mario was in Nottingham and Dante in London, so I phoned both of them and told them to come up here, and we've stayed together ever since.

Jim was working at the Red House on the Quayside, downstairs in the Steak House, and upstairs we opened a little room, a little restaurant where we introduced 'Veal Milanese' and a few pasta dishes. It went well eventually, but the owner wasn't interested, so when Jim started up Jim's Inn in Northumberland Street we followed him there.

For the first four years in England you were under contract, and so long as you got it renewed every year you were okay. But then Dante happened to talk to someone who said if you have money and you apply to the Home Office they'll give you a restaurant permit just like that. So the three of us pooled all our savings, about £700 which was a lot of money then, and we leased a place in Low Fell. We called it Dante's and all the cream of Newcastle came. But Mario and I didn't stay there very long, because

Dante had these financial backers and people used to say you'll end up working for them, you'll never be boss.

We went back down to London, but always with the intention of opening a place in Newcastle. We worked at the Otello in Frith Street, near Gennaro's. In Soho there were a whole lot of Italians then, chefs and waiters, because those were the years when all the trattorias were starting up. If you said you were going to Newcastle, they'd say: Where's that – Scotland? They just didn't understand. But we knew it would catch on.

We scoured the whole of Newcastle for months and months looking for a place, and eventually a little café down the Quayside came up, only a few tables, and we nearly went for that. But then the solicitor told us about this antique shop here in Collingwood Street, and from the day we put the notice in the window saying 'Italian restaurant opening soon' we were never alone. We did it up in a very rustic style, whitewashed walls, strings of onions, a couple of pictures, Chianti bottles, with one very big table in the middle and four others. We opened on September 8, 1965 and it took off straightaway. The first night we had 150 people booked, because we knew most of Newcastle by then.

'Restaurant' comes from the Latin verb 'restaurare', to relax. Going to a restaurant isn't the same as catching a train – you go to a restaurant because you want to relax, you want to be with your friends, enjoy the meal, the atmosphere, the service and all sorts. That's what I believe, and perhaps that's why I've lasted such a long time.

We learned from our mothers, our grandmothers. I can still smell my mother's beans cooking when I came in from school. One chicken had to last for everybody. Creativity! I wonder these days what would happen if a famine started. Everyone would die, we no longer know how to survive.
(Pasqualino Fulgenzi, one afternoon at the 'Roma', 2008)

The arrival of the moderately priced friendly Italian restaurant was in tune with the times. By the mid-1960s most people had a bit more spending money, and with a more hedonistic approach to life particularly among the young eating out became both more desirable and more affordable. In the course of the Seventies the Italian establishments in central Newcastle swelled to a dozen, among them 'The Italian Job' in Dean Street, an astute move by a local English entrepreneur, the first outsider to exploit the Italians' evident success in marketing their country's appealing image and cuisine. All these novel busy eateries were staffed by a lively colony of new immigrants, young and ambitious, not a few of whom went on to open their own premises within the city and beyond. Like the *garzoni* of old, most were recruited as likely lads by the new restaurant *padroni* from their own home towns and set to 'slave' for long hours and not much money in the kitchens or waiting at table. So, little by little, Italian restaurants and pizzerias began mushrooming all over the region, in Sunderland and Durham, in Darlington and Middlesbrough, and in smaller centres like Hexham and Yarm. By 1982 the Italian eateries in Newcastle and Gateshead alone had surged to 22, just exceeding the count of Indian restaurants, and not too far behind the 25 Chinese restaurants and chop suey houses.

Teesside's first Italian restaurant was Joseph's, in Linthorpe Road, Middlesbrough, founded in 1969. Its namesake, Giuseppe Arceri, was born in the Sardinian mining town of Iglesias and had been a miner himself before escaping to another life as a tinplate worker in Swansea, and finally a steel worker for Dorman Long. His Middlesbrough experiment became the first link in a remarkable North East catering connection with Sardinia, or rather with one small inland town in the south of the island: Arbus, near Cagliari, the hometown of Giuseppe's wife, Maria Addis. Over time, Maria's parents and all but one of eight brothers and two sisters followed her here and between them all they have seeded a remarkable 'spaghetti tree'. Brothers Eliano and Paolo worked at first at Joseph's and then went on to open new restaurants with their mother and father, first Mamma Vittoria's in Linthorpe Road, and next Papa Luigi's in Yarm. In the mid-1970s, brothers Sergio, Adriano and Efisio left Teesside to start up Adriano's in Gosforth and then the renowned Da Vinci in Jesmond, Newcastle, not far from the pioneering Pizzeria Francesca, thereby helping to propel this genteel leafy neighbourhood toward its current status as a hugely popular alternative venue to the city centre for diners-out, now dense with Italian (and pseudo-Italian) eating places. In their turn, Giuseppe and Maria's own four sons have also made names for themselves in the region's Italian restaurant scene, not least Paolo Arceri, who with Peter Gowling in 1980s Newcastle began building up the Joe Rigatoni's chain of restaurants which within ten years were dotted all over the southern half of our region and beyond, from Darlington right down to Ripon. The family's success has inevitably drawn other *paesani* over here, several starting up new enterprises in their turn. Some of the best-known restaurants in the region today, such as Pani's in Newcastle, Sardi's in Darlington, and Sassari in Middlesbrough, are Sardinian foundations.

By 1992, thirty years after the Dante served up its first *spaghetti bolognese,* more than 50 Italian restaurants and pizzerias were spread all over Tyneside. A seeming triumph, except that the wealth of lunchtime half-price pizza or pasta deals and early evening happy hours suggested that all might not be so well. The fact is, of course, that by this time the always lively and productive competition between Italians had generated formidable external rivals, not just the first few of countless fast-food franchises like Pizzaland and the US-based Pizza Hut but an ever-growing number of non-Italian local pasta and pizza joints and takeaways, all cashing in on this phenomenal revolution in our food preferences. Other factors also weakened the Italians' hold on their once unassailable market position. With an economy at last as strong as Britain's to provide employment for most of the population back home, there was no longer an inexhaustible supply of eager young cooks and waiters straight from Italy. To keep pace with demand the *padroni* were having to recruit from new sources, often freshly arrived immigrants from less prosperous Mediterranean countries who were willing to work for cash in hand. Despite its early achievements, therefore, by the time the pasta and pizza revolution was evolving into a global industry the Italian restaurant network here simply could not generate either the manpower or the single-minded sacrifice typical of new settler families which characterised for instance the new wave of Indian and Chinese catering ventures that so rapidly penetrated the North East's remotest localities and suburbs, a phenomenon comparable to the Italians' own dedicated conquest of our towns and collieries in the golden age of the ice cream parlour. Tellingly too, by now some of these other ethnicities were beginning to invest in ice cream vans.

Even more threatening to the Italians' old hegemony, and more recent still, is the formidable entrepreneurism of immigrants from the Middle East and North Africa, those whom in the context of this chapter it is tempting to call the 'newest Italians' since their numberless pizza and kebab takeaways jostling for custom in every second street and housing estate up and down the region are not only invariably kitted out in the red-white-green Italian national colours (which are also those of Iran) but also often assume Italian or pseudo-Italian names. Why the disguise, I have sometimes asked, why not promote your own good food under your own name? Because Italians make the best pizza, I'm usually told. But some also add: because Muslims are not particularly liked here. A poignant and troubling reflection of the long road the Italians have come since they too were made to feel intruders.

Already back in the 1970s some of the earliest Italian restaurants in the North East were emulating the Chinese and Bangladeshis by adding a takeaway service, and within a few years several newly arrived young Italians also began experimenting with takeaway pizza joints in still untouched smaller localities like Washington and Willington. Maybe they showed the way, but all have vanished now. As long as twenty-five years ago I happened to drop into 'La Casa' in Linthorpe Road, Middlesbrough – 'Italian Takeaway Pizza Pasta Kebab Burgers' – and was told no one connected with it was Italian. Today you can eat Italian all over Stockton, or what passes for Italian, but since the demise of Rocco's not one place is owned by an Italian. Just off the High Street, in the first short stretch of Yarm Lane where Giacomantonio Pacitto opened his ice cream shop a hundred years ago, are crammed half-a-dozen pizza, kebab and parmo takeaways all run by 'newest Italians' trading under such names as Casanova, Marina, Siciliano ('Contemporary Italian Cuisine'), and Gino ('A Taste of Italy').

In this profitable free-for-all of multiple identities pledging 'a taste of Italy' other immigrant entrepreneurs, again largely from the Middle East and particularly Iran, but also from Albania, have been buying up or starting up more upmarket Italian-style spots on quite a scale. The process began, in the North East at least, with local businessmen acquiring Italian restaurants when the founders failed or were ready to retire to Italy, and from this it is but a small step to opening up one's own entirely new 'ristorante', a reflection on a local scale of what was shortly to happen nationally with the now seemingly unstoppable spread of British Italian-look chains and franchises like 'Ask', 'Bella Italia', 'Strada' and 'Zizzi', all now well represented in the North East. Discounting the many 'newest Italians' proliferating right across town, my own home city of Durham boasts a choice of 15 Italian or Italian-themed restaurants in its very small town centre alone, far outnumbering the sprinkling of Spanish, Indian and Thai alternatives: 8 of the 15 are run by Italians, 3 by non-Italians, and 4 are branches of national chains.[4] This balance still just in favour of the genuinely Italian-owned is probably unique in the North-East, but unfortunately does not mean all eight provide anything like authentic Italian fare.

Fast food joints and brutally standardised fodder for tourists are not hard to come by in Italy itself today, and yet as everyone knows Italians still take enormous pride in their cuisine, particularly in its numerous specific regional identities, each time-honoured dish a treasured amalgam of tradition and ritual inseparable from the very notion of the quality of life. All the same, a common characteristic of restaurants in Italian hands anywhere abroad is that the longer they last the less Italian they become. With no large and fastidious Italian clientele to satisfy, recipes and ingredients soon get adapted and standardised to come closer to 'what the natives want', as a newly arrived Italian chef in Newcastle despairingly put it to me. Some very obvious local departures from the Italian norm which would bemuse or dismay a first-time visitor from Italy are pre-cooked soggy pasta drowned in red gravy, meat and vegetables served on the same plate never excluding potatoes, pizzas as limp and insipid as greased sliced bread, deep-fried garlic mushrooms, deep-fried almost everything, the absence from most menus of Italian standards such as veal and tripe and squid, canned music of numbers that went out of date in Italy forty years ago, jealously guarded grated Parmesan(?) cheese never entrusted to customers to handle themselves, and the quaint custom (universal in Britain but how did it start?) of volunteering to pepper everything on your plate from an outsize grinder that nearly dwarfs the Tower of Pisa. True, the same obliging drift toward acclimatisation and standardisation happened long ago with Chinese and Indian restaurants in Britain too, but in their case there has so far

The pasta war hots up: photos taken on the same August day in Newcastle, 1992.

A 'newest Italian' in Bishopton Lane, Stockton 2007.

Ethnic restaurant rivalry: Bigg Market, Newcastle 2012.

been a sufficient reservoir of new immigrants to keep them in the hands of genuine natives.

In our hands-on era of MasterChef and Jamie Oliver we are finally getting to know more and expect better of Italian food, and indeed there are now some reasonable, and even reasonably good, Italian restaurants in the North East where not just the owner but none of the personnel are Italian. One Italian restaurateur in Newcastle only half jokingly suggested to me his threatened species should form an exclusive club with a special window-sticker declaring 'Genuine Italian Restaurant' along the lines of the *Associazione Verace Pizza Napoletana*, the Genuine Neapolitan Pizza Association, which in the face of pizza's globalisation (Texan, Mexican, Hawaian, Piri-Piri, Tandoori...) only validates as authentic the simplest handmade wood-oven-baked pizza margherita or pizza marinara. Fair enough, I suppose, so long as it's never forgotten that nowhere more than in a restaurant is the proof of the pudding in the eating, for sadly all too many of our established 'genuine' Italian eateries are proof of how dangerously complacent has become the old claim that only Italians can cook Italian. In the present economic climate the days are surely numbered for not a few fossilised relics, some of which have not dreamt of changing their menus (in pidgin Italian) for years and years.

Faced with so much fierce competition and canny emulation, if it is not to perish there are only two ways for an Italian restaurant to go: upmarket or down the fast food road. The dilemma is hardly new. By the early 1980s Newcastle's most exclusive Italian restaurant, L'Aragosta, felt constrained to flag up its 'reasonable prices', while others strove to keep abreast of the accelerating times of grab-a-bite by introducing takeaway facilities or stressing the 'fast and pleasant service beside good food'. A decade later, yellow-pages adverts for Tyneside show the Da Vinci in fashionable Jesmond bucking the trend by promoting its 'fresh ingredients, great care, international experience' and the newly founded Il Piccolo in relatively remote Prudhoe luring discerning customers from far and wide by defiantly advertising its 'classic Italian cuisine – no pizzas!'

In retrospect it is clear that the 1970s and 80s were the Golden Age of the Italian restaurant in the North East, when a limited number vied for a captive market in very profitable competition. The illustrations on the next pages give a good idea of some of the fun they had too, consciously or unconsciously applying the innovative London restaurant designer Enzo Opicella's dictum: 'A restaurant to be successful must have atmosphere, and atmosphere is created by people who know each other. If it's going to thrive a restaurant must have a party every night.' In Newcastle, Giuseppe Pignataro and Nico Arpone (starring on the front cover!) soon extended their popular La Stalla pizzeria to add a disco and even laid on coach outings for staff and customers. In the Tyneside Italian football championship, which was generally a close-run thing between the La Stalla team and its initiator Benito Gianfreda's La Capannella, their many regular Geordie customers provided a devoted fan base as well as extra team players. One year the restaurants got together to stage a costume re-enactment of the historic 1909 match in Turin which made West Auckland the world champions. But of course the greatest party of all was when Italy won the 1982 World Cup and Italians all over the region took to the streets almost like a coming of age.

In retrospect, too, like all golden ages that was also an age of innocence, when there was still something exotic about cave-like interiors with fishnets and bunches of plastic grapes suspended from the ceiling, and wax-encrusted Chianti-bottle candlesticks on check tablecloths, and '*O sole mio*' and '*Torna a Sorrento*' on the record player, and real genuine handsome young Italians to greet you warmly with 'Buona sera, signorina' as though you must be fluent in their language or couldn't wait to learn it. It was commerce, yes, but this time, unlike the cafés and temperance bars of old, Italians were not making money out of the natives while drawing as little attention as possible to their quaint origins; instead they were confidently, even exuberantly, promoting 'Italianità' as both liberating and chic. And in the process, if admittedly at the risk of fashioning new stereotypes, they made a crucial contribution to the social acceptance of Italians that had been so set back by the grim war years. Together with their country's glamorous leading role at the upper end of the global consumer industry in almost everything from cars to fashion, and the new freedom over here for almost all to travel to Mediterranean destinations and experience that gracious world for themselves, they finally helped to lay to rest, one hopes, the dismal days when to most Brits all Ay-Ties were either Greasy Waiters or Fat Mamas.[5] And as will always happen when preconceptions are at last overcome, we too have benefitted. If it's true you are what you eat, we are all Macaronis, we are all Worm-Eaters now!

Friendly rivalry: outside Dante Calzini's 'Wheatsheaf' in Ponteland, about 1979, before the start of the annual cycle race between Italian restaurant teams, La Capannella, L'Aragosta, and La Stalla. Front, kneeling: 'Alex' Cuscani, unidentified girl, Benito Gianfreda with giant pizza, Judy, Vincenzo with bike. Second row, standing, left to right: Luciano, Dante Calzini, Luciano and Mario in L'Aragosta T-shirts, Daniele, unidentified, former Chinese pilot Jimmy (with flag) who worked in various Italian restaurants, Pino Graziani, Nico Arpone, Colin, Alan Murphy, Peppino Puspi, these last five all in La Stalla T-shirts.
(Photo and identifications: Nico Arpone).

Nico Arpone at La Stalla. As well as his astounding table leaps (see book cover!) Nico also dazzled customers with his daring balancing acts.

Benito ('Benny') Gianfreda wipes away a mock tear as he hands the football trophy to Mario Fantin in 1983. For six years Benny's team had won the Tyneside Italian championship, until hairdresser Mario persuaded his regular customer Johnny Heenan (behind) to use his Newcastle United contacts to field an unbeatable side. The big after-match dinner at Benny's La Capannella included Antipasto Lost, Leg of Pork alla Rage of Benny, Gateau alla Fiddled Cup. (NCJ Media Ltd.)

'THE SECRET OF SUCCESS'

I've spent my entire life in restaurants, it's the one thing I know how to do. My grandfather was a cook, my father was a cook, and you could say I was born in a restaurant, seeing my mother was working in my father's place in Catania all the time she was pregnant with me. In 1968 we left Sicily and went to Rome, and my parents eventually opened a place in Ostia Lido, the beach resort.

One day my father happened to bump into an old friend in a bar who told him that another friend he used to work with was in England now, in Sunderland, and he'd opened a restaurant there: La Gondola. My father rang him up and Nino said, 'Things are good here, there's plenty of business and not too many of us. There are just two Italian restaurants in the whole city.' 'So if I come, do you reckon I'd have a chance?' 'Sure'. So my father goes straight home and says to my mother, 'Pack my bags, I'm going to England!' That was January 1976 and he was 51. My father was never able to sit still, he needed to keep moving, create. When he left he said to my mother, 'Give me three months, then come on up too', and he took my younger brother Maurizio with him, who was just 16.

He got work in the Pinocchio in Sunderland, very famous then, and it was good money. So he phoned home, the flat we rented: 'Sell the furniture, sell everything, and come up here!' That was a fantastically beautiful summer, I don't remember another like it ever again in England! I arrived on the first of May, a Saturday, and on the Tuesday I was a waiter in a restaurant in Durham, the De Medici. After three months I too joined the Pinocchio. Meantime my father had fixed up Maurizio in a hotel by the sea in Roker, since he wanted someone in the family with good English and a boy can pick it up in no time. Maurizio was on £18 a week, I remember, and I was on £27, but with tips I was getting more like £100. Sterling was very strong compared with the lira then.

In 1978 we took our first big step. We leased premises in Sunderland, a restaurant called La Sicilia belonging to Vincenzo Barbaro who had the hairdresser's here in Durham. My father and mother were in the kitchen, and me and Maurizio out front. But it didn't go, just Fridays and Saturdays, but nothing

Father and son: Umberto and Giovanni Viglianisi at home in Sicily after Umberto's retirement from the North-East restaurant circuit

during the week. It was in the wrong place, over the bridge near the stadium, whereas in the centre of town everyone was doing well. After two years we gave up, we'd lost everything we had. My father went to The Italian Job in Newcastle for £250 a week, plus the taxi back to Sunderland. In 1980 just two chefs in all Newcastle were taking that kind of money. I was waitering there when this Englishman asked me to help him open a new place in Peterlee, The Colosseum, right in the centre of town, for twice what I was getting. I lasted four months. Why? Because he had the English mentality, not the Italian. I told him first impressions matter, we have to create a nice setting, Italian, give it atmosphere. Yes, yes, he said, and went and got cheap MFI chairs that fell apart when you sat on them, and horrible half-plastic curtains, and bought his meat where it was cheapest. People were complaining.

But by then my father and I had taken another place in Sunderland – Marcello's – and we turned it into the most famous restaurant for miles around. Nino along with a chef from Naples called Marcello had tried to make a go of it, but when it didn't succeed he sold it on to the manager of a building society who put in a waiter from Catania to run it. But it still didn't take off. So my father says, 'I'll buy it and pay you back so much a week'. Well, we took that place to the stars, it was a fabulous success, always packed. We could seat nearly 80, it was right under the Conservative Club, lots of famous people came.

By 1983 I was hankering to do my own thing. I was married with two children, and it was time to create something of my own. I didn't have enough money for the place I found in Durham, but then Jim, one of our regulars, said, 'I'll put up the money, and you do what you want!' And so with Fabio Campolillo and Jim as sleeping partner we opened the famous Giovanni and Fabio. It was a success from Day One, and we were together there 16 years.

In 1995 I also opened La Spaghettata in the centre of town. I wanted to do something for the students. Students want to be able to eat for no more than a tenner, the food and the wine. My partners thought I was crazy, they didn't even want to come in at first, and yet I managed to create the first restaurant in Durham where you could eat for £3.50, with a free salad selection too, and they kept coming back for more. What a success that was, I took the place to the stars, it was fantastic.

Only now we had two boats to keep afloat. I was putting everything into La Spaghettata and meantime Giovanni and Fabio was starting to go under. Because a good restaurant is created by the person up front. My father was different, he was a great cook, but it was my mother who kept their places going. The food has to be up to scratch, but it's not everything, it's a good waiter that makes a restaurant. You have to take hold of the customer right on the door and keep him two or three hours, that's the secret of success. If the food's good that's a bonus, because the package needs to be perfect. I've always thought there are two important reasons why a customer comes in: first because he's worked 8 hours in the office or a shop, and second because he wants to free up, switch off, have a good time for a couple of hours, forget all his troubles. And we're there to give him that chance – Come on in then, we'll see to it you have a good time the next two hours, we'll take your mind off it all! So if you've that ability to carry the customer with you, you're going to be a success. He needs to feel at home, somewhere he can relax, and you have to sense whether he wants to share a joke with you or only wants to say 'Good evening, how are you?' You have to grasp at once what type he is. And I got lucky there, everyone says so, I'm a good front man.

(Giovanni Viglianisi in Durham in 2009, reminiscing at his 'Enoteca' specialising in Italian fine wines, his final venture after forty years in restaurants. 'Giovanni and Fabio' long ago morphed into Gabriele Ferola's 'Bistro Italiano' (see overleaf).

THREE RECIPES FOR A SUCCESSFUL ITALIAN RESTAURANT

Joseph De Giorgi, who began working in his father's kitchens at the age of 11: *More than anything I think the Italians brought democracy to eating out, made it a social activity, an egalitarian activity, where you had students, artists, manual workers and professionals all eating the same food, and sharing the same environment and the same conviviality. Don Vito's was an everyman's restaurant, with customers sitting at long tables, and that was a big change. Too often the English want their pasta soft, bland, not spiced, but ever since we started in the 1970s we've never dumbed it down – we've made our own bread, bought fresh ingredients from the market every morning, and kept it simple yet distinctive in the best tradition of southern Italian food. Even now the English tend to underestimate Italian cooking. We try to exceed customers' expectations, pass on our passion and pleasure in food, because we believe all the money should go on the plate, not on cloth napkins and expensive wines.*

Joseph and Mario De Giorgi at one of their latest creations, Pasqualino's, inside the Theatre Royal, Newcastle. Since 1978, when Mario turned Don Vito's into one of Newcastle's most popular restaurants, the family, who originate from Galatone near Lecce in the heel of Italy, have launched other very successful ventures, most of them in the same capacious building on Pilgrim Street, including the bar-restaurant Secco which was voted 'best Italian outside of London' by Harden's UK Restaurants in 2006.

Roberto Pani, who with his brother Walter manages Pani's restaurant: *For the sake of our idea of the business we have always tried to take on Italian staff – Sardinians if possible – because that is our image, our identity. And in fact I've found that customers prefer to be served by Italians. In recent years the best Italian restaurants in England have been evolving toward a more regionally based cuisine rather than the traditional standard menu – otherwise all do the same thing and everyone copies everyone else. A lot of our food is unique to Sardinia, even our antipasti, and our sandwiches made with carasao flatbread. So if I'm going to recommend an unfamiliar dish I know to be delicious, like our four-colour pasta twists called maloreddus, or fregula cun cocciua, a kind of Sardinian couscous with clam sauce, the customer has to have complete trust in me. That's another reason why the personal touch is very important to us. My wife Barbara, who is a teacher, even gives free Italian classes here in the restaurant.*

Roberto, Patrizia, and Chicco Pani, from Arbus in Sardinia, at their restaurant in High Bridge, Newcastle. Pani's, which opened in 1995, is in the best Italian tradition an entirely family concern: here five Pani brothers and their sister Patrizia work together in a youthful and informal atmosphere toward which local Italians gravitate naturally. In the coffee-bar area customers can read Italian newspapers and watch Italian TV. Originally a small café, it has expanded into a capacious restaurant specialising in Sardinian cuisine.

Gabriele Ferola, in conversation at the Bistro Italiano, after thirty years in the North East: *It was much easier for Italian restaurants long ago, when the English knew nothing about Italian food and a great many essential ingredients were unobtainable. Now customers are more sophisticated, they know Italy at first hand, they know Italian food is about a lot more than pizza and pasta. Today there is no excuse for poor quality, for now you can get all the best Italian products even if it means paying a bit extra. For me, a good restaurant needs three essentials: passion, authentic produce, quality. In most other Italian restaurants these days ninety per cent of the staff is not even Italian, but I always try to employ Italians, above all in the kitchen. Customers sometimes say to me they have eaten even better here than in Italy.*

Gabriele Ferola, from Sorrento, at his Bistro Italiano in Claypath, Durham. After working as a chef in a succession of Italian restaurants, Ferola founded his Ristorante Gabriele in Bishop Auckland in 1986. The Bistro Italiano, a small restaurant with tightly packed tables and a superb menu, including lavish antipasti and great fish dishes, first opened in 2000.

285

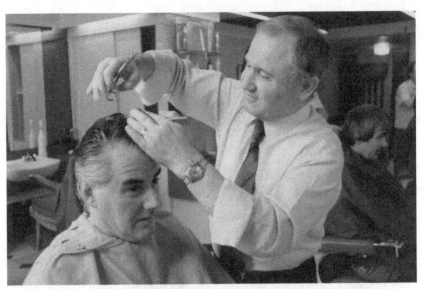

Mario Fantin, from Latina, at work in his Salon 66 in Blackett Street: 'I believe I gave the people of Newcastle something they never had before – and the people they are so nice to recognise all this'. Mario and his first three colleagues, also from Latina, all married Geordie assistants who worked alongside them.

'We created some things that went all over the country': Vincenzo Barbaro (centre) launches his Italian Salon in Durham, 1969, with latest recruits from his native Sicily, Giovanni Cultrera (left) and Filippo Di Simone. The Italian barbers brought back traditional skills, in particular deft work with comb and razor or scissors rather than a swift shearing with electric clippers. In time Giovanni and Filippo each founded their own businesses.

Hairdressers

By the 1920s Italian barbers and hairdressers in London and Glasgow were numerous enough to form their own professional associations, yet I have not found even a trace of their presence in the North East until long after World War II, in fact only a year or two before the Dante restaurant first opened its doors in Gateshead. Predictably, at a time when self-respecting hair stylists looked to France, pre-war local trade directories occasionally come up with a French flavour ('Estelle' 'Madame Marcelle') but never Italian. Another 1960s novelty was therefore the arrival of Italian hairdressers in our region, and they too helped to revolutionize our set ways.

The first came as skilled professionals recruited directly from Italy by some of our most forward-looking hairdressers. Benny Lloyd in Middlesbrough led the way, I'm told, followed by Douglas Darrell in Newcastle, and Jack Brown in Durham. Most of these young immigrant men went on to launch their own businesses, singly or more often banding together, once they had found their feet and completed the four-year ban on migrants working for themselves.

From the late 1950s British hairdressing began an enduring phase of intense innovation. This was the time of the freeing up of women's hairstyling associated with the names of Freddie French and Vidal Sassoon, the era in which the music of Elvis and soon our own Beatles and Rolling Stones finally got even the British male to let his hair down a bit too, particularly at the back and sides. Amid the general emancipation the Italians too had their own distinct impact, not only with their styling skills but in their own personal stylishness. Together with his compatriots at his newly opened Salon 66 (named for its founding year) Mario Fantin's inaugural present to the Geordies was the Roman Look, 'how the emperors of Rome wore it'. 'The day after we featured it on local television,' Mario recalls, 'they were queuing down the street here to have it done.'

The Italian trade apprenticeship was long, beginning as early as twelve and requiring at least five years' experience. The first trained hairdresser to arrive on Tyneside from Italy was Mario's first employer, Luigi Bernardelli of Mantua, now a sprightly octogenarian who keeps a close eye on the family's several restaurants. He owes his entire career, he says, to his sister whom he helped out before he had any training at her ladies' hairdresser in Santa Margherita on the Italian Riviera. 'Listen, Luigi' she said one day, 'you get on so well with women, why don't you take this up as a profession? Women bring you their charm, their beauty, their money – a man could hardly do better, could he!' He has done better and better in his adopted country. Within twenty years he possessed three salons in Newcastle, half-a-dozen more in Sunderland, and noting the growing appeal of all things Italian was going into restaurants as well. Lino's in Sunderland and Michelangelo's in Newcastle were the first, and still today three of Tyneside's best known restaurants are run by the family: Prima and Sabatini's (formerly Michelangelo), both in the Quayside district of Newcastle, and the Ristorante Fratelli in Ponteland. But now here is 'Mr Luigi' looking back on his early years in Newcastle.

'THERE WAS NOTHING UP HERE'

I answered an advert in the Corriere della Sera, *and left on New Year's Eve 1959 at 11 p.m. from Milan station. It took two days. Douglas Darrell, who was 22 at the time, had come up from London and was opening shops in Newcastle and needed hairdressers. He wanted Italians because he liked Italy and had worked alongside Italians in London, and he knew an Italian has a certain flair for a lot of things. I only intended to come here for six months, most of all for the language.*

Luigi Bernardelli (front) at the opening of the Michelangelo restaurant, Newcastle 1980, together with an expert Italian staff poached from the Gosforth Park Hotel. (NCJ Media Ltd)

I was an emigrant, yes, but I have to say I never felt like an emigrant, someone just arrived from nowhere. I was a nice-looking lad and I worked hard. A certain way of conducting yourself is what makes the difference. You've got to put yourself across, make an impression, that's the important thing. In fact ever since I first arrived I've always been 'Mr Luigi', never Luigi. To them I was somebody. And I wasn't a barber, which is simpler, I was a ladies' hairdresser. They're two very different things – because a woman will want her hair long or short, curled or straight, fringe to the left, fringe to the right, and the fashion's always changing. Bouffons were the thing then.

After a year all my work was beginning to pay off. I'd won over a lot of clients, people like the mayor's wife who brought along a lot of her friends, top people at the time, and they're the ones that gave me the incentive to start up something of my own. You couldn't work for yourself until you'd been here four years[6], and you had to report to the police every two weeks. But I got married before, and that's how I was able to open my own place at the end of '63 – 'Luigi' in Northumberland Street. I'd saved up a bit but it was a big shop, £60 a week rent, so I still had to borrow £1,500 from the bank, the cost of a house then. But they all trusted me. I had to do up the place – presentation is everything – paint the entrance, lay the lino, put in my Calypso bar where people could get a coffee. I opened the week before Christmas. The basins were in, but the dressing tables with the mirrors hadn't even arrived. My first clients came from Darrell's salon, most of them followed me. I took £70 that week, just working Friday and Saturday. But I'd only ever been a worker, I'd never been in business before with all the costs to worry about: rent, staff, suppliers. But eventually it took off. I was on my own at first, then I got two girls in to work with me, and I even incorporated another floor where I set up a men's hair stylist's – 'Man About Town'. For that I got in a lot of Italians, first Mario and Giorgio in1964, then Agostino and Carlo, and Giuseppe who later opened his restaurant La Stalla. After a couple of years Mario and Giorgio opened their own salon in Blackett Street – great rivals of mine, because they were good and they took some of my business with them. Then Carlo left to set up Salon 70 in Sunderland, leaving me with just two barbers! So I had to go off to Naples to recruit more. In those days, fifty years ago, it was impossible to find good English staff, there was nothing up here. Then people started going to Rimini and such places, started eating spaghetti, drinking wine, expanding their horizons, and so then they wanted a bit of Italy here. That's why I wanted to promote Italians. We washed hair, gave manicures, did face packs, all the proper treatment, and we kept afloat because we brought something high-class to the North East.

Another man with strong ambitions, though less fortunate in some of his later restaurant ventures, was Vincenzo Barbaro, a trained hairdresser from Catania recruited in 1960 by Jack Brown of Framwellgate Moor, Durham, when he too decided to 'go Italian'. Anyone who knew 'Vince', who died in 2003, will sorely miss his infectious exuberance, his fantastic waistcoats, and his indelible Italian accent. 'When I first came I thought this was a mute country,' he remarked in a conversation I taped in 1990, 'so quiet, so calm, so organised. Nobody shout, nobody push like in Sicily. Whenever I spoke all thought I gone mad!' His first independent venture was a shop in the pit village of Sacriston in 1962 catering for both gents and ladies, then a busy salon in Durham Market Place, and later yet another in the Royal County Hotel. In 1965 he was delighted ('with my pidgin English') to be elected chairman of the Durham Branch of the National Hairdressers' Federation. Vince won many awards for his creativity, and with top north-east hairstylists like Benny Lloyd and David Aston founded and led an artistic group which practised new styles together in each others' salons and then put on public displays, often for local charities: 'You cannot believe the progress the English made in such a short time. All was harmony, no jealousy. We created some things that went all over the country.' Today his son Domenic and granddaughter Sophia continue in Durham in the profession he loved.

The arrival of Italian hairdressers in the 1960s was a one-off phenomenon. There has been no significant renewal. In a few years it will be like Camy Rea said of the nearly extinct Italian ice cream vendor: 'We have lost that individual charm of the Italian coming round.' For the moment though, many readers will have their own favourite Italian hairdresser. When my hair is nearly blinding me I make my way to 'Filippo and Mario' in Meadowfield, both former Barbaro protégés. While Filippo Di Simone sculpts my mop to a brush we catch up on the gossip to the soothing sounds of Classic FM. Filippo is on his own now, because after the two had worked very contentedly side by side for 17 years Mario Annunziata died in 2006. His barber's chair is still there, as though he'd just popped out for a moment, except that the postcards round his end of the long mirror have vanished too. Filippo, who speaks of himself as 'one of the old brigade who all ended up having English wives, and English kids, and now even grandchildren', will, if pressed, concede that the English have in the meantime become 'quite good' at the profession. In hair creativity, and hair as business, Britain in fact now leads the world, even if some of its best-known practitioners have names like Angelo Seminara and Toni Mascolo.

HOW TO LOOK A CUT ABOVE THE REST

Gone are the days when you sidled into the barber's on a Saturday morning for your weekly trim. Gentlemen's hairdressing was a manly business then. No hairnets, hairdryers, receptionists and such nonsense. No pretty manicurists to do your nails, no fancy prices.

Then along came these new-fangled foreign barbers' shops and put the kibosh on the traditional English barber and the traditional English short back and sides.

At first the English were suspicious. These foreigners want to make fancy men of us, they thought, as they tried to stick grimly to their British haircuts.

Some men still do stick to their English barbers, of course. In fact what's happened now is that the men have divided completely into three types, all because of hair.

The first type is the manly man. The sort of person who would never dream of paying more than 4s

6d for a haircut because it's unmanly. This type isn't usually attractive to women because he spends so much time being masculine and doing masculine things.

The second type you have to beware of too. He's the one who gets his wife to do it for him. Too mean, or too poor, to have it done professionally. I'm not a haircutting wife, so I can pass on rapidly to the third type of man who is my favourite. He's the one who realises that hair is important, as clothes are important to a man, and is prepared to take time and trouble over making his topknot look attractive.

So, not afraid of being thought effeminate, he marches in boldly to his Italian barber's and settles himself down to a session, knowing he will be in good hands (and good scissors).

He comes out, not looking a freak and wanting to hide himself away for a day or two, but looking groomed and immaculate and confident.

Why should it have taken an influx of foreign barbers to make the British realise that a haircut could be a pleasant experience?

It has taken the Italians to teach British men that a bit of pampering isn't necessarily going to turn them into a race of pansies.

(Abridged from a cutting from a local paper kept by Mario Fantin, about 1970.)

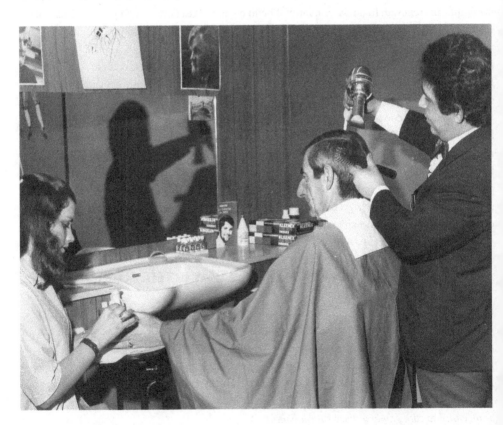

Vincenzo Barbaro and manicurist at work in the Italian Salon, Durham, during the 1960s: 'It's a clean profession, and you get to chat with people all the time, and I enjoy that'

'Their own personal stylishness': Gigi and Pino Campoli at the opening of their 'Roma' salon, Sunderland, 1986. The brothers, who first worked at Salon 70, opened other branches in Durham and Chester-le-Street.

Carlo and Agostino Petrucci at Salon 70, Sunderland, their first venture after finding their feet at Luigi's in Newcastle. The brothers went on to develop the 'Capo' chain of gents and ladies hairdressers in the Sunderland area, and founded an outstandingly successful clothing chain (see page 297).

Mauro, Guido, and Nicola Battista outside their salon in Princes Road, Middlesbrough, 2013. At 21, Guido exchanged the life of village barber in Liscia in the southern Apennines for furnace worker in Swansea. Made redundant from Dorman Long, he joined Benny Lloyd's gents salon before opening his own salon in Russell Street from which other Italian hairdressers have graduated to form local businesses. At 79, with a 20-strong staff managed by his son and daughter, Guido still shows no sign of wanting to retire.

In business: second and third generation Italians

Today, in the highly competitive world of own-brand ice cream, apart from the sustained success of Mark Toney's of Newcastle, Minchella's of South Shields, Pacitto's of Redcar and Stockton, and Greco's, the biscuit manufacturer in Middlesbrough, few of the once big local Italian families remain in business, and then generally but as a shadow of their former selves: the names, the evocative photographs on the walls, still speak of the great times, but the premises are now updated cafés with no ice cream production of their own: Forte's in Berwick, Marchetti's in Ashington (Mario's), Dragone's in Felling, Maggiore's in Sunderland (Louis café), Citrone's in Chester-le-Street, Bianco's in Hartlepool. An exception is the ever-popular Crescent Cafe in Seaton Delaval, still flourishing on its enduring reputation for superb ice cream.[7] The passing of Bertorelli's Riviera café in Newbiggin-by-the-Sea in 2004, virtually unchanged since it opened in 1937, and in 2009 Parisella's café in Wingate (John's café), featuring the very last old-style carved wooden cubicles in our region, are sad reminders of the impossibility of survival without renewal.

In the 1960s a number of new immigrants, generally with family connections to the old migration, took to our streets as independent van operators, or 'mobilers', buying their stock wholesale from long established producers such as Rea of Middlesbrough, Fella of Sunderland, or Nichol Rea in Benwell. This latter-day revival still has a very few veterans, but almost no successors. 'I never used to think of my age and just took it for granted that I would continue doing the job I loved until I took my last breath,' lamented Vincenzo Pellegrino, among the last of the veterans, when acute arthritis forced him to retire in 2009: for forty years his Austin BMC van had been a daily sight on the streets of Byker. One street-vending ice cream enterprise of that time which has not succumbed is that founded by ex-steelworker Donato Gregorio and his wife Elena (whose story was given on pages 235-6), now carried on by their sons whose vans are encountered all over Tyneside.

These van operators had arrived in the midst of a long boom for all self-employed ice creamers. Food scarcity and the persistent rationing of sugar-based products after the war had done nothing for the quality of ice cream, which remained reliant on ready-mix ICP (ice cream powder) and wartime expedients such as dried eggs and dried milk, but did wonders for the independent ice man's income. The ice cream ban had been lifted as early as 1944, but with sweets rationed for another ten years ice cream of any calibre was one of the few cheap treats going and was in huge demand in or out of season. To beat the government's milk and cream controls farmers and ice-creamers collaborated in a thriving underground 'white' market. The combination of high takings and new legislation outlawing the sale of handmade ice cream (sinking the old barrel freezer for ever) encouraged even the most cautious small producer to finally invest in up-to-date machinery and thus equip himself for what soon looked unmistakably like a Second Ice Age. Some 'continuous freezers' on the market at the time could churn out 120 gallons of ice cream an hour. Horses and carts were retired as family enterprises in the hands of a younger generation went over to motor vans. With their new fleet of specially equipped vans Seghini's of Blyth was able to cover nearly every residential street between Morpeth and Longbenton in a single day.

At first the only curbs on the general bonanza were steeper taxes on profits and more intrusive powers granted to the taxman, which sent the bad old habits of biscuit-tin safes and haphazard accounting the way of the barrel freezer, though some old firms never recovered from the shock. Further blows to the smaller maker and vendor were the imposition of purchase tax on ice cream at 22.5% in 1962, and ten years later VAT at point of sale, long-feared consequences of the industry's failure to convince government that its product is 'more than a treat, a food.' Here in the North East, the customary fierce rivalry between van operators kept the street price artificially low, and combined with our perverse British preference for the pre-packaged mass-produced article ultimately eroded everyone's profits.

The coup de grâce was delivered by our newest consumer age of domestic freezers and supermarket special offers, conveniencies which have quite literally decimated the numbers of ice cream vans tinkling for custom on our back streets. As for the village cafés founded long ago by the earliest immigrants, the few lone survivors have all fallen victim to the community deterioration that followed on the final cruel and swift succession of pit closures. But most old · hands will agree that the passing in the late 1980s of Notarianni's parlour in Sunderland and Rea's ice cream empire in Middlesbrough marked the real end to it all, the quiet conclusion of a century-long Italian success story that touched every city and town in the North East, and very nearly every village. The Appendix to this book is its roll of honour, if hard graft and strong personalities are considered worth honouring.

'Fish and chips, and a raincoat: the only two things nobody can go without in England.' So would muse Lorenzo Bimbi, from Castelnuovo near Barga, co-founder of what was to become the region's largest independent chain of fish restaurants, marvelling in the early days after he arrived from Italy at how people would come every night, often the very same people, for fish and chips. Yet now it seems he may have been mistaken, for this primal fast-food trade unique to our islands in which Italian immigrants in Scotland and Ireland and to some extent the North East played a leading role almost from the moment fish married chip is no longer as secure as it used to be.

Most chip shop proprietors are content to remain small fry, sticking to a single family-run outlet relying on a loyal local clientele. But from just such modest beginnings Lorenzo and Maria (Mary) Bimbi, and in time their sons James and Albert, built up a considerable empire of over a dozen upmarket fish restaurants in town centres right across the region from Ashington and Newcastle to Durham and Darlington. Mary, who lived to 104, was born into the trade in the Scottish border town of Annan, and worked tirelessly right into her nineties in the family's popular coffee shop in North Road, Durham. Today the family firm which for three decades made Bimbi's a synonym for famously 'scrumptious' fish and chips is no more, killed off by the spread of trendier national fast food franchises and the plethora of pizza and kebab takeaways. Another entrepreneurially minded Tuscan from the Barga region, whose forebears had a long connection with Scotland and the North East, was Enrico Biagioni. During the 1970s, as well as running the busy Broadway café in Darlington, he and his wife Romana built up a chain of 'Eric's Fish Bars' in South Durham.

As we have seen in earlier chapters, Barga and its environs were a major source of immigrants to Britain, originally as roving plaster statuette vendors, and then, like their rivals from Ciociaria, at the forefront of the move out of street trading into ice cream parlours and chip shops, particularly in Scotland. Astonishingly, by 1930 up to 80 per cent of all Scotland's fish friers were of Italian origin, almost without exception from either the Barga region or Ciociaria. Just as happened with ice cream, families with a background in fish frying moved down to our region in search of new markets, settling mostly in Northumbria. Today, due to its long connection with Britain, Barga has the distinction of being the only place in Italy

Second-generation beneficiaries of the Second Ice Age at the annual Ice Cream Alliance divisional dinner dance at the Coatham Hotel, Redcar, in the 1950s. Tony Rovardi is far left, Camy Rea to the right of the mayoress of Middlesbrough, and centre, kneeling, is Carmen Paleschi. On one copy of this photograph an unknown hand has scored: 'The Ice Cream Federation Dance, every year to stop the ice cream war'.

Third generation achievers: Connie Coia, only daughter of Biagio Coia (inset), photographed in Spennymoor on her wedding day in 1954, with her six brothers and her widowed mother, Maria Lanni. After living the life of a wandering musician Connie's grandfather opened an ice cream shop in Paisley before settling in Spennymoor in 1904. Her father, a leading light in the northern division of the Ice Cream Alliance and generous sponsor of the Spennymoor United soccer team, wanted his children to enjoy the benefits of the kind of education he never had. All seven subsequently entered the professions: four doctors, one solicitor, and two head teachers.

July 1961: Wedding procession of Carlo and Anna Rea at Vallefredda, near Arpino. Postwar regeneration of the old migratory links is well exemplified by this couple who committed to working and raising a family in the North East. Though born in Arpino, both had close family members who had worked in Middlesbrough and Newcastle in earlier times. Carlo and Anna, who until retirement ran their own ice cream concern, have for long been dedicated activists in the Newcastle Anglo-Italian Association.

The Dragonaires: in the late 1970s these sons of well-known local ice cream families teamed up to form one of the North East's most popular dance bands. From left to right: John Valente, lead singer and mandolin, with his Dragone brothers-in-law and nephews, Arthur, Michael, Frankie and Joe. (Photo: NCJ Media Ltd).

Gateshead 1983: Michael Quadrini, the younger son of one of Newcastle's leading ice cream families, greets the arrival of his latest purchase for lavish restyling as a floating nightclub. The Caledonian Princess, a former Sealink ferry, was renamed the Tuxedo Princess after Quadrini's Tuxedo Junction, Newcastle's most luxurious nightclub at the time. (Photo: NCJ Media Ltd)

Mary Bimbi (née Bacci), born in Annan in 1906 but educated in Italy, with sons James (right) and Albert in Durham in 1993 outside one of the family's many local fish restaurants at the height of their success. An indefatigable worker until her 90s, Mary died in 2009 aged 104.

John Citrone after receiving the
Masters Mr Universe trophy in
1994. As a young man John built a
personal gym above the family ice
cream factory in Elm Street, Chester-
le-Street, and here his friend Arnold
Schwarzenegger came from Austria at
the age of nineteen to train for six
months before going on to world fame.
(Photo: NCJ Media Ltd).

The brothers Giancarlo and Tullio Petrucci outside Tucci's
clothing store in High Street West, Sunderland, about 1990.
Among the handful of Italians who have set up clothing shops in
the North East the most successful have been the hairdressing
brothers Carlo and Agostino Petrucci (see illustration on page
291) who from 1987 together with Carlo's sons Tullio and
Giancarlo ran this men's clothing shop next door to their 'Salon
70'. Before its sale to Box Bros in 2007, the Tucci branded
fashion chain included major stores in Sheffield, in Grainger
Street, Newcastle, and at the Bridges Shopping Centre,
Sunderland.

Tullio Petrucci (right) now partners another second-generation Italian, Paul Gabriele, in this long established
Chester-le-Street family's import business specialising in supplying coffee and coffee machines to predominantly
Italian caterers in the region.

Even in these days of home freezers and superstore bumper choc ice offers, the self-employed driver of a single ice cream van who is loyal to his patch and his customers can make a relatively good living. And a good life too, humanly speaking. Well-known and well-liked in all the back lanes and housing estates around Bishop Auckland and Shildon, Gino Rossi from Valvori, a hamlet near Montecassino that has supplied generations of immigrants to the North East including many in his own family, has seen innumerable sweet-toothed children grow up to become mums and dads, and now grans and granddads, who even on a rainy winter's evening at the sound of Gino's famous 'Match of the Day' chimes will still pop out for a cornet or a packet of tabs. 'Who would want to run a restaurant, with all their big worries about staffing and overheads?' says Gino. 'I am one man, I come and go as I please, when I please'. He still remembers how he took £32 the first day he went out in 1969, far more than a week's wages for a miner. In 1990, after his original van had clocked up 240,000 miles, seldom going more than four miles from home, he bought his present van whose brightly painted bodywork is now an historic memento of the heady excitement of 'Italia 90', the one World Cup which Gino was certain his country could not fail to win.

where you can be sure of finding good old British fish and chips, and served up by true experts, at least in the month of August when this very picturesque town in the heart of the North Tuscan Apennines stages a fortnight-long *Pesce e Patate* festival. Needless to say, no kebabs or burgers are also on offer in the big Fish and Chips marquee.

Newcastle's reputation for great night life owes a lot to the business flair of Michael Quadrini, the youngest son of second-generation Italians who made Quadrini's a big name in ice cream on Tyneside after the war. Michael started out driving a van for the family firm, but always said his ambition was to be a millionaire. In 1978, after cutting his teeth on various catering ventures in Newcastle and also in Manchester he launched the plush Tuxedo Junction nightspot in New Bridge Street, Newcastle. Nine years later he capped a reputation for providing imaginative entertainment for Tynesiders by opening the Tuxedo Princess, the celebrated floating nightclub moored under the Tyne Bridge on the Gateshead side of the river which like its successor the Tuxedo Royale was for long one of the town's most conspicuous icons.

Wild stories of Italian mafia penetration were rife at the time of the North East's only case of gross criminality concerning people of Italian extraction: the murder of Angus Sibbett, an employee of millionaire businessman Vince Landa, found shot dead in the back seat of his Jaguar outside the little village of Hett in County Durham in January 1967. The movie *Get Carter* was partly inspired by a novel which drew on the case. Landa, who had assumed this surname 'because no-one could ever remember a name like Luvaglio', had made a fortune from installing and controlling gaming machines in the region's hundreds of working men's clubs. His disappearance after the so-called One-Armed Bandit Murder made him Britain's most wanted man. Michael Luvaglio, his younger brother, and Dennis Stafford, another Landa business associate, received life sentences. A high-profile 'Stafford is innocent' campaign ensued. One day, after living very comfortably abroad for eleven years, Landa walked into Chester-le-Street police station and gave himself up pleading guilty to a little matter of tax fraud, seeing by then all other charges against him had been dropped. Months later, Michael Luvaglio and Dennis Stafford were released still protesting their innocence, until Stafford suddenly confessed he had pulled the trigger, only to rapidly retract the claim... But at this point it is high time to stand up for the integrity of the North East's Italians by reminding readers that although the Luvaglio brothers made most of their money in the North East they are second-generation Italians from London's East End, and it was down there they acquired their fruit-machine know-how while working for the Kray twins!

Our second and third generation Italians, or Anglo-Italians, have not only made a name for themselves in business, for which their upbringing well prepared them. In sport, there is the unique figure of champion body builder John Citrone, of the Chester-le-Street Citrones, who though only 5' 3" has won eight Mr Universe titles. In his fifties he made an extraordinary comeback to win again as veteran master virtually every year between 1994 and 2002. Back in pre-war times, other second-generation working-class Italian lads such as Alfie Paolozzi of Newcastle and Joe Baldasera of the Sunderland branch of the family gained a big name in the north for their boxing prowess.

The Italian street-musicians of yore were not all mere organ-grinders, for many descendants of 'original Italians' speak of relatives who possessed exceptional ability on the accordion, the bagpipes, the fiddle, the mandolin, or had great singing voices. Some of their talented offspring who grew up here and understood the culture joined local orchestras and bands or did solo turns round the region's music halls and picture palaces, including no doubt the New Hippodrome and Palace of Varieties in Darlington, now the Civic Theatre, built by Rino Pepi, a Florentine quick-change artiste and impersonator who made a second career here in the north as a theatre impresario. One instance is the versatile musician Colombo Riani of Houghton-le-Spring (mentioned in chapters 6 and 7) who had two gifted sons: Furio, a talented boy soprano, and Osvaldo ('Ozzie') who played with big bands in Sunderland before settling for the famed Oxford Galleries in New Bridge Street, Newcastle, under the celebrated band leader Antonio Volpi, or rather Peter Fielding as show business knew him[8]. More recent years have seen popular amateur bands like Osvaldo Moscardini's 'Mandoleers' or the 'Dragonaires' of Felling, the all-family Dragone-Valente team which for long was in great demand at charity concerts and club functions all over the region. Status Quo's Francis Rossi was not born in the North East, but he is the grandson of Gennaro Rossi who opened a temperance bar in Annfield Plain a century ago. The only locally-born musician from a similar background to gain comparable fame far beyond our region is the rock-singer and songwriter Chris Rea whose family were once ice cream's biggest players on Teesside. His Irish mother was a church organist, and his uncle Gaetano was famed for his tenor voice.

Since so many of our region's people of Italian descent owe their presence here to their street-musician forbears' discovery of the earning powers of *la crema*, it seems fitting to conclude a section dedicated to the achievements of later generations with Chris Rea's reflections on his earlier incarnation as an ice cream man. Though clearly very personal to him, the singer's memories will resonate strongly with other sons and daughters of families who first came to prominence in the Ice Age.

'I USED TO BE AN ICE CREAM MAN'

I went through a long period where I never once thought about ice cream, I actually forgot what I did. One day I was with my own family in a restaurant, and we all had an ice cream. And as we were eating this ice cream I began explaining why there are two different types of vanilla. Words were coming out involuntarily, completely separate from myself – they say that's what happens when you're about to go mad – and I heard these words coming out of my mouth: 'I used to be an ice cream man'.

It was quite, quite frightening. I then became interested in that part of my past again, but it was as if it had happened to somebody else.

Dad was a distant figure, autonomous, a cross between the Pope and Mussolini. He was very Italian, as were all of my uncles, although they were second generation. My grandfather had come from Italy via New York and Panama: how he finished up in Middlesbrough is beyond me.

Every other summer we would go to Italy for three whole months, where there were wonderful comings and

Chris Rea, whose output in both music and film has at times drawn on his Italian heritage, promotes his first single while still working for the family ice cream firm.
(Middlesborough Gazette)

soulful goings, music, warmth, inspiring light, great smells, passionate but non-violent life... and then I was suddenly dropped back in Middlesbrough, into cold back streets, where no one was Italian. And that was very disorientating. I remember my first day at grammar school, being the only person who was me. Everybody else was like everybody else, and there I was, tanned, in a freezing cold playground in the middle of Middlesbrough, wondering what on earth I was doing there.

There was a strong work ethic that went with the Italian connection. The family business was an ice cream factory and coffee bar. There was an ice cream committee, a very serious affair. It was like the United Nations. Once a month, everyone in the business would meet at a country club outside town. They would have lunch, then go into a conference room and thrash out all their different grievances, and settle territorial differences concerning ice cream vans.

My father used to control the wholesale of many ice-cream items in Middlesbrough, he was central distributor for most of the region. If you fell out with him or the committee, you could find it difficult to get hold of cones.

The shop itself was classic Fifties, big Italian coffee machines, Formica everywhere, and a juke box in the corner. I had to work in the coffee bar on weekends. I started at 12, as a table clearer. I wore a white Bri-Nylon coat with Mr Really Good written on it.

Nothing was ever clean enough for my father. You could never clean as good as he could, you could never clean as fast and as thorough as he could. I would listen to the waitresses in the coffee bar, endlessly talking about their drunken husbands, bad backs and heart attacks, and that made me incredibly depressed.

In my teenage years I was involved in making the ice cream. Great big hundredweight bags of sugar would arrive at our factory, and 60lb blocks of lard, white vegetable fat. Cutting up the fat was a horrible job. You plunged in long knives to prise it into smaller pieces, and these would be put into a 100-gallon vat, which you would then fill up with hot water. The vat was sleeve heated, so the walls became red hot, and your arms were constantly burnt and blistered.

When you had emptied the sugar and the milk powder into the mix, then you had the horrible job of mixing and delumping, which made your hands go red and purple. You then added the secret ingredients, the family secret ingredients that had been prepared either by my father or a trusted member of the family. That was a very serious procedure, because this was the actual flavour of the ice cream: it was that blend which dictated what this white mass was going to become.

I became very strong from the ice cream factory, but it gave me a weight problem for life, because it developed me physically far beyond my body frame – my chest and shoulders are massive.

Going into the business drove my father and me a lot further apart. I wanted us to get out of the ice cream business; I would have levelled the lot, and moved into restaurants or fast food. My idea always earned a rebuke, 'Just get on with your work, Chris, we have no time for these crazy dreams.' We never did agree. We never agreed on anything.

In the beginning I had an intense desire to know everything about the business. Over a period of years there was a long, inevitable waning of interest. And when I left the business, one of my brothers took my place.

About six years ago, the shop was sold and my father retired. He and I don't really talk now. He's remarried, he has his new family, and I've got mine; our lives are very different. I suppose once upon a time he was my father, and I was his son, now we're just a pair of adults.

(*The Independent*, 29 November, 1993, slightly abridged.)

The situation today

As far back as 1969 statisticians noticed that more Italians were leaving Britain than arriving. The phenomenon was worldwide, for the heartening reason that in little more than ten years the homeland had undergone profound economic and social changes for the better. As the economy grew and grew, the same urge which brought impoverished peasants over here to chance their luck in the Victorian Age or to work for the first time in factories after World War II impelled their counterparts instead to invest their reserves of hope and energy in their own country as the new land of opportunity. Despite its current woes, Italy is still one of the ten largest economies in the world and the kind of lowly jobs millions of Italians were glad to find anywhere else until half a century ago are taken up eagerly in their own country by new arrivals from all over the globe – totalling at least four million according to latest estimates.

Most Italians who have come to Britain in more recent times are therefore beneficiaries of this rapid material transformation, with generally much higher levels of education than their parents, and certainly their grandparents, and with aspirations far removed from those of the unskilled migrant labourers of the early postwar years. Some are high fliers who have made career moves to Britain in sectors like international business and finance, others are skilled professionals who have made the most of the unrestricted movement of labour between EU member states. Thousands more are full- or part-time students hoping to improve their career prospects back home by spending time in an English-speaking environment. In addition there is a very considerable drifting population of young people chasing all kinds of temporary work in our cities who are here simply to enjoy the personal challenge of living abroad, making a little bit of money, and hopefully improving their English along the way. London is the chief attraction, but other cities including Newcastle are catching on. Mindful of the priorities of earlier immigrants, I asked one 26-year-old who characteristically lives by picking up casual work in local Italian bars and restaurants, 'Are you trying to save up?' 'No, I live for the moment, because I'm only passing through. I like the life, moving around, meeting new people, practising my English. Much better than work in an office, or on an assembly line like my father. I might try Spain next.'

Young single men who arrived in the North East in the 1960s on Ministry of Labour work permits as hairdressers or to toil in the kitchens and dining-rooms of our grander hotels already shared something of this more relaxed approach to the migrant experience, generally depicting themselves as driven not by dire necessity like 'mere emigrants' but by an adventurous compulsion to experience a different culture – indeed not a few say they were here as much for the women as for the money! 'I found the more liberal attitudes very exciting', recalls Nicky Sparacio who came to England in 1970 after studying at catering college in Genoa. 'I was able to be a hippy, have long hair and still get a job – things were much more restrictive in Italy.' Church influence in a country in which divorce was only legalised that same year (a century after this country) was still very strong, particularly in the countryside, and respect for conventional values and tradition had a deep hold on personal as well as national life.

The bulk recruitment of southern Italian labour had ceased by 1960, and the subsequent more modest influx of workers to Britain was for the most part a spontaneous consequence of the extraordinary success of the Italian restaurant formula. At the same time Italy's rising standard of living was beginning to bring more and more over here as tourists or for longer stays as language students. The latter novelty, which rapidly expanded into an industry for its British operators, had begun back in the mid-1950s when middle-class Italians who were themselves not yet in the habit of travelling abroad started sending their children to language schools in England or placing them with families as au pairs as an investment in their advancement within their own suddenly much more fluid society. Experience of foreign countries was a valued asset for management jobs in Italy's largest companies and also in the numerous export-driven small family manufacturing firms which underpinned the new prosperity.

By 1990 the early post-war immigrants had reached retirement age and few newcomers were replacing those who chose to return home.[9] It was at this juncture, during the decade 1983-93, some sixty years after the fascist regime had set up the network of state-backed emigrant institutions described in chapter 6, that government in Italy once again sought to intervene actively and politically in the lives of the millions of citizens abroad. Rapid recovery from the worst and longest recession since the great post-war economic boom, plus the ruling centrist coalition's determination to perpetuate itself, supplied both the cash and the incentive to woo the worldwide diaspora with a series of initiatives ultimately intended to win full participation in Italy's electoral process for all citizens abroad, on the presumption that most expatriates would vote for stability and continuity within the home country.

Italian national politics are felt to be much too remote and impenetrable to be of great interest to most Italians who settle or grow up abroad, but not so the issue of national identity. Therefore easily the most popular feature of the campaign to reach out to the potentially immense reservoir of useful new voters was a series of measures enacted to facilitate the acquisition of Italian citizenship for those who had renounced it or had not previously qualified. These culminated in 1992 in the granting of the right of dual nationality to more or less anyone in the world who could prove they had a drop of Italian blood, since in Italian law nationality is determined not by place of birth (*ius soli*) but the nationality of the parents (*ius sanguini*). Dual citizenship is not recognised by most states in the European Union, but Britain is an exception, and unsurprisingly many here took up the offer. For third or even fourth generation Anglo-Italians the chance to hold two passports may be little more than an exotic novelty, but for sons and daughters born here and brought up by Italian parents it offers legal recognition of their very real sense of being both one thing and the other.

The long-planned incorporation of this vast global electorate in the national parliamentary system came to nothing in 1993 when its proponents failed to win the necessary two-thirds majority which would have permitted a change in the constitution to create extra seats for émigré representatives in both houses of parliament. Nonetheless, the ten-year-long more or less nationalistic crusade had galvanised consular officials, inspired Italian Catholic missions to rally the patriotic faithful, and had given other active members of the emigration some sense that their scattered communities still mattered to the state they were born in. One notable bureaucratic result was that once again, as sixty years earlier, emigrants were relabelled 'Italians abroad' (*Italiani all'estero*) to signal they were not considered forever lost to the homeland.[10]

All these efforts of officialdom to recoup the emigrant population coincided with more spontaneous initiatives all over Britain to revitalise the sense of a community of Italians. After all, by this time the 'new Italians' here were not so young anymore, they had more free time on their hands, and they had much to be proud of. By dint of hard work most had achieved a reasonable level of well-being and none had failed to note how much in the meantime the image of their own country had risen in the appreciation of the average Briton. Even when well integrated here, even with no desire to return to Italy except for holidays, their origins still mattered.

Italians in our region were especially motivated to organise on their own behalf because of the North East's relative isolation from the centres of official Italian representation in the north, Liverpool in earlier times, and Manchester since 1969. Ever since the more or less forgotten *fascio* clubs of the Thirties there had been nothing apart from the annual social events of the northern division of the Ice Cream Alliance to bring together at least some elements of the very scattered Italian population. Unlike some other provincial centres with denser numbers like Bedford or Peterborough, nowhere in the North East was there an Italian church or mission, no club, no drop-in centre, around which to build a sense of communal identity and allegiance. Most dispiriting of all, because of a mistaken perception that the Italian presence here was negligible or dwindling, even the consular agency in Newcastle had been allowed to lapse.

For those who sought to do something about the organisation and welfare of their fellow countrymen, it was no easy task to gain the support or even interest of the state authorities in Manchester[11], but years of persistent lobbying by a determined group of postwar settlers in Middlesbrough and enthusiasts from the 'old' community on Tyne and Wear, both with backing from the Bradford Italian Catholic mission, did finally produce results. A paramount demand from both groupings was the provision of Italian language classes for the children of immigrant families, a principal obligation of the Italian consular service in Britain ever since 1971.

In its active years, the Middlesbrough 'Italia' Anglo-Italian Association, founded in 1985, played an exemplary role. Led by a few dedicated individuals from within the community of former steelworkers, and drawing on the strong sense of collective identity stemming from a shared life experience, it was able to stage well-attended larger communal events as well as run fortnightly Sunday evening socials in St Patrick's church hall which regularly attracted a core of forty to fifty members. The mainly British-born younger generation's participation was encouraged through the language classes and children's parties and by putting together a team to enter the Italian northern region five-a-side football league under the auspices of the Manchester consulate, an event it won on more than one occasion. True to the association's constitutional commitment to provide moral and material support and benefits advice for 'the elderly, the sick, the bereaved, needy families, and the unemployed', the committee very conscientiously addressed the plight of ageing members of the community and others who had lost out in the general advance to more comfortable circumstances. In 1991, for instance, the association was helping in a small way about thirty members, including an out-of-work widower with three children and a widow living on a state pension in one room. Unfortunately, due to the difficulty of enthusing another generation of activists the association folded in 2005.

The Anglo-Italian Association of Newcastle, founded thirty-four years after the war by enthusiasts mostly from long-established 'original Italian' families, is a much looser affiliation

The Newcastle Anglo-Italian Association committee displays a donation toward cancer work at the Freeman Hospital in 2005. Centre, standing between two representatives of the Charlie Bear charity: Betty Risi (with bear) and Joe Risi, president. Others, from left to right: Pat Angelucci, Rosalinda Wright (Quadrini), Elena Valente, Angela O'Neill (Quadrini), Anna Rea, Tina Rea, Josie Rea, Carlo Rea. Kneeling: Paul Risi and Armando Angelucci (right), Italian consular agent for the North East.

World Cup fever at a Saturday morning language class for British-born Italian children held in the Italian Department, Durham University, 1990. Similar free courses sponsored by the Manchester consular authority were organised in Newcastle and Middlesbrough at this time, but then phased out when Italian government policy shifted to part-funding Italian language classes within the normal school curriculum.

Christmas festa dei bambini organised by the Middlesbrough Anglo-Italian Association at the International Centre, Abingdon Road, 1992.

(Above) Lunchtime bingo at the Amici d'Italia circle, Newcastle, 2012.

(Left) Newcastle Anglo-Italian Association dinner dance, St James's Park stadium, 2008.

with no constitution and no formal membership mechanics. Among its prime movers back in 1979 were third-generation scions of traditional ice cream families who valued their Italian roots, notably John Valente of Sunderland and Joe Risi of Newcastle (still its president), British Italians who in their youth had served in the war and had no reason to feel inhibited about the Italian connection, least of all at a time when the country had become a leading mass tourist destination and a byword for stylish modernism. These days the association is heavily reliant on a very few long-serving committee members to sustain a significant presence in the teeth of the scepticism of newer settlers who tend to view it as stuck in the past and 'not Italian anymore'. Nonetheless the association can count on selling 250 tickets for its prestigious annual dinner dance which attracts participants from both the old and new immigrations, sometimes whole families. Furthermore, given its long and lone history of steadfast networking the committee can quickly drum up an impressive following for less formal fund-raising events, generally also involving a meal with entertainment. Profits from ticket sales and raffles go to local and international charitable causes, and in the case of natural disasters like the earthquake in L'Aquila or the Far Eastern tsunami the association has demonstrated it has the capacity to raise thousands of pounds. Activists have special reason to be proud of their record in the 1980s and 1990s when hard campaigning successfully restored a consular presence in Newcastle (Simonetta Manfredi, consular agent from 1990) and convinced the Manchester consulate to finance extra-curricular Italian classes for immigrants' children. Though now privatised, the consulate's *Sezione didattica* (Education Section) is its sole extra-mural activity to survive the axe in 2011. With Italian Foreign Ministry funding it continues to sponsor professional teachers from Italy who work with a number of schools in our region, mainly Catholic primary schools, to provide Italian language classes as part of the general curriculum.

In 2002, with help from consular agent Maria Pia Fontana, local Italians of retirement age wanting something more regular and homely – a bite to eat and a chat together over a game of cards in the old familiar tongue – founded the Amici d'Italia association which meets every Tuesday lunchtime in the Irish club in St Andrew's Street, Newcastle ('the Italian club in the Irish club in Chinatown'). As the name implies, 'Friends of Italy' welcomes all comers, mostly first-generation Italians and their spouses and friends, and it's here that along with a few descendants of the old migration can be found a representative cross-section of veterans of the postwar emigration, both men and women: former steelworkers, retired restaurateurs, ice creamers and hairdressers and their wives, former women hospital workers, and even a 'war bride'. Here old friendships have been strengthened and new ones cemented through regular contact as well as local outings and even several collective holiday trips to Italy.

Apart from their personal economic circumstances, much else has improved for the men and women who left Italy forty and fifty years ago. Low cost flights, satellite TV, mobile phones, make it far easier to be an Italian here while still maintaining living links with the old country. Having learned through hard experience and strength of character to move back and forth easily between separate languages and allegiances, most who have achieved a reasonable level of affluence recognise that they now have the best of both worlds. Philosophically, a lifetime's migrant experience has led the majority to identify far more positively than the insular British with the social ideals of the European Union, in particular that of national differences co-existing peacefully within a community of equals.

The minority who go back to Italy for more than a holiday do not always have an easy homecoming. The country they left behind is very different now. The once thriving home village seems lifeless and empty outside the holiday season, depleted by emigration and urbanisation, or has grown into a sizeable and almost unrecognisable town, or has been absorbed into a vast conurbation. If a community of sorts remains it is not the remembered community with the old inclusiveness and mutual dependency in adversity whose strengths could still be relied on among other *paesani* in England. Having lived long as 'Ay-ties' over here they may even feel like foreigners in their own land too, half-alien 'Inglesi', while their children if they accompany them can find it hard to adapt to small town life in southern Italy where most of the families have come from but good jobs are so few. Many youngsters drift back to England where they grew up and were educated.

In doing so they are joining an increasing number of Italians who have set out to make another life in Britain, particularly in cosmopolitan London.[12] While traditional immigration continues to some extent, at least from southern Italy and almost entirely in the catering sector, most of those arriving now are part of a much more privileged emigration that has certain parallels with that touched on in the earliest chapters: the cosmopolitan merchants and bankers, the clerics and military engineers, the scholars and artists and political and religious refugees of medieval and renaissance times and later.

While this transformation is in good part due to the much stronger political and commercial ties with Italy which have evolved ever since Britain entered 'Europe' in 1973, it is now becoming more and more difficult to distinguish from a 'brain drain' of growing numbers of skilled professionals in business, finance, academia, IT, etc, who are over here because of the drastically diminished job market at home for highly educated young people which is perhaps the most dismal outcome of the stagnation the country has endured for the past decade and more, a bitter reality check on the assumption of perpetual betterment such as we too have experienced in the UK.

Though the North East has one of the lowest populations of resident Italians the consequences of this extended period of the economic and moral doldrums synonymous with the long reign of Silvio Berlusconi are detectable in our region too. Recently I have spoken to an Italian professor of physics at Durham University who finds funding for high level research much easier to come by over here, a medical researcher at Newcastle's Centre for Life, a married couple from Milan making a good career as artists, and a young woman from Venice taking an MA in Social Studies at Northumbria University who tells me that among the Italian friends she has in the North East are an NHS doctor and an engineer besides other fellow graduates from Italian universities who prefer to pursue more advanced studies in our region. Armando Angelucci, the current Italian consular agent, has also spoken to me of doctors trained in Italy who as EU citizens have elected to make a career here (including two in the Freeman hospital's transplant unit), in addition to accountants and chemical engineers, business people and representatives of firms supplying Italian goods, and ever increasing numbers of academics and postgraduates at our region's six universities.

These are today's 'new Italians', not compelled by poverty, not burdened with feelings of inadequacy, not made to feel intruders, but here for the short or long duration of their own free choice as citizens of Italy and Europe. Truly now, for reasons Mussolini could never have foreseen and our own politicians and bureaucrats will assuredly never recognise, 'Italians abroad' rather than immigrants.

Coda

Searching for an appropriate conclusion from the long perspective which seeking to understand the lives of Italians in North East England has helped me to gain, and thinking back over the many illuminating interviews and discussions we have had with numerous people who actually lived parts of the story I have presumed to relate, two moments in particular spring to mind.

In 1992 a young woman born to Italian parents in Middlesbrough, and therefore according to Italian law entitled to an Italian passport, had this to say in answer to the inevitable question: Do you feel more Italian or more English?

At school when I was seven or eight we used to have to write down where our mother and father were from, and what nationality we were, and I was so confused. I remember scratching my head and thinking, Where am I from, where am I from, I don't know what I am! I was frantic – am I English, am I Italian, I don't know! The teachers used to have to help me to decide what I was. Of course they always said I was English. That helped because you don't want to be different to other children.

But now I don't mind, I like being from a different background, I like being different and not the same as everybody else. I like the fact that I have my knowledge of the language, and the food as well, and the fact that I've got relatives in Italy I can visit. I think it's more interesting. My life is English, but I think when it comes to emotions and feelings my personality is Italian. I like my double identity, the freedom it gives.

In fact I believe a lot of English people would like to be Italian. I know a lot of my friends always say, 'Oh I wish I was Italian!'

In the same year we talked to a much older woman who had moved with her parents from Italy to the North East in the hungry 1920s. When asked what she thought life was like now in the old country she answered in a way which marked her as the product of very different times, times that all the later chapters of this book have sought to recover: 'Credo che tutti vivono bene e il mangiare non gli manca, e vivono meglio là che noi qui.'

'I think they all live well and there's plenty to eat, and they have a better life there than we have here.'

That will be the day, when each one of all the hundreds of millions from all over the world impelled to live and work in other lands today can say the same about their own country and know they are not dreaming.

BOOKS AND SOURCES

Bulk recruitment and the steelworkers. Most information is from oral sources. The relevant Ministry of Labour files are in the National Archive under LAB 8. *The Colliery Guardian* for 1951-2 and 1955 carries brief reports on foreign labour in the mining industry. The five Durham NUM lodges openly opposed to the employment of Italians in 1955 were Wheatley Hill, Blackhall, Chopwell, Thrislington, and Eden.

The pasta and pizza boom. The classic work is A. Capatti and M. Montanari, *Italian Cuisine: A Cultural History* (2003), but equally recommended is John Dickie's *Delizia! The Epic History of Italians and their Food* (2007). Alastair Scott Sutherland's *The Spaghetti Tree: Mario and Franco and the Trattoria Revolution* (2009) is an entertaining and well-informed account of the rise of the Italian restaurant scene in Britain.

Hairdressers. Information from oral sources and the local press.

In business. Again, sources are oral memory and the local press. The central role played by Italian immigrants in the fish and chip trade is explored in J.K. Walton, *Fish and Chips and the British Working Class 1870-1940* (1992).

The situation today. How this long-established ethnic minority in Britain most typically struggles to preserve its identity is considered in the later chapters of Terri Colpi's *The Italian Factor* (1983), and from a more openly feminist perspective in both Anne-Marie Fortier's study of institutional and individual attitudes among the London Italian community, *Migrant Belongings: Memory, Space, Identity* (2000), and Azadel Medaglia's *Patriarchal Structures and Ethnicity in the Italian Community in Britain* (2001). However, Chiara Ghilardi's work on attitudes among the North East's women of Italian descent considerably diverges from these other writers' common findings of a deeply entrenched traditional mentality affecting even second generation Italians. Instead she discovered a broader and bolder outlook which along with the high incidence of intermarriage with the British in our region can probably be put down to the absence of a large concentration of Italian settlers within any one area of the North East, so that sooner or later integration is accepted as the only realistic survival option for the majority of those committed to making a life here (C. Ghilardi: *La collettivita' italiana nel nord est dell'Inghilterra*, unpublished graduate dissertation for the University of Pisa, 1994).

Italy's twentieth century growth spurt: four generations of Reas. Domenica Rea (right) was born in Blandford Street, Newcastle, 27 October 1904. (Photo: Anna Rea, taken in Arpino in about 1982.)

APPENDIX

THE GOLDEN AGE OF ICE CREAM PARLOURS

Distribution of Italian family catering businesses in the North East 1918-1950

Here is the proof of the remarkable extent of Italian immigrant enterprise in our region in the heyday of the 'Ice Age'. Listed are solely owners of ice cream businesses and parlours, cafés, 'refreshment rooms', confectionery shops, and fish and chip businesses. Though carefully pieced together from many sources, both written and oral, the absence of a full historical record inevitably means there must be inaccuracies below as well as omissions (notably of Italian street-vending operations which generally did not figure in the trade directories). While it was not unusual to find more than one Italian business on the same main street (see Ashington's Station Road!), recurring addresses and also surnames reflect the fact that premises changed hands not only within families but between colleagues, and many families ran more than one business. To complicate matters further, the presence in our region of members of large clans with the same surname and from the same locality in Italy (e.g. Rea, Valente) means that persons with identical surnames may not necessarily be from the same family or even closely related. Even allowing for all these variables it seems there must have been as many as 300 Italian-owned catering businesses in the North East in 1930, and still about 250 in 1950. A surprising number of these Italian-owned 'shops' continued right into the last quarter of the twentieth century. A miniscule few (*marked with an asterisk*) still survive at the same address (printed first below) in the hands of descendants of the original owners. Other survivors or revivals at new addresses today are Risi's of Newcastle, now on the Quayside, Pacitto's of Stockton, now in Dovecot Street, Maggiore's of Sunderland, in Park Lane (Louis cafe), Bianco's of Hartlepool, now on Middleton Road, and Greco's, the biscuit manufacturers of Middlesbrough, now in Greta Street.

Alnwick
Beccarelli, Market Place
Corvi, Clayport Street
Fontanella, Bondgate
Forte, Bondgate
Gasparini, Market Place & Fenkle Street
Orefice, Narrowgate
Parisella, Narrowgate
Valente, Bondgate

Alston
Petritzich

Amble
Costella, Queen Street
Ghini, Queen Street
Poggi, Leazes Street

Annfield Plain
Di Palma, Front Street
Rossi, Front Street

Ashington
Bacci, Station Road
Badiali, Station Road
Bertorelli, Station Bridge
Cecchini, Station Road
Cosimini, Acacia Terrace & Seventh Avenue
Di Mascio, Milburn Road
Fella, Laburnum Terrace
Gallone, Station Road
Limberti, Hawthorn Road
*Marchetti, Station Road & Poplar Street
Marchi, Hawthorn Road & Station Road
Mazzolini, Station Road
Nardini, Hawthorn Road & Third Avenue
Notarianni, Milburn Road & Laburnum Terrace
Pieroni, Station Road & Myrtle Street
Rossi, Milburn Road
Sassetti, Alexandra Road

Bedlington
Antonino, Ridge Terrace
Bacci, Market Place & Ravensworth Terrace
Bertorelli, Glebe Road & Front Street
Moscardini, Ravensworth Terrace

Berwick-on-Tweed
Azzali, Bridge Street
Corvi, West Street
De Duca, Bridge Street
*Forte, Hide Hill & Bridge Street
Signorini, Castlegate

Billingham
Panico, Station Road
Scarmiglia, The Green

Birtley
Di Duca, Dalmeney Terrace
Tomassi, Durham Road

Bishop Auckland
Bonini, Newgate Street
Di Palma, Gibbon Street & Newgate Street
Gabriele, Bondgate & George Street
Panicca, Market Place
Panzieri, Princes Street
Rea, Bondgate
Rossi, Newgate Street
Santi, Newgate Street
*Zair (Zaira), Bondgate

Blackhall Colliery
Pieroni, Middle Street & New Coast Road

Blackhall Mill
Figliolini

Blackhill
Parisi, Derwent Street

Blaydon
Lunatici, Church Street
Perna, Cowan Street & Tyne Street
Saporiti, Church Street

Blyth
Giacopazzi, Regal Street
Martino, Croft Road & Park Road
Motroni, Regent Street
Rea, Bowes Street, Union Street, Bondicar Terrace & Market Place
Seghini, Regent Street, Plessey Road & Waterloo Road

Boldon Colliery
Brucciani, Front Street

Brandon
Rinaldi

Browney Colliery
Rinaldi, Browney Lane
Valente, Browney Lane

Chester-le-Street
*Citrone, Front Street
Staffieri, Bridge End
Tomassi, Front Street

Chopwell
Figliolini, Derwent Street

Consett
Dimambro, Front Street & Medomsley Road
Figliolini, Church Street
Massarella, Front Street
Rossi, Newgate Street, Shakespeare Street & Church Street

Coundon
Ranaldi

Coxhoe
Iannuccelli, Front Street
Panico, Church Street & Front Street

Crook
Moscardini, Church Street & Addison Street
Notarianni, Hope Street
Rinaldi, Hope Street
Tazioli, Bridge Street & South Street
Vincenti, Commercial Street & Hope Street

Darlington
Biagioni, Horse Market
Di Duca, Parkgate & Priestgate
Di Luca, Victoria Road
Di Mascio, Market Place & Northgate Road
Di Paolo, Post House Wynd & Green Bank Road
Giacinto, Wilson St
Jannarelli, Skinnergate, Bondgate & Yarm Road
Martino, Duke Street
Minchella, Albert Road
Rea, Harrowgate Hill
Rissetto, High Northgate
Valente, Mount Street

Dawdon
Questa, Swinebank

Dipton
Di Palma, Front Street

Durham
Dimambro, Claypath, Gilesgate, Elvet Bridge & North Road
Gallone, North Road
Rossi, North Road
Valente, North Road

Eaglescliffe
Pacitto
Panico

Easington Colliery
Donnini, Seaside Lane
Equi, Seaside Lane
Fiori, Seaside Lane
Moscardini, Tyne Terrace
Passerotti, Seaside Lane

Easington Lane
Jaconelli, High Street

Esh Winning
Manattini

Evenwood
Santi

Fencehouses
Gallone, South Crescent
Minchella, George Street

Ferryhill
Cocozza, Darlington Road, South Road & Beach Crescent
Panico, Cornforth Lane
Rea, Chilton Buildings

Fishburn
Santi, Clayton Terrace

Gateshead
Andrucci, Askew Road West
Costantino, Durham Road
Crolla, Saltwell Road
Di Cucco, Chandlease Street
Dipreta, Sunderland Road
*Dragone, Felling High Street
Forte, Dunston
Gazzilli, Askew Road West
Mancini, Swan Street
Marcantonio (Mark Toney), Trinity Street, Sunderland Road & Durham Road
Pacitti, Askew Road
Pezzone, Sunderland Road & Collingwood Street
Pittiglio, Trinity Street
Reale (Riale), Sunderland Road

Grangetown
Lanni, Bolchow Road

Hartlepool
Amerigo, Musgrave Street, Grace Street & Hart Lane
Annonio, Stainton Street
Bianco, Grace Street, Whitby Street & Turnbull Street
Bonini, Northgate Street
Colarossi, Oxford Street & Studley Road
Di Cosimo, Corporation Road & Northgate Street
Di Duca, Elwick Road & Lynn Street
Di Passio, Millbank Crescent & Northgate Street
Facchini, Stranton Place, Streatham Street & Northgate Street
Martini, Albert Street
Pontone, Hart Road & York Road
Rossi, Lynn Street
Vincenzo, Lynn Street & Freeman Street

Haswell
Facchini, Front Street
Baldasera, Front Street

Hesleden
Colletta

Haverton Hill
Sera, Cowpen Road

Hebburn
Fionda, Bewick Street, Caledonian Street & Carr Street
Franchi, Hedgeley Road
Fusaro, Station Road & Tennant Street
Nardone, William Street

Hetton-le-Hole
Bianco, Richard Street, Front Street & Market Street
Fascia, Front Street
Massarella, Station Road

Hexham
*Fiori, Market Place & Fore Street
Gasparini, Mary's Chare
Risi, Mary's Chare & Gilesgate

Horden Colliery
Pontone, Blackhill Terrace
Saporiti, Blackhill Road

Houghton-le-Spring
Dimambro, Durham Road
Jaconelli, Newbottle Street
Riani, Newbottle Street

Jarrow
Colletta, Ormond Street
Fionda, Nixon Street
Rea, Grange Road, Walter Street & Ormond Street
Risi, Ferry Street, Western Road & Staple Road
Rumi, High Street

Langley Moor
Rea, High Street
Sacco, High Street

Langley Park
Citrone, Front Street
Massarella, Front Street
Tomassi, Front Street

Leadgate
Dimambro, Front Street
Di Palma, Front Street

Middlesbrough
Biesi, Cannon Street
Borzamato, Cannon Street
Borsumato, Newport Road & Princes Road
Capaldi, Snowdon Road
Costantino, Newport Road
De Lucchi, North Ormesby Road
Greco, Suffield Street
Lanni, Linthorpe Road
Lucantoni, Newport Road
Martino, Cannon Street & Newport Road
Minchella, Cannon Street
Nardone, Newport Road
Pacitto, Linthorpe Road
Panico, Hill Street
Ranaldi, Station Street
Rea, Linthorpe Road & Albert Park
Risi, Borough Road
Salvatore, Newport Road
Scappaticci, Gresham Road & Russell Street
Villa, Hill Street

Morpeth
Bertorelli, New Market & Newgate Street
Guazzelli, West Market Street
Resteghini, Newgate Street

Murton Colliery
Brunini, Victoria Street
Pioli, Church Street & Cookson Terrace

Newbiggin-by-the-Sea
Bertorelli, Front Street & North Seaton Road

Newburn-on-Tyne
Marchetti, Station Road
Nardini, Station Road

Newcastle
Allegretti, Shields Road
Bertorelli, Blackett Street & Westmorland Road
Capaldi, Elswick Road & Percy Street
Casali, Westmorland Road
Costella, Haymarket

D'Amerigo, Hendon Road
Fantozzi, Scotswood Road
Gabriele, Prospect Place
Gazzilli, Heaton Road
Giordano, Trafalgar Street
Giovannone, Welbeck Road
Gizzonio, Prudhoe Street
Jaconelli, Blenheim Street
Jaffrate, Blandford Street
*Marcantonio (Mark Toney), Percy Street, Grainger Arcade, Stepney Bank & Shields Road
Paolozzi, Robinson Street
Pernice, Starbeck Avenue
Prosperini, Shield Street
Quadrini, Elswick Road & Two Ball Lonnen
Quaglieri, Weatherley Street
Rea, Barrack Road, Raby Street, Scotswood Road, West Road, Condercum Road & Larch Street
Reale (Riale), Buckingham Street & West Road
Risi, Byker Bank, Grainger Arcade, Wilfred Street & Shields Road
Rossi, Pink Lane
Sebastianelli, Harriet Street
Sivori, Trafalgar Street
Tassi, Clarence Street

New Silksworth
Questa, Blind Lane

North Ormesby
Rea, Derwent Street

North Shields
Longino, Charlotte Street
Rinaldi, Wellington Street
Romanelli, Percy Square
Tomaselli, Bird Street
Vassallo, Clive Street & New Quay

Oxhill
Rossi, Eden Terrace

Pelton
Capaldi, Front Street

Philadelphia
Massarella

Prudhoe
Quarzi, Front Street

Redcar
Gallone, Esplanade
*Pacitto, Esplanade
Rea, Esplanade
Scappaticci, Esplanade
Todisco, High Street

Roker
Guidi, Queens Parade
Notarianni, Queens Parade

Rowlands Gill
Guazzelli, Station Bridge Road

Ryhope
Maggiore, Ryhope Street
Tricchi, Ryhope Street & St Paul's Terrace

Ryton-on-Tyne
Marchetti, Jubilee Terrace

Sacriston
Dimambro, Front Street
Gallone, Front Street

Seaburn
Guidi, the Promenade
Notarianni, the Promenade

Seaham Harbour
Di Mascio, Church Street
Pacitto, Adolphus Street
Passerotti, Princess Road
Pioli, Rutherford's Buildings
Questa, Church Street
Rosa, North Railway Street
Valente, North Terrace & New Arcade

Seahouses
Gasparini

Seaton Carew
Facchini, Front Street
Pontone, The Front
Silvestro, The Front

Seaton Deleval
*Arrighi, Avenue Crescent

Sedgefield
Capitano
Miele

Shildon
Bellezza, Church Street
Granelli, Church Street
Ranaldi, Cheapside

Shotton Colliery
Baldasera, Front Street
Passerotti, Front Street

South Bank
Di Mauro, Nelson Street
Fionda, Oxford Street

South Moor
Bove, Park Road
Citrone, Park Road

South Shields
Capaldi, Derby Street
D'Ambrosi, Ocean Road & Sunderland Road
Figliolini, Ocean Road
*Franchi (Colman), Ocean Road, South Eldon Street & Roman Road
Gabriele, Laygate Lane
Giannandrea, Park Street
Jannetta, Woodbine Street & Regent Street
Mancini, Ocean Road & James Mather Terrace
*Minchella, Ocean Road, King Street, & Prince Edward Road
Notarianni, King Street
Petrozzi, Derby Street, Taylor Street & Tennyson Street
Porretta, Victoria Road
Santilli, Mile Road End
Staiano, Tennyson Street

Valente, King Street & Ocean Road
Vassallo, Eldon Street

Spennymoor
Alonzi, Dean Street
Coia, Cheapside & Coronation Buildings
Di Mascio, Cheapside
Gallone, North Street
Giovannone, Gerard Street

Stanley
Biagioni, Front Street & Station Road
Equi, Front Street
Moscardini, Front Street
Niro, Front Street
Vincenti, Station Road & High Street

Stockton
Caira, Dovecot Street & High Street
Capitano, Yarm Lane & Albert Street
Di Duca, Lindsay Street
Ferri, Northcote Street
Massarella, Bishopton Lane & Yarm Lane
Pacitto, Yarm Lane
Petricca, Oxford Street
Rossi, High Street
Serrecchia, Rutland Terrace
Sperduti, Maritime Road
Tortolano, Hardwick Terrace & Norton Road

Sunderland
Ascione, New Grey Street
Baldasera, Peacock Street & High Street East
Ciarella, Prospect Row
Colletta, Market Street
D'Amerigo, Hendon Road
Fascia, Moor Street & Southwick
Fella, Silksworth Row
Franciosi, High Street East & Borough Road
Giraldi (Ciaraldi), Brady Street & Church Street North
Guidi, Silksworth Row & Roker Avenue
Luti, Hendon Valley Road
Maggiore, Crowtree Road & Trimdon Street
Minchella, Sans Street & Coronation Street

Notarianni, High Street
Palumbo, Hylton Road, Hendon Road & High Street West
Pieri, Carley Road
Pompa, High Street West & Hylton Road
Prenelle, Trimdon Street
Pucci, Coronation Street
Questa, Dundas Street
Rossi, High Street East
Someo, Moore Street
Tognarelli, Hylton Road & Trimdon Street
Valente, Market Street, Moor Terrace & Roker Avenue

Thornaby-on-Tees
Di Pucchio, New Street
Paleschi, George Street & Eldon Street
Rossi, Wilson Street

Thornley
Baldasera, Hartlepool Street

Trimdon
Baldasera

Tow Law
Marchetti, High Street

Tweedmouth
Forte, Main Street
Nardone, Main Street
Parisella, Main Street & Kiln Hill

Tynemouth
Bertorelli, Percy Street

Wallsend
Marchi, High Street West
Rossi, High Street
Togneri, Station Road

Washington
Forte, Station Road & Victoria Road
Rossi, Front Street

West Auckland
Rea, Front Street

West Cornforth
D'Orazio, High Street
Pierotti, High Street
Santi, High Street

Wheatley Hill
Baldasera, Front Street
D'Orazio, Front Street

Whitley Bay
Bertorelli, Station Road, Park Terrace & Pleasure Gardens
Capaldi, Marine Avenue
Di Mascio, John Street
Gallone, Marine Avenue
Gizzonio, Marine Avenue
Pantrini, Park Terrace
Rea, Esplanade
Risi, Esplanade
Torre, Marine Avenue

Willington
Rea, Commercial Street

Wingate
Facchini, Front Street, North Road & Station West
Gallone, Front Street
Parisella, Front Street
Scarniglia, North Road

Witton Park
Quadrini, Main Street

Yarm
Pacitto

Endnotes

Chapter 2

1   Now in the possession of Richard Tarelli whose great-great-grandfather Matteo Tarelli could well have worked on it when apprenticed to his father's brothers Antonio and Carlo Tarelli at 41, Dean Street, Newcastle, in 1849-50. The family was from Cardano, near Menaggio on Lake Como (see following note). Matteo went on to complete his apprenticeship with Vittorio Mastaglio, and after eleven years in Newcastle opened his own toy and fancy goods shop in High Row, Darlington.

2   While Antonio and Carlo prospered abroad, their brother Giovanni struggled to run the family's small farm in Cardano, at times labouring for a neighbouring landowner to work off crippling debts, including one incurred to buy his son Matteo's exoneration from conscription after his escape to Newcastle: 'Remember, after my death you will all have to thank me for having managed to give all of you your freedom'. Giovanni died in March 1857. In his last letter, weakened by long ill health and still laden with debts, he reported that poverty was emptying the village: 'young men and old men of fifty and sixty are leaving for "La Merica" [America], up to four or five per household and even entire families, if they can raise the money for the voyage'.

3   Jill Allibone, in her book on Salvin, suggests that when Salvin suffered a nervous collapse 'the strain of controlling his Italian craftsmen and integrating their work with his own no doubt contributed to his breakdown'!

4   Wearside's Bianchis descend from Antonio Bianchi, also from Lombardy, who married his cousin Maria in 1871 after working some ten years in her father Gaetano Taroni's shop on Sunderland High Street.

Chapter 3

1   Other Italian 'professors of language' in nineteenth-century Newcastle: Ludovico Bompiani, a 47-year-old widower in Blackett Street (1851), and Giovanni Basini, 'interpreter / professor of languages', aged 40, with English wife and family in Matford's Entry (1861). Count De Mancini, the Italian consul, was another (see later in this chapter).

2   The dinners are now held at St James' Park stadium or the Marriot Hotel (see final chapter).

3   The sword was purchased from Heeley's of Birmingham, and the telescope from John English, Grey Street, Newcastle. Both are engraved: 'Presented to Giuseppe Garibaldi by

the People of Tyneside, friends of European Freedom. Newcastle-on-Tyne, April, 1854'.

4　There is a story that Garibaldi got his thousand red shirts cheaply from a Newcastle warehouse.

5　Launched in August 1860 (note date) by John Rogerson & co, for passenger service on the Tyne.

6　The consular office was later restored to an Italian, though only at vice-consular level, and remained in the care of Italian appointees until June 1940, when Italy entered the war against Britain. Names with dates of appointment: vice-consul Enrico Stella (1868), vice-consul David Segre (1879), vice-consul Carlo Pallotti (1886), vice-consul R. Rizzetto (1891), consular agent V.A. Montaldi (1899), consular agent V.A.Montaldi Jnr (1911), consular agent Renato De Carolis (1914), consular agent Francesco Valle (1923), consular agent Nestore Tognoli (1928), upgraded later to vice consul.

7　The local press regularly quoted freight costs for coal and coke out of Tyne, Wear and Tees to Genoa, Naples, Livorno, Civitavecchia, Messina, Palermo, Venice and Trieste.

Chapter 4

1　Certain families noted for their beauty, in particular from Picinisco in Ciociaria, came to specialise in working as artists' models. By 1900 some 200 professional models in Britain's art academies and studios were Italian.

2　Carpena was from the Val Taro, Lertoria (originally probably Lertora) almost certainly from the hills around Chiavari, on the Ligurian side of the same section of the Apennines.

3　The Italian anthropologist Cesare Lombroso (1836-1909) was the inventor of an influential but now entirely discredited physiology of 'criminal types'.

4　The Child Protection Act became law in 1889. Within Italy, on the heels of repeated attempts to legislate against child trafficking in the old Duchy of Parma and Piacenza, the employment of children under 18 (other than one's own) in vagrant occupations became illegal in 1873. But enforcement was another matter. The reality of almost universal dependency on child labour was implicit in united Italy's first legislation for compulsory schooling (1877) which set the age limit at nine.

5　After vice-consul Rizzetto's departure, the Newcastle post was downgraded to a consular agency dependent on the Italian consul-general in Liverpool who had ultimate responsibility for the whole of the north. On Montaldi's death in 1911 the latter went out of his way to praise his Newcastle colleague's unfailing support and 'generous initiatives' on behalf of his fellow-countrymen. He was succeeded by his hard-drinking son, Vittorio Amedeo Jnr, who within three years resigned in disgrace after squandering the family fortune.

6　The requirement to list each child's age and place of birth can provide a fascinating glimpse into the peregrinations of the parents. For instance Girolamo Cavazzi and his wife Albertina, street musicians from the province of Piacenza who settled permanently in Trafalgar Street, Newcastle, had earlier tried their luck in Prussia where their first child was born (1879), then London (1881 census) where they can have stayed at most a couple of years seeing the second child was born in Newcastle in 1883. For her superb singing voice and diminutive stature Albertina was nicknamed 'the Little Nightingale'. See page 98 for a vivid recollection of the couple in their seventies.

Chapter 5

1 The legend dies hard, to the point of having him live nearly as long as Methuselah: 'Marco Polo introduced ice cream to Europe in the 17th century' (*Newcastle Evening Chronicle*, 1st July, 1999). Another enduring myth credits the Venetian adventurer with bringing the first spaghetti back from China.

2 The precise census figures for Italians in Britain were 9,909 (1891), 20,332 (1901), 20,771 (1911). Life stories retold to us by descendants of the North East's 'original Italians' confirm that the boom years for arrivals in our region were 1890-1905.

3 As late as 1934, Hartlepool council (seconded by 130 other borough councils) was demanding better controls on premises and handlers. A law of 1937 stipulated that the three successive processes of boiling, cooling, and freezing had to be conducted in separate rooms, and the 1938 Food and Drugs Act finally made the registration of ice cream premises compulsory everywhere. Even so, long after World War II schoolchildren were still being warned that eating ice cream from barrows and small shops was dangerous. To counter these enduring suspicions, as pictures in this chapter show, the claim 'Pure Ices' was universal on carts and shop fronts from very early times.

4 Both villages kept on sending migrants to the North East until very recent times. At the grocer's on the central square in Valvori customers could receive a cheery 'Ta-ra!' on leaving. The proprietor, Isidoro Di Meo, had spent twenty years touring the coastal towns around Tynemouth in his 'Mr Eddie' ice cream van, years he described as the happiest of his life. His brother Armando keeps up the 'Mr Eddie' tradition to this day.

5 The 1881 census discovered Mario Rigari, 67 and blind, 'formerly traveller with peep show', living in Matford's Yard with his English wife and son.

Chapter 6

1 The Pro-Italia committee, sponsored by the UK government and supported by individual contributions and regular flag days, had raised money for refugees in the Italian war zone and for Italian soldiers' and sailors' families in Britain, including the costs of repatriation. Longer lasting products of the wartime alliance, the British-Italian League (1916) and Friends of Italy (1918), along with the worldwide Italian state-sponsored Dante Alighieri Society, would soon become cosy homes for British as well as Italian enthusiasts of fascism.

2 Members were called *fascisti*. *Fascio*, literally 'bundle', was a standard term for extra-parliamentary protest groups long before Mussolini, but in associating the word with the ancient Roman *fasces*, a bundle of rods bound round an axe carried as an emblem of state authority, the movement forged a potent emotive symbol for its mission to restore 'Roman' domination of the Mediterranean, represented as Italy's historic right and destiny following the achievement of national unification and then victory in the Great War.

3 The London *fascio*, the brainchild of two Italian lecturers at London University, claimed to be the first of its kind abroad. The Manchester *fascio* was also inspired by an Italian lecturer at the university. The authority and evident conviction of such 'persons of culture' as well as respected Catholic priests ministering to the community was an important factor in the reception of fascism by the largely poorly educated immigrant population. From early on the London

fascio boasted such distinguished members as the Italian consul-general and tyre magnate, Giorgio Pirelli, Prince Piero Colonna of Hambros bank (later fascist governor of Rome), and the physicist Guglielmo Marconi (honorary president of the London *fascio* from 1927).

4. The Ministry of Foreign Affairs' own figures in 1927 were actually 9.2 million Italians abroad, 7.7 million of them in the Americas.

5 'As far as our consular services are concerned, Newcastle is a much more important centre than Liverpool because of its important coal export to Italy and its more numerous Italian colony, and because the number of our vessels docking in that port is probably ten times that of Liverpool'. (Renato De Carolis, Liverpool vice-consul, 3 January 1925). Newcastle was a four-hour train journey from Liverpool, and consular officials often emphasised its relative isolation. As a former consular agent for the North East with business interests in Newcastle, De Carolis knew the city well and had married a local woman who was apparently a notable pianist.

6 'Superdrug' on the corner of Northumberland Street stands on the site of Saville House.

7 In March 1936 Tognoli alarmed Liverpool by announcing he would have to resign to look for more remunerative work since the trade embargo had nullified his income from his commercial activities and the consular salary was too little for a family to live on. Only the promise of a salary increase persuaded him to stay. The British sanctions against Italy were lifted as soon as decently possible, in July 1936.

8 Pietro Casali's at 16, Westmorland Road.

Chapter 7

1 The government estimated 18,000 Italians over the age of 16. The last census, in 1931, gave 21,719 Italians, so the estimate allowed for an observable decrease in the later Thirties and the run-up to the war. It may have some bearing on the 'loyalty' of those remaining that even after the experiences examined in this chapter very few opted to return to Italy after the war.

2 These are the standard figures quoted, but notoriously uncertain. 734 Italians were on board.

3 Giuseppe Saporiti (Horden Colliery), Colombo Riani (Houghton-le-Spring), and Antonio Greco (Middlesbrough) whose brother Tullio was among the drowned.

4 The experience is memorably recorded in Bernard Moscardini's *La vacanza*.

5 Decoded as 'I Trust And Love You' by the Italians in their attempts to 'fraternise'. The green uniforms were another source of grievance since many co-operators felt their new allegiance should entitle them to Italian army uniform just like their comrades assisting the Allies in Italy.

Chapter 8

1 The precise figure for the 1971 UK census was 108,930, of whom it is estimated up to 70% owed their presence to the bulk recruitment schemes and the new migration chains which quickly evolved out of them. Between 1950 and 1960, the decade of mass recruitment, Italian immigration to Britain averaged 8,000 a year.

2 The North East acquired a significant connection with Bradford when the Italian Catholic Mission, founded there in 1950, also assumed pastoral duties toward migrants in our region.

3 Francesco Marini's restaurant in Grainger Street; Giovanni Terzaghi at the Old Robin Hood Inn, Pilgrim Street; Giuseppe Ferrario at the Prince of Wales, Wellington Street;

Clerico Vitali at the Wellington Hotel, Pudding Chare, succeeded by F. Merlo who also opened the café-restaurant 'Roma' in the neighbouring Bigg Market. On the strength of its name alone the latter must surely have served something of an Italian description.

4 With no apparent irony the most recent English-owned restaurant on the list markets itself as 'Durham's Little Italy', while in nearby West Rainton the latest addition to the locally owned Tavistock Italia's chain was promoted as 'a welcome new arrival from Italy'.

5 It is my strong recollection that among the war generation anti-Italian prejudice persisted at all levels of society for a very long time. In 1963, when senior members of my own university of Durham first suggested Italian Studies should have a place in the curriculum I am told the Vice-Chancellor cut short further debate by spitting out contemptuously, in atrocious Italian, probably the only phrase he knew: *E' pericoloso sporgersi!* i.e. 'It is dangerous to lean out of the window'.

6 The restriction was waived for immigrants who married a British national before the four year Ministry of Labour contract expired.

7 In 2013 Di Meo's 'Delaval Ices', the family's subsidiary in Whitley Bay, won the ICA award for the UK's best vanilla ice.

8 Volpi, born in Chatham of Italian parents, starred at the Oxford Galleries from 1932 to 1948. He gained a decoration from Mussolini in 1935 for his setting of the fascist youth song *Il balilla all'estero* together with Colombo Riani, and during the war turned out a number of very popular Jingoistic compositions for the Allied cause.

9 The 1991 UK census showed a 16.5% fall in the Italian-born population from the peak recorded 20 years earlier: 1971: 108,930; 1981: 97,848; 1991: 91,011. Italian Foreign Ministry estimates which as always included all residents with Italian parentage were consistently at least double these figures, e.g. 196,000 in 1984. That up to 80% had origins in southern Italy is a consequence not only of the bulk recruitment schemes but of the uneven development of the Italian economy which has never succeeded in eradicating much higher unemployment levels in the south and islands.

10 For example, the *Comitati dell'Emigrazione Italiana,* the Italian Emigration Committees elected by ballot from 1986 to represent community interests within every consular district were soon renamed Committees for Italians Abroad, *Comitati Italiani all'Estero.* Though heralded with much fanfare from officaldom, these grandly titled committees of emigrant activists with no powers and no funds have inevitably proved a bureaucratic charade.

11 The main consular office for northern England was transferred from Liverpool to Manchester in 1969. In 2011, in a cost-cutting exercise which has deprived northern England of full consular representation after a period of more than a century, the Manchester office was downgraded and its major responsibilities were devolved to London. The Greater Manchester area, with about 5,000 nationals, has the highest count of Italians in the north of England. The present estimate for the North East is 3,000.

12 After a twenty-year decline from the peak recorded in the census of 1971, the graph of Italian-born residents in the UK started climbing again in the decade 1991-2001, rising more steeply in the most recent decade to reach its highest-ever recorded level in the 2011 census, a 32% increase in just ten years: 1991: 91,011; 2001: 107,244; 2011: 144,295. Half this population is concentrated in the Greater London area. One telling indication of the very different make-up of the newest influx is that Chelsea and Kensington are now among the London boroughs with the highest density of Italian residents. Italian consular records of first and second generation Italians living in England and Wales alone amount to approximately 250,000.

Valente family, Browney Colliery, in the 1920s

Printed in November 2021
by Rotomail Italia S.p.A., Vignate (MI) - Italy